Library of
Davidson College

MINOAN LINEAR A

MINOAN LINEAR A

by

David W. Packard

UNIVERSITY OF CALIFORNIA PRESS
Berkeley / Los Angeles / London 1974

University of California Press
Berkeley and Los Angeles, California
University of California Press, Ltd.
London, England

Copyright © 1974 by The Regents of the University of California

ISBN: 0-520-02580-6
Library of Congress Catalog Card Number: 73-85794

Printed in the United States of America

PREFACE

This book does not set out to identify the language of Linear A. Those in search of comprehensive "decipherments" have at least four recent attempts from which to choose, according to whether they prefer to have the Minoans speaking Greek, Hittite, Indic, or North-West Semitic. What languages were used in Crete before the arrival of the Mycenaeans is still a matter for conjecture—some of those named above are possible—but I believe we can make progress in the study of Linear A without basing our argument on a hypothetical identification of the language.

A cogent "etymological" interpretation of the texts would have been decisive, but few believe that this has been achieved. The history of scholarship on Linear B before the decipherment provides guidance as to what sort of research is likely to be productive at the present state of our knowledge. The scholars who contributed most towards Ventris's eventual success were Bennett and Kober. Bennett did fundamental work in establishing the signary, in editing the tablets, in preparing indices, and in developing a system of classification which groups together tablets dealing with similar subjects. None of this involved any premature claim to have deciphered the script. Raison, Pope, and a few others have been making important recent contributions for Linear A in the first three areas. In Chapter Two of the present work I have tried to develop a preliminary classification of the Hagia Triada archives. In view of the paucity of material, I have no illusions of approaching the admirable elegance and exactness of Bennett's classification of Linear B; but recognizable divisions exist, and the attempt to find them has been unjustly neglected. I hope at least to have demonstrated that there is enough material to allow some simple conclusions. Intensive contextual study of the Linear B tablets made it possible before the decipherment to predict with considerable accuracy which sign-groups represented personal names, occupational terms, and so forth. This provided a valuable discipline on future etymological speculation. A decipherer who presents a list of Egyptian and Semitic "personal names" in Linear A ought to have an explicit theory of how to recognize a personal name on a Minoan tablet. This important preliminary step has too often been ignored.

In addition to helping with the classification of the Knossos tablets, Kober was able to show how inflection could be used as evidence for the Linear B phonetic values. In her 1948 article she correctly deduced the phonetic relationships between about a dozen signs. The problems of Linear A today are not identical with those of Linear B twenty five years ago, and the range of available evidence is different; but we can still profit from Kober's example by resisting the temptation to resort too soon to the "etymological method." In Chapters Three through Five, I have addressed myself to the question of non-etymological evidence for the Linear A phonetic values.

Eight appendices provide various compilations which, I hope, will prove useful to scholars holding diverse views about Linear A. Each appendix is preceded by a brief explanatory introduction.

My initial idea for a statistical study of the Linear A phonetic values originated in 1966 in a Harvard University seminar on computational linguistics taught by Susumu Kuno who generously provided computer time for much of my preliminary analysis. Without his early assistance and encouragement my work on Linear A could hardly have begun. With the addition of a section on the classification of tablets, the study was subsequently expanded into a doctoral dissertation under the guidance of G.P. Goold, himself one of the first scholars to attack Linear A after the decipherment of Linear B. I presented a preliminary report at the Mycenological Congress in Rome in 1967 but postponed further work on Linear A in the hope that the Zakro tablets, discovered five years earlier, would soon be published.

During 1972, I repeated much of the analysis using an improved text and brought the work up to date in other ways. Further delay would undoubtedly have made additional improvements possible. Raison and Pope have announced their new *Corpus du Linéaire A,* and we may hope that the Zakro tablets will eventually be published. Moreover, the final editions of the Knossos and Pylos tablets are scheduled to appear within five years; and Chadwick, in the meantime, is preparing a second edition of *Documents in Mycenaean Greek* which will include an up-to-date index of sign-groups. His index would have served my purposes better than Morpurgo's excellent but somewhat dated *Mycenaeae Graecitatis Lexicon,* but I have at least been able to collate her *Lexicon* with the newest edition of *The Knossos Tablets.*

I was not able to examine the original Linear A documents in Crete but have consulted photographs and the careful drawings by Pugliese Carratelli. In my earlier work I relied heavily on Brice's transcriptions. The knowledge that Pope and Raison had already been at work for several years on a new edition based on repeated autopsy of the documents in the Heraklion Museum dissuaded me from any thought of producing a completely new edition. Their recently published *Index* implies great divergence from earlier editors. The publication of their *Corpus* will resolve many doubts, but for the present we must reconstruct their text from their *Index*. I have discovered more than two hundred places where they differ from Brice. On the assumption that the *Index* contains essentially the same readings which will appear in the *Corpus*, I have adopted the *Index* as my basic standard text. I have not, however, ignored Brice's readings either in my text or in the appendices where they are marked with a special symbol. Pope and Raison very generously made available to me a preliminary copy of their *Corpus*; but since I consulted this only at a very late stage in my work, it should be assumed that the *Index* constitutes my basic text.

It will be obvious that computer methods have a major role in this research. I hardly need to emphasize that my conclusions do not possess any special validity simply because a computer was involved. Clerical tasks such as counting and collating can be carried out rapidly by a computer, which makes it feasible to formulate and test a wider range of hypotheses; but the underlying arguments can be understood, and should be presented, with no reference to the machine. To avoid possible misunderstanding on this point, I have deliberately excluded any mention of the computer from my text. Recognizing, however, that some readers may approach this book with more interest in computer techniques than knowledge of Minoan epigraphy, I have included in Chapter One a general survey of Aegean writing.

The book itself, both text and appendices, was set in type by the author using computer photocomposition. Camera-ready copy was prepared on an RCA Videocomp at *The Los Angeles Times*. This method of typesetting scholarly books, especially those requiring unusual alphabets or difficult page formats, has important advantages in cost, flexibility and speed and deserves to become more widely known. The development of my program for photocomposition was partially supported by an earlier grant from the American Philological Association. I have described this program in an article to appear in the journal *Scholarly Publishing*.

The programs for the analysis of the Minoan and Mycenaean material were written first in 1967 for an IBM 7094 computer at Harvard. They were subsequently rewritten in 1971-1972 for an IBM 360/91 computer at the University of California, Los Angeles. I wish to thank both universities for their support of my computational work.

I also wish to thank Professor G. Buccellati who advised me on several Akkadian problems, Dr. C. Saporetti whose help has been of great value, and Dr. Paola Negri who kindly provided me with a copy of her unpublished University of Rome dissertation. Several persons have read the manuscript in varying stages of completion: David Wilson, Professors E.C.H. Carterette and J. Puhvel, and above all Professors G.P. Goold and M. Pope. I am grateful to all of them for their extremely helpful comments, but none should be held responsible for any of my follies.

David W. Packard

University of California
Los Angeles

CONTENTS

List of Figures 11
List of Tables 12
Bibliography 13
Chapter One: Introduction
    Aegean Literacy 19
    The Linear A Inscriptions 22
    The Homogeneity of Linear A 23
    The Linear A Writing System 23
    Previous Publication on Linear A 25
    Typographical Conventions 29
Chapter Two: Classification of Tablets
    General Principles 38
    The A Series 41
    The B Series 51
    Lists of Agricultural Commodities 56
    The C Series 56
    The D Series 57
    The E Series 58
    The F Series 60
    The G Series 61
    The H Series 61
    The X Series 62
    Clusters of Sign-Groups 62
    Word Classes 64
Chapter Three: The Phonetic Values
    Introduction 67
    Types of Evidence 70
    Statistical Control 72
    Alternation at the End of Words 75
    Alternation Internal to Words 78
    Alternation at the Beginning of Words 79

Chapter Three: The Phonetic Values (continued)
    Frequency Distribution 80
    Pure Vowel Signs 80
    Consonant-Plus-Vowel Signs 81
    Linear B Parallels 90
    Summary of Evidence 93

Chapter Four: Individual Signs
    L 32 103
    L 43 104
    L 57 104
    L 61 106
    L 69 107
    L 72 and 94 107
    L 79 108
    L 83 108
    L 86 110
    L 98 110
    L 100 110

Chapter Five: Hints About the Phonology of the Minoan Langauge
    The Vowels 112
    The Consonants 115

Appendices
    Appendix A: Alternations within Linear A 123
    Appendix B: Parallels with Linear B 139
    Appendix C: Parallels with Hypothetical Phonetic Values . . . 155
    Appendix D: Random Decipherments of Linear A 178
    Appendix E: Linear A Sign Frequency 193
    Appendix F: Linear B Sign Frequency 206
    Appendix G: Linear B Sign Frequency by Word Class 223
    Appendix H: Linear A Sign-Groups in Transliteration 255

LIST OF FIGURES
(Pages 30-37)

1. The Five Branches of Aegean Writing: a) Cretan Pictographic seal (P. 24) reproduced from page 153 of *Scripta Minoa* I, by A.J. Evans (Oxford University Press, 1909). b) Linear A Tablet (HT 7) reproduced from *Le epigrafi di Haghia Triada in lineare A* by G. Pugliese Carratelli (supplement to the journal *Minos*, 1963). c) Linear B Tablet from Pylos (PY An 5) reproduced from *The Pylos Tablets* by E.L. Bennett, Jr. (Princeton University Press, 1951). d) Cypro-Minoan tablet from Enkomi reproduced from Figure 2 of "A Second Inscribed Clay Tablet from Enkomi," by P. Dikaios, *Antiquity* 27(1953)233-237. e) Dedication to Apollo in the Classical Cypriot Syllabary reproduced from Figure 88 of *Les inscriptions chypriotes syllabiques* by O. Masson (Boccard, 1961).
2. Drawings of Linear A Tablets by Pugliese Carratelli (for source, see Fig. 1) with transcriptions into L numbers and into conventional phonetic values.
3. Drawings and Transcriptions of Linear A Tablets (cont.).
4. Drawings and Transcriptions of Linear A Tablets (cont.).
5. The principal Linear A phonetic signs. The numbering of the signs follows Raison-Pope (1971).
6. Selected Linear A ideograms, ligatures, and numeric signs. The numbering of the signs follows Raison-Pope (1971).
7. The Linear B syllabary reproduced from *The Knossos Tablets* (4th ed.) by J. Chadwick, J.T. Killen, and J.-P. Olivier (Cambridge University Press, 1971).
8. The Classical Cypriot Syllabary reproduced from Figure 1 of *Les inscriptions chypriotes syllabiques* by O. Masson (Boccard, 1961).

LIST OF TABLES

1. Sign-Groups in A Series Lists (p. 48).
2. Lists Sharing Sign-Groups with A Lists (p. 50).
3. Items in B Series lists (p. 54).
4. Items in E Series Lists (p. 59).
5. Tablets Listed by Class and Scribe (p. 65).
6. Linear B Total Frequency (p. 85).
7. Linear B Initial Percentage (p. 86).
8. Linear A Complete Frequency (p. 87).
9. Linear A Frequency (4 x 10) (p. 88).
10. Linear A Initial Percentage (p. 89).
11. Linear B Words in Linear A (p. 92).
12. Evidence for Phonetic Values (p. 95).
13. "Morphological" Evidence by Decipherment (p. 97).
14. Parallels between Linear A and B (p. 98).
15. Confirmation by Phonetic Value (p. 99).
16. Confirmation by Sign (p. 101).
17. Non-Final Vowels in Linear B (p. 118).
18. Consonants in Linear B (p. 119).

BIBLIOGRAPHY

Bennett E.L. Jr. 1950. "Fractional Quantities in Minoan Bookkeeping," *American Journal of Archaeology* 54:204-222.
——— 1963. "Names for Linear B Writing and for its Signs," *Kadmos* 2:98-123.
——— 1972. "Linear B Sematographic Signs," *Acta Mycenaea I* [*Minos* 11] 55-72.
Billigmeier J.C. 1969. "An Inquiry into the Non-Greek Names on the Linear B Tablets from Knossos and their Relationship to Languages of Asia Minor," *Minos* 10:177-183.
Branigan K. 1969. "The Earliest Minoan Scripts—the Pre-palatial Background," *Kadmos* 8:1-22.
Brice W.C. 1961. *Inscriptions in the Minoan Linear Script of Class A.* Oxford.
——— 1962a. "Some Observations on the Linear A Inscriptions," *Kadmos* 1:42-8.
——— 1962b. "The Writing System of the Proto-Elamite Account Tablets of Susa," *Bulletin of the John Rylands Library* 45:15-39.
——— 1963. "A Comparison of the Account Tablets of Susa in the Proto-Elamite Script with those of Hagia Triada in Linear A," *Kadmos* 2:27-38.
——— 1967. "The Structure of Linear A, with some Proto-Elamite and Proto-Indic Comparisons," *Europa. Festschrift für Ernst Grumach* (ed. W.C. Brice). Berlin.
——— 1971a. "The Kindred Linear A Signs, L48, L79, and L83," *Kadmos* 10:28-34.
——— 1971b. "Epigraphische Mitteilungen: Linear A," *Kadmos* 10:174.
Caskey J.L. 1969. "Lead Weights from Ayia Irini in Keos," *Archaiologikon Deltion* 24:95-106.
——— 1970. "Inscriptions and Potters' Marks from Ayia Irini in Keos," *Kadmos* 9:113-117.
Chadwick J. 1967. *The Decipherment of Linear B* (2d ed.). Cambridge.
——— 1968. "The Organization of the Mycenaean Archives," *Studia Mycenaea* (ed. A. Bartonek). Brno.

―――― 1969. "Linear B Tablets from Thebes," *Minos* 10:115-137.

―――― 1972. "The Classification of the Knossos Tablets," *Acta Mycenaea I* [*Minos* 11] 20-54.

―――― & L. Baumbach. 1963. "The Mycenaean Greek Vocabulary," *Glotta* 41:157-271.

―――― , J.T. Killen, & J.P. Olivier. 1971. *The Knossos Tablets* (4th ed.). Cambridge.

Chapouthier F. 1930. *Les écritures minoennes au palais de Mallia* (Études Crétoises 2). Paris.

Daniel J.F. 1941. "Prolegomena to the Cypro-Minoan Script," *American Journal of Archaeology* 45:249-282.

Davis S. 1967. *The Decipherment of the Minoan Linear A and Pictographic Scripts.* Johannesburg.

Deimel A. 1928-1933. *Sumerisches Lexikon, II Teil, Vollständige Ideogramm-Sammlung.* Rome.

Deroy L. 1962. *Initiation à l'épigraphie mycénienne.* Rome.

Dikaios P. 1953. "A Second Inscribed Clay Tablet from Enkomi," *Antiquity* 27:233-237.

―――― 1971. *Enkomi: Excavations 1948-1958.* Mainz.

Diringer D. 1968. *The Alphabet* (3d ed.). New York.

Dow S. 1954. "Minoan Writing," *American Journal of Archaeology* 58: 77-129.

―――― 1968. "Literacy: The Palace Bureaucracies, The Dark Ages, Homer," in *A Land Called Crete* (Smith College Studies in History 45). Northampton, Mass.

―――― 1973. "The Linear Scripts and the Tablets as Historical Documents. (a) Literacy in Minoan and Mycenaean Lands," *Cambridge Ancient History* (vol. II, part I, pp. 582-608). Cambridge.

Evans A.J. 1909. *Scripta Minoa I.* Oxford.

Frisk H. 1960-1972. *Griechische etymologisches Wörterbuch.* Heidelberg.

Furumark A. 1941. *The Mycenaean Pottery: Analysis and Classification.* Stockholm.

―――― 1956. *Linear A und die altkretische Sprache.* Berlin (mimeographed).

Geiss H. 1970. *Abbreviations and Adjuncts in the Knossos Tablets.* Berlin.

Gelb I.J. 1963. *A Study of Writing* (2d ed.). Chicago.

Georgiev V.I. 1963. *Les deux langues des inscriptions crétoises en linéaire A.* Sofia.

―――― 1968. "L'état actuel du déchiffrement des textes en linéaire A," *Atti e Memorie del Primo Congresso Internazionale di Micenologia* I, 355-382. Rome.

Goold G.P. & M. Pope. 1955. *Preliminary Investigations into the Cretan Linear A Script.* Cape Town (mimeographed).

Gordon C.H. 1966. *Evidence for the Minoan Language.* New Jersey.
——— 1969. "Minoan," *Athenaeum* 47:125-135.
Graham J.W. 1964. "The Relation of the Minoan Palaces to the Near Eastern Palaces of the Second Millennium," *Mycenaean Studies* (ed. E.L. Bennett Jr.). Madison.
Grumach E. 1961. *Review of* Brice (1961). *Gnomon* 33:737-744.
——— 1963. *Bibliographie der kretisch-mykenischen Epigraphik.* Munich.
——— 1964. "The Structure of the Cretan Hieroglyphic Script," *Bulletin of the John Rylands Library* 46:346-384.
——— 1967. *Bibliographie der kretisch-mykenischen Epigraphik. Supplement I (1962-1965).* Munich.
——— 1968. "The Minoan Libation Formula—Again," *Kadmos* 7:7-26.
——— 1969. "Die kretischen und kyprischen Schriftsysteme," *Handbuch der Archäologie: Allgemeine Grundlagen der Archäologie* (ed. U. Hausmann). Munich.
——— 1970. "The Structure of Minoan Linear Scripts," *Bulletin of the John Rylands Library* 52:326-345.
Heubeck A. 1957. "Linear B und das ägäische Substrat," *Minos* 5:149-153.
Hester D.A. 1968. "Recent Developments in Mediterranean 'Substrate' Studies," *Minos* 9:219-235.
Hood M.S.F. 1967. "The Tartaria Tablets," *Antiquity* 41:99-113.
Hooker J.T. 1967. "The Beginnings of Linear B," *Europa. Festschrift für Ernst Grumach* (ed. W.C. Brice). Berlin.
Householder F.W. 1961. "Early Greek -j-," *Glotta* 39:179-190.
Hutchinson R.W. 1962. *Prehistoric Crete.* London.
Jeffery L.H. 1961. *The Local Scripts of Archaic Greece.* Oxford.
Jucquois G. 1969. "L'évidence des déchiffrements du linéaire A," *Muséon* 82:507-516.
Kamm R. 1965a. "Über die Bruchzahlen der Linear A-Schrift," *Orbis* 14:546-559.
——— 1965b. "Eine statistische Grundanalyse der minoischen Linear-A-Schrift," *Orbis* 14:237-249.
——— 1965c. "Über den Lautstand der minoischen Linear A-Schrift an Hand einiger Ritualtext- und Hagia Triada-Wörter," *Orbis* 14:410-432.
——— 1966. "Beweise für phonetisch-silbischen Charakter der kretish-mykenischen Linearschriften," *Orbis* 15:541-558.
——— 1967a. "Systematik der Hagia Triada-Ideogramme und -Ligaturen," *Minos* 8:130-148.
——— 1967b. "The World of the Hagia Triada Tablets," *Orbis* 16:242-268.
Kenna V.E.G. 1960. *Cretan Seals.* Oxford.
Kober A. 1948. "The Minoan Scripts: Fact and Theory," *American Journal of Archaeology* 52:82-103.

Labat R. 1962. "Le rayonnement de la langue et de l'écriture akkadiennes au deuxième millénaire avant notre ère," *Syria* 39:1-27.
────── 1963. *Manuel d'épigraphie akkadienne.* Paris.
Landau O. 1958. *Mykenisch-Griechische Personennamen.* Göteborg.
Leemans W.F. 1954. *Legal and Economic Records from the Kingdom of Larsa.* Leiden.
Lejeune M. 1966. "Doublets et Complexes," *Proceedings of the Cambridge Colloquium on Mycenaean Studies* (ed. L.R. Palmer & J. Chadwick). Cambridge.
Levi D. 1969. "Sulle origini minoiche," *La Parola del Passato* 127:241-264.
Marinatos S. 1967. "The 'Volcanic' Origin of Linear B," *Europa. Festschrift für Ernst Grumach* (ed. W.C. Brice). Berlin.
────── 1969. *Excavations at Thera II.* Athens.
────── 1971. "Thera Excavations 1970," *Athens Annals of Archaeology* 4:66-74.
Masson E. 1967. *Recherches sur les plus anciens emprunts sémitiques en grec.* Paris.
────── 1969. "La plus ancienne tablette chypro-minoenne (Enkomi 1955)," *Minos* 10:64-77.
Masson O. 1957. "Répertoire des inscriptions chypro-minoennes," *Minos* 5:9-27.
────── 1961. *Les inscriptions chypriotes syllabiques.* Paris.
────── 1968. "Ecritures et langues de la Chypre antique," *Archäologischer Anzeiger* 1967[1968]:615-619.
Meriggi P. 1956. *Primi elementi di minoico A* (Supplement to *Minos*). Salamanca.
Morpurgo A. 1963. *Mycenaeae Graecitatis Lexicon.* Rome.
Morpurgo-Davies A. & G. Cadogan 1971. "A Linear A Tablet from Pirgos, Mirtos, Crete," *Kadmos* 10:105-109.
Mylonas G. 1962. "The Luvian Invasions of Greece," *Hesperia* 31:284-309.
Myres J.L. 1951. "The Purpose and the Formulae of the Minoan Tablets from Hagia Triada," *Minos* 1:26-30.
Nagy G. 1963. "Greek-like Elements in Linear A," *Greek Roman and Byzantine Studies* 4:181-211.
────── 1965. "Observations on the Sign-Grouping and Vocabulary of Linear A," *American Journal of Archaeology* 69:295-330.
Neumann G. 1957. "Zur Sprache der kretischen Linearschrift A," *Glotta* 36:156-158.
────── 1958. "Zwei minoische Gefässbezeichnungen," *Glotta* 37:106-112.
────── 1960. "Minoisch Kikina "die Sykomorenfeige" *Glotta* 38:181-186.
────── 1961. "Weitere mykenische und minoische Gefässnamen," *Glotta* 39:172-178.

Olivier J.-P. 1967. *Les scribes de Cnossos*. Rome.

Packard D.W. 1967. "A Study of the Minoan Linear A Tablets," (unpublished doctoral dissertation, Harvard University).

——— 1968. "Contextual and Statistical Analysis of Linear A," *Atti e Memorie del Primo Congresso Internazionale di Micenologia* I, 389-394. Rome.

——— 1971. "Computer Techniques in the Study of The Minoan Linear Script A," *Kadmos* 10:52-59.

Palmer L.R. 1958. "Luvians and Linear A," *Transactions of the Philological Society* 75-100.

——— 1963. *The Interpretation of Mycenaean Greek Texts*. Oxford.

——— 1965. *Mycenaeans and Minoans* (2d ed.). New York.

——— 1968. "Linear A and the Anatolian Languages," *Atti e Memorie del Primo Congresso Internazionale di Micenologia* I,339-354. Rome.

Peruzzi E. 1960. *Le iscrizioni minoiche*. Florence.

Pope M. 1958a. "The Linear A Question," *Antiquity* 32:97-99.

——— 1958b. "The Language of Linear A," *Minos* 6:16-23.

——— 1962. "The Date of Linear B," *Kretika Chronika* 15-16:310-319.

——— 1964. *Aegean Writing and Linear A*. Lund.

——— 1966. "The Origins of Writing in the Near East," *Antiquity* 40:17-23.

——— 1968. "The First Cretan Palace Script," *Atti e Memorie del Primo Congresso Internazionale di Micenologia* I,438-447. Rome.

Pugliese Carratelli G. 1945. "Le iscrizioni preelleniche di Haghia Triada in Creta e della Grecia Peninsulare," *Monumenti Antichi* 40:422-610.

——— 1955. "La decifrazione dei testi micenei e il problema della lineare A," *Annuario della Scuola Archaeologica di Atene* 30-32[n.s. 14-16(1952-1954)]:7-21.

——— 1958. "Nouve epigrafi minoiche da Festo," *Annuario della Scuola Archaeologica di Atene* 35-36[n.s. 19-20(1957-1958)]363-388.

——— 1963. *Le epigrafi di Haghia Triada in lineare A* (Supplement to *Minos*). Salamanca.

Raison J. 1960. "Du nouveau sur la chronologie du linéaire A," *Bulletin de l'Association Guillaume Budé* 1960:315-324.

——— 1962. "Pour un corpus du linéaire A," *Kadmos* 1:49-58.

——— 1967. "Pour un corpus du linéaire A (ii)," *Europa. Festschrift für Ernst Grumach* (ed. W.C. Brice). Berlin.

——— & M. Pope 1971. *Index du linéaire A*. Rome.

Reich J.J. 1968. "The Rôle of the Naturalistic Signs in the Minoan Hieroglyphic Script," *Atti e Memorie del Primo Congresso Internazionale di Micenologia* I,448-461. Rome.

Ruijgh C.J. 1970. "L'origine de signe *41 (*si*) de l'écriture linéaire B," *Kadmos* 9:172-3.

Schachermeyr F. 1962. "Luwier auf Kreta?" *Kadmos* 1:27-39.

Setatos M. 1969. "Comparaison des tablettes mycéniennes sur la base d'une statistique phonétique," *Minos* 10:96-108.

Tsédakis J.G. 1967. "Zeugnisse der Linearschrift B aus Chania," *Kadmos* 6:106-109.

Ventris M. & J. Chadwick. 1956. *Documents in Mycenaean Greek*. Cambridge.

Was D.A. 1971. "Numerical Fractions in the Minoan Linear Script A—I: The Evaluation of the Fraction Signs," *Kadmos* 10:35-51.

Webster T.B.L. 1964. *From Mycenae to Homer* (2d ed.). New York.

Wiseman D.J. 1953. *The Alalakh Tablets*. London.

Wyatt W.F. 1968. "The Mycenaean Ideogram 120 GRANUM," *Kadmos* 7:100.

Xénaki-Sakellariou A. 1958. *Les cachets minoens de la collection Giamalakis* (Études Crétoises 10). Paris.

Young D. 1967. "Linear B Documents at Andreapolis: A Case-Study in Ventrisian Multivalency," *Europa. Festschrift für Ernst Grumach* (ed. W.C. Brice). Berlin.

CHAPTER ONE

INTRODUCTION*

Aegean Literacy

The scripts in use during the Aegean Bronze Age form an independent group, distinct from the contemporary Egyptian and Babylonian systems.[1] Four major branches are attested during the second millennium: the Cretan Hieroglyphic Script, Linear A, Linear B, and Cypro-Minoan. By the end of the Bronze Age this family of scripts had fallen out of use, and Greece remained illiterate until the introduction of the Phoenician alphabet several centuries later. A single descendant of the earlier Aegean scripts survived in the first millennium on the island of Cyprus in the form of the Classical Cypriot Syllabary.

The earliest branch of Minoan writing is the so-called Cretan Hieroglyphic or Pictographic script which, to avoid confusion with Egyptian Hieroglyphics, would more accurately be termed simply the "First Cretan Palace Script."[2] Most of the known inscriptions are on seal stones; but a variant of the script is attested at Knossos, Phaistos, and Mallia on clay accounting documents (tablets, bars, and labels) which are similar to

---

* Recent surveys: Pope (1964), Grumach (1969), Raison-Pope (1971, xii-xxxvii).

[1] The isolated and independent character of Minoan literacy is affirmed most recently by Dow (1973, 582-583). Pope (1966) finds the orthodox view of independent evolution unsatisfactory and argues for a common origin for all the scripts on the periphery of the Cuneiform area. According to him, Minoan has ultimate links with Egyptian and Hittite Hieroglyphs, Proto-Elamite, and the Indus Valley scripts. See also note 48 below. Apparent early examples of writing in the Balkans (Hood 1967) also show certain resemblances to the Minoan scripts. The influence of Egyptian Hieroglyphics is obvious in the shape of a few of the Cretan Pictographic signs (Evans 1909, 240).

[2] As suggested by Pope (1968).

those written in Linear A.³ The script begins at the time of the foundation of the first palaces in the MM I period (about 2000 B.C.) and continues into the early part of MM III (perhaps down to 1650 B.C.).⁴ Since the inscriptions are all extremely short, the prospects for decipherment are discouraging; and there is fundamental disagreement about so basic a question as whether the script is ideographic or phonetic.⁵ About two dozen of the Hieroglyphic signs resemble signs occurring later in Linear A and B, and the same sequence of five signs occurs both on Hieroglyphic seals and on Linear A religious inscriptions.⁶ It is difficult to see how this could occur if the first script were purely ideographic and the second syllabic. In any case, the obvious ideographic use of four signs to designate agricultural commodities on a Hieroglyphic tablet has an exact parallel in Linear B where these same signs represent wheat, oil, olives and figs. They also occur (in the same order) on several Linear A tablets.⁷

The second Cretan palace script is Linear A. Despite its obvious resemblance to the earlier script it is not easy to document a natural development from one to the other. Linear A was in use at Phaistos as early as 1850 B.C., long before the disappearance of the first script; but the bulk of the surviving texts date from the destruction of the palaces at the end of LM Ib (around 1450 B.C.) with a smaller number assignable to MM III and none securely dated after 1400 B.C.⁸ Linear A is attested at all the major Minoan sites. Outside of Crete, two short inscriptions come from the islands

---

[3] The majority of the Hieroglyphic inscriptions are published by Evans (1909) and Chapouthier (1930); a few more by Xenaki-Sakellariou (1958) and Kenna (1960). Further bibliography: Grumach (1963, 17-23) with supplement (1967, 5-6) and the yearly *Epigraphische Mitteilungen* published in the journal *Kadmos*. Reich (1968, 460n) refers to a projected (computerized) "complete corpus of the Minoan Hieroglyphic inscriptions," while Raison-Pope (1971, xv) mention a "nouveau *Corpus* de l'hiéroglyphique" in preparation by J.-P. Olivier and J.-C. Poursat.

[4] Branigan (1969) discusses the precursors of writing in the Early Minoan period and the social and economic conditions which led to the creation of the scripts.

[5] Evans (1909, 245-250) thought that the script was essentially phonetic though he proposed complex ideographic interpretations for some symbols. Grumach (1964) and Reich (1968) support an ideographic analysis, while Pope (1968) argues that the script is syllabic.

[6] Tables of parallel signs: Ventris-Chadwick (1956, 33), Pope (1968, 438), Raison-Pope (1971, xiv). For the repeated "Minoan Libation Formula" see Grumach (1968).

[7] The Hieroglyphic tablet is P 121; the Linear A is HT 91 (cf. HT 14, 21, 114, 116).

[8] For the dating of Linear A see Raison (1960). Pugliese Carratelli (1958, 387) and Hutchinson (1962, 71) make the suggestion that Linear A was at first the official palace script at Phaistos, where it is attested far earlier than elsewhere, and that it only later spread to the rest of Crete. Pope (1968, 446) finds the differences between Hieroglyphic and Linear A so large as to suggest that they were brought to Crete on separate occasions, perhaps from Anatolia or the Syrian coast.

of Thera and Melos; and recent excavations on Keos and Thera are yielding important new evidence of Linear A literacy on both of these islands.[9]

The Linear B script was used by the Mycenaean Greeks at Pylos, Mycenae, and Thebes for accounting documents in the Greek language. Its use in Crete is restricted almost entirely to Knossos at the time of the Greek occupation in the LM II period.[10] The script is modeled either directly on Linear A or on a near relative of Linear A. The latter view gains support from the observation that some of the Linear B signs are more ornate than their assumed Linear A ancestors (e.g., *ka, ku*), and the Linear B ideograms for men correspond to Hieroglyphic prototypes rather than Linear A ideograms known at Hagia Triada. A widely held theory states that the Mycenaean Greeks devised Linear B in Crete at the time of their conquest of Knossos in LM II, basing it on the current version of Linear A. A rival theory holds that the Greeks on the mainland had encountered Minoan writing earlier in their trade with Crete and had adapted it to their own language, perhaps already in the Shaft-Grave period. On this theory the Mycenaeans would have brought the already existing Linear B script with them from the mainland when they took Knossos. In an important epigraphical study Pope has shown that Linear B has the closest affinity with the version of Linear A current in MM III. This fact makes it highly doubtful that Linear B was created at Knossos in LM II, but the matter is still *sub judice*.[11]

The island of Cyprus has a long history of syllabic writing closely affiliated with the Aegean scripts. From the end of the Geometric Period down to the Hellenistic Age the Classical Cypriot Syllabary (deciphered in the last century) was used for Greek and for the yet unidentified Eteocypriot language. Many of the signs of this syllabary resemble Linear B; but only a few have the same phonetic value, and the spelling conventions, though similar, are not identical.[12] During the Bronze Age a related script known as Cypro-Minoan was widely used in Cyprus and is attested also at Ras Shamra on the coast of Syria. This script differed with time and place, and

---

[9] Literacy on Keos: Caskey (1970); on Thera: Marinatos (1971, 72).

[10] A few short Linear B inscriptions have recently come to light in Western Crete near the modern Chania (Tsédakis 1967). According to the traditional chronology, a gap of 200 years separates Linear B at Knossos (end of LM II, around 1400 B.C.) from Linear B at Pylos (end of LH IIIb, around 1200 B.C.). This gap may narrow somewhat as a result of recent controversy over the date of the Knossos tablets. For references see Grumach (1969, 247).

[11] Pope (1962). Chadwick (1969, 116) also favors the hypothesis of mainland creation. Further speculation by Hooker (1967) and Marinatos (1967).

[12] O. Masson (1961) offers, in addition to a valuable introduction, a collection of texts in the Classical Cypriot Syllabary together with transliteration and commentary.

may have been used for more than one language. The documents include clay tablets inscribed with continuous (possibly literary) texts and at least seventy mysterious inscribed clay balls. Cypro-Minoan is presumably the ancestor of the Classical Cypriot Syllabary despite a gap of several centuries in our documentation.[13]

The presence of Cypro-Minoan at Enkomi as early as 1500 B.C., at least a century before the earliest Linear B at Knossos, suggests that some form of Linear A rather than Linear B is the ancestor of the Cypriot scripts. The study of the syllabary confirms this conclusion.[14] If so, the Classical Cypriot Syllabary may represent a separate line of descent from Linear A, and may therefore contain evidence independent from Linear B for the structure and phonetic values of Linear A.

The Linear A Inscriptions

Nearly 150 clay tablets, by far the largest collection of Linear A texts, were discovered in the archives of the small palace at Hagia Triada, a site in southern Crete. Many of these, unfortunately, are fragmentary; hardly 30 are complete or nearly complete. Several more tablets have been found at Knossos, Phaistos, Tylissos, Palaikastro, and at a few other sites in Crete. In addition to the tablets, there are a number of small clay sealings from Phaistos, about 60 short inscriptions from various sites on stone, metal and clay objects (libation vessels, double axes, scraps of pottery, etc.), and a few short graffiti scratched on stucco wall facings.

Mention should be made of the discovery in 1963 of a dozen more Linear A tablets in the palace at Kato Zakro. Ten years later these were not yet published or available for study.[15] Still more tablets have been found recently at Arkhanes and Mirtos.[16]

Whereas the clay tablets are clearly administrative or commercial documents, many of the remaining inscriptions have a religious context. The range of Linear A literacy is somewhat wider than that of Linear B, which seems restricted entirely to commercial use; but it cannot equal the diversity typical of Near Eastern palace economies. It can safely be assumed that no surviving Minoan document contains epic poetry, royal epistle, or historical

---

[13] An older study is Daniel (1941). There is as yet no collected *Corpus* of Cypro-Minoan, but O. Masson (1957) has gathered references to the scattered publications up to that date. See also O. Masson (1968). Dikaios (1971, 881-889) discusses the inscriptions from Enkomi. Especially important is the discovery there of the first Cypro-Minoan "inventory."

[14] Daniel (1941). For a summary of recent views see O. Masson (1961, 34-38).

[15] Preliminary announcement in *Kadmos* 3(1964)183.

[16] Arkhanes: Brice (1971b); Mirtos: Morpurgo-Davies & Cadogan (1971).

annals. It is entirely possible, however, that the Minoans wrote also on perishable materials such as papyrus.[17]

The Homogeneity of Linear A

Since Linear A has a wide chronological and geographical distribution, the question may be raised whether all the texts are in a single language. The many repeated sign-groups and formulae within the Hagia Triada tablets confirm that this group is homogeneous. The group clearly includes also the cretulae which share with the tablets at least four sign-groups.[18] The tablets from other sites and the inscriptions on vases also share a few sign-groups with the Hagia Triada tablets.[19] The religious inscriptions, however, have little in common with the commercial documents.[20] The only viable link between Hagia Triada and the religious inscriptions is KU.PA$_3$.NA.TU on HT 47 and 119 beside]KU.PA$_3$.NA.TU.NA.TE[on a libation bowl from Apodoulou (AP Z 2).

A divergence between commercial and religious vocabulary could account for this lack of common sign-groups, but it is equally reasonable to imagine separate languages. Brice notes significant differences between the shapes of the signs at Hagia Triada and elsewhere,[21] and Georgiev, as mentioned below, considers that two separate languages are represented.[22] In Appendix E below, I have tabulated the frequency of each sign separately for the Hagia Triada tablets and for the remainder of Linear A. The divergence in percentage in some cases (e.g., L22, L32, L52, L75, L91) is large enough to arouse doubts about complete homogeneity, but the statistics are not conclusive.

The Linear A Writing System

The signs of Linear A may be divided into four categories: numerals and metrical signs (the Lm series), phonetic signs (those of the L series which occur in groups), ligatures and composite signs (the Lc series), and ideograms (those of the L series which stand in isolation). The distinction between phonetic signs and ideograms is not always clear.

Easiest to recognize are the numbers which are employed according to a

---

[17] Dow (1954, 1968, and 1973) discusses Minoan and Mycenaean literacy in its broader context. The Cypro-Minoan inscriptions from Enkomi, unlike the Cretan tablets, contain long continuous texts which Ventris thought might be poetic (Dikaios, 1953, 237).
[18] KA.KU.PA, KU.MI.NA.QE, PA.SE.JA, 87.DU.
[19] Raison-Pope (1971, xxi).
[20] They contain several internally recurrent phrases (Brice 1961, plate XXa).
[21] Brice (1961, 2).
[22] Georgiev (1963).

decimal system, with units represented by vertical dashes, tens by horizontal dashes (less often by dots), hundreds by circles, and thousands by circles with rays. Certain signs which occur in conjunction with numerals are commonly regarded as fractions. Some scholars have assigned definite values to these signs, but little is securely known about them except that they are alien to the Linear B metrical system.[23] The fundamental difference between the Linear B metrical signs and these Linear A fractions is that in Linear B each metrical symbol may be followed by an integer, while the Linear A fractions occur without such integers. From this it is inferred that where the Linear B scribe would write 10 gallons, 2 quarts, 3 cups, his Linear A counterpart would have written 10 11/16 gallons (which he would have expressed as $10+1/2+1/8+1/16$ gallons). It is, however, going beyond the evidence to deduce from this that the Linear A signs are fractional in any abstract sense. These Linear A signs could refer to equally concrete units of measure, the only difference being in the ratio between adjacent units. In Linear B this ratio is always greater than two to one. The Linear B series of dry measures, for example, shows the ratio 1, 1/10, 1/60, 1/240. It might be necessary, therefore, to fill the second measure as many as nine times. If the Linear A ratio were 1, 1/2, 1/4, 1/8, 1/16, 1/32, 1/64, etc., it would never be necessary to fill any measure more than once. Eight symbols would be required to reach the same discrimination as three in Linear B, but the actual measuring could be performed more efficiently since in the worst case the Linear A system would require eight measurements against seventeen in Linear B. The occurrence of some of these Linear A fractional signs ligatured with ideograms such as GRAIN (Lc 2, 4, 6, 7, 8, etc.) suggests that at least some of the signs are in fact metrical rather than fractional. We may, however, leave undecided the precise nature of these fractions—it may well turn out that several distinct types of signs are included under this term.[24]

Certain signs which appear in isolation, normally in headings or followed by numerals, seem to be ideograms identifying the items numbered.[25] As in Linear B, most of these ideograms probably represent agricultural com-

---

[23] Bennett (1950) first explained these Linear B metrical symbols. Kamm (1965a) and Was (1971) have recently studied the Linear A fractions.

[24] Several signs appear on small weights from Keos (Caskey 1969). A careful study of these weights and the lead weights from Thera and Vappheio (Marinatos 1969, 48-50) might lead to a better understanding of the metrical system underlying this puzzling group of signs.

[25] Bennett (1963, 113-116) prefers the term "fiscal sign" which is logically more correct than "ideogram" in the Akkadian and Egyptian sense. These Linear A signs, though very common, seem restricted to "fiscal" environments.

modities. No Linear A ideogram is so obvious as the Linear B ideogram for man or horse, but several of the most frequent Linear A ideograms are common not only to Linear B but also to the Cretan Hieroglyphic script. Surprising is the absence of ideograms referring to the livestock so common in the Linear B tablets (unless L48 and L113 depict animals).

The remaining signs, slightly under 100 in number, seem to be phonetic since they appear in various permutations in groups of from two to six or more signs.[26] The number of these phonetic signs is far too large for an alphabet, so it is reasonable to assume that each sign represents a syllable. A system which included signs for consonant-plus-vowel-plus-consonant (e.g., *par, lam*) would require hundreds of signs. Linear B and the Classical Cypriot Syllabary, both derived ultimately from some form of Linear A, use signs restricted to the pattern consonant-plus-vowel (e.g., *pa, pe pi*) except for the pure vowels which have separate signs. The natural hypothesis that Linear A follows the same pattern gains support from the nature of the internal alternations, parallels with Linear B, and frequency distribution discussed in Chapter Three.[27] To assume a basic continuity of structure between the two linear scripts is not to exclude the possibility that the spelling conventions are different or that Linear B makes use of full syllabic writing in cases where Linear A prefers ligatures or other ideographic mechanisms.

Previous Publication on Linear A

The Linear A tablets from Hagia Triada were uncovered shortly after 1900, but their publication was delayed more than forty years. Pugliese Carratelli produced the first edition of the tablets in 1945.[28] The difficult task of establishing a reliable inventory of signs was begun by him, and his edition laid the foundation for subsequent research. He issued an edition of the Hagia Triada material on a more limited scale in 1963.[29] This edition is especially valuable for the careful drawings of the tablets.

In 1961 Brice published a more complete edition of Linear A based on this earlier work and on the notes which Myres and Evans had compiled for

---

[26] The average phonetic group is about three signs long. A few scholars have held the unlikely view that Linear A contains no phonetic signs. For references and a discussion see Pope (1964, 6-7) and Kamm (1966).

[27] Signs for vowel-plus-consonant, which exist in Cuneiform, are a logical possibility. Consonant clusters (like *nwa* and *pte* in Linear B) should not be ruled out, but this phenomenon is of very restricted occurrence in Linear B and probably has a special explanation (see p. 115).

[28] Pugliese Carratelli (1945).

[29] Pugliese Carratelli (1963).

the projected *Scripta Minoa III*.³⁰ Some aspects of Brice's readings and signary now need revision, but his work for a decade has been the standard edition of Linear A.

Raison and Pope have announced a new *Corpus du linéaire A*. This work will undoubtedly become the standard edition when it is published. For the present we must reconstruct their readings from their *Index du linéaire A* which has already appeared.³¹

After the decipherment of Linear B in 1952, interest naturally centered on Linear A. Since about 50 of the Linear A signs have plausible counterparts in Linear B, the obvious first step was to transliterate as much as possible of the Linear A texts using these values to see whether anything comprehensible would emerge. In 1955 Goold and Pope issued a progress report describing their preliminary work on Linear A and outlining the chances for decipherment. They included an index of Linear A sign-groups and a list of comparisons between Linear A and Linear B syllabic groups.³² In the following year Furumark described his own attempt at applying Ventris's method independently to Linear A. The limited material did not allow him to achieve conclusive results, but his insistence on the priority of contextual analysis has often been ignored by later researchers.³³ Neither Goold and Pope nor Furumark had ventured to identify the language of the tablets, but other scholars soon came forward with suggestions.

Gordon first proposed that the texts contain a Semitic language, at one time identifying it as Akkadian.³⁴ This theory of Semitic affinity has received a good deal of public notice and has been taken up by a few other scholars in a tentative way.³⁵ A brief summary will afford some insight into the nature of the evidence presented. An attempt to identify the language of the texts must deal first with the few words whose meaning can be controlled by their context. The word for 'total,' transliterated as KU.RO³⁶ is the clearest example. It resembles the Semitic root *kull- meaning 'all' (Akkadian *kalu*,

---

³⁰ Brice (1961). The collection of alternate readings contained in Raison (1962 and 1967) is now superseded by Raison-Pope (1971).

³¹ Raison-Pope (1971).

³² Goold-Pope (1955).

³³ Furumark (1956).

³⁴ Gordon has published a long series of articles on his "decipherment." A convenient summary may be found in Gordon (1966). Gordon (1969) attempts to answer the many (often unfavorable) reviews.

³⁵ Including at one time Pope (1958a, b) though he is by no means committed to a Semitic solution.

³⁶ Or KU.LO since in Linear B the *r* series also represents *l*. The meaning of this word is established by the many cases of numerical summation introduced by it.

kullatu, Hebrew *kol*). Although this particular root is not normally used for totaling in Akkadian, the equation is plausible enough semantically.

The words written above the ideograms for pots on HT 31 bear some resemblance to Semitic: QA.PA$_3$, SU.PU, KA.RO.PA$_3$, SU.PA$_3$.RA and PA.TA.QE. For the second, third and fourth of these words, Ugaritic names for vases have been suggested as parallels: *sp, krpn, spl*. A major difficulty with these and other Semitic parallels is that vowels are often ambiguous in Semitic writing. Such parallels reduce to two or three consonants, and it is easy to underestimate the probability of coincidence. Names for vessels, in any case, are often loan words, and it would hardly be surprising if Crete and Ugarit shared some commercial vocabulary.

Morphological evidence, as Gordon himself admits, would be more convincing since isolated lexical items can easily be dismissed as loan words. Typical of such morphological "evidence" is Gordon's suggestion that *u*- serves as a prefix in Linear A like a Semitic copula *u*-.[37] It is true that L97=U in Linear A is very frequent initially (as is to be expected with a pure vowel), but there are no examples of the same word appearing both with and without this alleged prefix. There are, in fact, a good number of apparent prefixes and suffixes in Linear A (see Appendix A) which may prove valuable in identifying the language, but *u* does not seem to be among them. Gordon's hypothetical copula *u*- is based on an incomplete word U-JA-[following a word he interprets as a verb JA.TA.100.88. This is hardly conclusive.

Gordon has presented a list of about two dozen Semitic vocabulary items (excluding proper names) in Linear A. Even if some of these identifications were valid, they would not form an impressive proportion of the over five hundred distinct words on the tablets and miscellaneous inscriptions. No comprehensive case for a Semitic language has yet be constructed.[38] There are a few Semitic loan words in Linear B, and some Semitic words may have been borrowed also by the language of Linear A.[39]

The second major candidate for the language of Linear A has been Luvian, championed most vigorously by Palmer[40] who would place Luvians

---

[37] Gordon (1966, 28).

[38] Jucquois (1969) presents an instructive chart listing Gordon's translations beside those of rival decipherers for many of the same words and phrases.

[39] Semitic loan words in Greek are discussed by E. Masson (1967).

[40] Palmer (1958; 1965, chap. ix; 1968). Palmer acknowledges that his theory is "a possibility . . . merely as a working hypothesis" (1968, 339) as distinct from Gordon (1966, viii) who "aims at providing qualified scholars with all the evidence they need for understanding the Northwest Semitic character of Minoan." The comprehensive Hittite decipherment by Davis (1967) is not on a par with Palmer's studies.

on the Greek mainland as well as in Crete during the Middle Bronze Age. The difficulties associated with the hypothesis of a Luvian invasion of the mainland have been emphasized by Mylonas.[41] As for Crete, the excavators of the 'Luvian' palace at Beycesultan were confident that Minoan palace architecture was heavily indebted to Luvian models, but Graham has cast serious doubt on many of the alleged similarities.[42] Luvians in Crete remain hypothetical, though recently published seals from the Luvian area show remarkable parallels with Minoan seals from contemporary Phaistos.[43]

Georgiev proposes to read the Hagia Triada tablets as Greek (the 'Phaistian' dialect), and the religious inscriptions as Hittite.[44] With a more limited goal, Neumann has drawn attention to some possible lexical survivals from the language of Linear A in later Greek.[45] Nagy has also attempted to isolate "Greek-like" elements in Linear A.[46]

Kamm has studied the syllabary, fractions, and ideograms, but his own identification of the language of Linear A (Indic) does not yet have many supporters.[47]

Brice, in addition to editing the texts, has written a series of papers comparing the structure of the script and the organization of the tablets with Near-Eastern counterparts. He does not share the commonly held view that Linear A contains a syllabary.[48]

This brief review of work to date on Linear A illustrates the precariousness of attempts to link Linear A with other known languages. Sign-groups have been found in Linear A which could be interpreted as Semitic, as Luvian and as Greek. This fact is not itself a *reductio ad absurdum* of the etymological method since, as far as lexical items go, elements of any of these languages could be present in Linear A. Isolated lexical correspondences, however, can be misleading, especially since the spelling rules are flexible enough to make it possible to find plausible

---

[41] Mylonas (1962).

[42] Graham (1964). Luvians in Crete are discussed by Schachermeyr (1962). The hypothesis that Linear A may contain an Anatolian language has been suggested with varying degrees of confidence also by Furumark (1956), Pugliese Carratelli (1955), and Peruzzi (1960).

[43] Levi (1969).

[44] Georgiev (1963 and 1968).

[45] Neumann (1957, 1958, 1960, and 1961).

[46] Nagy (1963 and 1965).

[47] Kamm (1965a, 1965b, 1965c, 1966, 1967a, 1967b). Many of his observations have interest independent of his linguistic hypothesis.

[48] Brice (1962a, 1962b, 1963, 1967).

"yields" in several languages.⁴⁹ Etymological analysis can serve a useful role in isolating "Greek-like" or "Luvian-like" elements, but no one has yet been able to interpret a significant portion of the Linear A corpus with reference to any known language. It is equally possible that the language of Linear A is not attested elsewhere. In either case, there is a need to carry the *internal* analysis of the texts and syllabary further than has been done in the past. The present study attempts to carry forward such internal analysis in two directions. The first part is a preliminary contribution towards a contextual classification of the Hagia Triada archives. The second attempts a detailed and critical investigation into the problem of the phonetic values.

Typographical Conventions

Linear A sign-groups are transliterated according to the phonetic equivalents given on page 67 and Figures 5 and 6, with use of L numbers reserved for signs with no parallel in Linear B. Use of this convention does not imply endorsement of the phonetic values, but even specialists will find it easier to remember KU.MI.NA.QE than 98-76-26-91. Linear A sign-groups are distinguished by capitals with a period separating the signs (KU.PA$_3$.NU), to avoid confusion with Linear B in lower-case italics with a hyphen separating the signs (*ka-pa$_3$-no*). Ideograms in Linear A have English names (MAN) as opposed to Latin (VIR) for Linear B. Sign-groups in Linear B are cited from Morpurgo's *Lexicon* where further references can be found.⁵⁰ Linear A readings are those of Raison-Pope (1971) unless otherwise stated, and references to inscriptions follow their numeration.

---

⁴⁹ For an entertaining demonstration of the ambiguities of the Linear B spelling conventions, see Young (1967).
⁵⁰ Morpurgo (1963). But note that *56, *66 and *43 are here transcribed *pa$_3$*, *ta$_2$*, and *ai*. Where the fourth edition of *The Knossos Tablets* differs from Morpurgo, I have normally cited the newer reading with a fuller reference.

a) Three-sided Pictographic Seal from Knossos

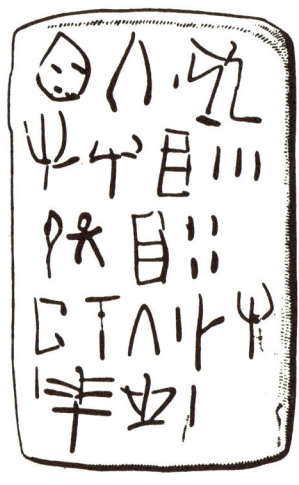 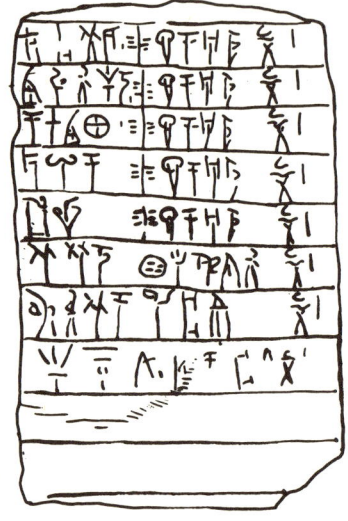

b) Linear A Tablet

c) Linear B Tablet

 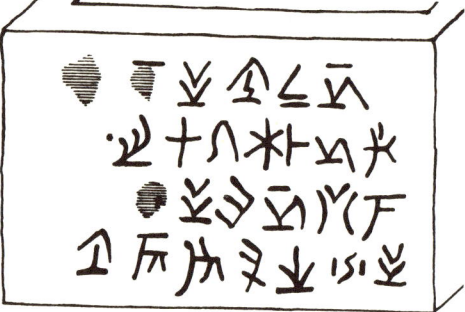

d) Cypro-Minoan Tablet

e) Classical Cypriot Script

Figure 1. The Five Branches of Aegean Writing

[Full credits for all figures appear on page 11]

1. L29.L97.L102.L74
2. L82 , L92 , L54.L23 '5' [?] Lm9 [
3. L92.L6 '56' L92.L103
4. '27' Lm9 L98.L101.L60 '16' Lm9
5. L30.L57.L85 '19' L100.L93.
6. L61.L57 '5'
7. L98.L22 '130' Lm9

1. KA.U.DE.TA
2. WINE , TE , RE.ZA '5' [?] 1/x [
3. TE.TU '56' TE.KI
4. '27' 1/x KU.DO.NI '16' 1/x
5. DA.SI.L85 '19' I.DU.
6. NE.SI '5'
7. KU.RO '130' 1/x

HT 13 (G Series)

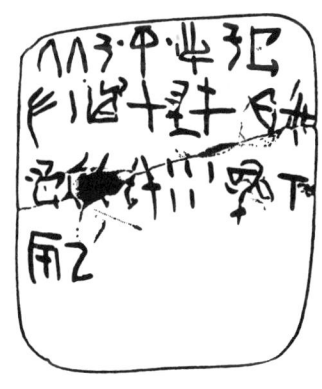

1. L78.L78.L98 , L42 , L100.L98.L74
2. L71 '1' Lc29 Lm19 Lc122 Lm19 L90 Lm19
3. Lc24 [Lm28?] L44 '5' Lc109 Lm18
4. L82 Lm23

1. TI.TI.KU , WHEAT , I.KU.TA
2. CYPERUS '1' Lc29 1/x OIL+RI 1/x L90 1/x
3. OIL+TA [1/x] L44 '5' Lc109 1/x
4. WINE 1/x

HT 35 (E Series)

Figure 2. Linear A Tablets with Transcription

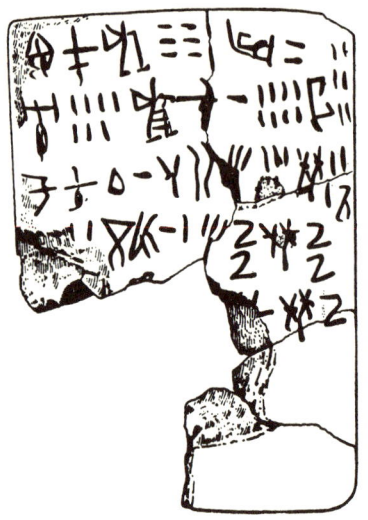

1. L29.L2 L99 '60' L35 '20'
2. L52 '7' L126 '18' L74 '6'
3. L98.L22 '110' L31.L58 L71 '5' L60 '3' Lm7
4.] L81.L83 '11' L71 Lm24 L60 Lm24
5.]Lm9 L60 Lm23

1. KA.PA MAN '60' SHIP? '20'
2. A '7' MAN '18' TA '6'
3. KU.RO '110' SA.RA$_2$ CYPERUS '5' FIGS '3' 1/x
4.] JE.L83 '11' CYPERUS 1/x FIGS 1/x
5.]1/x FIGS 1/x

HT 94 (B and C Series)

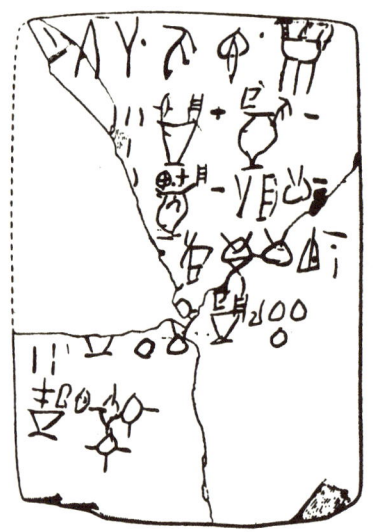

1.]L78.L31 , L64.L45 , Lc45
2.]'5' Lc63 '10' Lc64 '10'
3.]'1' Lc65 '10' L31.L32.L95 '20'
4.]'10' L103.L102.L95.L9.L26
5. '4' LcX '400' Lc66 '300'
6. Lc67 '3000'

1.]TI.SA , PU.KO , TRIPOD+JE
2.]'5' POT+QA.PA$_3$ '10' POT+SU.PU '10'
3.]'1' POT+KA.RO.PA$_3$ '10' SA.JA.MA '20'
4.]'10' KI.DE.MA.L9.NA
5.]'4' POT+? '400' POT+SU.PA$_3$.RA '300'
6. POT+PA.TA.QE '3000'

HT 31 (F Series)

Figure 3. Linear A Tablets with Transcription

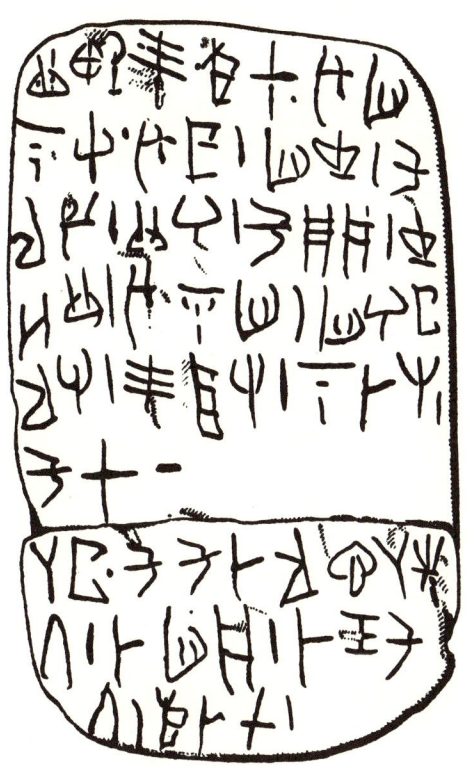

1. L95.L29.L72.L92 , L103.L22 , L97.L76.
2. L26.L57 , L97.L59 '1' L76.L6 '1' L98.
3. L53.L100 '1' L95.L55 '1' L98.L1.L25 '1' L6.
4. L68.L95 '1' L97.L51.L76 '1' L76.L55.L74.
5. L53.L54 '1' L92.L32.L54 '1' L26.L30.L54 '1'
6. L98.L22 '10'
7. L31.L74 , L98.L98.L30.L53 L45.L31.L24.
8. L78 '1' L30.L76.L25 '1' L30.L61.L98.
9. L78 '1' L103.L30.L22 '1'

1. MA.KA.RI.TE , KI.RO , U.MI.
2. NA.SI , U.SU '1' MI.TU '1' KU.
3. RA.I '1' MA.RU '1' KU.PA$_3$.NU '1' TU.
4. L68.MA '1' U.DI.MI '1' MI.RU.TA.
5. RA.RE '1' TE.JA.RE '1' NA.DA.RE '1'
6. KU.RO '10'
7. SA.TA , KU.KU.DA.RA KO.SA.KE.
8. TI '1' DA.MI.NU '1' DA.NE.KU.
9. TI '1' KI.DA.RO '1'

HT 117 (A Series)

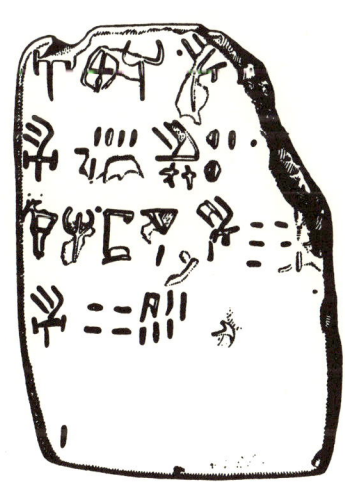

1. L52.L29.L55 , Lc14 '20'[
2. Lc12 '18' Lc13 '3' [
3. L103.L54.L74.L26 Lc14 '50'
4. Lc12 '47'

1. A.KA.RU , OIL+1/x '20'[
2. OIL+A '18' OIL+L44 '3' [
3. KI.RE.TA.NA OIL+1/x '50'
4. OIL+A '47'

HT 2 (C Series)

Figure 4. Linear A Tablets with Transcription

Figure 5. The Principal Linear A Syllabic Signs

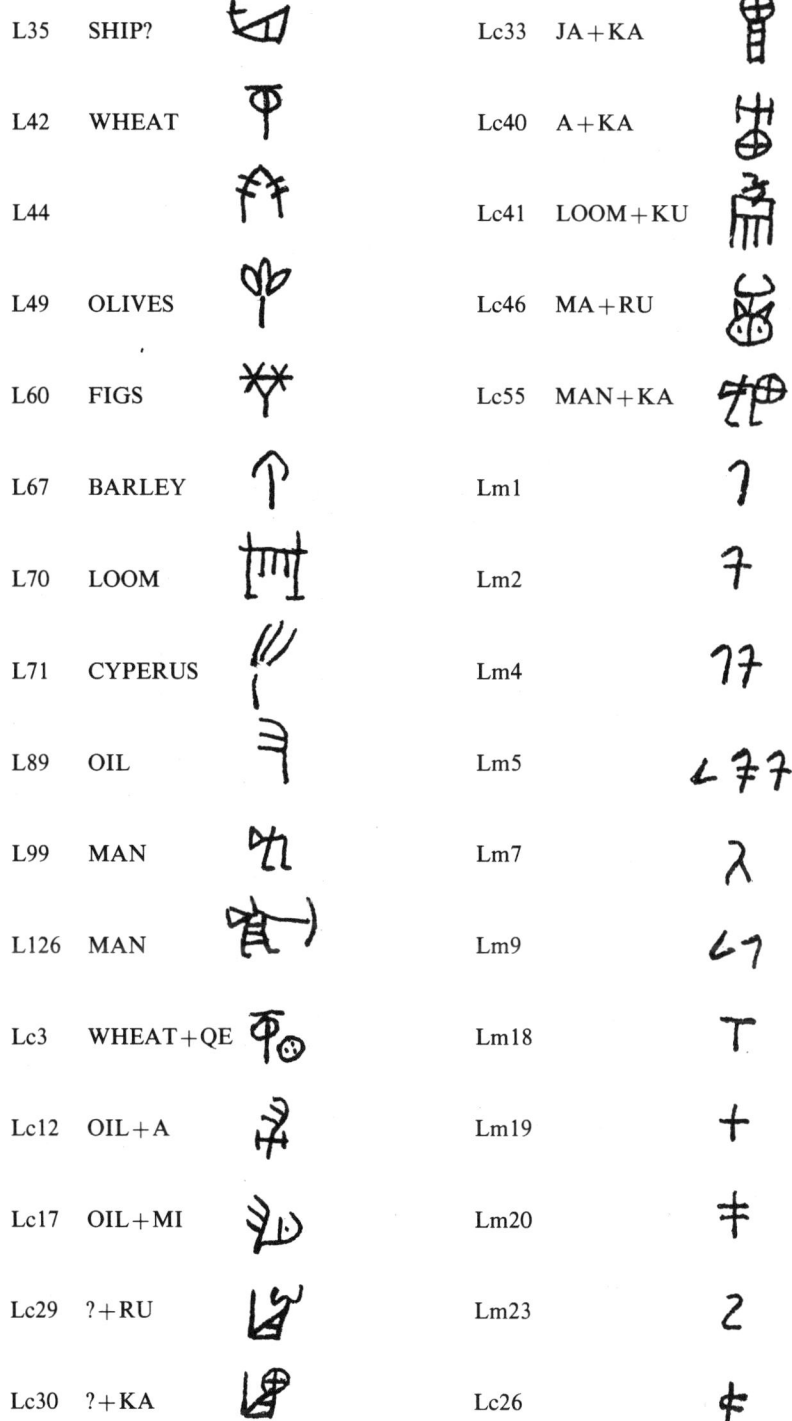

Figure 6. Some Linear A Ideograms, Ligatures, and Fractions

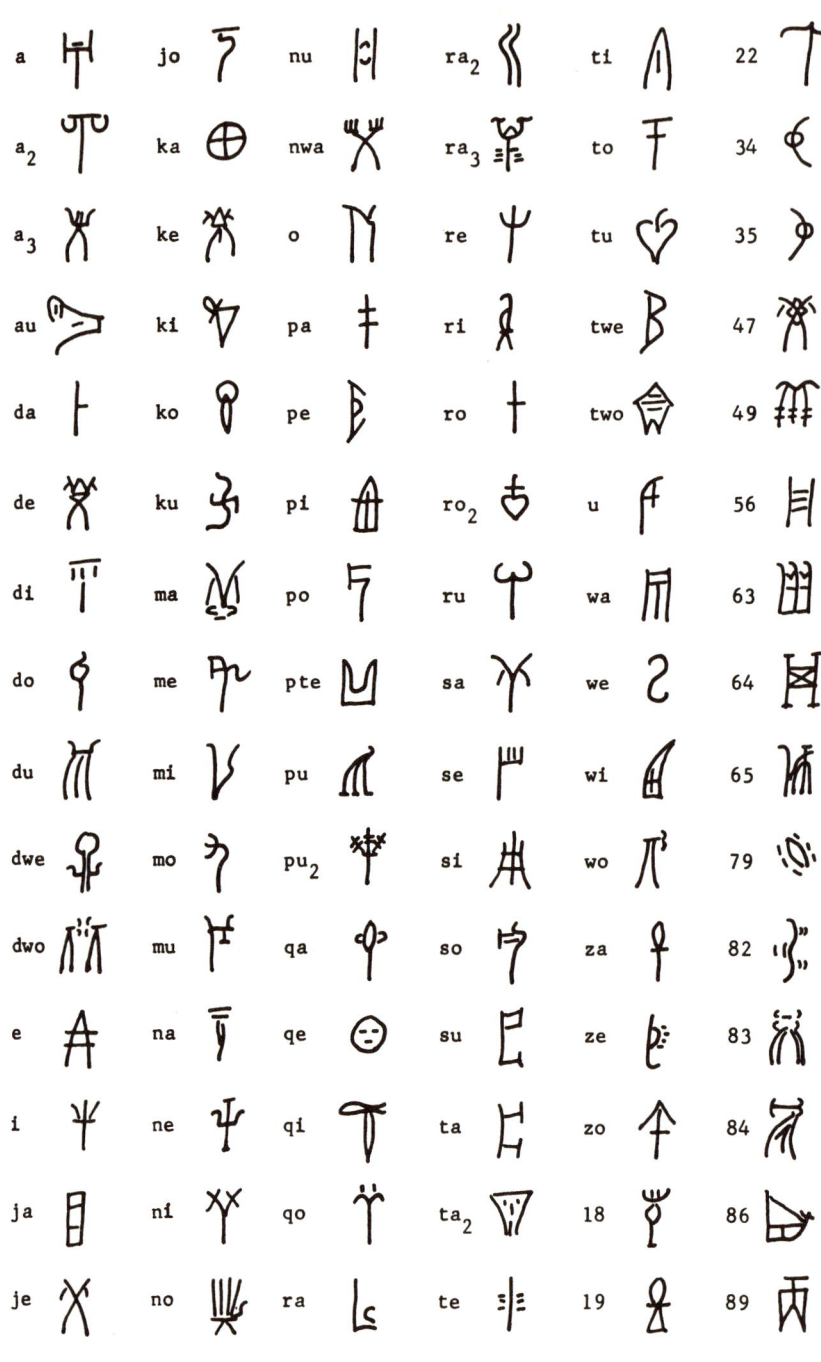

Figure 7. The Linear B Syllabary

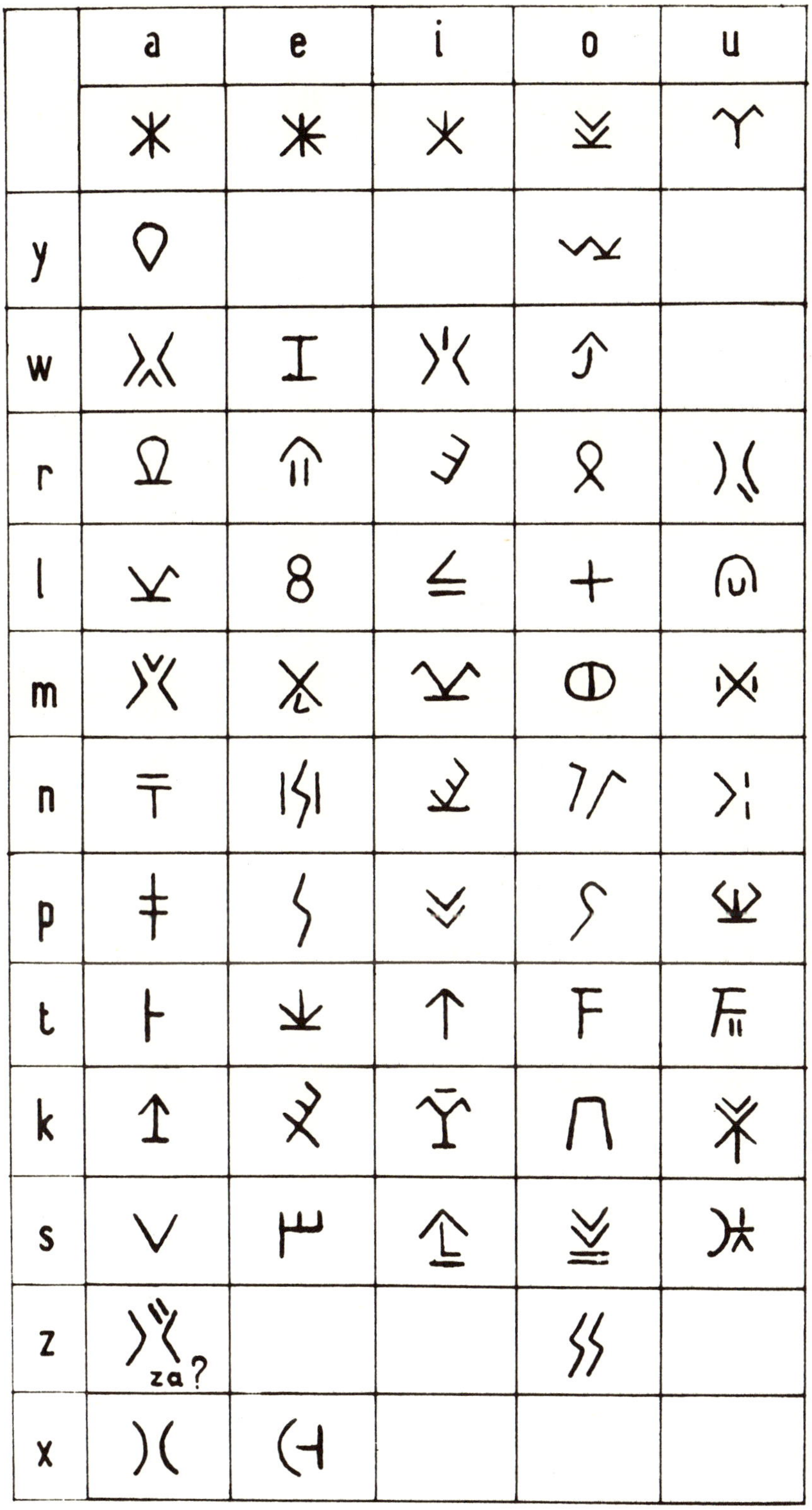

Figure 8. The Classical Cypriot Syllabary

CHAPTER TWO

CLASSIFICATION OF TABLETS

General Principles

Several years before the decipherment of Linear B, Bennett produced a remarkably accurate classification of the Pylos (and later the Knossos) tablets according to their apparent subject matter.[1] His criteria for assigning tablets to the various classes included recurrent formulaic phrases and ideograms as well as the scribal hands; but he could not read a single syllabic sign and refrained from speculation about the language of the tablets. His success might have encouraged others to attempt a similar analysis of Linear A, but the tablets are far less formulaic and the ideograms less clearly pictorial. Even more discouraging is the paucity of material. There are fewer than 150 fragmentary tablets from Hagia Triada compared with over 3000 at Pylos and Knossos. Recognizable subdivisions, nonetheless, exist within the Hagia Triada archives, and these have not yet been sufficiently explored. The tentative classes proposed below are not intended as a full counterpart to the system in use for Linear B, but they provide a framework for the contextual study of the tablets. Especially important is the possibility of isolating clusters of words which occur in the same general environment on tablets of the same class. Such groups of words have a reasonable chance of being homogeneous or at least falling within a limited semantic sphere. Chadwick, speaking of Linear B, stresses the importance of independent contextual analysis for evaluating a potential decipherment: "If a word so identified as an occupational term turns out, when transcribed phonetically to mean 'cow-herds,' this confirms the interpretation. On the other hand, interpretations which do not agree with this preliminary classification are at once suspect, due allowance being made for errors."[2]

---

[1] Bennett first presented his classification in 1947. For a summary of the Linear B classes, see Deroy (1962, chap. iv) and Palmer (1963, 4-8). Chadwick (1968 and 1972) discusses possible improvements, and the latest edition of the Knossos tablets (Chadwick-Killen-Olivier, 1971) introduces a few refinements; but the changes so far have been minor.

[2] Chadwick (1967, 46).

Myres published brief suggestions for classifying the Hagia Triada tablets according to the presence or absence in the heading of "principal sign-groups" and "transaction signs" and according to whether the items in the list (excluding numerals) are sign-groups, commodity signs, or both.[3] Brice offers a clearer but essentially identical scheme.[4] Such a classification may reflect the superficial organization of the tablet, but it takes no account of sub-groupings within the ideograms, or of the numbers and fractions which follow the items in the list. It also ignores clusters of identical sign-groups on different tablets. Further contributions toward a system of classification were made by Furumark who published his work only in outline, and by Peruzzi whose more extensive studies contain contextual analysis interspersed with etymological speculation.[5] However useful such linguistic analysis may be, it is best kept distinct from the contextual classification of the texts. Bennett's classification of Linear B was successful largely because he did not try to read anything.

The Linear B scribes often give visual emphasis to the logical structure of a document by writing introductory words in larger script and by disposing ideograms and numerals in vertical columns. Between sign-groups they normally insert word-dividers and avoid breaking a word at the end of the line. Uninscribed space frequently divides longer tablets into "paragraphs." The Linear A scribes, for the most part, are devoid of this sense of tidiness. Sign-groups, ideograms, and numbers spill over indifferently from one line to the next. In his hand-drawn transcription of each tablet, Brice introduces some clarity by aligning the items in rows and columns. Such transcriptions are an aid in visualizing the underlying structure of a tablet, but they represent an act of interpretation which can mislead. Brice underlines what he takes to be the "headings" and "subheadings." These distinctions are real ones, but since headings are not underlined on the tablets themselves, there is a danger of choosing the wrong division between heading and list. Within headings a dot often appears to serve as a word-divider, but such dots also occur elsewhere under obscure conditions. Since most sign-groups in the list are followed by numerals, the heading can be assumed roughly to consist of all initial sign-groups not followed by numbers. More complex structures are also possible, including apparent subheadings (e.g., HT 117). Some tablets (e.g., HT 119) may have no heading.

---

[3] Myres (1951).

[4] Brice (1961, 6) "based on his [Myres's] work."

[5] Peruzzi (1960, 31) sets out to analyze the Linear A inscriptions "ordinate secondo il contenuto." Furumark (1956) distinguishes classes A and B on the basis of ideograms. Kamm (1967a) makes some observations on classification of ideograms.

Too rigid a distinction between heading and list, however, may sometimes mislead. Given a scribal unwillingness to repeat an ideogram more often than necessary, one can easily imagine a tablet such as the following:

Phaistos, WHEAT	25
Knossos	30
Kydonia	20
Total	75

In the above tablet the sign-group in the heading is exactly parallel to the sign-groups in the list. It is unique only by being first. In other cases a sign-group in the heading might refer globally to every entry:

Zakro, WHEAT	
For spinners	10 1/2
For weavers	5
For carders	7 1/2
Total	23

A possible pattern for a more complex tablet might be:

Zakro, Monthy Rations	
For spinners	WHEAT 10 FIGS 10 WINE 10
For weavers	WHEAT 15 FIGS 20 WINE 17
For carders	WHEAT 20 FIGS 40 WINE 20
Total	WHEAT 45 FIGS 70 WINE 47

Many lists are totaled. The items counted or the substances measured in such lists must be commensurate or they could not be included under a single total. What is being totaled, however, is not necessarily named by the sign-groups which precede the numbers in the list. It might be mentioned in the heading, or perhaps deduced only from the context or filing place of the tablet. Three hypothetical tablets illustrate the difference:

At Knossos		Bakers		Workers	
Bakers	10	At Knossos	10	At Phaistos	40
Grooms	20	At Phaistos	15	Bakers	30
Smiths	40	At Mallia	10	With John	20
Total	70	Total	35	Total	90

In each case men are counted; but they are mentioned explicitly in the *list* in the first, and in the *heading* in the second and third. Moreover, the sign-groups in the third list are not strictly homogeneous, though they all describe men. A perhaps extreme example of this last principle is provided

by a text from the kingdom of Larsa dating around 1800 B.C. It lists
distributions of barley for various purposes:[6]

>3 s. food for the house
>6 qa for the goat
>5 qa for the ox
>.
>.
>.
>1 qa for groats
>1 qa for fine flour
>5 qa in a basket
>3 qa for (some kind of) flour
>.
>.
>.
>1/2 qa for beer
>... qa for the tailor

When confronted with a comparable list in Linear A, we must not infer that
houses, goats, oxen, groats, fine flour, baskets, beer, and tailors are literally
"homogeneous."

The major criterion used by Brice and Myres for classifying the Hagia
Triada tablets was the headings. Another potential indicator is the type of
item found in the list, including numerals and fractions. Still a third is the
scribal hands, recently identified by Raison and Pope.[7] One could begin by
dividing tablets into groups according to handwriting, but I have preferred
to reserve handwriting as a final test of classes arrived at by independent
means. The analysis will begin, therefore, by subdividing the tablets according
to the sign-groups, ideograms, and numbers in the *lists*. Headings
will then be examined to verify these groupings. Some tablets cannot be
classified by this procedure, and for them the heading must serve as
principal classifier. Finally, the classes will be tested against the tentative
identification of scribal hands published by Raison and Pope.

The A Series

We may assign to the A series those lists which consist of sign-groups all
followed by the numeral "1." Of these only HT 85b, 87, 88, 94a, and 117 are
substantially intact. The assumption that the sign-groups in these lists refer

---

[6] Edited and translated by Leemans (1954, 44-45), text number 30. Text number 51
lists food and fodder for boys, cattle, rams, a pig, and at least eight named individuals.

[7] Raison-Pope (1971, xx).

to personal names has much plausibility.⁸ Lists of personal names in Linear B are recognizable by the presence of the ideogram VIR or MULIER followed by the numeral "1"; but some Linear B name lists omit the ideogram and have a structure identical to these Linear A lists (PY Vn 865, KN Ap 482, As 1517, 1520). There appears to be no ideogram in Linear A which corresponds to VIR and MULIER in the function of enumerating individual names (for possible Linear A ideograms for MAN see page 51), but this may only reflect the general reluctance of the Linear A scribes to repeat superfluously the same sign-group or ideogram many times on the same list. Uneconomical repetition is a frequent phenomenon in Linear B (e.g., PY Cn 254, 655, Ep 212). The place name *ma-ro-pi* on PY Cn 655 is repeated at the beginning of twenty consecutive lines. One suspects that such a record, if written in Linear A, would mention the place only once, presumably in the heading.⁹ This same principle seems to govern the repetition of ideograms in lists. An ideogram which refers to all the numbers is apparently placed in the heading (HT 8, 9, 13, 115). The few cases where the same ideogram is repeated without a differentiating ligature more than once in one list can be explained by the necessity for clarity where several commodities are listed after one sign-group (HT 28, 116, 123). There is no objection, therefore, to neglecting the VIR ideogram in comparing these Linear A lists to lists of names in Linear B. Similarity of general structure, to be sure, is not conclusive. One can easily imagine a list which conforms in structure to these A series lists but does not enumerate personal names:

TAX COLLECTORS
At Knossos 1
At Phaistos 1
At Amnisos 1
At Kydonia 1
TOTAL 4

In the above (imaginary though plausible) tablet it would be wrong to deduce that the four sign-groups in the list are personal names, but it is not easy to substantiate this hypothetical example by pointing to an actual

---

⁸ Made first by Furumark (1956) though he did not use it explicitly as a basis for classification.

⁹ At least one Linear B scribe recognized the futility of these monotonous repetitions, for in PY Cn 328 he repeats the toponym *a-ka-na-jo* three times, but after writing the initial *a-* of the fourth repetition he omits the place name from the remaining ten entries (though leaving space on the tablet).

Linear B tablet in which words other than personal names are listed with the numeral "1" following each entry. It need not be the names themselves which are being counted. PY Vn 851, for example, seems to list a distribution of *de-mi-ni-ja* (bedding?), one to each name in a list:

> *de-mi-ni-ja*
> (name in dative) 1
> (name in dative) 1
> (name in dative) 1
>   etc.

It may be coincidental that the names here are all opposite the numeral "1," but things issued one at a time are very likely being issued to individual men. One Linear B tablet which might cast doubt on the identification of the A lists as lists of personal names is PY Cn 3 which begins:

> *jo-i-je-si me-za-na*
> *e-re-u-te-re di-wi-je-we qo-o*
> *a₂-ra-tu-a o-ka-ra₃*   BOS 1
> *pi-ru-te ku-re-we*   BOS 1
>   etc.

The sign groups in the list are probably place names and ethnics.[10] If the repeated ideogram BOS were omitted from each entry (as it might be in Linear A since it is already included in the heading as the sign-group *qo-o*) this would be a tablet where items other than personal names are followed by "1" in a list. Having illustrated the possibility that something other than personal names could occur on such lists, we must nonetheless conclude that these Linear A lists of the A series most likely enumerate individual men and women.

The sign-groups in these A series lists are printed in Table 1. They account for roughly 20% of the words preserved at Hagia Triada. Some appear more than once within the series as well as on other tablets.[11] The identification of all the sign-groups on these lists as personal names is not without some difficulty. In particular, it is suspicious that the monosyllables

---

[10] Palmer (1963, 176).

[11] For the inclusion of HT 122 see below. The adoption of the readings of Raison and Pope (rather than Brice) eliminated three additional links within the A series: A.RA.68 on HT 87 (also on HT 122); PA.JA.RE on HT 117 (also on HT 88); and SI.DA.RE on HT 49 (also on HT 122). From the photographs none of these readings of Brice seems impossible. Their repetition within the A series makes them attractive, but without examining the tablets in person I would hesitate to reject the opinion of Raison and Pope.

PA and DI seem to represent names. Linear A may not share Linear B's alleged aversion to writing words with a single sign. On the other hand, these monosyllables may resemble TA and DA or *ko-wo* and *ko-wa* in certain Linear B tablets like KN Ap 639. That tablet contains a long list of women, each followed by MULIER "1"; but interspersed among the names are entries of *ko-wa* "1" or *ko-wo* "1." In addition to "boy" or "girl," other meanings such as "helper" or "overseer" could be imagined for these Linear A monosyllables. They might be abbreviations for longer names, though personal names could be abbreviated to a single sign only at the expense of considerable ambiguity.[12]

Only five tablets of the A series have headings preserved. The heading to HT 85b is unique, but the headings to the four complete and totaled lists show remarkable similarity:

79.TU.NE MA.KA.RI.TE	(HT 87)
KI.RO	(HT 88)
KI.RO	(HT 94)
MA.KA.RI.TE KI.RO U.MI.NA.SI SA.TA 79.TU.NE	(HT 117)

In addition, the signs 79.TU.[on HT 94 should almost certainly be restored as 79.TU.[NE and taken as a sub-heading. The similarity in headings is a strong confirmation that we were justified in grouping these lists together on the basis of the structure of their lists.

In addition to the list of "names," most of these A series tablets contain another list (we may term it the "reverse"). A common element of these reverse lists seems to be some form of the MAN ideogram (L99 on HT 25, 85, and 122; L126b on HT 94; Lc55 on HT 88) and numbers greater than one without fractions. Two of the headings to these lists include the sign-group A.DU (HT 85 and 88). The similarity of these reverse lists is another confirmation of the homogeneity of the A series.

We may now ask which scribal hands are associated with the A series. Raison and Pope attribute HT 87, 94, and 117 to hand iii. These three tablets will form the Aa series. They have interrelated headings, have no monosyllables in the lists, and the entire group has only one "reverse" (on HT 94). HT 88, attributed to hand xvi (which has affinities with hand iii), shares one sign-group with HT 117 and has a heading which fits in with the

---

[12] The desire to avoid ambiguity is well illustrated in Linear B by the scribe of MY Ge 603 who abbreviates the spice names KO = *ko-ri-ja-da-na*, KU = *ku-mi-na*, SA = *sa-sa-me*, but writes *ka-na-ko* and *ka-da-mi-ja* in full to avoid the ambiguity of KA.

Aa series, but its reverse shares the sign-group A.DU with HT 85 by hand viii. These two tablets may be classified Ab. Both HT 25 and 49 are by hand xi and may therefore be linked as an Ac series. The remaining three tablets (HT 4, 55, and 127) are fragmentary and may be classed Ax.

One enigmatic tablet (HT 122) does not fulfill the major criterion for entry into this series since its list contains several numbers (all early in the list) greater than one, but secondary criteria strongly associate it with the A series. The last ten sign-groups in the list are all followed by the numeral "1," the list shares three[13] sign-groups with the A series, its reverse fits into the A pattern, and it is by the scribe of the "Aa" series (hand iii). On the basis of these indicators it may perhaps be classed Ad, but I have no easy explanation for its idiosyncrasies.

It is clear from Table 1 that many words on these A lists appear also on other tablets. If a sign-group represents a personal name on an A list, it presumably also has the same meaning on other lists although we cannot exclude the presence of occasional homographs, especially for short words. It will be convenient, therefore, to draw up a list of tablets which share sign-groups with the A lists. The presence of one personal name on a list does not allow the inference that all the entries are names, but it will often provide a starting point for the analysis of a tablet if we can note that one or more sign-groups on that tablet occur also within A lists. There is, then, *prima facie* evidence for the presence of at least one personal name on each tablet listed in Table 2. One tablet (HT 9) shares five sign-groups with the A lists, and six others share at least two each.

There is an independent way of testing the hypothesis that sign-groups in the A lists are personal names. Linear A sign-groups in some cases resemble names known in the Linear B tablets from Knossos. Since such comparisons will involve assumptions about the phonetic values of the Linear A signs, we must reserve them for Chapter Three. At this point it will be sufficient to anticipate the later section by remarking that at least five sign-groups in these A lists can be equated with personal names at Knossos, thus strengthening their identification as personal names in Linear A.

Linear B and Near Eastern tablets provide many analogous lists of names. By examining the purpose of keeping such lists in a Bronze Age palace economy, we may gain some notion of what kind of information these Linear A lists are likely to record.

Linear B lists of personal names are accompanied by the following sorts of information.

1) Place where the men or women are located. (PY An 5)

---

[13] Possibly five. See note 11.

2) Trade. (PY Vn 865)

3) Name of owner or overseer. (PY An 129, 340)

4) Ethnic origin as opposed to present location. (PY An 295)

5) Miscellaneous information such as "men having to take the field" (PY An 218),[14] or the name of the person in whose *ke-ro-si-ja* the man is a member (PY An 261, 616).

The Alalakh tablets also contain many lists of names.[15] The tablets have not yet been fully published, but the available descriptions are usually detailed enough to allow comparisons with Linear A and B. Many of the Alalakh tablets record the census of a single village (135, 136, 140, 141 etc.). The entries are subdivided according to social class and are accompanied sometimes by trade, origin (if not native to the village), and father's name. At Alalakh, as in Linear B, place names and occupational terms seem to be the most common rubrics. Personal names occur in headings, however, also at Alalakh (145 and 165 list men under charge of certain individuals).

A few observations are now possible about the headings to the Aa series. The heading to HT 117 is followed by two sub-headings. The sign-groups in the two sub-headings may be parallel to one of the sign-groups of the main heading. Two of the words in the main heading would be understood as implicit in each of the sub-headings. Two of many possible arrangements of word classes are:

```
Place Trade Month        Trade Place Month
  name   "1"               name   "1"
  name   "1"               name   "1"
Trade                    Place
  name   "1"               name   "1"
  name   "1"               name   "1"
Trade                    Place
  name   "1"               name   "1"
  name   "1"               name   "1"
```

In HT 87, the sign-groups 79.TU.NE and MA.KA.RI.TE occur together in the heading. It is therefore not likely that they are both place names or both trade designations. In HT 117, then, the sub-heading 79.TU.NE is probably not parallel to MA.KA.RI.TE in the main heading, so that the subheadings SA.TA and 79.TU.NE may belong to the same word-class as either KI.RO or U.MI.NA.SI. This last sign-group is involved in a similar pattern of

---

[14] Palmer (1963, 142)
[15] Wiseman (1953).

headings and sub-headings on HT 28a. U.MI.NA.SI, then, seems to have an affinity for major headings and may be a more general vocabulary term. KI.RO, SA.TA and 79.TU.NE would then form a group of related terms used as sub-headings.[16] It is easier to point out these parallels than to know how to interpret them. There is some slight reason to suspect that 79.TU.NE is a personal name since it occurs on HT 7 along with TA.NA.TI which is listed on HT 49, one of the less certain A lists. This is slim evidence, though a personal name is a possible component of a heading to a list of personal names both in Linear B and at Alalakh.[17]

Another, perhaps more likely, hypothesis is that these three words describe classes of men. If we are correct in restoring 79.TU.[NE as a sub-heading on HT 94 then these words will fall in the same word class as L35, a parallel sub-heading on that tablet, which is an ideogram characteristic of the B Series and presumably denotes a class of men.[18]

---

[16] If U.69.SI can be considered a spelling variant of U.MI.NA.SI (see p. 107), then HT 15 would allow another comparison. The only sign-groups on this tablet (KI.RO and U.69.SI) would then be paralleled in headings to the A series.

[17] On the possibility of overlap between personal names and geographical terms, it is worth quoting Leemans (1954, 89-90): "Like many small towns, also some towns in this [Akkadian] text may have been named after persons (founders, etc.)." Personal names themselves are often derived from toponyms (cf. *pa-i-ti-ja* in Linear B) and from occupational terms. It is perfectly plausible, therefore, that the same sign-group in Linear A might function both as a personal name and as an occupational term or place name.

[18] I am inclined, therefore, to agree with the reconstruction of lines 4-5 by Georgiev (1963, 53) and Kamm (1967b, 248) which takes L35 as a sub-heading followed by a single name RA.[X].ME.TE "1," followed by another sub-heading 79.TU.[NE and a name plus "1" in the broken area of the tablet.

Table 1: Sign-Groups in A Series Lists

Sign-Group	In A Series	Elsewhere
PI.TA.KE.SI	HT 87	
JA.RE.MI	HT 87	
DI.KI.SE	HT 87,117	
QE.SU.PU	HT 87	
KU.RU.KU	HT 87	
A.RA.WI/PI	HT 87	A.RA.68 (HT 122)
A.TU	HT 87	
KU.PA$_3$.NU	HT 88,117,49,122	HT 1,3
KA.96	HT 88	
PA.JA.RE	HT 88,117?	HT 8,29
SA.MA.RO	HT 88	HT 39
DA.TA.RE	HT 88	HT 62
TU.MA	HT 94	cf. TU.68.MA(HT 117)
PA.TA.NE	HT 94,122	
DE.DI	HT 94	
KE.KI.RU	HT 94	
SA.RU	HT 94	HT 86,95,123
U.SU	HT 117	
MI.TU	HT 117	HT 135
KU.RA.I	HT 117	
MA.RU	HT 117	
TU.68.MA	HT 117	
U.DI.MI	HT 117	
MI.RU.TA.RA.RE	HT 117	
TE.JA.RE	HT 117	(read PA.JA.RE?)
NA.DA.RE	HT 117	
KU.KU.DA.RA	HT 117	
KO.SA.KE.TI	HT 117	
DA.MI.NU	HT 117	
DA.NE.KU.TI	HT 117	
KI.DA.RO	HT 117	
KU.RE.96	HT 117	HT 39
U.DE.ZA	HT 122	cf. U.37.ZA 10,85
DA.SI.85	HT 122	HT 13,85a,99
TE.KI	HT 122	HT 13
JA.MI.DA.RE	HT 122	
SI.DA.RE	HT 122	HT 17
?.DI.RA	HT 122	HT 9
PA.DE	HT 122	HT 9

Table 1 (cont.)

Sign-Group	In A Series	Elsewhere
83.TU	HT 122	HT 9,119
DA.WE.DA	HT 122	HT 10,85,93
]RU.NI	HT 25	
U.RE.WI	HT 25	
DI.NA.U	HT 25	HT 9,16
A.RI.NI.TA	HT 25	
TU.QE.NU	HT 25	
DO.96.PU$_2$	HT 25	
DU.RU.WI[	HT 25	
]I.KI.RA	HT 25	
PA	HT 25,85	
]PU.RA$_2$	HT 49	
]TA.NA.TI	HT 49	HT 7,10,98
SU.KI[	HT 49	
TI.DU.NI	HT 49	
]SI.RA	HT 49	
A.RU	HT 49	HT 9
U?	HT 49	
L36	HT 49	
TU.SU.PU$_2$	HT 49	
KI.RE.TA$_2$	HT 85	HT 129
QE.KA	HT 85	HT 111
TE.TU	HT 85	HT 7,13
PA.KA	HT 85	
DI	HT 85	
ME.ZA	HT 85	HT 10
RE.DI.SE	HT 85	
WA.DU.NI.MI	HT 85	HT 6
MA.DI	HT 85	HT 3,69,97,118
QA.63.I	HT 85,122	HT 8
]83.TI.KA.A.RE	HT 4	
]TA.DU.WE.TE	HT 4	
SI.RE[	HT 4	
]TA.PI.SI.DI	HT 4	
]MA.RE	HT 55	
SI.RU	HT 55	
]DU.NE.MI	HT 127	
]10.DA.DE.KU	HT 127	

Table 2: Lists Sharing Sign-Groups with A Lists

Tablet	Sign-Groups in Common with A Lists
HT 1	KU.PA$_3$.NU(HT 49,88,117,122)
HT 3	MA.DI(HT 85),KU.PA$_3$.NU(HT 49,88,117,122)
HT 6	WA.DU.NI.MI(HT 85)
HT 7	TA.NA.TI(HT 49),TE.TU(HT 85)
HT 8	QA.61.I(HT 85,122),PA.JA.RE(HT 88,117?)
HT 9	A.RU(HT 49),7.DI.RA(HT 122),PA.DE(HT 122), 83.TU(HT 122),DI.NA.U(HT 25)
HT 10	ME.ZA(HT 85),TA.NA.TI(HT 49), DA.WE.DA(HT 122)
HT 13	TE.TU(HT85),DA.SI.85(HT 122),TE.KI(HT 122)
HT 16	DI.NA.U(HT 25)
HT 17	SI.DA.RE(HT 122)
HT 29	PA.JA.RE(HT 88)
HT 39	KU.RE.96(HT117),SA.MA.RO(HT 88)
HT 62	DA.TA.RE(HT 88)
HT 86	SA.RU(HT 94)
HT 93	DA.WE.DA(HT 122)
HT 95	SA.RU(HT 94)
HT 97	MA.DI(HT 85)
HT 98	TA.NA.TI(HT 49)
HT 99	DA.SI.85(HT 122)
HT 111	QE.KA(HT 85)
HT 118	MA.DI(HT 85)
HT 119	83.TU(HT 122)
HT 123	SA.RU(HT 94)
HT 129	KI.RE.TA$_2$(HT 85)
HT 135	MI.TU(HT 117)

The B Series

The criterion for assigning a list to the B series is the presence of the sign L99 or one of its variants L125, L126 and Lc55. These signs seem to depict men, though they do not closely resemble the Linear B ideograms VIR and MULIER. We shall refer to them as "MAN" ideograms, but for purposes of classification it will not be necessary to establish what the signs represent.

For the most part these signs stand in isolation in apparent ideographic usage, but in a few cases phonetic function is conceivable. The sequence L99-L100 occurs twice (HT 11a4 and 93a5) as does the more doubtful L100-L126 (HT 25b2 and 102.2, both uncertain readings). Since all four cases involve the simple addition of L100, they provide very little evidence for full phonetic usage. On HT 7a1, L99 is most naturally taken as the last element of the heading rather than as part of the following sign-group.

Two tablets (HT 28 and 93) containing these signs have a complex structure and must be treated separately. A third tablet (HT 102) probably belongs with these since it contains multiple ideograms in the list and shares sign-groups with HT 93. Four further tablets are fragmentary (HT 66, 68, 72, and 84). Of the remaining lists eight are totaled (HT 25b, 27a, 89, 94b, 97a, 100, 119, 127).[19] The items in these totaled lists are most likely to be homogeneous. They are listed in Table 3. Five more lists contain MAN ideograms but are not totaled (HT 11a4, 26b, 62, 88, 105). These items are listed in a separate column in Table 3.

In addition to the MAN ideograms about 50 other entries appear in these B lists. Seven of these are repeated twice: L35 on HT 27 and 94, L66 on HT 89 and 100, L8 on HT 97 and 119, KI on HT 97 and 100, Lc34 on HT 127 and 26, A on HT 94 and 100, L96 on HT 97 and 119. These repetitions lend confidence to the decision to classify the lists together.

L35 appears in two B lists (HT 27 and 94a). HT 11b may therefore belong with the B lists since it contains L35. Moreover, L99 appears on the reverse. HT 45, a very fragmentary tablet, has an entry 35.66 which may be a phonetic group. Since both L35 and L66 occur independently on B lists, however, it may be safest not to ignore the dot separating the signs and to view them as a compound ideographic usage of some sort. Brice reads Lc55 on HT 37.2, but the sign is not visible in the photograph or in Pugliese Carratelli's drawing. The tablet, nonetheless, may possibly have affinities with the B lists as it shares two items with those lists (A and KI). The numbers and heading of HT 26a resemble HT 26b which contains L99 and L35. Since HT 26a shares the sign-group TA.TI with HT 97, we are perhaps safe in classifying the entire tablet in the B series.

---

[19] The total on HT 97a is contained on the recently joined HT 109.

A few entries in B lists occur also in the A series: DI, MA.DI, 83.TU, and possibly DA.TA.RE. Elsewhere, the B items appear in headings or in lists normally accompanied by numbers greater than one. The fractions on HT 9 and 13 almost certainly reflect the WINE ideogram in the headings.

The headings to the B series include two instances of L56b (HT 27a and 89).[20] The sign-group KA.PA occurs on three B headings (HT 94, 102, and 105).

Four B lists are assigned to or near hand iii (HT 94, 97, 119, 127). No single hand is associated with the remainder of the B series.

The analysis of the B series lists shows that the entries appear to form a coherent group and does not contradict the view that they designate entities counted (in whole numbers) rather than measured (with fractions). The identification of these ideograms as MEN on the basis of their shape is consistent with the context in which they occur. It is further supported by the nature of the lists which appear on the same tablets with B lists. Some tablets have only a B series list. Others (HT 25, 88, 94, 127) include also an A list. In a third group (HT 27, 89, 94, 100) the B list occurs in conjunction with a list which contains agricultural ideograms (the C series, see below). These groupings would accord well with an interpretation of the B series ideograms as *classes of men*. In the second group, the B series list would itemize the men in larger categories while the A series list would enumerate particular individuals. The third group might then record rations paid out to, or commodities due from, various groups of men, just as the Ab series in Linear B records groups of women with their rations.

It is not easy to determine what distinctions are made by the various modifications of the MAN ideograms and by the various sign-groups and ligatures which occur in lists with them. The Linear B ideograms VIR and MULIER are of little help here since they do not make any fine distinctions at all and, in any case, do not resemble the Linear A signs. These Linear B ideograms seem to have closer affinity with several of the Cretan Hieroglyphic signs than with Linear A.[21] Some of the MAN ideograms seem to be wearing ceremonial robes (L125 and L126) though this may be illusory in view of the schematic nature of the signs. The detailed ritual preparations listed on the Linear B tablets might lead one to look for religious personnel in Linear A.

The most obvious need for distinguishing groups of men is by their

---

[20] Brice reads this sign also in two additional B headings (HT 84 and 97a).

[21] Compare Hieroglyphic signs no. 1 and 2 with Linear B VIR and VIRb. Parallels with Mycenaean vase painting cited by Peruzzi (1960, 54) are late and from Cyprus. They may reflect Minoan traditions but do not explain the variations in shape.

profession. In this connection it may be relevant to consider three signs which occur in B series lists along with various MAN ideograms: L8, L35 and L10. The first of these resembles the Linear B ideogram for bronze; the second looks like the prow of a ship, and the third may be based on the ideogram L67, perhaps BARLEY. It is tempting, though highly speculative, to interpret these as "men who work with bronze," that is, bronzesmiths (cf. *ka-ke-u* in Linear B); "men who work with boats," perhaps shipwrights (cf. *na-u-do-mo* in Linear B); "men who work with barley," or bakers of some sort (cf. *a-to-po-qo* in Linear B). The only occurrence of L10 outside of a B series list is on HT 127a where it precedes a sign-group which is followed by the numeral "1." This sign-group could be a personal name with the ideogram describing the profession, though such use of an ideogram is foreign to Linear B.

Table 3: Items in B Series Lists

Ideogram or Sign-group	Totaled B List	Other B List	Elsewhere
L99	25b,27a 94a,119	26,62,105 66,68,72,84	85a,93a,122b
L126a	25b,27a		102,108
L35	27a	11b?,26b?	45,94b
RE[	27a		
]I.MI.SA.RA	27a		
]QE	27a		
KI.DA[	27a		
]KI.DU.KU[	27a		
]SA.RA.DI	27a		
L66	89,100		41,45,132
Lc58	89		
MA.I.MI	89		
L125	89,100		
TA.RA	89		
A	94a,100.2?		37,39
L126b	94a,127		
TA	94a		
L8	97,119		
KA.NU.TI	97		
PA.I.TO	97		120.6
DI	97		3.3,20.3,32.3, 69.1,85b3,111,122
NA.TI	97		
MA.DI	97		85,118,170,3,69
L96	97,119		
KI	97,100		37,49,118
TA.TI	97		26
Lc55	100,97	88	
L10	100		
RI.MI.SI	119		
KO.JA	119		
KU.PA$_3$.NA.TU	119		47a
TI	119		
JA.138	119		
83.TU	119		9,122
8.96	119?		

Table 3 (cont.)

Ideogram or Sign-group	Totaled B List	Other B List	Elsewhere
L56b	127b		
KU?	127b		
Lc34	127b	26	
L88?	127b		126?,10?,110?,115
A.SU.JA		11a	
99.I		11a	93
TA$_2$		11a	
]TE.RO.NI		26	
KA.U.101.NI		26	
I.KA		26	91,93,102
87.35		26	
DA.TA.RE?		62	88
KA.KU		62	
I.TI		62	
KO[		62	
]NU		62	
]NU.TI		84	
RE.ZA		88	13
KI.KI.NA		88	

Lists of Agricultural Commodities

The next three series (C through E) contain ideograms which resemble Linear B ideograms for agricultural products. The major Linear A signs are: L60 (FIGS), L49 (OLIVES), L42 (WHEAT), L67 (BARLEY), L89 (OIL), L82 (WINE), and L71 (CYPERUS).[22] A large number of tablets contain these ideograms and it is not obvious how they should be classified. We might expect to find agricultural ideograms on tablets dealing with rations, tribute, land tenure, religious offerings, and in other similar contexts. When they appear on tablets of the B series, such ideograms most likely represent rations since those tablets seem to enumerate groups of men. HT 27 contains CYPERUS, FIGS, and WINE, HT 89 may list FIGS and WINE,[23] HT 94 enumerates CYPERUS and FIGS, and HT 100 lists CYPERUS, FIGS, WINE and OIL (with ligatures).

The C Series

This series consists of twenty-three tablets containing various agricultural ideograms: HT 2, 14, 18, 21, 28, 42, 44, 50, 58, 90, 91, 99, 101, 114, 116, 121, 125, 129, 130, 131, 137, 139, 140. Fractions are frequent. Particularly noteworthy is the large number of ligatures, especially those involving the sign L89 (OIL). The summation on HT 116 proves that at least several of these ligatured signs are similar enough in nature to have their total introduced by the plain unligatured ideogram.

The sign-group $SA.RA_2$ is repeated nine times in headings and sub-headings in the C series (HT 18, 28, 90, 99, 101, 114, 121, 125, 130). The single sign TE (sometimes referred to as a "transaction sign") occurs in five of these headings (HT 14, 21, 42, 91, and 116). Additional sign-groups which appear twice are: $PU.RA_2$ (HT 28 and 116), I.QA.85 (HT 44 and 131), and $KI.RI.TA_2$ (HT 114 and 121). This last sign-group is perhaps related to $KI.RE.TA_2$ which occurs on HT 129 and can be restored plausibly on HT 125. The sign-group KI.RE.TA.NA on HT 2 may be a further variant of the same basic word. Much more speculative is the

---

[22] The exact identification of these Linear A commodities is based largely on comparisons with Linear B ideograms. See Raison-Pope (1971, xv). These conventional identifications have some plausibility but are far from secure. The sign L71, in particular, has been identified as CYPERUS by Peruzzi (1960) and others, but it may be a grain. Goold-Pope (1955) identified L71 as BARLEY.

[23] Brice reads WHEAT, FIGS, and WINE in the fifth line of this tablet, but Raison and Pope reject the first and consider the second two uncertain.

identification of U.MI.NA.SI on HT 28 with U.69.SI on HT 140 (see page 107). More than half of the headings to the C series contain sign-groups that occur also as headings to other tablets in the same series.

One scribe (vi) wrote four of the C lists. Three additional scribes wrote two each (v, viii, and xiv).

The D Series

The D series contains lists with no ideogram except L42, simple or ligatured. There are nine such lists: HT 15, 36, 40, 43, 61, 102, 108, 120, 133. Two further tablets (HT 92 and 128) are included in this series by virtue of their structure, despite the fact that they contain the sign L67 in addition to L42.

The sign L42 occurs also on many C series lists in conjunction with other agricultural ideograms. It is clearly ideographic in usage despite one or two collocations which might conceivably be phonetic (on HT 34 and 93). In shape it bears a strong resemblance to the ideogram for wheat in Linear B, *120=GRANUM. The ancestor of these signs occurs on the Hieroglyphic tablet from Phaistos in a context reminiscent of the linear scripts.[24] In eight of these D lists, WHEAT is ligatured; in three cases two different ligatures occur on the same list. In Linear B, GRANUM is never ligatured, but these ligatures of WHEAT in Linear A should occasion no surprise in view of the many potential varieties and conditions of grain. At Alalakh at least nine types of grain are recorded: barley, barley meal, fodder barley, emmer, husked emmer, freshly gathered emmer, emmer for fine milling, vetches, vetches for horse fodder.[25] On the other hand, the distinction in Linear A may be one of quantity rather than type since several of the ligatured signs are fractional.

In Linear B, tablets with only the GRANUM ideogram fall into two or three main classes. Tablets like KN E 668 and KN E 749 list masculine ethnics followed by large quantities of GRANUM. It is not clear whether these tablets record rations to groups of men or payments from the inhabitants of various localities. In some cases (E 777) the ideogram LUNA seems to indicate that the tablets record monthly rations. The other main class of tablets with the ideogram GRANUM is the land tenure tablets of

---

[24] Ventris-Chadwick (1956, 30). The Linear B ideogram GRANUM gives the impression of being formed out of the phonetic signs *si* and *to* which calls to mind σῖτος, the Greek word for grain. Whatever the explanation for this striking etymological symbolism, the sign's parallel attestation in all three Minoan scripts virtually guarantees that it represents a grain of some sort in Linear A. See Ruijgh (1970), Wyatt (1968).

[25] Wiseman (1953, 81-93).

the E- series. Here GRANUM is used as a measure of land, and precedents can be found in both Sumerian and Akkadian texts for seed used as a standard of land measure.[26] It is conceivable, though not likely, that these Linear A texts also refer to land measurement.

The heading of HT 92 is parallel to that of HT 133, and the tablets are similar in structure except that HT 92 includes the ideogram BARLEY in addition to WHEAT. Since this ideogram probably also represents a grain (the identification as BARLEY is not certain) it seems legitimate to include HT 92 in the D Series.

The numbers which follow WHEAT in the D series are remarkably large, in six cases being above one hundred ('684' and '570' on HT 15, '207' and '134' on HT 40, '680' on HT 92, and '976' on HT 102). Except for totals, only fifteen tablets from Hagia Triada contain numbers as large as this. Six of these large numbers follow the ideogram WHEAT (HT 15, 21, 22, 40, 92, 102). Two more follow ideograms for vessels (HT 31 and 39), and three occur in the secondary sections of tablets in the E series (HT 32, 33, and 34). A relative scarcity of fractions also distinguishes this series from the C and E Series. Two of the tablets with fractions, HT 120 and 128, have a similar structure in that subheadings are followed by pairs of WHEAT ideograms.[27]

The headings to this series have only a small degree of overlap. The sign-group KI.RE.TA.NA is repeated on HT 108 and 120; and, as mentioned above, the heading formula of HT 92 is nearly identical to that of HT 133.

The tablets of this class were written by several different scribes. Only HT 40, 92 and 108 can be ascribed to a single hand (vi).

The E Series

Lists of the E series are distinguished from those of the C and D series by the presence of the signs Lc29, Lc30, Lc31, Lc108 and Lc109. Some of the agricultural ideograms discussed in the previous section appear also on these lists and, very rarely, a sign-group. There are ten lists in this E series. The fourteen signs which appear two or more times on these lists are listed in Table 4.

---

[26] Ventris-Chadwick (1956, 236).

[27] The last subheading on HT 120 is followed directly by the number since there was no space left on the tablet for an intervening ideogram.

Table 4: Items in E Series Lists

Item	Tablets on which the Item Appears								
L44	12	23				34?	35		
L60	12		30						
L67	12				33				
L71		23	30				35		
L82		23	30				35		60
Lc16	12								
Lc21		23		32			35?		
Lc22		23							
Lc24			30				35		
Lc29		23		32			35		81
Lc30					33				
Lc31						34			
Lc38			30						
Lc46	12								
Lc47	12								
Lc48	12								
Lc49		23							
Lc50					33	34			
Lc51						34			
Lc59					33				
Lc60					33				
Lc95		23							
Lc108		23		32	33	34			
Lc109	12	23	30	32	33	34	35	45	60
Lc121		23							
Lc122							35?		

Several of these lists seem to be divided into two sections, one of which is characterized by fractions and small numbers, the other by quite large numbers. In HT 32, 33 and 34 the division seems clear; in HT 23 the entries on the third line may also fit in with this pattern of large numbers, but it is possible that the dots on this line may not represent "10" as interpreted by Brice.[28] Three of these signs, L82, Lc108 and Lc109 are followed by small numbers and fractions on other E series lists, so it is not certain that they are parallel to the large quantities listed in the second part of HT 32, 33 and

---

[28] Brice (1961, iv).

34. These three sets of larger entries may have something in common with the lists of the A and B series. KI.RO (on HT 34) appeared three times in headings to A series lists, and L66 (on HT 33) occurred twice in B series lists. One component of Lc59 (on HT 33) is L56 which is part of the heading to two B series lists. Moreover, DI (on HT 32) appears in an A series list. Lc31 might also be compared with Lc58, an entry in a B series list. These larger entries in the E lists, then, may have some relationship to the lists of men and of men's names. The other entries, however, are all followed by fractions or by small numbers.

One may speculate about the meaning of the signs in the E series, but several facts must be kept in mind. Most important is the presence of FIGS, WINE and BARLEY in these lists.[29] This does not, of course, mean that the lists must be rations. Wine and honey were used in the preparation of aromatics, and all these commodities are attested in Linear B ritual offerings. The small quantities might suggest spices or dyes or ritual materials. A heading to HT 12 Lc46 (MA+RU) brings to mind the Linear B ligature for wool,[30] and L85 (a pair of scales) recalls Linear B *ta-ra-si-ja*, (talansia=*pensum*) frequent on tablets dealing with wool.[31] Wool would be appropriate in a context with dyes and spices (for anointing) or other ritual material. We can, however, do little more than speculate about the meaning of the entries in these lists.

Four tablets of this series (HT 30, 32, 33, and 35) are assigned by Raison and Pope to one scribal hand (iv).

The F Series

The F series contains tablets with more pictorial ideograms. HT 16 and 20 have similar lists and may be classified Fa because of the sign L70 which seems to represent an upright loom. The ligature Lc35 also occurs only on these two tablets. Both are by scribe vii. It is a curious fact that three items from this Fa series occur also on cretulae (KA.KU.PA, L70, and L16). HT 38 shows the similar signs Lc41 and Lc42 which not only resemble the Linear B ideogram for cloth, PANNUS, but are ligatured with the same phonetic signs as in Linear B.[32] The sign L85 on this tablet brings to mind Linear B *ta-ra-si-ja* common in wool contexts. Furthermore, HT 24 contains

---

[29] It is possible that some of these signs may have a phonetic rather than ideographic significance here.

[30] Ventris-Chadwick (1956, 314), Bennett (1972, 57-60).

[31] Chadwick-Baumbach (1963, 247) gloss *ta-ra-si-ja* as 'an amount weighed out and issued for processing.' Also in Akkadian texts, "The produce most frequently measured by talents was wool" (Leemans, 1954, 83).

[32] Ventris-Chadwick (1956, 36).

L85 as well as the sign Lc46 (MA+RU) which recalls the Linear B ligature for wool. All these tablets (HT 16, 20, 24, and 38) may be classified Fa and may be imagined to be connected somehow with the cloth industry.

HT 31 presents seven ideograms for pots with superscripted sign-groups. This will be classified Fb. HT 38 and 39 each have one pot ideogram with a superscripted sign or sign-groups. Since HT 38 shows elements of both the Fa and Fb series, Georgiev may possibly be correct in believing that the pots on HT 31 are associated with dye and the cloth industry.[33]

The G Series

In the previous five series, the ideograms occurred in the lists and were followed directly by numbers. In the G series the ideogram appears as part of the heading and presumably applies to each number in the list below. The fractions which often follow sign-groups in these lists are explained by the ideogram in the heading.

The Ga series consists of four closely related tablets, HT 9, 13, 17, and 19. Each begins with a sign-group followed by the sign TE and the ideogram WINE. Three of the lists contain fractions, and three contain the sign-group SA.RO. The last two tablets, which are by a single scribe (ix), are identical except for the numbers and the final sign-group. One further tablet, HT 62, may belong in this series since it also contains WINE and TE.

Tablets of the Gb series contain agricultural ideograms other than WINE in the heading and have fractions in the list. HT 8, 104, and 115 clearly meet these criteria. More problematical is HT 6, which contains fractions and TE but no clear ideogram unless the sign L60 is to be taken as FIGS.

The tablets HT 86 and 95 have nearly identical lists of sign-groups (for this cluster see page 62) as well as the ideogram WHEAT and fractions. These two tablets, which are by the same scribe (i), fall into the Gc series, as does HT 106 which shares two sign-groups with these tablets though it has the ideogram CYPERUS in its heading. Finally, though HT 10 does not contain an ideogram it does have fractions; and its list is headed by a member of the cluster.

The H Series

Tablets of the H series have no ideogram. Since few of these tablets are preserved intact, it is likely that many once contained an ideogram and properly belong in a different series. In their present state these tablets can be analyzed only on the basis of sign-groups they have in common with

---

[33] Georgiev (1963, 15-18).

other more securely classified tablets. The distinction between tablets with fractions, the Ha series, and those lacking fractions, the Hb series, is probably fundamental; but many tablets now in the Hb series might instead be in the Ha series if they were in a better state of preservation.

The X Series

The tablets of the X series are fragmentary and cannot be assigned to any other class.

Clusters of Sign-groups

Two tablets (HT 86 and 95) have almost identical lists and related headings.

Sign-Group	Tablet (parenthesis for heading)
KU.NI.SU	86,95,(10)
SA.RU	86,94,95,(123)
DI.DE.RU	86,95
QA.RA$_2$.WA	86
QE.RA$_2$.U	(1),3?,95
DA.ME	86,95,(106),(120)
MI.NU.TE	86,95,(106)

These sign-groups occur elsewhere primarily as headings. Four sign-groups in these two tablets (HT 86 and 95) are perfect matches; a fifth, DA.ME, differs only by the sign L42 which is surely to be read as WHEAT rather than as a phonetic sign. There is no evidence that L42 is ever phonetic. The remaining pair of sign-groups, QA.RA$_2$.WA and QE.RA$_2$.U (discussed on page 80) is important in assessing the phonetic values inferred from Linear B. The natural presumption is that they are variant spellings of the same word.

The headings and subheadings to these two lists have the sign-group A.DU in common. On the basis of both the list and the heading, therefore, we were justified in classifying these two tablets together in the Gc series. The ideogram WHEAT occurs near the beginning of each list, after KU.NI.SU on HT 86 and before DA.ME in HT 95. This suggests that WHEAT to be read with the entire list rather than as a special "determinative" to KU.NI.SU or DA.ME. Important in this respect is HT 106 where MI.NU.TE forms the first heading followed by CYPERUS, and DA.ME is the second heading. In HT 120, DA.ME also appears in a heading followed by WHEAT in the list. Since three sign-groups in this cluster occur with grain ideograms on other tablets, we may assume that all the items in these two lists are to be read with the ideogram.

A more extensive example of clustering can be observed in HT 7, 10, 13, 85a and 122a. The following chart lists the sign-groups which are common to two or more of these lists:

Sign-Group	Within Cluster	Elsewhere
DA.RE	7,10,85a	122b
TE.TU	7,13	(85b)
U.37.ZA	10,85a	
DA.WE.DA	10,85,122a	93
ME.ZA	10,(85b)	
TA.NA.TI	7,10	98,49
TE.KI	13,122a	
KU.DO.NI	13,85a	
DA.SI.85	13,85a,122a	99

The headings to these five lists are worth examining. In two cases (three including HT 122b) a sign appears which is provisionally identified as MAN (L99, Lc55). In HT 13, however, we find the ideogram wine. The sign-groups in these lists, then, if they are homogeneous, must be of such a nature that they can introduce both a list of men and a transaction in WINE. Geographical expressions would be the most obvious:

Workers Sent		Wine Received	
Phaistos	25	Phaistos	5 1/4
Knossos	44	Knossos	8
Tylissos	12	Tylissos	3 3/4

Personal names would be conceivable:

Men Receiving Wine		Foremen with Squads	
John	10 1/2	John	10
James	8	James	12
Peter	5 1/4	Peter	15

If the sign-groups in these lists were personal names, however, one might expect some of them to occur also on tablets of the A series. There is only one example, TA.NA.TI (HT 7, 10), which may be attested on HT 49, an incomplete A series list. One sign-group on HT 7, 79.TU.NE, does occur as a heading in two A series lists (HT 87 and 117). Here again, place names would fit well though personal names are possible. The length of the list would seem to exclude general vocabulary words.

Word-Classes

In the two major clusters discussed above, as in the A series, we were able to isolate groups of words likely to be homogeneous. It is tempting to carry this method further by assuming that all sign-groups in a single list are homogeneous, or that all headings and subheadings on a single tablet are parallel. Unfortunately, this method, if followed to its logical conclusion, will allow us to demonstrate that every sign-group is parallel to every other.

As an example of how such a word-class can be isolated we begin with A.KA.RU on HT 2. This sign-group appears as a heading on HT 86 in a position equivalent to DA.DU.MA.TA on HT 95. (On each of these tablets A.DU serves as a subheading.) Returning to HT 2, we note that KI.RE.TA.NA is parallel to A.KA.RU, which is also a subheading on HT 120, along with DA.U.120.I and PA.I.TO. The major heading to HT 120 consists of DA.QE.RA and DA.ME. Since DA.ME occurs on HT 86 in a list headed by A.KA.RU, it belongs probably to a different word-class. We may therefore assign DA.QE.RA to our word-class. KI.RE.TA.NA also occurs on HT 8 in the list. The other items in this list must be assigned to our group. We have been able to assign thirteen sign-groups to a single word-class, but the method is treacherous since a single false link can introduce a large number of unrelated sign-groups.

Table 5: Tablets Listed by Class and Scribe

Tablet	Class	Scribe	Tablet	Class	Scribe
HT 1	Ha	xvii	HT 41	X	
HT 2	C		HT 42	C	(vi)
HT 3	Ha		HT 43	D	xv
HT 4	Ax		HT 44	C	
HT 5	X		HT 45	E	
HT 6	Gb	(xii)	HT 46	X	
HT 7	Gd?	xii	HT 47	Ha	
HT 8	Gb	vi	HT 48	(joined to HT 27)	
HT 9	Ga		HT 49	Ac	xi
HT 10	Hb	(ix)	HT 50	C	
HT 11	B		HT 51	X	(xii)
HT 12	E	xii	HT 52	X	
HT 13	Ga	viii	HT 53	(fragment)	
HT 14	C		HT 54	X	
HT 15	D		HT 55	Ax	
HT 16	Fa	vii	HT 56	X	
HT 17	Ga	ix	HT 57	X	
HT 18	C	xiv	HT 58	C	viii
HT 19	Ga	ix	HT 59	(joined to HT 42)	
HT 20	Fa	vii	HT 60	E	
HT 21	C	(viii)	HT 61	D	
HT 22	D?,B?		HT 62	B,Ga	
HT 23	E	iii	HT 63	Ha	
HT 24	Fa		HT 64	X	xvii
HT 25	Ac,B	xi	HT 65	X	
HT 26	B		HT 66	B	xvii
HT 27	B,C?	xii	HT 67	X	
HT 28	C		HT 68	B	
HT 29	Ha		HT 69	X	
HT 30	E	iv	HT 70	X	
HT 31	Fb	ii	HT 71	(joined to HT 45)	
HT 32	E	iv	HT 72	B	
HT 33	E	iv	HT 73	(joined to HT 62)	
HT 34	E		HT 74	X	
HT 35	E	(iv)	HT 75	X	
HT 36	D	xvii	HT 76	(joined to HT 40)	
HT 37	G?		HT 77	(joined to HT 30)	
HT 38	Fa		HT 78	X	
HT 39	Fb	ii	HT 79	X	
HT 40	D	vi	HT 80	X	

Table 5 (cont.)

Tablet	Class	Scribe	Tablet	Class	Scribe
HT 81	E		HT 121	C	v
HT 82	X		HT 122	A	iii
HT 83	X		HT 123		i
HT 84	B		HT 124	(joined to HT 123)	
HT 85	Ab	(viii)	HT 125	C	xv
HT 86	Gc	i	HT 126	Ha	
HT 87	Aa	iii	HT 127	Ax,B	(iii)
HT 88	Ab,B	xvi	HT 128	D	iii
HT 89	B,C	(i)	HT 129	C	
HT 90	C	vi	HT 130	C	x
HT 91	C		HT 131	C	
HT 92	D	vi	HT 132	Ha	iii
HT 93	C	xiii	HT 133	D	(viii)
HT 94	Aa,B,C	iii	HT 134	(joined to HT 128)	
HT 95	Gc	(i)	HT 135	Ha	iii
HT 96	C	viii	HT 136	X	
HT 97	B	xvi (iii)	HT 137	C	
HT 98	Hb		HT 138	(joined to HT 137)	
HT 99	C,Hb	vi	HT 139	C	xiii
HT 100	B,C		HT 140	C	vi
HT 101	C	vi	HT 141	X	
HT 102	D,B	xiii	HT 142	X	
HT 103	Hb		HT 143	(joined to HT 140)	
HT 104	Gb	xiii	HT 144	X	
HT 105	B		HT 145	(joined to HT 140)	
HT 106	Gc	x	HT 146	X	
HT 107	X		HT 147	X	
HT 108	D	vi	HT 148	(joined to HT 140)	
HT 109	(joined to HT 97)		HT 149	(joined to HT 95)	
HT 110	X		HT 150	X	
HT 111	Ha		HT 151	X	(vi)
HT 112	X	x	HT 152	(joined to HT 130)	
HT 113	X		HT 153	(joined to HT 140)	
HT 114	C	v	HT 154	X	
HT 115	Gb	viii			
HT 116	C	xiv			
HT 117	Aa	iii			
HT 118	G				
HT 119	B	iii			
HT 120	D	i			

CHAPTER THREE

THE PHONETIC VALUES

Introduction

An initial obstacle to the study of the phonetic values is the lack of agreement about the inventory of distinct signs in Linear A. Pugliese Carratelli's system of L numbers provides a convenient means of citing the signs, but individual scholars have often introduced modifications. Brice, in his edition, combined signs which Pugliese Carratelli considered distinct and, less often, distinguished signs which he did not separate.[1] His most important innovation is to merge L94 with L72. A more radical proposal of Peruzzi to subclassify L100 as two distinct signs, one corresponding to Linear B *i*, the other to *no*, has been accepted by Gordon, Nagy and others. On the criteria so far proposed, however, it is far from easy to determine which sign the scribe intended.[2] In their *Index*, Raison and Pope do not divide L100 but maintain the old distinction between L72 and L94. I have adopted their numbering of the Linear A signs.[3]

---

[1] Brice (1961, Tables 1 and 2). Discussion in Grumach (1961). Brice (1971a) raises the possibility that L48, L79 and L83 should be conflated.

[2] Peruzzi (1960, 40-42).

[3] Unlike them, however, I have not hesitated to make frequent use of a conventional phonetic transliteration. This transliteration, based mainly on the *shape* of the signs, does not imply endorsement of the phonetic value: 1=PA$_3$, 2=PA, 6=TU, 22=RO, 23=ZA, 24=KE, 25=NU, 26=NA, 28=WI, 29=KA, 30=DA, 31=SA, 32=JA, 34=PU$_2$, 39=TO, 45=KO, 51=DI, 52=A, 53=RA, 54=RE, 55=RU, 56=PI, 57=SI, 58=RA$_2$, 59=SU, 60=NI, 61=NE, 62=QA, 64=PU, 74=TA, 75=WA, 76=MI, 77=SE, 78=TI, 81=JE, 84=ME, 86=TA$_2$, 91=QE, 92=TE, 93=DU, 94=WE, 95=MA, 97=U, 98=KU, 100=I, 101=DO, 102=DE, 103=KI. My choice of the value *si* for L57 calls for comment since the resemblance in shape between L57 and Linear B *si* is not immediately obvious. For my arguments supporting this value see page 104. The value *pa$_3$* is not certain for the Linear B sign *56, but little depends on its use here. Some additional problems, including the distinction between L72 and L94, are discussed in Chapter Four.

The identity in shape between signs in Linear A and Linear B has encouraged many scholars to assume a corresponding identity of phonetic value. This is a natural but highly uncertain hypothesis. A similar assumption vitiated much of the work on Linear B by the predecessors of Kober, Bennett and Ventris. Similarity between the shape of signs of the Classical Cypriot Syllabary and those of Linear B provided a starting point for many fruitless early attempts at decipherment. The fact that this method failed in the decipherment of Linear B has not discouraged the adoption of a similar strategy in the interpretation of Linear A. The following quotation illustrates, perhaps in an extreme form, the commonly held view that the links between Linear A and B are so much closer than those between Linear B and Cypriot that the past failures of this method can safely be ignored:

La comune asserzione che a segni identici della lineare A e B non devono necessariamente corrispondere i medesimi valori, ... si fonda sulla nostra esperienza di sistemi grafici diversi, anche se in rapporto di parentela fra loro, mentre qui si tratta della medesima scrittura.[4]

Within limits, this statement has a certain degree of truth. The two Cretan scripts, both in external appearance and in geographical and chronological proximity, are much closer to each other than to the Cypriot Syllabary. But the fact that the archives at Hagia Triada in Linear A and at Knossos in Linear B are separated by so few miles and so few years can mislead. If those who place the creation of Linear B on the Greek mainland in MM III are correct, the two scripts had time for many years of independent development before external circumstances brought them together again in Crete. In any case, the history of writing provides many examples, both ancient and modern, which demonstrate that borrowing the idea of writing or the shape of the signs need not involve borrowing every phonetic value.

Gelb lists six possible ways in which the forms and values of signs used in writing have been borrowed in historically attested writing systems.[5] His six categories are reproduced below (in quotes) with some supplementary remarks.

1) "The forms of the signs and their values are borrowed, as in the case of Greek from Phoenician."

Even here several signs received new values because of the differing phonological structure of the two languages and because of the Greek practice of systematically representing the vowels.

2) "The forms are all borrowed, but the values assigned are partly borrowed, partly freely invented, as in the case of Meroitic from Egyptian."

---

[4] Peruzzi (1960, 37).
[5] Gelb (1963, 143).

The monumental type of Meroitic script is obviously based on Egyptian Hieroglyphics, but only in a few cases (perhaps 6 out of 23) do the phonetic values correspond.[6]

3) "The forms and values are partly borrowed, partly invented, as in the case of South Arabic from some North Semitic writing."

4) "The forms are borrowed but the values given to the signs are new, as in the case of the Sauk or Fox writing and normally, of course, in cryptography in the so-called 'substitution cipher'."

Of the fifteen signs in the Fox alphabet (borrowed from the Latin cursive letters), eleven have values more or less identical with the Latin original, but four have new values.

5) "The forms are partly borrowed, partly invented, with new values, as found, for example, in the case of the Cherokee writing, built chiefly upon the forms of the Latin alphabet."

The Cherokee syllabary is composed of 85 signs. Most are based on the Latin alphabet, but none retains its Latin value. Diringer cites the Cherokee script as "one of the best examples of the borrowing of a form of writing without retaining the original phonetic values of the symbols concerned."[7]

6) "The forms are freely invented, with new values, as found in a large number of writings."

The above quotations from Gelb and Diringer suggest that the borrowing of symbols without retention of their phonetic values is not an uncommon event in the history of writing. A more conservative view is expressed by Jeffery in her study of the origins of the Greek alphabet.[8] She argues that an illiterate people when learning a method of writing will accept the entire system with little initial criticism. Expansion will occur by borrowing signs from other scripts and by creating doublets out of single signs rather than by giving entirely new values to existing signs which are phonetically "useless" for the new language. The examples she cites of the borrowing of alphabetic writing support this view, but an alphabet may be more adaptable than a syllabary. If the new language, for example, possesses additional vowels, an alphabet can be supplemented by a single new vowel sign; but the syllabary will require an entire series. Ad hoc spelling rules may bring temporary relief, but the motivation to restructure the entire system will be stronger.

In any case, there is no lack of historical precedent to encourage the suspicion that Linear A and B, while related formally, make different phonetic use of at least some signs. Historical analogy does not exclude the

---

[6] For the Meroitic script, see Diringer (1968, 140 and fig. 11.2).
[7] Diringer (1968, 129).
[8] Jeffery (1961, 1-5).

possibility that the scripts have identical phonetic values, but it underlines the importance of finding every piece of evidence which can be used in testing this hypothesis.

Types of Evidence

There are several ways in which these phonetic values could be confirmed. The best way, and the least likely at present, would be an independent and cogent decipherment of Linear A. Furumark expressed this goal in 1956 and made some attempt at reaching what he termed "eine von Linear B vollständig unabhängige Untersuchung und Deutung des Materials."[9] Laudable as such an intention may be, the possibility of a completely independent decipherment is frustrated by the small amount of Linear A available for study. If progress is to be made, we cannot ignore the evidence provided by the decipherment of Linear B. An uncritical borrowing of the phonetic values, however, is not the proper way to use this evidence. While we may be encouraged by certain preliminary indicators which seem to support the hypothesis of shared values, we must not hesitate to subject the evidence to a systematic scrutiny.

The inflected nature of the language of Linear B was recognized by Kober, and it was her brilliant insight into how to use this inflection as evidence for the phonetic values which formed the basis for Ventris's decipherment. She noted that an inflectional paradigm like the Latin second declension, when written syllabically, will show the following pattern.

a-mi-cus	*a-ni-mus*
a-mi-ci	*a-ni-mi*
a-mi-co	*a-ni-mo*
a-mi-cum	*a-ni-mum*

Such a pattern can be recognized with the syllables represented by arbitrary numbers.

1.2.3	1.7.8
1.2.4	1.7.9
1.2.5	1.7.10
1.2.6	1.7.11

Without knowing the phonetic values, we might suspect that signs 3, 4, 5 and 6 have one initial consonant, and that 8, 9, 10, and 11 have another. A further deduction would be that the vowels in signs 3 and 8 are identical but different from the vowel in signs 4 and 9 and so forth. After collecting

---

[9] Furumark (1956, 8).

several such inflectional paradigms in Linear B, Kober was able to draw up a small table in which signs in each row have the same (unknown) consonant, and signs in each column share the same (unknown) vowel. Her method led directly to Ventris's famous 'grid', and many of her specific observations were fully confirmed by the decipherment.[10]

This method worked well for Linear B since the corpus of inscriptions is large, since Greek is highly inflected, and since the spelling conventions of Linear B happen to bring out this particular kind of inflection. The same second declension written with different syllabic conventions would not have permitted such inferences about phonetic values:

am-ic-us	an-im-us
am-ic-i	an-im-i
am-ic-o	an-im-o
am-ic-um	an-im-um

The success of this method is therefore highly dependent on the conventions of the syllabary. The nature of the inflection is also important. A Semitic language, to take one example, might show a far less obvious pattern.

Spelling variation can also provide a highly useful confirmation for a phonetic value and was exploited by Ventris, but there should be contextual confirmation that two sign-groups are orthographic variants rather than unrelated words which superficially resemble each other.[11]

More than 100 groups of Linear A words are involved in alternations which superficially resemble inflection or orthographic variation. They are collected in Appendix A in three categories: (1) pairs where the first two signs are identical but the third is not, e.g., 30.74.53 and 30.74.54, (2) pairs where the last two signs are identical but not the beginning, e.g., 98.101.60 and 29.97.101.60, (3) cases where the first and third signs are identical but the second differs, e.g., 103.54.86 and 103.72.86. If these sign-groups are transcribed according to the phonetic values inferred from Linear B, some of the alternations take on a plausible appearance. The emergence of doublets such as KI.RE.TA$_2$ and KI.RI.TA$_2$ or DA.TA.RA and DA.TA.RE has been taken as confirmation that the Linear B phonetic values may be safely transferred to Linear A. We shall return to this question below.

Evidence based on possible morphological and orthographic alternation is internal to Linear A and requires no explicit identification of the language or

---

[10] Kober's contribution to the decipherment is duly recorded in Ventris-Chadwick (1956, 14-20) and Chadwick (1967, 35).

[11] Olivier (1967, 98-100) prints a list of spelling alternations in Linear B at Knossos. His study of the scribal hands now makes it possible to associate idiosyncratic spellings with specific scribes. See also page 114 below.

the meaning of any individual word. It is wise to maintain a deliberate distinction between the assessment of the phonetic values and the etymological interpretation of lexical items, but one class of external evidence does not depend on identifying the language. Personal names and place names tend to survive changes of language. English has been the standard language in California for more than a century, but the principal cities—San Francisco, Los Angeles, Sacramento, Santa Barbara, San Diego and San Jose—all have Spanish names. The tenacity of place names is world-wide and for this reason played a major role in the decipherment of Linear B.[12] The same phenomenon occurs with personal names; a large number of English-speaking Americans retain non-English names, and generations of Latin-speaking Romans kept Etruscan names.

Over 900 personal names and nearly 100 place names are attested on the Knossos Linear B tablets. Some of the names have Greek-like etymologies, but a large number do not. According to Landau's tabulation about 45% have not been associated with any known Greek name.[13] Of the remaining 55%, many identifications may be illusory since there is little contextual control over the etymology of a personal name. It is a natural assumption that many of these names reflect a pre-Greek population. The Linear B place names represent a wide geographical distribution in East and Central Crete and include the region of Hagia Triada where the Linear A archives were found. Since these Linear A documents precede the Linear B tablets at Knossos by only a few years, it would be surprising if personal names and place names were not common to the two groups.[14]

The Linear B phonetic values do, in fact, yield words in Linear A which are identical or similar to names known at Knossos. Several scholars have prepared lists of these parallels, but the correspondences have not been examined systematically and are usually presented simply to engender a general confidence in the validity of the Linear B values as a group.[15]

Statistical Control

The laws of probability suggest that some of this apparent evidence supporting the transferral to Linear A of the Linear B phonetic values may result from chance. The amount of such evidence which might be expected

---

[12] Ventris-Chadwick (1956, 22)

[13] Landau (1958, 237).

[14] If Palmer's dating of the Knossos tablets is correct, the gap would be increased somewhat, but this would not seriously reduce the likelihood of finding Linear A names in Linear B.

[15] See note 34 below.

to support an incorrect assignment of values ought therefore to be determined. Moreover, the set of phonetic values confirmed must be explicitly delimited. There is no reason to believe that confirmation of some phonetic values confirms by implication the entire group.

The "morphological" alternations, for example, must be considered as a group, and careful attention must be given to the problem of statistical control. Only a dozen consonants are distinguished in the Linear B orthography. Using these values for Linear A, if each of the twelve consonants occurred with the same frequency (which they do not), we could predict that one twelfth of the alternating pairs listed in Appendix A would share a common consonant by *chance* alone. This model is not strictly accurate, but its prediction of about eight coincidental pseudo-morphological alternations agrees well with the results of the random decipherments discussed below.

A similar approximate model can be devised to predict the number of matches with Knossos Linear B names which might occur with random phonetic values. Assuming that each script contains exactly 60 signs of equal frequency we can calculate what number of Linear A sign-groups will *happen* to share two signs and the consonant of the third sign with a Linear B word. There are just under 200 complete words in Linear A composed of exactly three signs and a few more than 1000 in Linear B. For any pair there is one chance in sixty that the first sign will match and one chance in sixty that the second will match. Since we only require the same consonant in the third sign the chance of a match here will be one in twelve. Coincidence up to the third consonant may then be expected in one pair out of 43,200 (60 times 60 times 12). Since there are 200,000 possible pairs (each of 200 Linear A with each of 1000 Linear B), we might then expect a total of about five random matches (200,000 divided by 43,200). This prediction, though based on inexact assumptions, is close to the actual results of the random decipherments to be described next.

In order to make these arguments from probability both more tangible and more exact, I have constructed nine deliberately invalid "random decipherments" to determine how much plausible "evidence" of various types can actually be found to certify the erroneous values.[16] We can use these fictitious decipherments as a control to determine whether the evidence supporting the use of the Linear B phonetic values in Linear A has any statistical significance.

---

[16] The major source of error in the naive model presented above is that all signs do not occur with the same frequency and that the same sign has different rates in initial, medial and final positions in a word.

Since the fictitious decipherments play a major role in the argument it is important to avoid misunderstanding about how they were constructed. The fictitious phonetic values are not truly random—they are assigned according to an explicit procedure which another investigator can reproduce—but they are intended to be *effectively* random for the specific use to which they are put. The nine "decipherments" fulfil the following conditions:

1) The same set of phonetic values is used in each decipherment but reshuffled. Each decipherment has signs for *ma* and *ja* but not for *mo* or *jo* since no Linear A sign resembles those Linear B signs.

2) The frequency of each value varies as little as possible from decipherment to decipherment. The value *na* is assigned in each case to a sign of about the same frequency. This tends to equalize from one decipherment to the next the probability of random matches.

3) Each decipherment is unique. No sign has the same value in any two decipherments, so that if a sign happens to receive the correct value in one of the ten decipherments, it must receive the wrong value in the other nine.

To produce the ten sets of phonetic values the Linear A signs were first arranged in order of descending frequency (see Appendix E) and then divided into ten groups, the most frequent ten signs, the next most frequent ten signs, and so forth. Within each group the phonetic values were rotated to produce the ten different decipherments, each value being assigned successively to the next less common sign with the tenth sign in each case moving up into first position. The first set is based on the Linear B phonetic values; the remaining nine are all different. Appendix D lists in full the phonetic values used in these random decipherments together with the plausible "supporting evidence" consisting of internal alternations and matches with Linear B.

This method of selection, though not random, should have no tendency to maximize the amount of apparent confirmation. I have used it deliberately in preference to true "random numbers" in order to remove any suspicion in the minds of non-technical scholars that the values are deliberately biased. Anyone can easily understand how these sets of values were picked, and anyone can reproduce them. Random values chosen by other methods would perhaps allow more rigorous statistical analysis, but similar results would be expected with nearly any set of unbiased values.[17]

---

[17] An earlier version of this monograph (Packard, 1967) made use of a different set of random decipherments since the signs were initially ordered according to their frequency in Brice (1961) rather than Raison-Pope (1971). The proportion of random confirmations was similar.

Alternations at the End of Words

There are 39 groups of Linear A words which share two or more initial signs (see Appendix A). Some of these groups may represent inflection, though it is difficult to discern a regular pattern in the alternations. Many are undoubtedly illusory. In every language there will be unrelated words which begin with the same two syllables (e.g. Latin *amabo, amarus, amazon*), and the ambiguity of the Minoan writing system could produce many more. The groups most likely to be significant are the five in which at least the first three signs are identical. Three of these, when transcribed according to the Linear B phonetic values, have the same consonant in the first alternating sign.

I.PI.NA.MA[	APZ2a1(I13)
I.PI.NA.MI.NA	PKZ10(I6)
JA.SA.SA.RA.MA.NA	KNZ10a(I8)
JA.SA.SA.RA.ME	PSZ2c(I1),TLZ1(I16)
]SU.KI.RI.TA	PHW18
SU.KI.RI.TE.I.JA	HTZ158b(I17)

The first sign-group is on a libation table from Palaikastro, the second on a libation bowl from Apodoulou; and the second pair involves the so-called "Minoan libation formula." The similar religious context strengthens the association. Of the last pair, one is on a sealing from Phaistos, the second on a pithos from Hagia Triada.[18]

These correspondences can be taken as partial confirmation of the phonetic values *ma, me, mi, ta* and *te*. Only the consonants *m* and *t* are supported by these alternations; the value of the vowel in each case is left open. It is not impossible that even these parallels could be coincidental. The sixth and seventh "random decipherments" each resulted in two such alternations (Appendix D).

In the remaining 34 pairs only the first two signs are identical. With the Linear B phonetic values seven of these have a common consonant in the third sign:

A.TI.KA.A.MI.KO	ZAW2.1(III8)
A.TI.KI.TA.A.	TYZ4(II18)

---

[18] I have adopted the reading SU.KI.RI.TA on PHW18 which Raison-Pope (1971, xv) consider "à la rigueur possible," though they prefer SU.KI.WE.TA. It is not clear why they divide SU.KI RI.TE.I.JA into two sign-groups. Pope points out (in a letter) that the rarity of L72 (and L94) in initial position could be cited to support the reading I have printed.

DA.TA.RA	6a1
DA.TA.RE	88.5,62.2
KA.U.DE.TA	13.1
KA.U.DO.NI	26b2
KI.RE.TA.NA	8a5,108.1,120.4,(2.3)
KI.RE.TA$_2$	129.1,85b1
KU.PA$_3$.NA.TU	47a1,119.3
]KU.PA$_3$.NA.TU.NA.TE[	APZ2b1
KU.PA$_3$.NU	1a3,3.6,88.3,88.4,117a3,
WA.TU.MA.RE	128a2
WA.TU.MI	HTW206a(CRIV8)
KU.DO.NI	13.4,85a4
]KU.DO.NA[	64.1

The last alternation involves rejecting Brice's reading KU.DO "2" on HT 64.1.[19] The other sign-group on HT 64, RU.MA[, can be compared with RU.MA.TA on HT 99b. Another sign-group on HT 99b, DA.SI.85, appears next to KU.DO.NI on HT 85a and HT 13. This relation can be shown more clearly by a diagram. In each tablet only the relevant sign-groups are shown:

HT 64	HT 85a	HT 99b
]KU.DO.NA[	DA.SI.85	DA.SI.85
RU.MA[	KU.DO.NI	RU.MA.TA

This indirect association not only makes the alternate reading more convincing but also increases the value of the two sign-groups as evidence for the phonetic values *na* and *ni*.

For the pair KU.PA$_3$.NU/KU.PA$_3$.NA.TU there is some, though not conclusive, contextual control. The shorter sign-group seems to be a personal name appearing in three lists of the A series.[20] The longer sign-group occurs in a B series list (HT 119) as well as on a list which resembles a B series list (HT 47). In addition, the sign-group 83.TU appears on both HT 119 and HT 122 providing another link between the two words. The shorter word, then, could be a personal name while the longer word

---

[19] Raison (1962, 52) terms this reading "arbitraire."
[20] The significance of this alternation is highlighted by the occurrence in Linear B of the doublet *ka-pa₃-no/ka-pa₃-na-to*. See page 110.

could qualify a group of men. The relation need not be singular/plural though it could be. The fact that the longer form also occurs with a suffixed NA.TE[outside of Hagia Triada on a libation bowl from Apodoulou may suggest that the words are ultimately founded on a place name or perhaps a divine name.

Of the next pair, A.TI.KA.A.MI.KO/A.TI.KI.TA.A, one is scratched on the shoulder of a pithos from Tylissos, the other on a roundel from Kato Zakro. The commercial context is not unfavorable to a possible association, and the unusual presence of L52 (A) in non-initial position in each sign-group speaks strongly in favor of some relationship.

Of the pair KI.RE.TA$_2$/KI.RE.TA.NA each sign-group occurs as a heading to a list of the C series but also once as an entry in a list. (For the possible value of this alternation in determining the exact phonetic value of the sign TA$_2$, see page 110.)

As for the sign-groups DA.TA.RA/DA.TA.RE, the first appears in a heading followed by TE while the second sign-group is apparently a personal name (Table 1).

It may be useful by way of comparison to ask how many alternations at the end of words can be collected as "evidence" to support the fictitious values of the random decipherments. The seemingly significant alternations in favor of each of the ten decipherments are printed in Appendix D. Alternations are considered significant if the alternating signs have the same consonant according to that decipherment. Seven of the nine decipherments resulted in at least half as many plausible alternations as the Linear B phonetic values. The average, excluding the first, is 3.9 alternations. This indicates that we must be willing to accept as fortuitous a significant number of the alternations resulting from the Linear B values.

Many sign-groups consist of only two signs. Since Linear A has less than 100 phonetic signs, many of these short sign-groups will necessarily share the same initial sign. It is virtually impossible, therefore, to draw any reliable conclusions from alternations involving them, though contextual analysis occasionally indicates that several of these short sign-groups may be related. One such group cited by Furumark[21] is TE.KE/TE.KI. The first occurs on HT 85, the second on HT 13 and 122. HT 13 and 85a share two sign-groups, KU.DO.NI and DA.SI.85, while HT 85a and 122a share DA.WE.DA and DA.SI.85. These longer sign-groups provide a link between the lists and make it plausible that TE.KI and TE.KE are variant spellings of the same word, but they do not prove that they are. On each tablet there are several sign-groups which do not reappear on the other two, and the

---

[21] Furumark (1956, p. 15 of charts).

mere identity of initial sign could equally support the claim that TE.KE and TE.TU (also on HT 13) are identical. Two other groups of short words cited by Pugliese Carratelli[22] are KI.RA/KI.RO and SA.RA/SA.RA$_2$/SA.RO/SA.RU. These and other apparent alternations involving such short sign-groups are so likely to occur randomly that they offer no confirmatory evidence for the phonetic values.

Alternation Internal to Words

There are 26 alternations in which the first and third signs are identical but the second is not. Some of these could represent spelling variation or inflection internal to the word, but in only four cases the alternating signs share a common consonant according to the Linear B phonetic values:

KI.RE.TA$_2$	129.1,85b1
KI.RI.TA$_2$	114a1,121.1
DI.RA.DI.NA	PH1a(IV13)
DI.RE.DI.NA	98a2
A.SE.JA	115a4
A.SU.JA	11a3
WA.DU.NI.MI	6b1,85b4
WA.DI.NI	HTW207(CRIV1),

The only pair with strong contextual confirmation is the first. The tablet HT 129, headed by KI.RE.TA$_2$, presents a structure very similar to that of HT 114 and 121, each headed by KI.RI.TA$_2$. The identity of the next two sign-groups DI.RA.DI.NA and DI.RE.DI.NA is made plausible by their length though there are in Linear B many pairs of entirely unrelated sign-groups of this length which differ by one internal sign.[23] Both occur on tablets with fractions, one from Phaistos, the other from Hagia Triada.

Only one of the random decipherments produced internal alternation in a pair of words four signs long like DI.RA.DI.NA/DI.RE.DI.NA, but seven of the nine decipherments resulted in one or two alternations like KI.RE.TA$_2$/KI.RI.TA$_2$ (Table 13). One might hope to reach a finer discrimination by segregating the alternations into a priori categories such as "plausible" (*i/e, o/u, u/wa*) and "implausible" (*e/u, u/a* etc.), but such an arbitrary division contributes little (the random decipherments result in many "plausible" spelling variants).

---

[22] Pugliese Carratelli (1955).
[23] Several examples are: *a-ka-i-jo/a-ka-ta-jo, a-pi-da-ta/a-pi-qo-ta, a-ra-da-jo/a-ra-ka-jo.*

Alternation at the Beginning of Words

There are 42 groups of Linear A words which coincide in the final two or three signs. Here again the possibility arises that some of these groups may involve inflectional or orthographic alternation. With the Linear B phonetic values five pairs of sign-groups present patterns which could be interpreted as significant:

JA.DI.KI.TE.TE.PI	PKZ8a(I3)
A.DI.KI.TE.TE.PI	PKZ11a(I4)
JA.SA.SA.RA.ME	PSZ2c(I1),TLZ1(I16)
A.SA.SA.RA.ME	PKZ11b(I4)
JA.TA.I.88.U.JA	APZ1(I14)
A.TA.I.88.WA.JA	KOZ1a,PKZ12a(I5),
KU.DO.NI	13.4,85a4
KA.U.DO.NI	26b2
QA.KU.RE	HTW217a1(CRIV4)
QE.KU.RE	20.2

There are here three instances of an apparent A/JA alternation. Because of the length of the words and their similar religious context, it seems virtually certain that we are dealing here with a legitimate example of inflection or (more likely) orthographic fluctuation.[24] For the next pair, KU.DO.NI/ KA.U.DO.NI, it is impossible to find any obvious contextual confirmation, but an orthographic alternation KU/KA.U, if attested here, could be important evidence for the precise phonetic value of the sign KU (see page 110).

Once again the nine fictitious decipherments warn us against too facile an acceptance of short alternations as evidence for the validity of the phonetic values brought over from Linear B. Five random decipherments produced at least as many alternations as the Linear B values. The two short alternations in the first decipherment could easily be coincidental.

One more alternation should be mentioned which does not fit into our three categories. The tablets HT 95 and 86 are very closely related. Five of

---

[24] Another curious example of this same alternation is found in the F series where Lc40 (A+KA) on HT 38 is parallel to Lc33 (JA+KA) on HT 24. In Linear B there may be occasional confusion between *a* and *ja*; *a-sa-ro/ja-sa-ro, a-ke-te-re/ja-ke-te-re*.

the six sign-groups in each list have an exact counterpart in the companion tablet, and one word is common to a heading on each tablet. In each list there is only one sign-group which is not matched exactly on the other tablet. These two sign-groups, transcribed according to the Linear B values, are: $QE.RA_2.U$ and $QA.RA_2.WA$. It does not require great imagination to suspect that these sign-groups represent the same word. The contextual control seems so strong in this case that identity is almost assured. A similar alternation between WA and U occurs in the third pair cited on the previous page. An ambiguity between *wa* and *u* is attested in Linear B as well as in Cuneiform.[25]

The evidence provided by these putative alternations is summarized in Table 12. Some of the Linear B phonetic values are provisionally confirmed. This evidence will be collated with evidence from other tests to produce a list of signs whose Linear B phonetic value receives support from several independent kinds of evidence.

Frequency Distribution

The relative frequency of each syllabic sign can give some clue to its phonetic value. Such evidence is not entirely free from suspicion since it depends, at least partially, on the phonetic pattern of the unknown underlying language.

Pure Vowel Signs

The Linear B syllabary contains, in addition to signs of the pattern consonant-plus-vowel (*ka, ke, ki*), signs to represent pure vowels (*a, e, i*). These signs must be used at the beginning of a word or as the second element of a diphthong (or any pair of adjacent vowels), but in other positions the vowel is already included in the syllabic sign.[26] Pure vowel signs, therefore, might be expected to show a preference for the initial position in a word; the Linear B sign *a* is 92% initial, *e* is 70%, and *o* is 51% initial. The signs *i* and *u* which form diphthongs are only 36% and 11% initial.[27] A similar phenomenon can be observed in the Classical Cypriot Syllabary. In the great bronze tablet from Idalion[28] the sign *a* which

---

[25] For Linear B cf. *ra-wa-ra-ta/ra-u-ra-ta*, and for Cuneiform the place name at Alalakh *Wa-ri-a-du/U-ri-a-du* (Wiseman; 1953, 14).

[26] These are the only uses of the pure vowel signs in Linear B and the Classical Cypriot Syllabary. In Cuneiform such signs may have the function of representing internal *aleph* as well as indicating vowel length (e.g., KA-A = *kā*), or clarifying signs with ambiguous vocalism (e.g., BI-E = *be*).

[27] For these statistics only complete Linear B words were counted. See Appendix F.

[28] Inscription 217 in O. Masson (1961).

occurs in 25 distinct sign-groups is initial in 80% of them. The signs *e* and *o* are 55% and 50% initial respectively, but *i* and *u* are both only 15% initial. Of the remaining 46 signs only *ka* and *pa* show preference for initial position.

Since both Linear B and the Cypriot syllabary contain Greek, one could ascribe this pattern to the Greek language itself, but the high initial frequency of the pure vowel signs can be predicted from the structure of the syllabary. The vowel signs also show preference for initial position in Akkadian where the sign A (#579) is 78% initial, E (#308) is 50%, I (#142) is 74%, and U_2 (#318) is 60% initial.[29]

In addition to having a high word-initial percentage, the pure vowel signs in Linear B have a fairly high total frequency, ranging in rank from second to twentieth. This is likely also to reflect the nature of the syllabary rather than the distribution of sounds in the language. If *a* and *k*, for example, were equally common in the language of Linear B, the sign for *a* might still be more common than the sign for *ka* since initial *k* would be spread among five separate signs depending on the following vowel. Unless the average word contained five or more syllables (in Linear B the average is a little above three) the higher frequency of the consonant signs in non-initial position would not be able to mask the greater initial frequency of the pure vowels.

Appendix E shows for each Linear A sign the percentage of word-initial occurrences. The signs assumed to represent *a* and *u* (L52 and L97) show very strong preferences for initial position (82% and 77%) which helps to confirm them as vowels. The sign L100 is commonly taken as *i*, and its initial percentage of 44% is plausible enough for a pure vowel. The signs sometimes proposed for *e* and *o* (L44 and L87) are rare, and it is open to question whether they are phonetic signs at all. Since pure vowels should be among the most frequent signs in a syllabary, it seems probable that signs for *o* and *e*, if they exist in Linear A, have not yet been identified. Likely candidates will be frequent signs which prefer initial position, though all such signs need not be pure vowels. Some Linear B consonant signs show deceptively vowel-like distributions (*ku, po,* and *pu* are over 60% initial).

Consonant-Plus-Vowel Signs

Further evidence for phonetic values can be drawn from frequency distribution, though it is hard to find any theoretical justification for the

---

[29] According to information kindly supplied by Professor Giorgio Buccellati from a small sample of Old Babylonian letters. The Akkadian signs are cited here according to the numbers in Deimel (1928-1933).

necessary underlying assumptions. If the sign *da* were twice as common as *di*, one might predict that *ka* should be roughly twice as common as *ki* and that *ma* should be twice as common as *mi*. A similar prediction could be made that if *ta* is three times more common than *sa* then each sign with *t* should be roughly three times more common than the corresponding sign with *s*. The basis for these predictions might be termed a "hypothesis of symmetrical distribution" which states that the frequency of a sign is proportional to the overall frequency of its vowel and its consonant. Taken literally, this assumption is obviously false. Even if a language happened to show such symmetry at a certain period, it could easily be upset by consonant changes conditioned by the quality of the following vowel. It is perhaps surprising, then, that the frequencies of the Linear B signs do approximate such a distribution. In Table 6 the frequency of each Linear B sign is printed directly above the frequency predicted by the hypothesis of symmetry. The predicted frequency is obtained by multiplying the total count for that vowel by the total count for that consonant and dividing the result by the total of all signs. The predicted values automatically fulfil the condition of "symmetry."[30] A complication is introduced by the fact that some of the phonetic values (*ji, ju, qu, wu,* etc.) are unknown or missing. Since it would be misleading to assign a rate of zero to all such signs, I have used a method of iterative approximation which begins by assuming that each missing sign has a frequency of zero and then calculates its predicted frequency by the method described above. I then repeat the calculations using the new *predicted* rate as the *observed* rate (but only for the missing signs). The predictions stabilize after about a dozen iterations. The number printed in square brackets below the predicted frequency is chi-square (the square of the difference between the observed and predicted rates divided by the predicted rate). A higher value of chi-square indicates a more significant divergence between predicted and actual rates.[31] Most of the predictions agree fairly well with the actual frequencies, though the low rate of *je* is especially striking.

---

[30] The ratio between the predicted rate of *ka* and *ke* is identical with the ratio between predictions for *da* and *de, pa* and *pe,* and so forth. Moreover, there is a fixed ratio, for example, between the prediction for each sign containing *p* and the corresponding sign containing *t*.

[31] Chi-square here is not serving in its traditional function as a statistical test of the validity of an hypothesis. No one could seriously propose symmetry as an accurate predictor of frequency distribution; and the total chi-square for these tables is extremely high despite the large number of degrees of freedom. Chi-square here serves only as a relative indicator drawing attention to those frequencies which differ most radically from symmetry.

Table 8 shows the frequency of each of the Linear A signs identified on page 67. Once again, the predicted "symmetrical" frequency and chi-square are printed directly under the observed count. Estimated rates are calculated for missing signs.[32] Only a few predicted frequencies in Table 8 disagree strongly with the observed rates (*je, ke, ku, re, ri, we*). It may be noted that the rate of L100 coincides well with the prediction for *i* but not with that for *no*. The rate of L72 (23) is lower than the prediction for *ri* (50.5), while the rate of L94 (23) is higher than the prediction for *we* (10.3); but if we follow Brice and include L94 under L72, the combined total of 46 agrees well with the prediction for *ri*. The prediction for *ne* is 22.9. Of the two signs sometimes given this value, L57 occurs 46 times, while L61 occurs 24 times. This latter sign better fulfils the prediction. As for L57, I have proposed the value *si* for entirely different reasons (see page 104). The prediction for *si* (32.7) is not far from the actual rate of L57 (46 occurrences).

We can obtain a more accurate prediction by reducing the number of missing phonetic values. Table 9 shows the frequencies and predictions for Linear A without the incomplete *j-, q-, z-,* and *-o* series. The new prediction for *si* (38.1) is even closer to the frequency of L57, while the prediction for *we* (6.3) is further from L94.

The percentage of word-initial occurrences can be an indicator for consonant signs as well as for vowels. In Linear B, signs beginning with *n-* tend to avoid initial position (*na*=9% initial, *ne*=18%, *ni*=0%, *no*=4%, *nu*=5%), while signs with *d-* more often start a word (*da*=34% initial, *de*=22% *di*=57%, *do*=32%, *du*=42%). This pattern is reasonably consistent though there are exceptions (*so*=3% versus *su*=51%; *to*=18% versus *tu*=49%). In Table 7 the percentage of word-initial occurrences of each Linear A sign is printed above its percentage predicted on the basis of symmetry. Predictions are also obtained for missing signs. It is clear that the *n-* series has a low initial frequency in Linear A (as in Linear B). The initial percentage of L57 is 37%, far above the prediction of 5.1% for *ne*.[33] The sign L61, the other claimant for the phonetic value *ne*, has an initial percentage of 9.1%, which agrees much better with the remainder of the *n-* series in Linear A. The predictions for *ri* (11.7%) and for *we* (18.1%) are too close to allow any clear inferences.

---

[32] Kamm (1965b, 241) also calculates expected frequencies for missing signs. His results differ from mine, but since he does not explain his method of calculation I am unable to find the cause of our disagreement. One cause, but not the only one, is that he begins with higher observed frequencies for the identified signs. See Appendix E below.

[33] It agrees better with the predicted initial ratio for *si* (26%).

In concluding this discussion of frequency distribution we must emphasize again the lack of any firm theoretical foundation for these tests. Although the frequencies of many signs follow a consistent and predictable pattern, disagreement with this pattern is only partial and inconclusive evidence against a phonetic value.

Table 6: Linear B Total Frequency

	-a	-e	-i	-o	-u
pure vowel	627 614.6 [0.2]	543 490.2 [5.6]	324 406.8 [16.8]	418 605.9 [58.2]	428 222.3 [190.1]
d-	244 204.8 [7.4]	191 163.4 [4.6]	125 135.6 [0.8]	147 201.9 [14.9]	73 74.1 [0.0]
j-	559 488.2 [10.2]	76 389.4 [252.2]	— 323.1	724 481.2 [122.4]	— 176.6
k-	435 453.9 [0.7]	422 362.0 [9.9]	241 300.4 [11.7]	449 447.4 [0.0]	181 164.2 [1.7]
m-	249 220.1 [3.7]	274 175.5 [55.1]	140 145.6 [0.2]	145 216.9 [23.8]	30 79.6 [30.9]
n-	258 297.6 [5.2]	237 237.3 [0.0]	193 196.9 [0.0]	355 293.3 [12.9]	90 107.6 [2.9]
p-	276 296.2 [1.3]	208 236.3 [3.4]	296 196.1 [50.9]	254 292.0 [4.9]	94 107.1 [1.6]
q-	116 131.1 [1.7]	135 104.6 [8.8]	54 86.8 [12.4]	147 129.3 [2.4]	— 47.4
r-	582 584.4 [0.0]	459 466.1 [0.1]	426 386.8 [3.9]	590 576.1 [0.3]	168 211.4 [8.9]
s-	191 227.4 [5.8]	116 181.4 [23.6]	298 150.5 [144.4]	201 224.2 [2.4]	60 82.2 [6.0]
t-	608 536.3 [9.5]	501 427.8 [12.5]	304 354.9 [7.3]	510 528.7 [0.6]	119 194.0 [29.0]
w-	310 394.7 [18.1]	393 314.8 [19.3]	221 261.2 [6.2]	436 389.1 [5.6]	— 142.8
z-	47 52.0 [0.5]	36 41.5 [0.7]	— 34.4	62 51.3 [2.2]	— 18.8

Table 7: Linear B Initial Percentage

	-a	-e	-i	-o	-u
pure vowel	92 59.6 [17.5]	70 50.6 [7.3]	36 43.5 [1.3]	51 37.6 [4.7]	11 68.4 [48.2]
d-	34 42.9 [1.8]	22 36.4 [5.7]	57 31.3 [21.0]	32 27.0 [0.9]	42 49.2 [1.0]
j-	3 1.6 [1.2]	0 1.3 [1.3]	— 1.1	1 1.0 [0.0]	— 1.8
k-	42 46.3 [0.4]	27 39.3 [3.8]	33 33.8 [0.0]	34 29.2 [0.7]	66 53.2 [3.0]
m-	35 37.6 [0.1]	36 31.9 [0.5]	24 27.4 [0.4]	14 23.7 [3.9]	55 43.1 [3.2]
n-	9 8.2 [0.0]	18 7.0 [17.1]	0 6.0 [6.0]	4 5.2 [0.2]	5 9.4 [2.1]
p-	51 59.2 [1.1]	51 50.2 [0.0]	28 43.2 [5.3]	61 37.3 [15.0]	67 67.9 [0.0]
q-	52 46.7 [0.6]	43 39.6 [0.2]	37 34.1 [0.2]	18 29.4 [4.4]	— 53.6
r-	16 14.2 [0.2]	12 12.0 [0.0]	9 10.3 [0.1]	3 8.9 [3.9]	22 16.3 [1.9]
s-	30 25.9 [0.6]	11 22.0 [5.5]	18 18.9 [0.0]	3 16.3 [10.9]	51 29.7 [15.1]
t-	12 26.3 [7.8]	19 22.4 [0.5]	17 19.2 [0.2]	18 16.6 [0.1]	49 30.2 [11.5]
w-	25 25.8 [0.0]	14 21.9 [2.8]	28 18.8 [4.4]	16 16.3 [0.0]	— 29.6
z-	24 30.2 [1.2]	38 25.6 [5.9]	— 22.0	13 19.0 [1.9]	— 34.6

Table 8: Linear A Complete Frequency

	-a	-e	-i	-o	-u
pure vowel	72 72.0 [0.0]	? 30.1	65 49.1 [5.1]	? 13.0	26 41.8 [6.0]
d-	57 62.5 [0.4]	15 26.1 [4.7]	51 42.6 [1.6]	15 11.3 [1.1]	41 36.3 [0.6]
j-	60 45.1 [4.9]	4 18.8 [11.7]	? 30.7	? 8.1	? 26.2
k-	52 57.6 [0.5]	6 24.1 [13.6]	45 39.3 [0.8]	8 10.4 [0.5]	54 33.4 [12.5]
m-	52 48.5 [0.2]	14 20.3 [1.9]	36 33.1 [0.2]	? 8.7	? 28.2
n-	73 54.7 [6.0]	? 22.9	28 37.3 [2.3]	? 9.9	23 31.8 [2.4]
p-	46 33.5 [4.5]	? 14.0	21 22.9 [0.1]	? 6.0	9 19.5 [5.6]
q-	17 27.4 [4.0]	22 11.5 [9.5]	? 18.7	? 4.9	? 15.9
r-	62 74.0 [1.9]	55 31.0 [18.5]	23 50.5 [14.9]	21 13.4 [4.2]	51 43.0 [1.4]
s-	47 48.0 [0.0]	18 20.0 [0.2]	? 32.7	? 8.6	31 27.9 [0.3]
t-	64 70.5 [0.6]	35 29.5 [1.0]	59 48.1 [2.4]	4 12.7 [6.0]	40 41.0 [0.0]
w-	17 24.7 [2.4]	23 10.3 [15.4]	12 16.8 [1.4]	? 4.4	? 14.3
z-	10 9.9 [0.0]	? 4.1	? 6.8	? 1.8	? 5.8

Table 9: Linear A frequency (4 x 10)

	-a	-e	-i	-u
pure vowel	72 69.3 [0.1]	? 26.7	65 53.9 [2.3]	26 39.8 [4.8]
d-	57 59.9 [0.1]	15 23.1 [2.8]	51 46.6 [0.4]	41 34.4 [1.3]
k-	52 57.3 [0.5]	6 22.1 [11.7]	45 44.6 [0.0]	54 33.0 [13.4]
m-	52 47.2 [0.5]	14 18.2 [1.0]	36 36.7 [0.0]	? 27.1
n-	73 52.7 [7.8]	? 20.3	28 41.0 [4.1]	23 30.3 [1.8]
p-	46 32.3 [5.8]	? 12.4	21 25.1 [0.7]	9 18.6 [4.9]
r-	62 85.7 [6.6]	55 33.0 [14.7]	? 66.7	51 49.2 [0.1]
s-	47 49.0 [0.1]	18 18.9 [0.0]	? 38.1	31 28.1 [0.3]
t-	64 72.3 [1.0]	35 27.8 [1.8]	59 56.3 [0.1]	40 41.6 [0.1]
w-	17 16.3 [0.0]	? 6.3	12 12.7 [0.0]	? 9.4

Table 10: Linear A Initial Percentage (4 x 10)

	-a	-e	-i	-u
pure vowel	82	?	44	77
	73.4	32.5	55.5	74.0
	[0.9]		[2.3]	[0.1]
d-	45	25	22	25
	36.5	16.1	27.5	36.7
	[1.9]	[4.8]	[1.1]	[3.7]
k-	43	17	40	40
	43.6	19.3	32.9	43.9
	[0.0]	[0.2]	[1.4]	[0.3]
m-	23	8	22	?
	24.1	10.6	18.2	24.2
	[0.0]	[0.6]	[0.7]	
n-	9	?	13	10
	11.5	5.1	8.7	11.6
	[0.5]		[2.0]	[0.2]
p-	47	?	50	57
	55.7	24.7	42.1	56.1
	[1.3]		[1.4]	[0.0]
r-	14	7	?	17
	15.5	6.8	11.7	15.6
	[0.1]	[0.0]		[0.1]
s-	37	6	?	42
	34.6	15.3	26.2	34.9
	[0.1]	[5.7]		[1.4]
t-	13	16	18	29
	23.7	10.5	17.9	23.8
	[4.8]	[2.8]		[1.1]
w-	47	?	25	?
	41.0	18.1	30.9	41.3
	[0.8]		[1.1]	

Linear B Parallels

The first desideratum is an exhaustive list of identical or similar sign-groups in the two linear scripts (with Linear A signs transcribed according to their values in Linear B). Such a list is presented in Appendix B.[34] Those parallels which seem most plausible are collected in Table 11. Only a few sign-groups are identical, but in many cases the initial two signs are identical as well as the consonant of the third sign. It seems reasonable to disregard the final vowel or an obvious Linear B suffix in making these comparisons since a non-Greek name might be accommodated to a Greek inflectional pattern.

It has been common to cite parallels in which one (or more) of the internal syllables shows a different vowel.[35] While it is conceivable that internal vowels could be altered in the process of transmission from Linear A to Linear B, these less exact parallels must be viewed with great scepticism. If vowels are ignored, the random decipherments produce hundreds of matches between Linear A sign-groups and complete Linear B words at Knossos. The Linear B values produce more (see the second list in Appendix B) but not by an impressive margin.[36]

For the purpose of confirming the phonetic values, the most significant parallels are those involving Linear B sign-groups attested at Knossos as personal names or as place names. The chance of error is further reduced by requiring both sign-groups to be complete and longer than two signs. On this criterion fifteen matches can be found: three which are exact, eight in which the final vowel differs, and four which differ by a recognizable Linear B suffix (*i-jo, e-u*) or by a double final vowel. The average random decipherment produced only about three such matches (see Appendix D). More parallels can be cited, but these are the most reliable and should be kept distinct from the others.

---

[34] Tables of parallel names have been published by Goold-Pope (1955, xiv), Landau (1958, 269-271), Gordon (1969, 127) and others. Many of these lists are seriously flawed by faulty readings of Linear A and B sign-groups and by very imprecise criteria for admission. A typical example is the list of twenty names in Gordon (1969, 127). A.WE.SU / *a-wa-so* and KE.KI.RU / *ki-ke-ro* have unequal vowels; KU.KU.DA.RA / *ku-ku-da-ro* is a misquotation—the Linear B word is *ku-ka-da-ro*, another case of unequal vowels; *ku-pa₃-na-to* and *ku-pa₃-no* are misquotations—in each case the initial sign is *ka*.

[35] See, for example, the lists by Landau and Gordon cited in the previous note.

[36] It would have been pointless to include in Appendix D the hundreds of matches which arise in each random decipherment when vowels are disregarded. If we exclude incomplete sign-groups and Linear B words not attested at Knossos (as in the second list in Appendix B) the second random decipherment produces 129 such matches, the third 176, and the fourth 100.

Two exact matches with Knossos names (*ma-di* and *pa-de*) involve sign-groups of only two signs. Because of the probability of coincidence when dealing with such short words, these are not persuasive. The average random decipherment yields more than three.

Going beyond the disciplined limits of the Knossos names one can point to still more parallels. Three matches with complete Knossos words other than names compare favorably with an average of less than one for the random decipherments. These have some confirmatory value. The four matches with sign-groups at Pylos, on the other hand, are nearly worthless since the average random yield is almost three. This last figure shows clearly that the parallels with the highest statistical significance are those involving names at Knossos. This is entirely plausible. From historical considerations, one would not expect to find many Minoan names at Pylos, but in the Knossos archives they should cause no surprise. The few parallels with Linear B on the mainland may possibly prove valuable at a later stage of interpretation, but they are not acceptable as evidence for the phonetic values.

Table 11: Linear B Words in Linear A.

Linear A		Linear B	
Knossos names			
A.KA.RU	2.1,86a1	a-ka-re-u	
A.RA.NA.RE	1a4	a-ra-na-ro	
A.SA.RA$_2$	89.1	a-sa-ro	
DA.MI.NU	117a8	da-mi-ni-jo	(place)
KI.DA.RO	117a9	ki-da-ro	
KU.DO.NI	13.4,85a4	ku-do-ni-ja	(place)
KU.RU.KU	87.4	ku-ru-ka	
PA.I.TO	97a3,120.6	pa-i-to	(place)
PA.JA.RE	8b4,88.4,29.2,	pa-ja-ro	
QA.QA.RU	93a4,118.2,122b3,	qa-qa-ro	
QA.RA$_2$.WA	86a3	qa-ra$_2$-wo	
SA.MA.RO	88.4,39.3	sa-ma-ri-jo	
SU.KI.RI.TA	PHW18	su-ki-ri-ta	(place)
TA.NA.TI	7a4,10b4,98a2,	ta-na-to	
TE-JA-RE	117a5	te-ja-ro (?)	
Knossos Miscellaneous			
KA.SA.RU	10b3	ka-sa-ro	
KI.RI.TA$_2$	114a1,121.1	ki-ri-ta	
DI.DE.RU	86a3,95a4,96b4	di-de-ro	(name?)
DI-KA-TU[	52a2	di-ka-ta-jo	(ethnic?)
RA.RI.DE[	113.1	ra-ri-di-jo	
Pylos and Mycenae			
A.RE.SA.NA	TEZ2	a-re-sa-ni-e	Pylos
I.JA.TE	PHZ4(II12)	i-ja-te	Pylos
I.KU.TA	35.1	i-ku-to	Mycenae (name)
KA.NU.TI	97a3	ka-nu-ta-jo	Pylos (name)

Summary of Evidence

The evidence which may support the validity of each Linear A phonetic value transferred from Linear B is summarized in Table 12. Frequency distribution has been omitted since it bears primarily on a few signs.

It would be useful to find a means of judging for each sign how compelling this evidence is, but it is not apparent how much weight should be given to each kind of evidence. A very rough estimate of the amount of evidence favoring each sign might be obtained by counting the number of alternations or parallels which involve that sign, but this procedure would not reflect the unequal value of the various types of evidence. A parallel involving a rare sign such as QE is less likely to occur randomly than one involving a common sign like RA. Furthermore, the various types of confirmation do not all possess the same degree of reliability. It is easy to agree that an exact parallel with a Linear B name is more significant than one in which internal vowels differ; but is one exact match worth two or four or six inexact ones? Is evidence from "morphological" alternations more or less significant than parallels with Linear B names? The nine random decipherments provide a useful control. Those types of evidence should be valued most highly which discriminate most clearly between the random phonetic values and the values borrowed from Linear B.

Table 13 summarizes the alternations within Linear A resulting from the random decipherments. The figures at the bottom of the table may be helpful in appraising the relative worth of the several classes of evidence. The total number of alternations from all nine random decipherments is followed by the average and by the ratio of this average to the figure for the first (Linear B) decipherment. A large ratio indicates a large confirmatory value for this class of alternation. A relative "weight" (from 0 to 10) is assigned on the basis of this ratio.

Evidence from the Linear B names at Knossos distinguishes much more clearly the random values from the Linear B values. Table 14 includes the same calculations as the previous table. The Linear B phonetic values produce substantially more parallels than any of the random decipherments, which demonstrates conclusively that at least some of the Linear B phonetic values are valid for Linear A. It does not, however, prove that they are all correct or even that every value is correct which is involved in one or even two parallels with the Knossos names. In each random decipherments there are signs confirmed more than once by parallels with Linear B.

In the far right column of Table 12 a figure is computed which may give some indication of the degree of confirmation attaching to each sign. This figure is not intended to be understood as a true test of statistical significance. It is obtained by multiplying the figures in the first nine columns by 10, 5, 4, 10, 0, 10, 2, 10, and 2 respectively. These multipliers reflect the "weight" of each class of evidence (see Tables 13 and 14).

In Table 15 each Linear A phonetic value is listed together with the "significance" of its confirmation according to each of the ten decipherments. This same information is organized in Table 16 according to sign rather than phonetic value. The values *si* and *ne* are omitted from these tables since those assignments are not based only on the shape of the signs.

An example may illustrate the meaning of these last tables. The traditional equation L23=ZA has no support from internal alternations or matches with Linear B. Does this cast suspicion on the assignment? Since there is no phonetic value in Linear A with which ZA could alternate the only possible confirmation will be from matches with Linear B. Table 15 shows that only one random decipherment produces confirmation for a sign with the value *za*, and according to Table 16, the sign L23 is never confirmed for *any* value. The lack of support for the equation L23=ZA is therefore not at all remarkable. The evidence confirming each sign must be evaluated in the light of the potential alternations and matches with Linear B. This potential is a function of the frequency of the sign in Linear A, the number of other signs which have the same consonant, the frequency of the phonetic value in Linear B, and many other factors. The random decipherments give us a method for judging the background "noise" against which the alleged confirmatory evidence must assert itself.

Table 12: Evidence for Phonetic Values.

| Sign | Linear B | | | Alternations | | | | | | Signi- |
| | Names | | Misc. | Initial | | Medial | | Final | | ficance |
	4=	3=	3=	3=	2=	3=	2=	3=	2=	
A		1	2	3						50
I		1								5
U								(1)	(1)	(12)
DA		2								10
DE		1							1	7
DI		1								5
DO		1							1	7
DU										0
JA		2		3						40
JE										0
KA		1	1		1				2	13
KE									1	2
KI	1	1	1						1	21
KO										0
KU		3			1					15
MA		1					2		1	27
ME							1			10
MI		1					1		1	17
NA	1	1							1	17
NI		1								5
NU		1							1	7
PA		2								10
PE										0
PI										0
PU										0

Table 12: Evidence for Phonetic Values (cont.)

Sign	Linear B		Alternations						Signi-ficance
	Names 4=	Misc. 3=	Initial 3=	Initial 2=	Medial 3=	Medial 2=	Final 3=	Final 2=	
QA		3	1						15
QE			1						0
RA	1					1		1	22
RE	1	2			1	1		1	34
RI	1		1			1			16
RO		2							10
RU	4	1							24
SA	2	1							14
SE						1			2
SU	1					1			12
TA	1	1					1	1	27
TE		1					1		15
TI		1							5
TO		1							5
TU									0
WA		1					(1)	(1)	5 (17)
WI									0
ZA									0
TA$_2$		1						1	6
RA$_2$		2							10
PA$_3$									0
PU$_2$									0

Table 13: "Morphological" Evidence by Decipherment

Decipher-ment	Final 2=	3=	Medial 2=	3=	Initial 2=	3=
Lin. B	7	3	2	1	2	3
2	4	0	1	0	2	0
3	5	0	1	0	2	0
4	4	0	2	1	2	0
5	3	0	1	0	1	0
6	2	1	0	0	0	0
7	4	2	0	0	1	0
8	5	0	2	0	3	3
9	4	0	1	0	1	0
10	4	0	1	0	4	0
Total 2-10	35	3	9	1	16	3
Ave. 2-10	3.9	0.33	1	0.11	1.8	0.33
Ratio 1/2-10	1.8	9	2	9	1.1	9
Weight	2	10	2	10	0	10

Table 14: Parallels between Linear A and B

Decipherment	Knossos Name 4=	Knossos Name 3=	Knossos Other 3=	Pylos etc. Misc.
Lin. B	2	13	3	4
2	0	4	1	0
3	0	3	0	3
4	0	2	1	0
5	0	2	1	6
6	0	2	0	6
7	0	3	0	2
8	0	2	1	4
9	0	6	3	3
10	0	3	0	1
Total 2-10	0	27	7	25
Ave. 2-10	0	3	0.8	2.8
Ratio 1/2-10	—	4.3	3.8	1.4
Weight	10	5	4	0

Table 15: Confirmation by Phonetic Value

Value	Decipherment									
	1	2	3	4	5	6	7	8	9	10
A	50	15		12		5	5		15	4
I	5	5	2			5				5
U	(12)	2					5		7	
DA	10	2		2	6		5		4	
DE	7		2	4				2	11	
DI	5		2				5		2	
DO	7		2		2					
DU		2		7				2		5
JA	40		7	12	5	5		5	5	4
JE										
KA	13		5				10	5	9	
KE	2									
KI	21							2		
KO								2		
KU	15	5								5
MA	27					2			4	
ME	10				4				4	
MI	17	4				7			5	
NA	17		2	6	4			2		5
NI	5			2						
NU	7			2				7		
PA	10		20	5			10	9	5	2
PI						10	10		5	
PU									2	

Table 15: Confirmation by Value (cont.)

Value	Decipherment									
	1	2	3	4	5	6	7	8	9	10
QA	15						5		5	
QE										
RA	22	5		4	5	5	14	35	5	12
RE	34	5	7			5	4	32	2	2
RI	16	5			5				2	
RO	10		7				10			
RU	24			5				2	5	
SA	14	2						2	8	
SE	2	2			2			2		
SU	12								4	
TA	27	4		14	7			6		5
TE	15				4	2	2	2	10	
TI	5	21	2	5			2	5	9	
TO	5									
TU		2	2			2				
WA	5 (17)						2	2	2	5
WE		2					2		5	
WI								2		5
ZA					5					
PA$_3$					5	10			6	2
PU$_2$										
RA$_2$	10	5	5				10	4		4
TA$_2$	6	4			2				5	

The Phonetic Values

Table 16: Confirmation by Sign

Sign	Decipherment									
	1	2	3	4	5	6	7	8	9	10
L1 (PA$_3$)		5		4	2		5	2	5	
L2 (PA)	10	2						2		
L6 (TU)		2							4	
L22 (RO)	10		5				2			
L24 (KE)	2									
L25 (NU)	7			2		2			5	
L26 (NA)	17	5	7	2		5	14	6		4
L28 (WI)					2					
L29 (KA)	13	2						2	2	
L30 (DA)	10	21	7	4	7	5	5	2		2
L31 (SA)	14		2			2		2		2
L32 (JA)	40	5						32	4	
L39 (TO)	5									
L51 (DI)	5		5					9	8	
L52 (A)	50				6			35		5
L53 (RA)	22	4	2	12	4		4		9	4
L54 (RE)	34	2	2	12	5					5
L55 (RU)	24								5	
L56 (PI)					4			2	5	
L58 (RA$_2$)	10		2							2
L59 (SU)	12								7	
L60 (NI)	5							7		
L62 (QA)	15	2			5			2		5
L64 (PU?)									5	
L68		4			5			2		

Table 16: Confirmation by Sign (cont.)

Sign	Decipherment									
	1	2	3	4	5	6	7	8	9	10
L72 (RI)	16						2			
L74 (TA)	27	5		6		5	5	5	5	12
L75 (WA)	5					10	10		11	
L76 (MI)	17						5		4	
L77 (SE)	2		7						2	
L78 (TI)	5			14		5			2	
L84 (ME)	10		2				10		6	4
L86 (TA$_2$)	6									
L88								2	2	
L91 (QE)				2					10	
L92 (TE)	15	4			5					
L93 (DU)				5			5		9	
L94 (WE)		5						2	5	
L95 (MA)	27		2	7			10	2	5	
L96										5
L97 (U)	(12)						2			
L98 (KU)	15	5		5	5	5			15	5
L100 (I)	5	15	2				2	5	5	5
L101 (DO)	7							5	4	
L102 (DE)	7					10	10			
L103 (KI)	21		20					5		5

CHAPTER FOUR

INDIVIDUAL SIGNS

Introduction

Tables 12 through 16 at the end of the previous chapter summarize the evidence confirming each Linear A phonetic value. This chapter contains detailed observations about certain specific signs. Discussion here does not imply that a sign's phonetic value is more or less highly confirmed than the average (the degree of confirmation is stated in the tables). Some of the arguments advanced in this chapter are more speculative than those presented earlier.

L 32

The identification of this sign as JA receives strong support from internal and external evidence. There is little doubt that the sign has a value not far removed from *ja* in Linear B, but there may be some difference in the precise phonetic value or in the spelling conventions which govern the use of the sign. In Linear B, *ja, je,* and *jo* most often follow signs ending in *-i*. In the majority of cases this *j* seems merely a conventional indication of a non-distinctive glide intervening between the *i* and the following vowel, but in some cases *j* may correspond to a distinct phoneme of limited distribution.[1] The rather rare instances of phonemic *j* are far outweighed by the others. Nearly 60% of all instances in Linear B occur after *i*. In the Classical Cypriot Syllabary, signs in *j* have become entirely restricted to positions following *i*, though in Eteocypriot *j* seems to have a different distribution and may be phonemic.[2] The vowels which precede the sign JA within Linear A sign-groups are tabulated in the following chart:

Vowel:	*a*	*e*	*i*	*o*	*u*
Count:	14	7	9	1	8
Expected:	16(42%)	5(13%)	9(24%)	1(3%)	7(18%)

---

[1] The phonemic status of *j* in Linear B is discussed by Householder (1961).

[2] O. Masson (1961, 53, 71). For Eteocypriot cf. *ta-le-ya* and *a-ya-i-a-?-?-ko-ti* (inscriptions #194 and #205).

The expected counts are based on the hypothesis that the distribution of vowels before JA is the same as that in Linear A as a whole (percentages in parentheses). It is clear that the occurrence of JA is not determined by the preceding vowel.[3] The sign has no obvious preference for following an *i*. It is therefore a reasonable inference that JA is not functioning merely as a conventional glide in Linear A. There is only one possible instance of the sequence *-i-a*: PA.SI.A on HT 45b3.[4] If J- is always phonemic in Linear A, however, it is hard to know what to make of the apparent alternation between JA and A cited on page 79.

L 43

This sign appears in only one sign-group, RA.43.TI. The Linear B sign which bears some resemblance to this sign, *64, itself occurs only in one word, *a-*64-ja/o,* both at Knossos and Pylos. This provides meagre material for speculation, but one curiosity is worth recording. A phonetic value su_2 for each of these signs would result in the following parallels:

| RA.SU$_2$.TI | 17.1,19.1 | *ra-su-to* | KN toponym |
| A.SU.JA | 11a3 | *a-su$_2$-jo* | KN name |

The Linear A sign-group RA.43.TI occurs as a heading, a context favorable for identifying it as a toponym. It would naturally be of interest to find the Linear B place name *ra-su-to* on a Hagia Triada tablet, but this phonetic value is purely speculative. The rarity of its counterpart *64 in Linear B, however, may imply that it represents a "substrate" sound retained only as a conservative spelling in non-Greek personal names.

L 57

This sign has often been taken as the Linear A counterpart of *ne* in Linear B, but the correspondence in shape is not close. Both Goold-Pope and Nagy list the equation as uncertain; and in their index Raison and Pope do not offer any transliteration.[5] Since L57 occurs in nearly fifty sign-groups, the determination of its phonetic value is considerable importance for the interpretation of the texts. One alternation within Linear A affords support for the value *ne*:

---

[3] A chi-square test gives a likelihood of nearly 80% that the variation observed could occur by chance alone.

[4] The two possible examples in Brice's edition, RI.A (V 2) and I.A.SI (I 7), are not accepted by Raison and Pope.

[5] Goold-Pope (1955, fig. 1), Nagy (1965, 296), Raison-Pope (1971, xv).

| NA.DA.RE | 117a5 |
| NE.DA.RE | 17.3, 122a5 |

This pair has some contextual support, but the random decipherments show that isolated alternations of this kind are of small value as confirmatory evidence. A more promising value for this sign may be *si*. This value results in three possible alternations within Linear A:

A.SU.JA	11a3
A.SE.JA	115a4
A.SI.JA.KA	28a1, 28b1
PI.TA.KA.SE	21.1
PI.TA.KE.SI	87.2
SI.KI.RA	8a4
I.KI.RA	25a5

The above alternations are admittedly not conclusive, but they are supported by three parallels with Linear B at Knossos:

MA.SI.DU	43.1	*ma-si-dwo*	KN
SI.KI.RA	8a4	*si-ki-ro*	KN
SI.MI.TA	96a2	*si-mi-te-u*	KN name

The second two Linear B sign-groups are not listed by Morpurgo since they are recent readings adopted in the fourth edition of *The Knossos Tablets*.[6]

This value is further supported by a consideration of the shape of the sign. The canonical form of the Linear B sign bears only a distant resemblance to L57, but some versions are much closer. Examples of *si* in Linear B with a single cross-bar are common (scribes 107, 114, 124, 126 etc. in Olivier 1967, tables), and in many cases the sloping side-strokes are mostly above the cross-bar, though never entrely above as in L57. The closest parallel is perhaps between *si* written by Olivier's scribe 124 and the shape of L57 on HTZ161(II10) and PHZ4(II12). One could easily imagine a prototype of L57 developing into Linear B *si*.

Finally, it will be recalled that L57 fits badly into the frequency distribution charts if given the value *ne* (page 83). The value *si* results in a better agreement both with the expected total frequency and with the expected initial percentage.

---

[6] *Si-ki-ro* on U8210 and *si-mi-te-u* on Am827 and V1583.

In an earlier paper[7] I presented my identification of the value *si*. Part of that evidence depended on epigraphical readings of Brice which have now been corrected by Raison and Pope. My argument is therefore somewhat weaker, but I believe that the balance of probability still favors the value *si*.[8]

If L57 is *si* then a sign with the value *ne* remains unidentified. An obvious candidate is L61. A few scholars have made this identification, retaining two distinct signs for *ne* in Linear A; and L61 is transliterated as *ne?* by Raison and Pope. As far as correspondence in shape is concerned, L61 is almost as close to *ne* in Linear B as is L57.

L 61

A correspondence in shape with Linear B *ne* could be imagined,[9] but there is no "yield" from this value in Linear A. The value *ne* results only in one curious alternation:

4.RA$_2$.DI.NE	6a4
]DI.RA.DI.NA	PH1a1(IV13)
DI.RE.DI.NA	98a2

The sign L4 occurs only here. It might conceivably be a variant or archaic version of DI, but some distinction must be intended since DI appears in this sign-group in its normal form.

The value *ju* produces two "yields":

PA.RA.JU	115a4,115b1	*pa-ra-ja*	KN and PY
PA.TA.JU	94b1,122a6	*pa-ta-ja*	KN

Kamm points to an alternation within Linear A which results from this value:[10]

JU.MI.NA	115a3,135a1
U.MI.NA.SI	28a1,117a1

It is therefore without conviction that I follow Raison and Pope in

---

[7] Packard (1968).

[8] In his intervention after my talk Pope stated: "In 1964 M. Raison pointed out to me the possibility that *si* was the correct phonetic value to be assigned to L57. His arguments were quite distinct from those just put forward by Mr. Packard." These remarks are printed at the end of Packard (1968).

[9] Especially as written by scribes 102, 104, and 124 (Olivier, 1967, tables). Both signs may be based on the Cretan Hieroglyphic sign P40 (Evans, 1909, 197).

[10] Kamm (1965b, 243).

transcribing this sign as *ne,* rather than using the attractive but speculative value *ju.*

L 69

Two alternations within Linear A allow the hypothesis of the phonetic value *mina* for this sign:[11]

U.MINA.SI	15.1,140.1
U.MI.NA.SI	28a1,117a1
PI.MINA.TE	116a4
]41.MI.NA.TE[12]	APZ2a2(I13)

The sign may perhaps represent a crescent moon. If so, one might compare the similar Linear B ideogram LUNA and the widespread Indo-European words for moon and month based on the root *men.* If further confirmation could be found for this value, it would not only provide important evidence for the linguistic affinities of Linear A, but would introduce a new structural principle, the bisyllabic (or at least biconsonantal) sign, into the syllabary. Such far reaching conclusions cannot possibly be sustained by the very modest evidence cited above for this phonetic value.

L 72 and L 94

Theoretically L72 has a small slash or loop at the center while L94 is a simple smooth reverse "s," but the variants merge almost imperceptibly into each other, and a good case can be made for recognizing only a single sign.[13] Pugliese Carratelli's original distinction between the two signs is maintained by Peruzzi, Nagy, and Raison and Pope who compare them respectively to *ri* and *we* in Linear B, but is abandoned by Meriggi who treats both as *we,* by Brice who lists both as L72, and by Georgiev who transliterates all variants as *ri.*[14] The superficially parallel sign-groups A.94.SU on HT 118 and A.72.SU[on PH13 could be identical, but there is no contextual control.

The value *ri* for L72 is confirmed by an internal alternation KI.RI.TA$_2$/KI.RE.TA$_2$ (see page 78), but there are only two uncommon signs with

---

[11] This value is mentioned by Furumark (1956, 24) without any explanation of how it was reached.

[12] The sign L41 does not occur at Hagia Triada but seems to be the same sign as L56=PI. See Raison-Pope (1971, xxxiii).

[13] Raison-Pope (1971, xxxiii).

[14] Peruzzi (1960, 35); Nagy (1965, 296); Raison-Pope (1971, xv); Meriggi (1956, 15); Brice (1961, Table 1); Georgiev (1963, 8).

which WE could alternate. This first sign-group has a possible parallel in *ki-ri-ta* at Knossos which is not a name. The best match with Linear B is:

]SU.KI.94?/72?.TA PHW18   *su-ki-ri-ta*   toponym

This match is especially attractive because of its length (no match of this length occurred in all the random decipherments) and because the Linear B word is a toponym; but the shape of the sign is closer to L94, at least in the opinion of Raison and Pope.

Evidence from frequency distribution is never conclusive, but it tends to support the view of Brice and others that L94 should not be separated from L72. This evidence was discussed in an earlier chapter (see page 83).

L 79

This sign occurs in only three (possibly four) sign-groups. This provides little material for analysis, but one comparison may be relevant. The word 79.TU.NE occurs twice as a heading (HT 87, 117, both A series) and may possibly be a variant spelling for QE.TU.NE which also serves as a heading in HT 12. The Linear B sign for *qi* is somewhat similar in shape to L79.[15] The phonetic value *qi* for L79 would imply an alternation between QE.TU.NE and QI.TU.NE which is plausible since an *e/i* ambiguity is attested in various writing systems.

L 83

Though not a common sign, L83 is by no means the rarest with nine occurrences in six distinct words, securely initial in two, apparently initial in two, and final in two. The relatively high percentage of word-initial occurrences creates a presumption in favor of identifying L83 as a pure vowel sign, while the modest total frequency points to a vowel sound of only limited distribution.

The apparent alternation of L83 with L52=A at the beginning of the following Linear A sign-groups may suggest a tentative connection.

]83.TI.KA.A.RE[4.1
]A.TI.KA.A.MI.KO   ZAW2.1
]A.TI.KI.TA.A   TYZ4

The first word is on a fragmentary Hagia Triada tablet, the second on a small clay roundel from Kato Zakro, and the third on the shoulder of a large jar from Tylissos. There is little possibility for exact contextual control,

---

[15] Brice (1971a, 32) also notes the similarity in shape.

but the unusual presence of L52=A in non-initial position in all three sign-groups is a persuasive indication of some relationship.[16]

Another short doublet may offer additional confirmation for the alternation L52/L83.

    83.TU   9a2,9b3,119.4,122a6
    A.TU   87.5

Both of these sign-groups appear in lists followed by the number "1", and they could represent the same personal name.[17] Such short sign-groups are not by themselves strong evidence (see page 91), but here they confirm a pattern observed in longer words.

A phonetic value for L83 of a_2 or *ai* would fit well with these possible spelling alternations as well as agreeing with the distribution of the sign in predominantly initial position.

Three parallels with Linear B names at Knossos offer further confirmation for the hypothetical value *ai*.

    83.TU   9a2,9b2,119.4, *ai-to*
    83.TU.JA   115b3   *ai-ta-jo*
    ]83.TI.KA.A.RE[4.1   *a-ti-ka*

In an earlier paper I cited also the following match, but the Linear B reading has since been rejected.[18]

    ]83.KI.TA$_2$ 122b6   *ai-ki-ta*

It is not obvious what pictorial origin this sign has, if any; but Meriggi[19] calls it a "testa equina," and Nagy compares it to a goat's head.[20] If one chooses to view L83 as a goat, a confrontation with Greek αἴξ αἰγός 'goat' will suggest itself, but the identification of L83 as *ai* does not depend on recognizing a goat in the shape of the sign. In any case, αἴξ lacks a clear Indo-European pedigree and has no certain cognate beyond Armenian *ayc*.[21] This "acrophonic" derivation, even if accepted, need not imply anything about the language of Linear A except that it is "Mediterranean."

---

[16] The sign L52 is 82% initial.
[17] It appears, however, that the same scribe wrote HT 87, 119, and 122 (Raison and Pope's hand iii).
[18] Packard (1968, 392). The new reading is *ai-ki-po* on KN U4478.
[19] Meriggi (1956, 17).
[20] Personal communication. One might compare several goat heads on Cretan Hieroglyphic tablets: Chapouthier (1930, 24). Sign number 65 in Evans (1909) has less curved horns than the examples at Mallia and seems closer to L83.
[21] Frisk (1960-1972, 42).

L 86

That this sign, transcribed as TA_2, could have a sound resembling *tana* is suggested by the following alternations:

KI.RE.TA$_2$	85b1,129.1
KI.RE.TA.NA	2.3,8a5,108.1,120.4
TA$_2$.TI.TE	PK1.3(IV5)
TA.NA.TI	7a4,10b4,49a1,98a2

Of the first pair, both sign-groups occur as headings to lists which contain grain ideograms followed by numbers and fractions. This is slender evidence, but a value *tana* or perhaps *tna* would be consistent with L69 as *mina* or *mna*.[22]

L 98

This sign corresponds in shape to *ku* in Linear B. There are indications, however, that the sign may have a value perhaps closer to *ka* than to *ku*.

KU.PA$_3$.NU	1a3,3.6,	*ka-pa$_3$-no*	KN name
KU.PA$_3$.NA.TU	47a1,119.3	*ka-pa$_3$-na-to*	KN name
A.KU.TU	TY3b7(IV9)	*a-ka-to*	KN name
KU.PA.JA	116a1	*ka-pa-jo*	KN
KU.PA$_3$.WE/RI.JA	24a1	*ka-pa-ri-jo*	KN name

This phenomenon may be connected with an apparent Linear A doublet:

KU.DO.NI	13.4,85a4
KA.U.DO.NI	26b2

L 100

An attempt was made by Peruzzi to distinguish in L100 two signs, one corresponding to Linear B *i*, the other to *no*. It seems very difficult, however, to find a consistent criterion on which the distinction can be made.[23] The value *i* may be supported by the high ratio of initial occurrences

---

[22] One might be tempted to carry this hypothetical biconsonantal series even further by proposing that L82, the ideogram for wine, has the phonetic value *wina* in its few possible phonetic uses. I place no value on the resulting match between Linear A PU.82 and the Pylos name *pu-wi-no*.

[23] Raison-Pope (1971, xxxiv).

(44%). Only four of the most common 25 signs have such high initial ratios, and two are the vowels A and U (see Appendix E). The most striking "yield" of the value *i* for L100 is PA.I.TO as the Cretan place name Phaistos. Another possible toponym would be I.TA.NU as the place known in later Greek as Ἴτανος. This toponym seems to occur in Linear B as *u-ta-no* which has been taken along with a few isolated facts to imply an *i/u* ambivalence in the pre-Greek nomenclature of Crete.[24]

The value *no* for L100 results in four good parallels with Linear B words at Knossos.

NO.SA.RI	PH6.4(IV16)	*no-sa-ro*	KN name
KU.RA.NO	117a2	*ku-ra-no*	KN name
KI.TA.NO	123a1	*ki-ta-no*	KN
A.TA.NO	PRZ1b(I17)	*a-ta-no*	KN name

This is impressive evidence for the value *no*, and it is difficult to decide whether such evidence is sufficient to overturn the equation L100=I. The fact that NA, NI, and NU, unlike L100, show a very low proportion of word-initial occurrence, inclines me to retain the value *i* for L100. This assignment is suggested also by the weakness of the -*o* series elsewhere in Linear A, though this second argument is dangerously close to being circular.

---

[24] Palmer (1963, 41).

CHAPTER FIVE

HINTS ABOUT THE PHONOLOGY OF THE MINOAN LANGUAGE

The previous chapter has dealt with phonetic values on an individual basis. We have deliberately postponed the question whether a systematic modification in the structure of the Minoan syllabary may have taken place in the process of its adaptation to Linear B. The most obvious motivation for restructuring would be the adaptation of the script to the needs of a new language.[1] The language for which the Minoan syllabary was first created may have differed significantly from Greek in its repertory of vowels and consonants. In adapting the script to Greek, a certain degree of ambiguity could be tolerated—ambiguity is indeed universal in writing systems—but the difficulties may have been so severe that a reform was mandatory.[2] There are hints both in Linear A and in Linear B that the Minoan language may have differed in phonetic structure from Greek, but such hints must be used with great caution as evidence for Linear A, especially since there is no way of knowing whether the language of the Hagia Triada tablets is identical with the language for which the Minoan syllabary was first devised.

The Vowels

The frequency of the Linear A signs is displayed in Appendix E. The weakness of the *o* series is immediately striking. Only two signs (RO and DO) occur with any strength, a disparity which cannot be attributed to chance. Signs with the vowel *e* also show some weakness though not nearly so pronounced. It will be remembered that no signs have been reliably identified as representing the pure vowels *e* and *o*.

Evidence from internal alternations does not bear on the vowels in most

---

[1] The Sumerian script, for example, was modified to suit the sounds of Akkadian. See Labat (1963, 13-17).
[2] So Dow (1954, 117).

cases. Doublets like DA.TA.RA/DA.TA.RE would tend only to imply that the signs RA and RE contain the same consonant, not that the consonant is *r* and certainly not that the vowels are *a* and *e*. Names common to the two scripts, however, would be expected to reflect the sounds more accurately, except that in a final syllable the vowel might be assimilated to the Greek inflection. It is therefore of great interest to find that the parallels between Linear A and Linear B names from Knossos listed in Table 11 furnish almost no example of a non-final sign containing the vowels *e* or *o*. The non-final vowels in these parallels are: *a* 21, *e* 1, *i* 5, *o* 1, *u* 4. This fact should not be ignored in seeking an explanation for the weakness of these vowels in Linear A.[3]

The lack of an *o* series or an *e* series in the Linear A syllabary would not, in itself, permit any deduction about the phonetic structure of the language. Underdifferentiation is exhibited in many contemporary syllabaries. But shortcomings in the Linear A script cannot explain the weakness of *e* and *o* in the Linear B names which seem to be inherited from the Minoan substratum.

If the Minoan language were in fact characterized by a weakness (or total lack) of syllables with *e* and *o*, one might expect this to be reflected in Linear B at Knossos. The elements at Knossos most likely to reflect the pre-Greek substratum are place names and personal names. General vocabulary words might be expected to contain a smaller proportion of non-Greek elements, though even here the proportion may not be small. Something might be learned, therefore, from a comparison of the relative frequency of the Linear B signs in various classes of words at the different geographical locations.

Appendix G presents a series of graphs showing the relative frequency of each Linear B sign in each of seven classes of words (from left to right): Pylos place names, Pylos names, Pylos total, Linear B total, Knossos total, Knossos names, Knossos place names. These graphs, if interpreted with caution, may give some clue to the phonetic structure of the non-Greek substratum at Pylos and at Knossos. The center bar in each graph represents the average for all of Linear B: toward the left are those classes of words assumed to be most typically Pylian, to the right those most typically Cretan. The bars for toponyms, at the extreme left for Pylos and the extreme right for Knossos, are often based on small samples, but the others have a

---

[3] The random decipherments, however, show almost the same proportions: *a* 31, *e* 5, *i* 12, *o* 0, *u* 6. The explanation for this fact is partially the weakness of signs transliterated with the vowel *o* in Linear A and partly the weakness of the vowel *e* in names at Knossos. See below.

secure statistical basis, and in many cases the toponyms continue a trend evident already in the personal names.

The bar graphs themselves represent for each category the *relative* number of occurrences of each sign in relation to the total number of signs in that category. The absolute number of occurrences is listed on the facing page as total, initial, medial and final. The figures used in compiling the graphs are those presented in tabular form in Appendix F. These graphs should prove valuable in analyzing various aspects of the Bronze Age substrata, but for the present discussion it is sufficient to notice that signs with the vowel *e* show a marked drop at the Knossos side. This phenomenon may be connected with the apparent weakness of *e* in Linear A. The vowels *a* and *u* seem to become stronger in names and place names at Knossos. Signs with *o* are slightly weaker in the Knossos names than in the total Linear B corpus, but the distinction is not clear enough to rule out coincidence.

Setatos has compiled statistics on sign frequency which are in certain respects similar to those just cited.[4] He separates Knossos, Pylos and Mycenae, but does not attempt to distinguish names or places from general vocabulary words. He also detects a weakness of *e* at Knossos but draws a different conclusion. For him this difference reflects a difference of dialect within the Greek element. It is not unlikely that some such difference exists within the Greek at the various palaces, but statistics broken down into word classes clearly show that the variation in vowel frequency between Pylos and Knossos is far greater in names than in general vocabulary and clearest of all in the geographical terms. For this reason I feel confident in ascribing the discrepancy mainly to a Minoan substratum.

A further source of information about the phonology of the Minoan substratum is in the idiosyncrasies of scribal spelling in Linear B at Knossos. The hypothesis of a three vowel graphic system for Linear A might lead one to expect vestigial ambiguity between *i* and *e*, and between *o* and *u*. Such fluctuation exists:[5]

a₃-ke-wa-to	*a₃-ki-wa-to*
qa-me-si-jo	*qa-mi-si-jo*
de-ko-to	*di-ko-to*
o-wa-si-jo	*u-wa-si-jo*
to-ma-ko	*tu-ma-ko*
to-ni-ja	*tu-ni-ja*

---

[4] Setatos (1969).

[5] These examples are drawn from the catalogue of scribal spelling variation at Knossos collected by Olivier (1967, 98-100).

The Consonants

Since there is reason to doubt that the Linear A syllabary distinguishes five vowels, one might also wonder whether the same consonants are represented as in Linear B (*d, j, k, m, n, p, q, r, s, t, w, z*). An alternative possibility is that Linear A has a graphemic repertory unlike that of Linear B and that some of the Linear A phonetic values may have no parallel in Linear B and vice versa.

It is often pointed out that the Linear B script is not perfectly adapted to the Greek language. Among other shortcomings, it ignores phonemic oppositions which are important in Greek (*t/th, p/ph/b, k/kh/g, l/r*). A possible though very uncertain inference is that these sounds were not distinguished by the language for which Minoan writing was invented. Certain distinctions, on the other hand, which are more or less redundant from the point of view of Greek are present in the so-called homophones (*ta/ta₂, ra/ra₂, pa/pa₃,* etc.). These signs may have originally expressed oppositions which were important in the Minoan language but which are at best marginal in Greek. We must emphasize, however, that the imperfections of a script are not reliable evidence for the nature of the language for which it is used.[6]

Several scholars have tried to evaluate these clues to the phonology of the Minoan language. Palmer, on the basis of the Mycenaean homophones, postulated for Minoan two additional consonant series, one palatalized and one labialized. Minoan signs from the first series would then survive in Linear B *ta₂* (=*tja*), *ra₂* (=*rja*), *pa₃* (=*pja*), *za* (=*kja*), and possibly *pte* (=*pje* which in Greek develops into *pte*). The second series would appear as *qa* (=*kwa*), *nwa, two, dwo, dwe, twe*.[7] It seems significant that these homophones are strongest in the *a-* series.

One might develop a unified explanation which covered both the weakness of the two Linear A vowel series and the hypothetical extra consonant series in Linear B (as postulated by Palmer) by imagining that the Greeks used some of the superfluous consonant signs to form the needed vowel series. Palatalized *tu*, for example, might be used for *to*. If two of the original vowel series were split up in this way (*i* and *u*), the third would be left more or less intact and could result in the preponderance of the homophones in the *a* series in Linear B. The possibility of such a restructuring merits further study.

---

[6] Daniel (1941, 264) cites the example of Hurrian which was once thought to contain less phonemic oppositions than it actually does because of the underdifferentiation of the script.

[7] Palmer (1963, 38). For a critique of Palmer's view, see Lejeune (1966).

The comparison of Linear B with the Cypriot Syllabary may permit still another deduction. Linear B distinguishes voiced stops only in the dentals (special sign for *d* but not for *b* or *g*). This lack of symmetry is unusual, especially since the Cypriot Syllabary does not have signs for *d* as distinct from *t*. This suggests that the *d*- series is an innovation in Linear B taken over perhaps from a related but not identical Minoan sound. Cypriot, on the other hand, unlike Linear B, distinguishes *r* from *l*. This could be explained by the postulation of a Minoan sound between *d* and *l* expressed by a series of Linear A signs which Linear B adopted to represent *d* as opposed to *t*, but Cypriot used for *l* as opposed to *r*. A true *d* sound (a voiced dental stop), if it existed in Linear A, might then have been written *t* as in Cypriot. Such an *l/d* ambivalence is documented not only in Greek but also in other ancient languages of the area.[8] This hypothesis is superficially attractive, but there are additional facts whose interpretation it only confuses. The Cypriot sign for *ta* is identical in shape with Linear B *da* which is not what the theory would predict. In addition, Linear B *ro/lo* appears in Cypriot as *lo* rather than as *ro*. If the *d* series in Linear A represented a Minoan sound close to *l* one might expect Linear B scribes at Knossos occasionally to represent this Minoan *l/d* sound with their *r* (=*l*) series. The following correspondences are probably coincidental.

Linear A	Linear B	
KI.DA.TA	*ki-ra-di-*[	KN
SI.DA.RE	*si-ra-ro*	KN place
WI.DI.NA	*wi-ri-ne-we*	KN name

Another, perhaps less unlikely, hypothesis is that this supposed Minoan *l/d* sound was written with the Linear A *r* signs but occasionally heard and written *d* in Linear B. The Cypriot evidence is more favorable to this theory since Cypriot *lo* is clearly derived from the (Linear A) prototype of Linear B *ro*. Three sign-groups in Linear A resemble names known at Knossos if *d* in Linear B is imagined to reflect a sound written *r* in Linear A.

A.RI.NI.TA	*a-di-nwa-ta*
SA.MA.RO	*sa-ma-da*
A.KA.RU	*a-ka-de*

The precariousness of these parallels is, however, underlined by the fact that two of these same Linear A words can be found in Linear B with the expected spelling in *r* (*sa-ma-ri-jo, a-ka-re-u*).

There is another way to explain the anomalous voiced dental series in Linear B. It is possible to imagine that Linear A distinguished two types of

---

[8] Heubeck (1957).

dentals which differed in some way other than in voicing. Linear B may have used the extra dental series to distinguish voicing while Cypriot simply discarded the redundant signs. The Cypriot *t* series seems eclectic in that *ta* corresponds to DA in Linear A, but *ti* agrees with TI and *to* with TO. A case could also be made for equating Cypriot *tu* with DU. If true, this hypothesis would imply that the *d* series in Linear A is not necessarily voiced, and that the *t* series is not necessarily unvoiced. Six correspondences between Linear A and Linear B can be quoted if voicing is ignored.

A.KU.TU	*a-ku-do-i*	KN place
KO.A.DU.WA	*ko-a-ta*	KN name
SI.MI.TA	*si-mi-do*	KN name (As 607)
SI.DA.RE	*si-ta-ro*	KN name
DA.TA.RE	*da-da-re-(jo)*	KN place
I.JA.TE	*i-ja-di*	KN name

The evidence is inadequate to decide whether any of the above hypotheses is correct.

Table 17: Non-final Vowels in Linear B

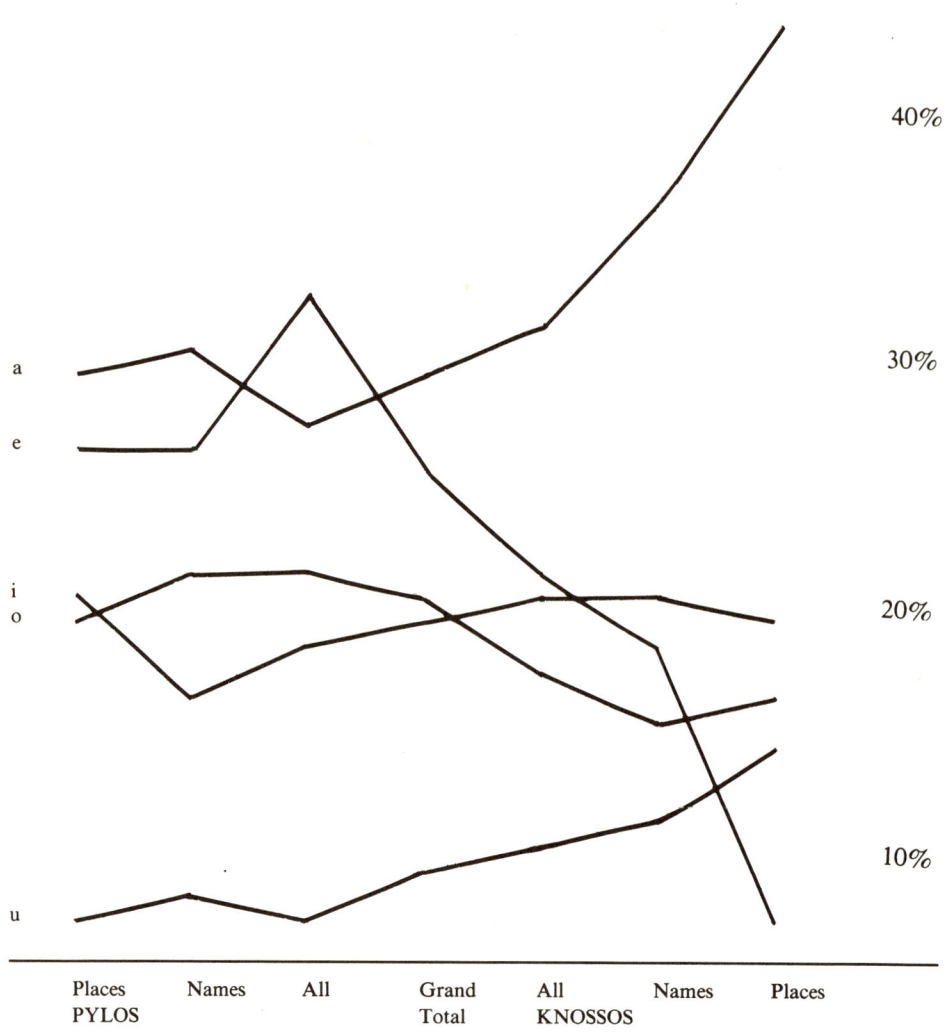

Table 18: Consonants in Linear B

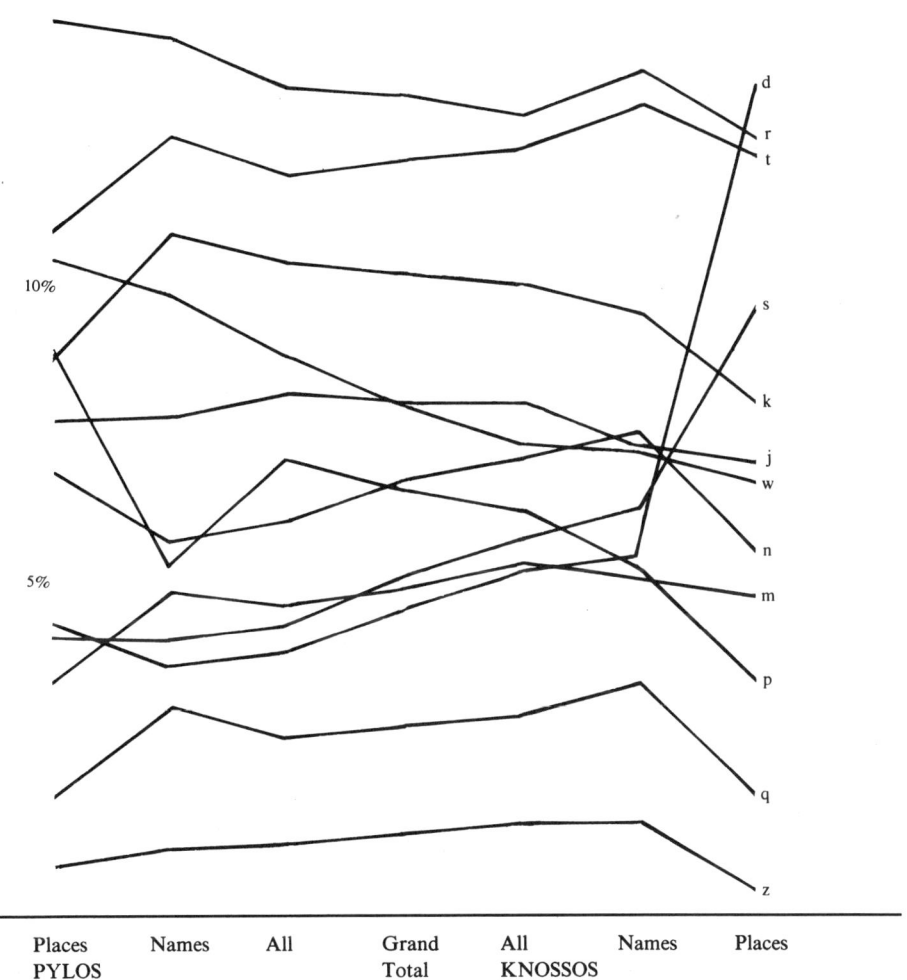

APPENDICES

APPENDIX A

This appendix collects pairs of Linear A sign-groups exhibiting alternations which could represent inflection or orthographic variation. Five types of alternation are listed: a) cases where the first two signs are identical, b) cases where the last two signs are identical, c) cases where the first and third are identical, d) cases where the sign-group occurs also with a suffix, e) cases where the sign-group occurs also with a prefix. The selection follows these criteria mechanically, with no attempt to segregate the plausible from the merely coincidental.

The sign-groups are transliterated according to the phonetic values used elsewhere in this book and listed on page 67 and Figures 5 and 6. The system of codes and references is explained in the introduction to Appendix H. Readings of Brice (1961) which differ from Raison-Pope (1971) are not included in this appendix.

Variation at the End of Sign-groups

A.DI.DA.KI.TI.PA.KU	*	C1	KNZ6(II1)
A.DI.KI.TE.TE.PI	*	C1	PKZ11a(I4)
A.KA.NU.WE.20	*	C1	KNZ7(II2)
A.KA.RU		C2	2.1,86a1,86b1?
A.RA.NA.RE		C1	1a4,47b1?
A.RA.PI	#	C1	87.5
A.RA.68		C1	122b3,87.5?,109.4?
A.RA.96	*	C1	109.4
A.RE.DA.I	*	C1	29.5
A.RE.NE.SI.DI.88.41	*	C1	KNZ13(V14)
A.RE.41.RE.NA	+	C1	ZAZ3.2
A.RU.DA.RA		C1	28b5,62.1?
A.RU.RA	*	B1	11a1
A.SA.DA.KA		C1	MAW5a1(III12)
A.SA.ME.NE	*	C1	ZAZ3.1
A.SA.RA$_2$	*	C1	89.1
A.SA.SA.RA.ME	*	C2	PKZ11b(I4),PRZ1c(I17)
A.SA.88.MA.I	*	C1	GOW1a1(III10)
A.TA.I.88.WA.JA	*	C3	PKZ12a(I5),TLZ1(I16),
A.TA.I.88.DE.KA	+	C1	ZAZ3.2
A.TI.KA.A.MI.KO	#	C1	ZAW2.1(III8)
A.TI.KI.TA.A	#	C1	TYZ4(II18)
DA.KU.NA		C1	103.4
DA.KU.SE.NE		C1B1	103.4,103.2
DA.SI.DI.JA		A1	126a3
DA.SI.85		C4	13.5,85a3,99b1,122a2
DA.TA.RA		C1	6a1
DA.TA.RE		C2	88.5,62.2*

Variation at End (cont.)

DI.NA.RO	*	C1	108.2
DI.NA.U		C6	9a3,9b5,16.1,25a1,
DO.DI.NA	*	C1	HTW210a(CRIV13)
DO.DI.RA		C2	HTW212a(CRIV11),
DO.96.DI		C1	101.1
DO.96.PU$_2$		C1	25a4
I.DA.A	+	C1	KOZ1b
I.DA.MA.TE		C2	ARZ1(V17iii),ARZ2(V17iv)
I.DA.PA$_3$		C1	PH6.4(IV16)
I.DU.NE.SI		C1	13.5
I.DU.TI	*	C1	104.2
I.DU.WI	*	C1	MA1a(IV10)
I.KU.RI.NA		C1	90.1
I.KU.TA	*	C1	35.1
I.NA.JA	*	C1	PKZ11(I4)
I.NA.JA.RE.68	*	B1	APZ2a2(I13)
I.NA.WA		C1	PH6.1(IV16)
I.41.NA.MA	*	B1	APZ2a1(I13)
I.41.NA.MI.NA	#	C1	PKZ10(I6)
JA.SA.SA.RA.MA.NA	*	C1	KNZ10a(I8)
JA.SA.SA.RA.ME	*	C2	PSZ2c(I1),TLZ1(I16)
KA.RO.NA		C1	11a2
KA.RO.PA$_3$		C1	31.3
KA.U.DE.TA		C1	13.1
KA.U.DO.NI		C1	26b2
KI.DA.RO		C1	117a9,27a4?
KI.DA.TA		C1	40.2

Variation at End (cont.)

KI.KI.NA		C1	88.2
KI.KI.RA.JA		C1	85b1
KI.RE.TA.NA		C3A1	8a5,108.1,120.4,2.3
KI.RE.TA$_2$		C2	129.1,85b1
KU.DO.NA	*	D1	64.1
KU.DO.NI		C2	13.4,85a4
KU.MA.RO		A1	96a5
KU.MA.96		C1	20.1
KU.PA$_3$.NA.TU		C2	47a1,119.3
KU.PA$_3$.NU		C9	1a3,3.6,88.3,88.4,117a3,
KU.PA$_3$.WE.JA		C1	24a1
KU.RU.KU		C1	87.4
KU.RU.MA	*	C1	115b3
MA.KA.I.SU	*	C1	PK1.7(IV5)
MA.KA.RI.TE		C2	87.1,117a1
PA.TA.NE		C2	94b1,122a6
PA.TA.QE		C1	31.6
PI.TA.JA		C1	6a2
PI.TA.KA.SE		C1	21.1
PI.TA.KE.SI		C1	87.2
PI.TA.RA	*	C1	96a4
QE.TU.NE		C1	12.3
QE.TU.SI	*	C1	PHW14a(III13)
RA.NA.TU.SU.PU$_2$.MI.WE	*	C1	PK1(IV5)
RA.NA.111	*	C1	115a2
SI.KI.NE	*	C1	116a5
SI.KI.RA		C1	8a4

Variation at End (cont.)

SU.KI.RI.TA	?	C1	PHW18
SU.KI.RI.TE.I.JA	?	C1	HTZ158b(II7)
TA.NU.144.JA	*	D1	PKZ13(II16)
TA.NU.144.TI	*	A1	KNZ10a(I8)
TU.RU.NU.SE.ME	*	C1	128a1
TU.RU.SA.RA$_2$.-.RE	*	C1	KOZ1b
WA.TU.MA.RE	*	C1	128a2
WA.TU.MI	*	C1	HTW206a(CRIV8)

Variation at Beginning of Sign-groups

KU.KU.DA.RA		C1	117a7
A.RU.DA.RA		C1	28b5,62.1?
JA.MI.DA.RE		C1	122a4
NA.DA.RE		C1	117a5
PA.DA.RE	*	C1	10a3
SI.DA.RE		C2	17.3,122a5,49a4?
KI.DA.TA		C1	40.2
TI.DA.TA	*	C1	123b2
JA.DI.KI.TE.TE.PI	*	C1	PKZ8a(I3)
A.DI.KI.TE.TE.PI	*	C1	PKZ11a(I4)
DO.DI.NA	*	C1	HTW210a(CRIV13)
DI.RA.DI.NA		A1	PH1a1(IV13)
DI.RE.DI.NA		C1	98a2
WI.DI.NA		C1	28a5
KI.DI.NI	*	C1	93a2
WA.DI.NI		C2	HTW208a(CRIV1),
DO.DI.RA		C2	HTW212a(CRIV11),
SO.DI.RA		C3	9a4,9b3,122a5
KU.DO.NI		C2	13.4,85a4
KA.U.DO.NI		C1	26b2
KO.A.DU.WA		C1	TY3b6(IV9)
NU.DU.WA		C1	40.1
PA.JA.RE		C2B2	8b4,88.4,29.2,TY3a4(IV9)
TE.JA.RE	*	C1	117a5
DI.DI.KA.SE	+	C1	ZAZ3.1
PI.TA.KA.SE		C1	21.1
I.KI.RA		C1	25a5
SI.KI.RA		C1	8A4

Variation at Beginning (cont.)

DA.KU.NA		C1	103.4
68.KU.NA	*	C1	KNZ6(II1)
KA.KU.PA		C3	16.1,HTW215a(CRIV6),
10.KU.PA	*	C1	HTW220b(CRV5)
QA.KU.RE	*	C1	HTW217a1(CRIV4)
QE.KU.RE		C1	20.2
JA.KU.TI		C1	KN1b1(IV1)
DA.NE.KU.TI		C1	117a8
A.KU.TU		C1	TY3b7(IV9)
SE.KU.TU		C1	115a3
KU.MA.RO		A1	96a5
SA.MA.RO		C1A1	88.4,39.3*
DA.DU.MA.TA		C1	95a1
RU.MA.TA		C1B1	99b2,29.1
I.41.NA.MI.NA	#	C1	PKZ10(I6)
NE.MI.NA		C1A1	115a3,135a1
DA.MI.NU		C1	117a8
QE.DE.MI.NU		C2	MA1a(IV10),MA1b(IV10)
DA.NA.SI		C1	126a1
U.NA.KA.NA.SI	+	C1	KOZ1c
U.NA.RU.KA.NA.TI	*	C1	PKZ11(I4)
TA.NA.TI		C3A1	7a4,10b4,98a2,49a2
DA.KU.SE.NE.TI		C1	104.1
SI.TU.NE.TI		C1	PK1.1(IV5)
A.RI.NI.TA		C1	25a3
I.DO.RI.NI.TA		C1	PH6.2(IV16)
TI.NI.TA		C1	27a1

Variation at Beginning (cont.)

KI.KI.RA.JA		C1	85b1
DE.NU.RA.JA		C1	115a1
MI.RU.TA.RA.RE	*	C1	117a4
QA.85.RA.RE		C1	96b1
JA.DI.RA.TI	*	C1	KN1a1(IV1)
PA$_3$.KA.RA.TI		C1	8a1
KU.RE.96		C1A1	117b1,39.2
SA.RE.96		C1	20.4
A.RI.NI.TA		C1	25a3
I.DO.RI.NI.TA		C1	PH6.2(IV16)
KI.RI.TA$_2$		C2	114a1,121.1
SI.RU.MA.RI.TA$_2$	*	C1	90.2
KU.RU.MA	*	C1	115b3
WE.RU.MA		C1	118.4
A.SA.SA.RA.ME	*	C2	PKZ11b(I4),PRZ1c(I17)
JA.SA.SA.RA.ME	*	C2	PSZ2c(I1),TLZ1(I16)
A.SE.JA		C1	115a4
PA.SE.JA		C3	93a8,HTW201(CRIV15)
DU.TA.DI	*	C1	19.3
RU.JA.TA.DI		C1	HTW208b(CRIV1)
A.TA.I	*	C1	PRZ1b(I17)
KI.TA.I		C1	123a1
KI.RE.TA.NA		C3A1	8a5,108.1,120.4,2.3
TI.TA.NA		C1	HTW220(CRV5)
DA.TA.RA		C1	6a1
PI.TA.RA	*	C1	96a4

Appendix A

Variation at Beginning (cont.)

QE.TU.NE		C1	12.3
SI.TU.NE	*	C1	HTW221a(CRV4)
79.TU.NE		C3	7b1,87.1,117b1
KU.PA$_3$.WE.JA		C1	24a1
PA.SA.WE.JA		C1	24a4
DI.WE.NA		C2	93a1,102.3
TA.WE.NA		C1	10b1
TU.79.WE.NA		C1	129.2
QA.63.I		C4	8a3,8b2,85b5,122a4
KA.RI.63.I		C1	98a4

Variation within Sign-Groups

PA.DA.RE	*	C1	10a3
PA.JA.RE		C2B2	8b4,88.4,29.2,
PA.RA.NE		C2	115a4,115b1,
PA.TA.NE		C2	94b1,122a6
TU.RU.NU.SE.ME	*	C1	128a1
TU.QE.NU		C1	25a3
DA.TA.RA		C1	6a1
DA.QE.RA		C2B1	6a6,120.1,57a1
DI.RA.DI.NA		A1	PH1a1(IV13)
DI.RE.DI.NA		C1	98a2
A.KU.TU		C1	TY3b7(IV9)
A.151.TU.134.RA	*	C1	PH2.1(IV14)
A.PU2.NA		C1	14.3
A.RA.NA.RE		C1	1a4,47b1?
A.SA.DA.KA		C1	MAW5a1(III12)
A.41.DA.85	#	C1	SIZ1
A.RE.DA.I	*	C1	29.5
A.RU.DA.RA		C1	28b5,62.1?
A.SA.SA.RA.ME	*	C2	PKZ11b(I4),
A.RE.SA.NA	+	C1	TEZ2
A.SI.JA.KA		C2	28a1,28b1
A.SU.JA		C1	11a3
A.SE.JA		C1	115a4
A.PA.RA.NE		C2	96a1,96b1
A.RU.RA	*	B1	11a1
A.MA.RA.TU	*	B1	SKZ1(II25)
A.RI.SU	*	B1	PH13(IV17vii)
A.WE.SU		C1	118.3

Appendix A

Variation within (cont.)

A.DI.KI.TE	*	B1	PKZ12a(I5)
A.DI.KI.TE.TE.PI	*	C1	PKZ11a(I4)
A.TI.KI.TA.A		C1	TYZ4
SI.TU.NE	*	C1	HTW221a(CRV4)
SI.TU.NE.TI		C1	PK1.1(IV5)
SI.KI.NE	*	C1	116a5
WA.DI.NI		C2	HTW208a(CRIV1),
WA.DU.NI.MI		C2	6b1,85b4
WA.TU.MI	*	C1	HTW206a(CRIV8)
WA.KA.MI.ZA.RE.NA	*	B1	PK1.3(IV5)
TI.DA.TA	*	C1	123b2
TI.NI.TA		C1	27a1
DU.TA.DI	*	C1	19.3
DU.ME.DI		C1	19.3
U.37.ZA		C3	10a2,10a4,85a3
U.DE.ZA		C2	122a1,122b3
KU.PA3.NA.TU		C2	47a1,119.3
KU.MI.NA.QE		C1D1	HTW214a(CRIV5),54a2
KU.RE.96		C1A1	117b1,39.2
KU.MA.96		C1	20.1
I.SA.RI		C1	PH6.4(IV16)
I.KU.RI.NA		C1	90.1
I.DO.RI.NI.TA		C1	PH6.2(IV16)
I.PA.85	*	C1	PA1(IV7)
I.QA.85		C2	44b1,131.2
KI.DA.TA		C1	40.2
KI.RE.TA.NA		C3A1	8a5,108.1,120.4,2.3
KI.RE.TA2		C2	129.1,85b1
KI.RI.TA2		C2	114a1,121.1

"Suffixes"

A.RU		C3	9a5,9b2,49a6,11a1?
A.RU.DA.RA		C1	28b5,62.1?
A.SE		C3	93a3,132.1,ZAZ3.1+
A.SE.JA		C1	115a4
83.TU		C4	9a2,9b3,119.4,122a6
83.TU.JA		C1	115b3
PA.SE		C2	18.1,27b4
PA.SE.JA		C3	93a8,HTW201(CRIV15)
KU.PA		C1	HTW220a(CRV5),110a2?
KU.PA.JA		C1	116a1
JA.DI		C1	PHW16a(III15)
JA.DI.KI.TE.TE.PI	*	C1	PKZ8a(I3)
SI.RU		C1	55a2,90.2?,PKZ11d(I4)?
SI.RU.MA.RI.TA$_2$	*	C1	90.2
PA$_3$.NI		C2	85a2,102.2
PA$_3$.NI.NA		C3	6b6,93a1,93a8
KU.MI	*	C1	110a1
KU.MI.NA.QE		C1D1	HTW214a(CRIV5),54a2
TI.DU	*	C1	TYZ1(V2)
TI.DU.NI		C1	49a4
A.RI		C2B1	PH6.1(IV16),PH6.3(IV16),
A.RI.NI.TA		C1	25a3
KA.KU		C1	62.2
KA.KU.PA		C3	16.1,HTW215a(CRIV6),
KA.PA		C4B2	6A1,8b3,94a1,102.1,105.1,
KA.PA.QE		C1	6a4

Appendix A

Suffixes (cont.)

SA.RO		C4	9a1,17.2,19.2,42.2,25b1?
SA.RO.QE	*	B1	73.3
A.RU		C3	9a5,9b2,49a6,11a1?
A.RU.RA	*	B1	11a1
QE.TI		C1	7a1
QE.TI.RA.DU		C1	58.1
JA.DI		C1	PHW16a(III15)
JA.DI.RA.TI	*	C1	KN1a1(IV1)
A.MA	*	C1	MA1b(IV10)
A.MA.RA.TU	*	B1	SKZ1(II25)
PA.DE		C3	9a2,9b2,122a5
PA.DA.RE	*	C1	10a3
I.NA.JA	*	C1	PKZ11(I4)
I.NA.JA.RE.68	*	B1	APZ2a2(I13)
SA.MA		C3	6b5,10a1,52a1,39.3?
SA.MA.RO		C1A1	88.4,39.3*
99.I		C2	11a4,93a5,62.5?
99.I.RU.JA	*	C1	7a2
A.RI		C2B1	PH6.1(IV16),PH6.3(IV16),
A.RI.SU	*	B1	PH13(IV17vii)
SI.MA		C1	PHZ4(II12)
SI.MI.TA		C1	96a2
RU.JA	*	C1	KNW26a(III17)
RU.JA.TA.DI		C1	HTW208b(CRIV1)
SI.TU.NE	*	C1	HTW221a(CRV4)
SI.TU.NE.TI		C1	PK1.1(IV5)

Suffixes (cont.)

JA.KU		C1	MA2b2(IV11)
JA.KU.TI		C1	KN1b1(IV1)
DA.KU.SE.NE		C1B1	103.4,103.2
DA.KU.SE.NE.TI		C1	104.1
I.TI	*	C1	62.3
I.TI.TI.KU.NI		C1	96a1
A.KU		C1	PA1.1(IV7)
A.KU.TU		C1	TY3b7(IV9)
A.TU		C1	87.5
A.TU.WE.SI.TI	*	C1	KNZ5(II4)
A.DU		C7	85a1,86a4,88.1,92.1,95b1,
A.DU.ZA	*	C1	PK1.2(IV5)
A.TA.I	*	C1	PRZ1b(I17)
A.TA.I.88.WA.JA	*	C3	PKZ12a(I5),TLZ1(I16),

Appendix A

"*Prefixes*"

JA.KU	C1	MA2b2(IV11)
A.JA.KU	C1	KNZ13(V14)
KA.RU	C1B1	97a1,75.1,84.1?
A.KA.RU	C2	2.1,86a1,86b1?
PA.RA.NE	C2	115a4,115b1,HTW221a(CRV4)?
A.PA.RA.NE	C2	96a1,96b1
SA.RA$_2$	C20B1	18.2,28a2,28b3,30.1,32.1,
A.SA.RA$_2$ *	C1	89.1
A.RE.DA.I *	C1	29.5
DA.I	C1	12.6,29.5?
KI.RA	C1	103.5
I.KI.RA	C1	25a5
RE.RO	C1	HTW212b(CRIV11)
KA.RE.RO	C1	HTW203(CRIV18)
SA.RU	C5	86a2,94b2,95a3,95b1,123a4
KA.SA.RU	C1	10b3
KU.PA	C1	HTW220a(CRV5),110a2?
KA.KU.PA	C3	16.1,HTW215a(CRIV6),
KI.RU	C1	MIZ1(II22IV)
KE.KI.RU	C1	94b2

Prefixes (cont.)

PA.JA		C2A1	41.4,PH1b1(IV13),MA4b
KU.PA.JA		C1	116a1
SU.PU		C1	31.2
QE.SU.PU		C1	87.4
NA.111		C1	155a2
RA.NA.111	*	C1	115a2
KI.RA		C1	103.5
SI.KI.RA		C1	8a4
NA.TI		C1	97a4,111b3?
TA.NA.TI		C3A1	7a4,10b4,98a2,49a2
MA.RE	*	C2	55a1,PH19.2+
WA.TU.MA.RE	*	C1	128a2
KU.PA		C1	HTW220a(CRV5),110a2?
10.KU.PA	*	C1	HTW220b(CRV5)
SA.DI		C1	111b1,100.2?
20.SA.DI	*	C1	PHW15(III14)
KU.RO		C30A5	9a6,9b6,11a3,11b5,13.7,
21.TO.KU.RO		C1	122b6
RU.JA	*	C1	KNW26A(III17)
99.I.RU.JA	*	C1	7A2

APPENDIX B

This appendix provides lists of sign-groups in Linear A which resemble sign-groups in Linear B. The first list contains sign-groups in which at least the first two signs and the consonant of the third sign are identical. The second enumerates parallels in which at least the consonants (but not necessarily the vowels) of the first three signs are identical. For reasons of space this second list is restricted to complete sign-groups and excludes Linear B words not attested at Knossos and Linear A words not accepted by Raison-Pope (1971). The third list is limited to parallels consisting of only two signs.

Linear A sign-groups are transliterated according to the values listed on page 67. The explanation of the code in the second column is given in the introduction to Appendix H.

References for Linear B words may be found in Morpurgo (1961) which served as the basis for these comparisons. I have collated the fourth edition of *The Knossos Tablets* with Morpurgo, and sign-groups not listed in the earlier lexicon are here marked with a plus sign. The code for the Linear B entries is divided into three columns. The first signifies the site (K=Knossos, P=Pylos, M=Mycenae, T=Thebes, +=Knossos not in Morpurgo); the second gives Morpurgo's tentative identification of probable word-class (N=personal name, P=place name, E=ethnic, G=god, Q=person qualifier); the third column indicates the state of preservation (A=incomplete at beginning, B=incomplete at end, C=complete, D=incomplete at both ends, X=additional doubts such as dotted letters).

This appendix results from a mechanical collation with no attempt being made to separate significant from fortuitous parallels. The problem of significance is treated in the text.

Parallels up to Third Consonant

Linear A	Code	Reference	Linear B	Code		
A.KA.NU.WE.20.DU	* B1	KNZ7(II2)	*a-ka-na-jo*	P		C
A.KA.RU	C2	2.1,86a1,	*a-ka-ra-no*	P		C
A.KA.RU	C2	2.1,86a1,	*a-ka-re-u*	PK	N	C
A.KA.RU	C2	2.1,86a1,	*a-ka-re-u-te*	P	P	C
A.KU.TU	C1	TY3b7(IV9)	*a-ku-tu-ru-wo*	K	N	C
A.MA.RA.TU	* B1	SKZ1(II25)	*a-ma-ru-ta*	P	N	C
A.MA.RA.TU	* B1	SKZ1(II25)	*a-ma-ru-ta-o*	P	N	C
A.NA.QA	A1	126a2	*a-na-qo-ta*	K	Q	C
A.PA.DU.PA	= D1	PKZ12d(I5)	*a-pa₃-da-ro*	K	N	CX
A.PA.RA.NE	C2	96a1,96b1	*a-pa-re-u*	K	N	CX
A.PA.RA.NE	C2	96a1,96b1	*a-pa-re-u-pi*	P	P	C
A.PA.RA.NE	C2	96a1,96b1	*a-pa-ri-ka-na-we-ja*	P	P	C
A.PA.RA.NE	C2	96a1,96b1	*a-pa-re*	+		B
A.PA.SE.PA	# D1	PKZ12d(I5)	*a-pa-sa*	P	N	B
A.PA.SE.PA	# D1	PKZ12d(I5)	*a-pa-sa-ki-jo*	K	N	C
A.PA.SE.PA	# D1	PKZ12d(I5)	*a-pa-si-jo-jo*	P	N	C
A.PU₂.NA	C1	14.3	*a-pu-ne-we*	P		C
A.RA.NA.RE	C1	1a4,47b1?	*a-ra-na-ro*	K	N	C
A.RE.SA.NA	+ C1	TEZ2	*a-re-sa-ni-e*	P		C
A.RE.SA.NA	+ C1	TEZ2	*a-re-se*	K		B
A.RE.SA.NA	+ C1	TEZ2	*a-re-su-ti-jo*	M	N	C
A.SA.ME.NE	* C1	ZAZ3.1	*a-sa-ma-o*	P	N	C
A.SA.ME.NE	* C1	ZAZ3.1	*a-sa-ma-to*	P		C
A.SA.ME.NE	* C1	ZAZ3.1	*a-sa-mi*	K		A
A.SA.ME.NE	* C1	ZAZ3.1	*a-sa-mi-to*	+		C
A.SA.RA₂	* C1	89.1	*a-sa-ro*	K	N	C
A.SI.JA.KA	C2	28a1,28b1	*a-si-ja-ti-ja*	P	P	C
A.TA.NU.WI.JA.WA	* B1	HTZ159(II8)	*a-ta-no*	K	N	C
A.TA.NU.WI.JA.WA	* B1	HTZ159(II8)	*a-ta-no-re*	P	N	C
A.TA.NU.WI.JA.WA	* B1	HTZ159(II8)	*a-ta-no-ro*	P	N	C
A.TI.KA.A	? C1	III8.1	*a-ti-ka*	K	N	C
A.TI.KA.A	? C1	III8.1	*a-ti-ke-ne-ja*	M	N	C
A.TI.KI.TA.A	? C1	II18	*a-ti-ka*	K	N	C
A.TI.KI.TA.A	? C1	II18	*a-ti-ke-ne-ja*	M	N	C
A.TI.KA.A.MI.KO	# C1	ZAW2.1(III8)	*a-ti-ka*	K	N	C
A.TI.KA.A.MI.KO	# C1	ZAW2.1(III8)	*a-ti-ke-ne-ja*	M	N	C
A.TI.KI.TA.A	C1	TYZ4	*a-ti-ka*	K	N	C
A.TI.KI.TA.A	C1	TYZ4	*a-ti-ke-ne-ja*	M	N	C
A.WA.TI.NA.RA₂	? C1	II13	*a-wa-ta*	P	N	C
A.WA.TI.NA.RA₂	? C1	II13	*a-wa-ti-ka-ra*	+		C
DA.MI.NU	C1	117a8	*da-mi-ni-ja*	P	EP	C

Appendix B

Parallels up to Third Consonant (cont.)

Linear A	Code	Reference	Linear B	Code		
DA.MI.NU	C1	117a8	da-mi-ni-jo	PK	EP	C
DA.TA.RO	? C1	116a1	da-ta-ra-mo	K	P	CX
DA.TA.RA	C1	6a1	da-ta-ra-mo	K	P	CX
DA.TA.RE	C2	88.5,62.2*	da-ta-ra-mo	K	P	CX
DI.DE.RU	C3	86a3,95a4,95b4	di-de-ro	K		B
DI.KA.TU	B1	52a2	di-ka-ta-de	K	P	C
DI.KA.TU	B1	52a2	di-ka-ta-jo	K	E	C
DI.KA.TU	B1	52a2	di-ka-ta-ro	K	N	C
DU.RU.WI	C1	25a4	du-ru-wo	K	P	A
I.JA.TE	C1	PHZ4(II12)	i-ja-te	P	Q	C
I.KU.TA	* C1	35.1	i-ku-to	M	N	C
I.KU.TA	* C1	35.1	i-ku-tu-re	+		C
I.MI.SA.RA	A1	27a3	i-mi-so-pi	K		B
I.MI.SA.RA	A1	27a3	i-mi-so	+		A
I.SU.KI	? C1	II7a	i-su-ku-wo-do-to	K	N	C
I.TA.NU	C1	28b6	i-ta-no	K		D
KA.NU.TI	C1	97a3	ka-nu-ta-jo	P	N	C
KA.SA.RU	C1	10b3	ka-sa-ro	K		C
KA.U.DO.NI	C1	26b2	ka-u-da	K	PN	C
KA.U.DE.TA	C1	13.1	ka-u-da	K	PN	C
KI.DA.RO	C1	117a9,27a4?	ki-da-ro	K	N	C
KI.RI.TA$_2$	C2	114a1,121.1	ki-ri-ta	K		C
KI.RI.TA$_2$	C2	114a1,121.1	ki-ri-ta-i	K		C
KI.RI.TA$_2$	C2	114a1,121.1	ki-ri-te-wi-ja	PK	Q	C
KI.RI.TA$_2$	C2	114a1,121.1	ki-ri-te-wi-ja-i	K	Q	C
KI.RI.TA$_2$	C2	114a1,121.1	ki-ri-te-wi-ja-pi	P	Q	C
KI.RI.TA$_2$	C2	114a1,121.1	ki-ri-ti-jo-jo	P		C
KI.RI.TA$_2$	C2	114a1,121.1	ki-ri-ta-de	+		C
KU.DO.NA	* D1	64.1	ku-do-ni	K		B
KU.DO.NA	* D1	64.1	ku-do-ni-ja	K	P	C
KU.DO.NA	* D1	64.1	ku-do-ni-ja-de	K	P	C
KU.DO.NA	* D1	64.1	ku-do-ni-jo	K	E	D
KU.DO.NI	C2	13.4,85a4	ku-do-ni	K		B
KU.DO.NI	C2	13.4,85a4	ku-do-ni-ja	K	P	C
KU.DO.NI	C2	13.4,85a4	ku-do-ni-ja-de	K	P	C
KU.DO.NI	C2	13.4,85a4	ku-do-ni-jo	K	E	D
KU.MI.NA.QE	C1D1	HTW214a(CRIV5),	ku-mi-no	M		C
KU.MI.NA.QE	C1D1	HTW214a(CRIV5),	ku-mi-na	M		C
KU.PA$_3$.NA.TU.NA	? D1	I13b1	ku-pa-nu-we-to	K	N	C
KU.PA$_3$.NU	C9	1a3,3.6,88.3,	ku-pa-nu-we-to	K	N	C
KU.PA$_3$.NA.TU	C2	47a1,119.3	ku-pa-nu-we-to	K	N	C

Parallels up to Third Consonant (cont.)

Linear A	Code	Reference	Linear B	Code		
KU.RU.KU	C1	87.4	ku-ru-ka	K	N	C
KU.RU.MA.I	? C1	115b3	ku-ru-me-ko-jo	K		C
KU.RU.MA.I	? C1	115b3	ku-ru-me-ni-jo	K		C
KU.RU.MA.I	? C1	115b3	ku-ru-me-no	PK	N	C
KU.RU.MA.I	? C1	115b3	ku-ru-me-no-jo	P	N	C
KU.RU.MA	* C1	115b3	ku-ru-me-ko-jo	K		C
KU.RU.MA	* C1	115b3	ku-ru-me-ni-jo	K		C
KU.RU.MA	* C1	115b3	ku-ru-me-no	PK	N	C
KU.RU.MA	* C1	115b3	ku-ru-me-no-jo	P	N	C
MA.RI.TA$_2$	? C1	90.3	ma-ri-ta	P	N	C
MA.RI.TA$_2$	? C1	90.3	ma-ri-ti-wi-jo	MPK	N	C
MA.SI.DU	C1	43.1	ma-si-dwo	K		C
PA.I.TO	C2	97a3,120.6,	pa-i-ti	K		B
PA.I.TO	C2	97a3,120.6,	pa-i-ti-ja	K	N	C
PA.I.TO	C2	97a3,120.6,	pa-i-ti-jo	K	E	C
PA.I.TO	C2	97a3,120.6,	pa-i-ti-ja	K	E	C
PA.I.TO	C2	97a3,120.6,	pa-i-to	K	P	C
PA.I.TO	C2	97a3,120.6,	pa-i-to	K	P	B
PA.I.TO	C2	97a3,120.6,	pa-i-tu	K		DX
PA.I.TO	C2	97a3,120.6,	pa$_3$-i-ti	K		C
PA.I.TO	C2	97a3,120.6,	pa$_3$-i-ti	K		BX
PA.JA.RE	C2B2	8b4,88.4,	pa-ja-ro	K	N	C
PA.JA.SA	D1	PH11b1(IV17iv)	pa-ja-so	K	N	C
PA.RA.TU	? C1	128a1	pa-ra-ti-jo	K	N	C
PA.RA.TU	? C1	128a1	pa-ra-to	K	N	C
PA.SA.RI.JA	? C1	24a4	pa-sa-ro	P		C
PI.JA.SU.MA.TI.TI	# A1	HTZ157	pi-ja-se-me	K	N	C
PI.JA.SU.MA.TI.TI	# A1	HTZ157	pi-ja-si-ro	K	N	C
PI.JA.TA.MA.TI.TI	= A1	HTZ157	pi-ja-to	K	N	A
PI.TA.KE.SI	C1	87.2	pi-ta-ke-u	P	N	C
PI.TA.KA.SE	C1	21.1	pi-ta-ke-u	P	N	C
QA.QA.RU	C3A1	93a4,118.2,	qa-qa-ro	K	N	C
QA.RA$_2$.WA	C1	86a3	qa-ra-we-ta	M	N	C
QA.RA$_2$.WA	C1	86a3	qa-ra$_2$-wo	K	N	C
RA.RI.DE	B1	113.1	ra-ri-di-jo	K	E	C
SA.MA.RO	C1A1	88.4,39.3*	sa-ma-ra	P	P	C
SA.MA.RO	C1A1	88.4,39.3*	sa-ma-ra-de	P	P	C
SA.MA.RO	C1A1	88.4,39.3*	sa-ma-ri-jo	K	N	C
SA.MA.RO	C1A1	88.4,39.3*	sa-ma-ri-wa	P	P	C
SA.MA.RO	C1A1	88.4,39.3*	sa-ma-ri-wa-ta	K	N	C
SA.MA.RO	C1A1	88.4,39.3*	sa-ma-ru	K	N	B

Parallels up to Third Consonant (cont.)

Linear A	Code	Reference	Linear B	Code		
SI.KI.RA	C1	8a4	si-ki-ro	+		C
SI.KI.TE	? C1	116a5	si-ki-to	K	N	C
SI.MI.TA	C1	96a2	si-mi-te-u	+		C
SU.KI.RI.TE.SE.JA	? C1	II7b	su-ki-ri	K		B
SU.KI.RI.TE.SE.JA	? C1	II7b	su-ki-ri-ta	K	P	C
SU.KI.RI.TE.SE.JA	? C1	II7b	su-ki-ri-ta	K		BX
SU.KI.RI.TE.SE.JA	? C1	II7b	su-ki-ri-ta-jo	K	E	C
SU.KI.RI.TE.SE.JA	? C1	II7b	su-ki-ri-to	K	N	C
SU.KI.RI.TE.SE.JA	? C1	II7b	su-ki-ri-ta-pi	+		C
TA.NA.TI	C3A1	7a4,10b4,	ta-na-ti	K		A
TA.NA.TI	C3A1	7a4,10b4,	ta-na-to	K	N	C
TA.PA$_3$.DU	* C1	PRZ1a(I17)	ta-pa-da-no	K		C
TE.JA.RE	* C1	117a5	te-ja-ro	K	N	CX
TE.JA.RE	* C1	117a5	te-ja-ro	K		A
TU.PA.DI.DA	C1	123b3	tu-pa$_3$-da-ro	K		C
WA.DU.NI.MI	C2	6b1,85b4	wa-du-na	K	N	C
WA.DU.NI.MI	C2	6b1,85b4	wa-du-na-ro	K	N	C
WA.DU.NI.MI	C2	6b1,85b4	wa-du-na-ro	K	N	BX
WA.DU.NI.MI	C2	6b1,85b4	wa-du-na-to	K	N	C
WI.JA.TA.MA.TI.TI	= A1	HTZ157	wi-ja-te-we	P	N	C
WI.JA.TA.MA.TI.TI	= A1	HTZ157	wi-ja-te-wo	P	N	C

A-B Parallels ignoring vowels

Linear A	Code	Reference	Linear B	Code		
A.KA.RU	C2	2.1,86a1,	*a-ka-re-u*	PK	N	C
A.KA.RU	C2	2.1,86a1,	*a-ke-ra-no*	K	N	C
A.KA.RU	C2	2.1,86a1,	*a-ke-ra-wo*	PK	N	C
A.KA.RU	C2	2.1,86a1,	*a-ke-re-mo*	K	Q	C
A.KA.RU	C2	2.1,86a1,	*a-ke-re-mo-no*	K	Q	C
A.KA.RU	C2	2.1,86a1,	*a-ki-re-u*	K	N	C
A.KA.RU	C2	2.1,86a1,	*a-ko-ra*	PK		C
A.KA.RU	C2	2.1,86a1,	*a-ko-ra-jo*	K		C
A.KA.RU	C2	2.1,86a1,	*a-ko-ra-ja*	K		C
A.KA.RU	C2	2.1,86a1,	*a-ko-ra-jo*	K	N	C
A.KA.RU	C2	2.1,86a1,	*a-ko-ro*	PK		C
A.KA.RU	C2	2.1,86a1,	*a-ko-ro-qo-ro*	K	N	C
A.KA.RU	C2	2.1,86a1,	*a-ko-ro-ta*	MPKQN		C
A.KA.RU	C2	2.1,86a1,	*a-ku-ri-jo*	K	N	C
A.KA.RU	C2	2.1,86a1,	*a$_3$-ka-ra*	K	N	C
A.KA.RU	C2	2.1,86a1,	*a-ki-ri-ja*	+		C
A.KA.RU	C2	2.1,86a1,	*a-ko-ro-da-mo-jo*	+		C
A.KU.TU	C1	TY3b7(IV9)	*a-ka-ta-jo*	PK	N	C
A.KU.TU	C1	TY3b7(IV9)	*a-ka-ta-ra-te-so-ke*	K		CX
A.KU.TU	C1	TY3b7(IV9)	*a-ka-to*	K	N	C
A.KU.TU	C1	TY3b7(IV9)	*a-ka-to-wa*	K	N	C
A.KU.TU	C1	TY3b7(IV9)	*a-ke-ta*	PK	N	C
A.KU.TU	C1	TY3b7(IV9)	*a-ke-ti-ri-ja*	PK	Q	C
A.KU.TU	C1	TY3b7(IV9)	*a-ke-to-ro*	K	Q	C
A.KU.TU	C1	TY3b7(IV9)	*a-ko-to*	K	N	C
A.KU.TU	C1	TY3b7(IV9)	*a-ku-tu-ru-wo*	K	N	C
A.KU.TU	C1	TY3b7(IV9)	*a$_2$-ke-te-re*	K		C
A.KU.TU	C1	TY3b7(IV9)	*a$_3$-ki-ta*	K	N	C
A.KU.TU	C1	TY3b7(IV9)	*a$_3$-ko-ta*	PK	N	C
A.PU$_2$.NA	C1	14.3	*a-pa$_3$-no*	K	N	C
A.PA.RA.NE	C2	96a1,96b1	*a-pa-re-u*	K	N	CX
A.PA.RA.NE	C2	96a1,96b1	*a-pe-re*	K		C
A.PA.RA.NE	C2	96a1,96b1	*a-pi-ra-wo*	K	N	C
A.PA.RA.NE	C2	96a1,96b1	*a-pi-re-jo*	K	N	C
A.RE.DA.I	* C1	29.5	*a-ra-da-jo*	K	N	C
A.RE.DA.I	* C1	29.5	*a-ro-do-ro-o*	K	GPN	C
A.RU.DA.RA	C1	28b5,62.1?	*a-ra-da-jo*	K	N	C
A.RU.DA.RA	C1	28b5,62.1?	*a-ro-do-ro-o*	K	GPN	C
A.RA.NA.RE	C1	1a4,47b1?	*a-ra-na-ro*	K	N	C
A.RI.NI.TA	C1	25a3	*a-ra-na-ro*	K	N	C
A.RE.SA.NA	+C1	TEZ2	*a-ra-si-jo*	K	N	C

A-B Parallels ignoring vowels (cont.)

Linear A	Code	Reference	Linear B	Code		
A.RA.WI	=C1	87.5	a-ro-we	K		C
A.RA.WI	=C1	87.5	a-ro-wo-ta	K	N	C
A.SA.ME.NE	*C1	ZAZ3.1	a-sa-mi-to	+		C
A.SA.RA₂	*C1	89.1	a-sa-ro	K	N	C
A.TA.I	*C1	PRZ1b(I17)	a-te-i-ja-ta	K	N	C
A.TA.I.88.WA.JA	*C3	PKZ12a(I5),	a-te-i-ja-ta	K	N	C
A.TA.I.88.DE.KA	+C1	ZAZ3.2	a-te-i-ja-ta	K	N	C
A.TI.KA.A.MI.KO	#C1	ZAW2.1(III8)	a-ti-ka	K	N	C
A.TI.KA.A.MI.KO	#C1	ZAW2.1(III8)	a-tu-ko	PK	N	C
A.TI.KI.TA.A	C1	TYZ4	a-ti-ka	K	N	C
A.TI.KI.TA.A	C1	TYZ4	a-tu-ko	PK	N	C
A.TU.WE.SI.TI	*C1	KNZ5(II4)	a-ta-wo	PK	N	C
A.WE.SU	C1	118.3	a-wa-so	K	N	C
DI.DI.KA.SE	+C1	ZAZ3.1	de-de-ko-wo	K		CX
DI.DI.KA.SE	+C1	ZAZ3.1	di-da-ka-re	K		C
DA.DU.MA.TA	C1	95a1	de-de-me-na	K		C
DA.DU.MA.TA	C1	95a1	de-do-me-na	K		C
DA.DU.MA.TA	C1	95a1	di-du-me	K		C
DU.DA.MA	C1	6b4	de-de-me-na	K		C
DU.DA.MA	C1	6b4	de-do-me-na	K		C
DU.DA.MA	C1	6b4	di-du-me	K		C
DI.DE.RU	C3	86a3,95a4,95b4	da-da-re-jo-de	K	P	C
DO.DI.RA	C2	HTW212a(CRIV11),	da-da-re-jo-de	K	P	C
DA.KU.NA	C1	103.4	di-ki-nu-wo	K	N	C
DA.KU.SE.NE	C1B1	103.4,103.2	da-ko-so	K	N	C
DA.KU.SE.NE	C1B1	103.4,103.2	de-ka-sa-to	K		C
DA.KU.SE.NE	C1B1	103.4,103.2	de-ke-se-u	K	N	C
DA.KU.SE.NE	C1B1	103.4,103.2	de-ki-si-wo	PK	N	C
DA.KU.SE.NE.TI	C1	104.1	da-ko-so	K	N	C
DA.KU.SE.NE.TI	C1	104.1	de-ka-sa-to	K		C
DA.KU.SE.NE.TI	C1	104.1	de-ke-se-u	K	N	C
DA.KU.SE.NE.TI	C1	104.1	de-ki-si-wo	PK	N	C
DI.KI.SE	C2	87.3,117b2	da-ko-so	K	N	C
DI.KI.SE	C2	87.3,117b2	de-ka-sa-to	K		C
DI.KI.SE	C2	87.3,117b2	de-ke-se-u	K	N	C
DI.KI.SE	C2	87.3,117b2	de-ki-si-wo	PK	N	C
DA.MI.NU	C1	117a8	da-mi-ni-jo	PK	EP	C
DA.QE.RA	C2B1	6a6,120.1,57a1	di-qa-ra	K	N	C
DU.RU.WI	C1	25a4	do-re-we	K	N	C
DU.RU.WI	C1	25a4	do-ri-wo	K		C
DU.SU.NI	C1	108.2	du-sa-ni	K	N	C

A-B Parallels ignoring vowels (cont.)

Linear A	Code	Reference	Linear B	Code		
DA.TA.RA	C1	6a1	*da-ta-ra-mo*	K	P	CX
DA.TA.RA	C1	6a1	*da-to-ro*	K	N	C
DA.TA.RE	C2	88.5,62.2*	*da-ta-ra-mo*	K	P	CX
DA.TA.RE	C2	88.5,62.2*	*da-to-ro*	K	N	C
DI.WE.NA	C2	93a1,102.3	*da-wa-no*	K	N	C
I.DO.RI.NI.TA	C1	PH6.2(IV16)	*i-da-ra-ta*	K		C
I.KU.TA	* C1	35.1	*i-ke-ta*	K	N	C
I.KU.TA	* C1	35.1	*i-ku-tu-re*	+		C
I.PI.NA.MI.NA	= C1	PKZ10(I6)	*i-po-no*	K		C
I.TA.NU	C1	28b6	*i-ti-nu-ri*	+		C
KU.DO.NI	C2	13.4,85a4	*ka-da-no*	K	N	C
KU.DO.NI	C2	13.4,85a4	*ku-do-ni-ja*	K	P	C
KU.DO.NI	C2	13.4,85a4	*ku-do-ni-ja-de*	K	P	C
KI.DI.NI	* C1	93a2	*ka-da-no*	K	N	C
KI.DI.NI	* C1	93a2	*ku-do-ni-ja*	K	P	C
KI.DI.NI	* C1	93a2	*ku-do-ni-ja-de*	K	P	C
KI.DA.RO	C1	117a9,27a4?	*ki-da-ro*	K	N	C
KI.DA.RO	C1	117a9,27a4?	*ki-do-ro*	K		C
KU.KU.DA.RA	C1	117a7	*ka-ko-de-ta*	K		C
KU.KU.DA.RA	C1	117a7	*ko-ki-da*	K	N	C
KU.KU.DA.RA	C1	117a7	*ko-ki-de-jo*	K		C
KU.KU.DA.RA	C1	117a7	*ku-ka-da-ro*	K	N	C
KI.KI.NA	C1	88.2	*ku-ka-no*	K	N	C
KE.KI.RU	C1	94b2	*ka-ka-re-a$_2$*	K		C
KE.KI.RU	C1	94b2	*ki-ke-ro*	K	N	C
KE.KI.RU	C1	94b2	*ko-ku-ro*	K	N	C
KE.KI.RU	C1	94b2	*ku-ka-ro*	K	N	C
KI.KI.RA.JA	C1	85b1	*ka-ka-re-a$_2$*	K		C
KI.KI.RA.JA	C1	85b1	*ki-ke-ro*	K	N	C
KI.KI.RA.JA	C1	85b1	*ko-ku-ro*	K	N	C
KI.KI.RA.JA	C1	85b1	*ku-ka-ro*	K	N	C
KU.MI.NA.QE	C1D1	HTW214a(CRIV5),	*ka-mi-ni-to*	K	N	C
KU.MI.NA.QE	C1D1	HTW214a(CRIV5),	*ka-mo-ni-jo*	K	N	C
KU.MI.NA.QE	C1D1	HTW214a(CRIV5),	*ku-mo-no-so*	+		C
KU.NI.SU	C4	10a1,86a1,95a3,	*ka-nu-se-u*	K	N	C
KU.NI.SU	C4	10a1,86a1,95a3,	*ko-no-si-jo*	K	E	C
KU.NI.SU	C4	10a1,86a1,95a3,	*ko-no-si-ja*	K	E	C
KU.NI.SU	C4	10a1,86a1,95a3,	*ko-no-so*	K	P	C
KA.NU.TI	C1	97a3	*ka-na-to-po*	K	N	C
KA.NU.TI	C1	97a3	*ka-ni-to*	K		C
KA.NU.TI	C1	97a3	*ku-ni-ta*	K	Q	C

A-B Parallels ignoring vowels (cont.)

Linear A	Code	Reference	Linear B	Code		
KU.PA.JA	C1	116a1	*ke-pu$_2$-je-u*	+		C
KU.PA$_3$.NU	C9	1a3,3.6,88.3,	*ka-pa$_3$-na-to*	K	N	C
KU.PA$_3$.NU	C9	1a3,3.6,88.3,	*ka-pa$_3$-no*	K	N	C
KU.PA$_3$.NU	C9	1a3,3.6,88.3,	*ku-pa-nu-we-to*	K	N	C
KU.PA$_3$.NA.TU	C2	47a1,119.3	*ka-pa$_3$-na-to*	K	N	C
KU.PA$_3$.NA.TU	C2	47a1,119.3	*ka-pa$_3$-no*	K	N	C
KU.PA$_3$.NA.TU	C2	47a1,119.3	*ku-pa-nu-we-to*	K	N	C
KU.RA.I	* C1	117a2	*ke-ra-i-ja-pi*	K		C
KU.RA.I	* C1	117a2	*ki-ra$_2$-i-jo*	K	N	C
KU.RU.KU	C1	87.4	*ku-ru-ka*	K	N	C
KU.RU.MA	* C1	115b3	*ka-ra-ma-to*	K		C
KU.RU.MA	* C1	115b3	*ke-ra-me-ja*	K	QN	C
KU.RU.MA	* C1	115b3	*ke-ri-mi-ja*	PK		C
KU.RU.MA	* C1	115b3	*ku-ru-me-ko-jo*	K		C
KU.RU.MA	* C1	115b3	*ku-ru-me-ni-jo*	K		C
KU.RU.MA	* C1	115b3	*ku-ru-me-no*	PK	N	C
KA.RO.NA	C1	11a2	*ka-ra-na-ta*	K	N	C
KA.RO.NA	C1	11a2	*ka-ru-no*	K		C
KA.RO.NA	C1	11a2	*ke-ra-no*	K		C
KA.RO.NA	C1	11a2	*ke-re-na*	K		C
KA.RO.NA	C1	11a2	*ki-ri-ne-to*	K	N	C
KA.RO.NA	C1	11a2	*ku-ra-no*	K	N	C
KA.RO.NA	C1	11a2	*ku-ru-ni-ta*	K	N	C
KA.RO.NA	C1	11a2	*ka-ra-na-ko*	+		C
KA.RO.NA	C1	11a2	*ku-ru-no*	+		C
KA.RO.PA$_3$	C1	31.3	*ki-ra-pa$_3$-so*	K		C
KA.RO.PA$_3$	C1	31.3	*ka-ri-pi-jo*	+		C
KA.RE.RO	C1	HTW203(CRIV18)	*ka-ra-re-we*	PK		C
KI.RE.TA.NA	C3A1	8a5,108.1,	*ke-ro-ta*	K		C
KI.RE.TA.NA	C3A1	8a5,108.1,	*ke-ro-te*	PK	Q	C
KI.RE.TA.NA	C3A1	8a5,108.1,	*ki-ri-ta*	K		C
KI.RE.TA.NA	C3A1	8a5,108.1,	*ki-ri-ta-i*	K		C
KI.RE.TA.NA	C3A1	8a5,108.1,	*ki-ri-te-wi-ja*	PK	Q	C
KI.RE.TA.NA	C3A1	8a5,108.1,	*ki-ri-te-wi-ja-i*	K	Q	C
KI.RE.TA.NA	C3A1	8a5,108.1,	*ko-re-te*	PK	Q	C
KI.RE.TA.NA	C3A1	8a5,108.1,	*ko-ro-ta$_2$*	K		C
KI.RE.TA.NA	C3A1	8a5,108.1,	*ko-ru-to*	K	N	C
KI.RE.TA.NA	C3A1	8a5,108.1,	*ki-ri-ta-de*	+		C
KI.RE.TA$_2$	C2	129.1,85b1	*ke-ro-ta*	K		C
KI.RE.TA$_2$	C2	129.1,85b1	*ke-ro-te*	PK	Q	C
KI.RE.TA$_2$	C2	129.1,85b1	*ki-ri-ta*	K		C

A-B Parallels ignoring vowels (cont.)

Linear A	Code	Reference	Linear B	Code		
KI.RE.TA$_2$	C2	129.1,85b1	*ki-ri-ta-i*	K		C
KI.RE.TA$_2$	C2	129.1,85b1	*ki-ri-te-wi-ja*	PK	Q	C
KI.RE.TA$_2$	C2	129.1,85b1	*ki-ri-te-wi-ja-i*	K	Q	C
KI.RE.TA$_2$	C2	129.1,85b1	*ko-re-te*	PK	Q	C
KI.RE.TA$_2$	C2	129.1,85b1	*ko-ro-ta$_2$*	K		C
KI.RE.TA$_2$	C2	129.1,85b1	*ko-ru-to*	K	N	C
KI.RE.TA$_2$	C2	129.1,85b1	*ki-ri-ta-de*	+		C
KI.RI.TA$_2$	C2	114a1,121.1	*ke-ro-ta*	K		C
KI.RI.TA$_2$	C2	114a1,121.1	*ke-ro-te*	PK	Q	C
KI.RI.TA$_2$	C2	114a1,121.1	*ki-ri-ta*	K		C
KI.RI.TA$_2$	C2	114a1,121.1	*ki-ri-ta-i*	K		C
KI.RI.TA$_2$	C2	114a1,121.1	*ki-ri-te-wi-ja*	PK	Q	C
KI.RI.TA$_2$	C2	114a1,121.1	*ki-ri-te-wi-ja-i*	K	Q	C
KI.RI.TA$_2$	C2	114a1,121.1	*ko-re-te*	PK	Q	C
KI.RI.TA$_2$	C2	114a1,121.1	*ko-ro-ta$_2$*	K		C
KI.RI.TA$_2$	C2	114a1,121.1	*ko-ru-to*	K	N	C
KI.RI.TA$_2$	C2	114a1,121.1	*ki-ri-ta-de*	+		C
KO.SA.KE.TI	C1	117a7	*ka-si-ko-no*	PK	Q	C
KA.SA.RU	C1	10b3	*ka-sa-ro*	K		C
KI.TA.I	C1	123a1	*ko-to-i-na*	K		C
KI.TA.I	C1	123a1	*ku-ta-i-jo*	K	N	C
KI.TA.I	C1	123a1	*ku-ta-i-to*	K	P	C
KA.U.DO.NI	C1	26b2	*ka-u-da*	K	PN	C
KA.U.DE.TA	C1	13.1	*ka-u-da*	K	PN	C
MA.KA.RI.TE	C2	87.1,117a1	*ma-ke-ra*	K	N	C
MA.KA.RI.TE	C2	87.1,117a1	*mu-ka-ra*	K	N	C
MA.KA.RI.TE	C2	87.1,117a1	*ma-ki-ro-ne*	+		C
MI.RU.TA.RA.RE	* C1	117a4	*ma-ri-ti-wi-jo*	MPK	N	C
MA.SI.DU	C1	43.1	*ma-sa-de*	K	P	C
MA.SI.DU	C1	43.1	*ma-si-dwo*	K		C
NA.DA.RE	C1	117a5	*no-da-ro*	K	N	C
PA.I.TO	C2	97a3,120.6,	*pa-i-ti-ja*	K	N	C
PA.I.TO	C2	97a3,120.6,	*pa-i-ti-jo*	K	E	C
PA.I.TO	C2	97a3,120.6,	*pa-i-ti-ja*	K	E	C
PA.I.TO	C2	97a3,120.6,	*pa-i-to*	K	P	C
PA.I.TO	C2	97a3,120.6,	*po-i-te-u*	K	N	C
PA.I.TO	C2	97a3,120.6,	*po-i-ti-jo*	K	N	C
PA.I.TO	C2	97a3,120.6,	*pa$_3$-i-ti*	K		C
PA.JA.RE	C2B2	8b4,88.4,29.2,	*pa-ja-ro*	K	N	C
PA$_3$.KA.RA.TI	C1	8a1	*po-ki-ro-nu-ka*	K		C
PA$_3$.KA.RA.TI	C1	8a1	*pu-ko-ro*	PK	N	C

A-B Parallels ignoring vowels (cont.)

Linear A	Code	Reference	Linear B	Code		
PA.RA.NE	C2	115a4,115b1,	*pi-ri-na-jo*	K	Q	C
PA.RA.NE	C2	115a4,115b1,	*pi-ri-no*	K	N	C
PA.RA.NE	C2	115a4,115b1,	*pu$_2$-ra-ne-jo*	K	N	C
PA.RO.SU	* C1	20.1	*pe-ru-si-nwa*	MK		C
PA.RO.SU	* C1	20.1	*pi-ra-si-ja*	K		C
PA.RO.SU	* C1	20.1	*pi-ri-sa-ta*	K	N	C
PA.RO.SU	* C1	20.1	*pu-ra-so*	K	N	C
PA.SE.JA	C3	93a8,	*pa-sa-ja*	K		C
PA.SE.JA	C3	93a8,	*pu-si-jo*	K	E	C
PA.SA.WE.JA	C1	24a4	*pi-sa-wa-ta*	K	QN	C
PI.TA.JA	C1	6a2	*pa-ta-ja*	K		C
PI.TA.JA	C1	6a2	*po-ti-jo*	K	N	C
PI.TA.KE.SI	C1	87.2	*pe-te-ki-ja*	K	N	C
PI.TA.KA.SE	C1	21.1	*pe-te-ki-ja*	K	N	C
PA.TA.NE	C2	94b1,122a6	*po-ti-ni-ja*	MPKG		C
PA.TA.NE	C2	94b1,122a6	*po-ti-ni-ja-we*	K		C
PA.TA.NE	C2	94b1,122a6	*po-ti-ni-ja-we-i-jo*	K		C
PA.TA.NE	C2	94b1,122a6	*po-ti-ni-ja-we-jo*	PK		C
PA.TA.NE	C2	94b1,122a6	*po-ti-ni-ja-we-ja*	K		C
PI.TA.RA	* C1	96a4	*pa-to-ro*	K	N	C
PI.TA.RA	* C1	96a4	*pe-te-re-wa*	K		C
PI.TA.RA	* C1	96a4	*po-ti-ro*	K		C
PI.TA.RA	* C1	96a4	*po-ti-ro*	K		CX
PI.TA.RA	* C1	96a4	*po-to-ri-jo*	K	N	C
PI.TA.RA	* C1	96a4	*po-to-ri-ka-ta*	K	N	C
PI.TA.RA	* C1	96a4	*pu-ta-ri-ja*	K		C
PI.TA.RA	* C1	96a4	*pu-te-ri-ja*	K		C
PI.TA.RA	* C1	96a4	*pu-to-ro*	K	N	C
PI.TA.RA	* C1	96a4	*pu$_2$-te-re*	PK	Q	C
PI.TE.RI	* C1	PKZ11b(I4)	*pa-to-ro*	K	N	C
PI.TE.RI	* C1	PKZ11b(I4)	*pe-te-re-wa*	K		C
PI.TE.RI	* C1	PKZ11b(I4)	*po-ti-ro*	K		C
PI.TE.RI	* C1	PKZ11b(I4)	*po-ti-ro*	K		CX
PI.TE.RI	* C1	PKZ11b(I4)	*po-to-ri-jo*	K	N	C
PI.TE.RI	* C1	PKZ11b(I4)	*po-to-ri-ka-ta*	K	N	C
PI.TE.RI	* C1	PKZ11b(I4)	*pu-ta-ri-ja*	K		C
PI.TE.RI	* C1	PKZ11b(I4)	*pu-te-ri-ja*	K		C
PI.TE.RI	* C1	PKZ11b(I4)	*pu-to-ro*	K	N	C
PI.TE.RI	* C1	PKZ11b(I4)	*pu$_2$-te-re*	PK	Q	C
QE.PI.TA	C1	6a6	*qe-pa-ta-no*	K	N	C
QA.QA.RU	C3A1	93a4,118.2,	*qa-qa-ro*	K	N	C

A-B Parallels ignoring vowels (cont.)

Linear A	Code	Reference	Linear B	Code		
QA.QA.RU	C3A1	93a4,118.2,	*qi-qe-ro*	K	N	C
QA.RE.TO	C1	132.1,111a1?	*qa-ra$_2$-ti-jo*	K	N	C
QA.RE.TO	C1	132.1,111a1?	*qi-ri-ta-ro*	K	N	C
QA.RA$_2$.WA	C1	86a3	*qa-ra$_2$-wo*	K	N	C
QA.RA$_2$.WA	C1	86a3	*qe-re-wa*	K	N	C
QE.TU.NE	C1	12.3	*qi-to-no-ro*	K	N	C
QE.TU.NE	C1	12.3	*qa-to-no-ro*	+		C
QE.TI.RA.DU	C1	58.1	*qi-ta-ro*	K	N	C
QE.TI.RA.DU	C1	58.1	*qo-te-ro*	PK	N	C
QE.TU.SI	* C1	PHW14a(III13)	*qe-te-se-u*	K	N	C
RU.MA.TA	C1B1	99b2,29.1	*re-me-to*	K	N	C
RI.TA.MA	C1	115a1	*ra-te-me*	K	N	C
SA.JA.MA	C1	31.3	*si-ja-ma*	K	N	C
SA.JA.MA	C1	31.3	*si-ja-ma-to*	K	GN	C
SI.KI.RA	C1	8a4	*sa-ka-ri-jo*	K	N	C
SI.KI.RA	C1	8a4	*su-ke-re*	K	N	C
SI.KI.RA	C1	8a4	*su-ke-re-o*	K	N	C
SI.KI.RA	C1	8a4	*su-ki-ri-ta*	K	P	C
SI.KI.RA	C1	8a4	*su-ki-ri-ta-jo*	K	E	C
SI.KI.RA	C1	8a4	*su-ki-ri-to*	K	N	C
SI.KI.RA	C1	8a4	*si-ki-ro*	+		C
SI.KI.RA	C1	8a4	*su-ki-ri-ta-pi*	+		C
SE.KU.TU	C1	115a3	*si-ki-to*	K	N	C
SA.MA.RO	C1A1	88.4,39.3*	*sa-ma-ri-jo*	K	N	C
SA.MA.RO	C1A1	88.4,39.3*	*sa-ma-ri-wa-ta*	K	N	C
SI.MI.TA	C1	96a2	*sa-ma-ti-ja*	K	N	C
SI.MI.TA	C1	96a2	*sa-me-ti-jo*	K	N	C
SI.MI.TA	C1	96a2	*sa-mu-ta-jo*	MPK	N	C
SI.MI.TA	C1	96a2	*se-me-tu-ro*	K	N	C
SI.MI.TA	C1	96a2	*si-mi-te-u*	+		C
SU.NI.KA	C2	HTW204a(CRIV2),	*si-nu-ke*	K	N	C
SI.RU.MA.RI.TA$_2$	* C1	90.2	*su-ri-mi-jo*	K	E	C
SI.RU.MA.RI.TA$_2$	* C1	90.2	*su-ri-mo*	K	P	C
SA.RA.RA	C1	30.3	*si-ra-ro*	K	P	C
TE.JA.RE	* C1	117a5	*te-ja-ro*	K	N	CX
TI.MA.RU.WI.TE	C1	PU1.1	*te-mi-ro*	K	N	C
TI.NU.JA	C1	115b2	*to-ni-ja*	K		C
TI.NU.JA	C1	115b2	*tu-ni-ja*	K	P	C
TA.NA.TI	C3A1	7a4,10b4,	*ta-na-to*	K	N	C
TA.NA.TI	C3A1	7a4,10b4,	*to-na-ta*	K	N	C

A-B Parallels ignoring vowels (cont.)

Linear A	Code	Reference	Linear B	Code		
TI.NI.TA	C1	27a1	ta-na-to	K	N	C
TI.NI.TA	C1	27a1	to-na-ta	K	N	C
TU.PA.DI.DA	C1	123b3	ta-pa-da-no	K		C
TU.PA.DI.DA	C1	123b3	tu-pa$_3$-da-ro	K		C
TA.PA$_3$.DU	* C1	PRZ1a(I17)	ta-pa-da-no	K		C
TA.PA$_3$.DU	* C1	PRZ1a(I17)	tu-pa$_3$-da-ro	K		C
TU.QE.NU	C1	25a3	tu-qa-ni-ja-so	K	N	C
TU.RU.NU.SE.ME	* C1	128a1	ta-ra-nu	PK		C
TU.RU.NU.SE.ME	* C1	128a1	te-re-no	K		C
TU.RU.NU.SE.ME	* C1	128a1	to-ro-no-wo-ko	K	Q	C
TU.RU.SA.RA$_2$.-.RE	* C1	KOZ1b	ta-ra-si-ja	MPK		C
TU.RU.SA.RA$_2$.-.RE	* C1	KOZ1b	tu-ri-si-jo	K	E	C
TU.RU.SA.RA$_2$.-.RE	* C1	KOZ1b	tu-ri-si-ja	K	E	C
TU.RU.SA.RA$_2$.-.RE	* C1	KOZ1b	tu-ri-so	K	P	C
TU.RU.SA.RA$_2$.-.RE	* C1	KOZ1b	ta-ra-sa-ta	+		C
TU.RU.SA.RA$_2$.-.RE	* C1	KOZ1b	te-ru-sa	+		C
TI.TI.KU	C2	35a1,ZAZ3.2#+	te-tu-ko-wo-a	K		C
TI.TA.NA	C1	HTW220(CRV5)	to-tu-no	K	N	C
TA$_2$.TI.TE	C1	PK1.3(IV5)	ta-ta-ta	K	PN	C
TA.WE.NA	C1	10b1	to-wa-no	K	N	C
TA.WE.NA	C1	10b1	to-wi-no	K	N	C
TA.WE.NA	C1	10b1	tu-wi-no	K		C
TA.WE.NA	C1	10b1	tu-wi-no-no	K		C
WI.DI.NA	C1	28a5	wa-du-na	K	N	C
WI.DI.NA	C1	28a5	wa-du-na-ro	K	N	C
WI.DI.NA	C1	28a5	wa-du-na-to	K	N	C
WA.DI.NI	C2	HTW208a(CRIV1),	wa-du-na	K	N	C
WA.DI.NI	C2	HTW208a(CRIV1),	wa-du-na-ro	K	N	C
WA.DI.NI	C2	HTW208a(CRIV1),	wa-du-na-to	K	N	C
WA.DU.NI.MI	C2	6b1,85b4	wa-du-na	K	N	C
WA.DU.NI.MI	C2	6b1,85b4	wa-du-na-ro	K	N	C
WA.DU.NI.MI	C2	6b1,85b4	wa-du-na-to	K	N	C
WI.TE.RO.I	* C1	25b1	wi-tu-ri-jo	K	N	C

Short A-B Parallels

Linear A	Code	Reference	Linear B	Code		
A.DE	? C1	IV10b	*a-de*	K		B
A.DU	C7	85a1,86a4,	*a-du*	K		B
A.DU	C7	85a1,86a4,	*a-du*	K	N	B
A.I	C1	115b4	*a-i*	K		A
A.KU	C1	PA1.1(IV7)	*a-ku*	K		BX
A.MA	* C1	MA1b(IV10)	*a-ma*	K		C
A.MA	* C1	MA1b(IV10)	*a-ma*	K		B
A.NU	* D1	PH13a1(IV17viii)	*a-nu*	K		B
A.PI	C1	KNZ16(V15)	*a-pi*	PK		CX
A.PI	C1	KNZ16(V15)	*a-pi*	PK		B
A.RA	? A1	IV11a	*a-ra*	K		D
A.RE	? C1	29.5	*a-re*	K	G	C
A.RE	? C1	29.5	*a-re*	K		B
A.RE	? C1	29.5	*a-re*	PK	P	B
A.RE	? C1	29.5	*a-re*	P		D
A.RI	C2B1	PH6.1(IV16),	*a-ri*	P		B
A.SE	C3	93a3,132.1,	*a-se*	K		A
A.U	? A1	46b2	*a-u*	K		BX
DA.I	C1	12.6,29.5?	*da-i*	K		B
DA.ME	C5	86a4,95a2,	*da-me*	K	N	BX
DI.DE	? C1	86b3	*di-de*	K	N	B
DO.RA	C1	PHW20	*do-ra*	P		C
I.JA	B1	KNZ10b(I8)	*i-ja*	K		A
I.KA	C3A1	26b4,91.1,	*i-ka*	K		BX
I.TA	? C1	25b1	*i-ta*	K		B
I.TA	? C1	25b1	*i-ta*	K	N	A
I.TA	? C1	25b1	*i-ta*	K		D
JA.QE	A1	KNZ17(I9)	*ja-qe*	K		A
KA.NA	C1B1	23a1,123b4	*ka-na*	M		B
KA.NA	C1B1	23a1,123b4	*ka-na*	K	N	A
KA.PA	C4B2	6a1,8b3,	*ka-pa*	PK		C
KA.RA	#C1	9b2	*ka-ra*	K		B
KA.RA	#C1	9b2	*ka-ra*	P		D
KA.RA$_2$	D1	139.3	*ka-ra*	K		B
KA.RA$_2$	D1	139.3	*ka-ra*	P		D
KA.RO	? D1	45a1	*ka-ro*	PK		C
KA.RO	? D1	45a1	*ka-ro*	K		B
KA.RO	? D1	45a1	*ka-ro*	K		B
KA.RO	? D1	45a1	*ka-ro*	P		D
KA.TI	C1A1	63.1,126b3*	*ka-ti*	P		C
KA.TI	C1A1	63.1,126b3*	*ka-ti*	M	N	B

Appendix B 153

Short A-B Parallels (cont.)

Linear A		Code	Reference	Linear B	Code		
KA.TI		C1A1	63.1,126b3*	*ka-ti*	K		A
KI.RA		C1	103.5	*ki-ra*	M	N	C
KI.RO		C13B1	1a1,15.4,	*ki-ro*	K		DX
KO.RU		C1	23a5	*ko-ru*	K		C
KO.WE		C1	11a3,62.5?	*ko-we*	K		D
KO.WE		C1	11a3,62.5?	*ko-we*	K		A
KU.DO	?	A1	64.1	*ku-do*	K		B
KU.DO	?	A1	64.1	*ku-do*	K	N	A
KU.KA	?	C1	110a1	*ku-ka*	M	N	C
KU.PA		C1	HTW220a(CRV5),	*ku-pa*	K		B
KU.RO		C30A5	9a6,9b6,	*ku-ro$_2$*	PK	N	C
KU.TA		B1	115b4	*ku-ta*	K		B
MA.DI		C4A2	85b5,97a4,	*ma-di*	K	N	C
MA.RI		B1	128a4	*ma-ri*	K	P	C
MA.RI		B1	128a4	*ma-ri*	K		B
MA.RI		B1	128a4	*ma-ri*	K		B
ME.TE	?	A1	94a4	*me-te*	P		B
ME.ZA		C2	10a5,85b3,	*me-za*	P		B
MI.TA		A1	128a3	*mi-ta*	M		C
MI.TA		A1	128a3	*mi-ta*	K		AX
MI.TI	?	A1	61.1	*mi-ti*	K	N	C
NI.SI	*	B1	140.2	*ni-si*	K		D
PA.DE		C3	9a2,9b2,122a5	*pa-de*	K	GN	C
PA.I	?	B1	I4d	*pa-i*	K		B
PA.JA		C2A1	41.4,	*pa-ja*	K	N	B
PA.KA	*	C1	85b3	*pa-ka*	MP	N	C
PA.RA		C1	128a1,	*pa-ra*	K		C
PA.RA		C1	128a1,	*pa-ra*	MK		B
PI.PI	?	C2	85a1,97a1	*pi-pi*	T	N	C
PU.RA$_2$		C2A1	28a3,116a2,49a1	*pu-ra*	K	N	B
PU.RA$_2$		C2A1	28a3,116a2,49a1	*pu-ra*	K	N	A
QA.SA	*	B1	111a1	*qa-sa*	K		D
RA.KI	*	C1	6b5	*ra-ki*	MK	N	A
RA$_2$.TI	?	A1	108.3	*ra-ti*	K		B
RE.RO		C1	HTW212b(CRIV11)	*re-ro*	P	N	A
RE.TA$_2$		A1	125.3	*re-ta$_2$*	K	N	A
RU.NA	*	A1	KN2(IV2)	*ru-na*	PK	N	C
RU.NA	*	A1	KN2(IV2)	*ru-na*	K		B
SA.MA		C3	6b5,10a1,52a1,	*sa-ma*	K		D
SI.MA		C1	PHZ4(II12)	*si-ma*	P	N	C
SI.PU		D1	HTZ161(II10)	*si-pu$_2$*	K	N	C

Short A-B Parallels (cont.)

Linear A	Code		Reference	Linear B	Code		
SI.RA		A1	49.5	si-ra	K		BX
SI.TA	*	A1	PH3a1(IV15)	si-ta	K		BX
SU.SE	?	C1	32.3	su-se	K	N	C
TA.NA	?	C1	120.5	ta-na	M		A
TA.PA		C1	104.1	ta-pa	K		B
TA.RA		C1	89.3,84.1?,	ta-ra	P		B
TA.RA		C1	89.3,84.1?,	ta-ra	K		A
TA.RA		C1	89.3,84.1?,	ta-ra$_2$	K		A
TA$_2$.ZA	?	C1	88.1	ta-za	K	N	C
TA$_2$.ZA	?	C1	88.1	ta-za	K	N	A
TA$_2$.ZA	?	C1	88.1	ta-za	K		B
TE.KE		C1	85a5	te-ke	P		C
TI.JA	?	C1	I3.2	ti-ja	K	N	AX
TI.JA	?	C1	I3.2	ti-ja	K		A
TI.SA		A1	31.1,39.5?	ti-sa	K		BX
TU.MA		C1	94b1,110b1?	tu-ma	K		B
TU.SA	*	A1	79.2	tu-sa	K		B
U.TA$_2$	*	C1	103.1	u-ta	K		B
U.TA$_2$	*	C1	103.1	u-ta	K		AX
WE.JA		A1	55b2	we-ja	K		A
WI.DU		A1	5.3	wi-du	K	N	BX
WI.SA	=	A1	113.1	wi-sa	P	N	B

APPENDIX C

This appendix enumerates matches between Linear A and Linear B which result from hypothetical *new* assignments of phonetic values for Linear A signs. Each hypothesis is of the form: "Let the Linear A sign x have the phonetic value y, but let all other signs maintain their conventional values." The hypothetical assignment is printed at the left, followed by the Linear A sign-group and its match in Linear B. An asterisk precedes the Linear A sign which receives the new hypothetical value. The full interpretation of the first entry will serve as an example. It reads: "If the Linear A sign L1 (conventionally PA$_3$) had instead the value DO, then the sign-group KU.PA$_3$.NU (which would now read KU.DO.NU) would match *ku-do-ni-ja* in Linear B.

Every possible phonetic value is assigned to each Linear A sign, but only matches which involve complete sign-groups are printed. The Linear B words are all attested at Knossos; Linear A reading are those of Raison-Pope (1971). For the format and identification of sign-groups see Appendix B.

The reservations expressed in the introduction to Appendix B apply with even more force here. A very large number of the matches printed in this appendix are coincidental and without significance. One of its values will be to illustrate once more the insidiousness of random correspondences. It will have the more important positive function of drawing attention to alternative phonetic values, especially for signs whose conventional value did not receive strong confirmation in Chapter Three.

Minoan Linear A

Hypoth.	Linear A	Code	Reference	Linear B	Code		
1=DO	KU.*PA$_3$.NU	C9	1a3,3.6,88.3,	*ku-do-ni-ja*	K	P	C
1=I	I.DA.*PA$_3$	C1	PH6.4(IV16)	*i-da-i-jo*	PK	N	C
1=KA	KU.*PA$_3$.NU	C9	1a3,3.6,88.3,	*ku-ka-no*	K	N	C
1=KE	SU.*PA$_3$.RA	C1	31.5	*su-ke-re*	K	N	C
1=PA	KU.*PA$_3$.NU	C9	1a3,3.6,88.3,	*ku-pa-nu-we-to*	K	N	C
1=QO	KA.RO.*PA$_3$	C1	31.3	*ka-ro-qo*	MPK	N	C
1=RA	KU.*PA$_3$.NU	C9	1a3,3.6,88.3,	*ku-ra-no*	K	N	C
1=RU	KU.*PA$_3$.NA.TU	C2	47a1,119.3	*ku-ru-ni-ta*	K	N	C
1=RU	KU.*PA$_3$.NU	C9	1a3,3.6,88.3,	*ku-ru-no*	+		C
1=SA	DU.*PA$_3$.NA	C1	115b2	*du-sa-ni*	K	N	C
2=*22	*PA.JA.RE	C2B2	8b4,88.4,29.2,	**22-ja-ro*	K		CX
2=A	*PA.TA.NE	C2	94b1,122a6	*a-ta-no*	K	N	C
2=AU	*PA.TA.NE	C2	94b1,122a6	*au-ta-na*	+		C
2=DA	*PA.DA.RE *	C1	10a3	*da-da-re-jo-de*	K	P	C
2=DA	*PA.JA.RE	C2B2	8b4,88.4,29.2,	*da-ja-ro*	K		C
2=DA	KU.*PA.JA	C1	116a1	*ku-da-jo*	K	N	C
2=E	*PA.RA.NE	C2	115a4,115b1,	*e-ra-ne*	K	Q	C
2=KA	*PA.TA.NE	C2	94b1,122a6	*ka-ta-no*	PK	N	C
2=KE	*PA.RA.NE	C2	115a4,115b1,	*ke-ra-no*	K		C
2=KE	A.*PA.RA.NE	C2	96a1,96b1	*a-ke-ra-no*	K	N	C
2=KI	*PA.DA.RE *	C1	10a3	*ki-da-ro*	K	N	C
2=KI	*PA.TA.NE	C2	94b1,122a6	*ki-ta-no*	K		C
2=KU	*PA.JA.RE	C2B2	8b4,88.4,29.2,	*ku-ja-ro*	K	N	C
2=KU	*PA.RA.NE	C2	115a4,115b1,	*ku-ra-no*	K	N	C
2=MI	*PA.TA.QE	C1	31.6	*mi-ta-qo*	K	N	C
2=MI	*PA.JA.RE	C2B2	8b4,88.4,29.2,	*mi-ja-ro*	K	N	C
2=NO	*PA.DA.RE *	C1	10a3	*no-da-ro*	K	N	C
2=O	*PA.DA.RE *	C1	10a3	*o-da-ra-o*	K		C
2=PA	*PA.JA.RE	C2B2	8b4,88.4,29.2,	*pa-ja-ro*	K	N	C
2=PA	*PA.I.TO	C2	97a3,120.6,	*pa-i-to*	K	P	C
2=PA$_3$	*PA.I.TO	C2	97a3,120.6,	*pa$_3$-i-ti*	K		C
2=PO	*PA.I.TO	C2	97a3,120.6,	*po-i-ti-jo*	K	N	C
2=PO	*PA.I.TO	C2	97a3,120.6,	*po-i-te-u*	K	N	C
2=PU$_2$	*PA.RA.NE	C2	115a4,115b1,	*pu$_2$-ra-ne-jo*	K	N	C
2=QA	*PA.DA.RE *	C1	10a3	*qa-da-ro*	K	N	C
2=QO	*PA.JA.RE	C2B2	8b4,88.4,29.2,	*qo-ja-ro*	K		CX
2=RO	KA.*PA.QE	C1	6a4	*ka-ro-qo*	MPK	N	C
2=RO$_2$	KU.*PA.JA	C1	116a1	*ku-ro$_2$-jo*	K	N	C
2=SI	*PA.RA.NE	C2	115a4,115b1,	*si-ra-no*	K	N	C
2=TA	*PA.RA.NE	C2	115a4,115b1,	*ta-ra-nu*	PK		C
2=TE	*PA.JA.RE	C2B2	8b4,88.4,29.2,	*te-ja-ro*	K	N	CX
2=TU	*PA.DA.RE *	C1	10a3	*tu-da-ra*	K	N	C

Appendix C

Hypoth.	Linear A		Code	Reference	Linear B	Code		
2=U	*PA.TA.NE		C2	94b1,122a6	u-ta-no	K	N	C
2=U	*PA.TA.NE		C2	94b1,122a6	u-ta-no	K	P	C
2=WI	*PA.RA.NE		C2	115a4,115b1,	wi-ra-ne	+		C
2=ZO	*PA.TA.QE		C1	31.6	zo-ta-qe	+		C
6=DO	A.KU.*TU		C1	TY3b7(IV9)	a-ku-do-i	K	P	CX
6=KU	*TU.SU.PU$_2$	*	C1	49a7	ku-su-pa	K		C
6=NA	A.KU.*TU		C1	TY3b7(IV9)	a-ku-na-i	+		C
6=RA	SI.*TU.NE	*	C1	HTW221a(CRV4)	si-ra-no	K	N	C
6=RA	QE.*TU.SI	*	C1	PHW14a(III13)	qe-ra-si-jo	K	G	C
6=RI	A.KU.*TU		C1	TY3b7(IV9)	a-ku-ri-jo	K	N	C
6=TE	QE.*TU.SI	*	C1	PHW14a(III13)	qe-te-se-u	K	N	C
6=WO	A.KU.*TU		C1	TY3b7(IV9)	a-ku-wo	K		C
7=A	*SO.DI.RA		C3	9a4,9b3,122a5	a-di-ri-jo	K	N	C
9=KA	SA.*9.RE	*	C1	29.4	sa-ka-ri-jo	K	N	C
9=MA	SA.*9.RE	*	C1	29.4	sa-ma-ri-jo	K	N	C
9=QA	SA.*9.RE	*	C1	29.4	sa-qa-re-jo	K	QN	C
9=U	SA.*9.RE	*	C1	29.4	sa-u-ri-jo	K	N	C
9=ZA	SA.*9.RE	*	C1	29.4	sa-za-ro	+		C
9=ZE	SA.*9.RE	*	C1	29.4	sa-ze-ro	K	N	C
20=DE	*20.*20.KU	=	C1	ZAZ3.2	de-de-ko-wo	K		CX
20=MA	*20.SA.DI	*	C1	PHW15(III14)	ma-sa-de	K	P	C
20=TO	*20.SA.DI	*	C1	PHW15(III14)	to-sa-de	+		C
20=WA	*20.*20.KU	=	C1	ZAZ3.2	wa-wa-ka	K	Q	C
22=A	KA.*RO.NA		C1	11a2	ka-a-na	K		C
22=DA	KA.*RO.NA		C1	11a2	ka-da-no	K	N	C
22=DA	SA.MA.*RO		C1A1	88.4,39.3*	sa-ma-da	K	PN	C
22=JA	PA.*RO.SU	*	C1	20.1	pa-ja-so	K	N	C
22=JO	U.TA.*RO	*	C1	116a1	u-ta-jo-jo	K	N	C
22=JO	U.TA.*RO	*	C1	116a1	u-ta-jo	K		C
22=MO	KA.*RO.NA		C1	11a2	ka-mo-ni-jo	K	N	C
22=NA	KA.*RO.PA$_3$		C1	31.3	ka-na-po	K	N	C
22=NA	PA.*RO.SU	*	C1	20.1	pa-na-so	K	PN	C
22=NO	U.TA.*RO	*	C1	116a1	u-ta-no	K	N	C
22=NO	U.TA.*RO	*	C1	116a1	u-ta-no	K	P	C
22=PA	KI.DA.*RO		C1	117a9,27a4?	ki-da-pa	K	P	C
22=PA$_3$	KA.*RO.NA		C1	11a2	ka-pa$_3$-no	K	N	C
22=QO	PA.*RO.SU	*	C1	20.1	pa-qo-si-jo	PK	N	C
22=RI	SA.MA.*RO		C1A1	88.4,39.3*	sa-ma-ri-jo	K	N	C
22=RI	KA.*RO.PA$_3$		C1	31.3	ka-ri-pi-jo	+		C
22=RO	KI.DA.*RO		C1	117a9,27a4?	ki-da-ro	K	N	C
22=RU	KA.*RO.NA		C1	11a2	ka-ru-no	K		C
22=SA	KA.*RO.NA		C1	11a2	ka-sa-no	K	N	C
22=TA	KA.*RO.NA		C1	11a2	ka-ta-no	PK	N	C

Minoan Linear A

Hypoth.	Linear A	Code	Reference	Linear B	Code		
22=TI	SA.MA.*RO	C1A1	88.4,39.3*	sa-ma-ti-ja	K	N	C
22=WA	PA.*RO.SU	* C1	20.1	pa-wa-so	K	N	C
24=A	*KE.KI.RU	C1	94b2	a-ki-re-u	K	N	C
24=A	*KE.KI.RU	C1	94b2	a-ki-ri-ja	+		C
24=MA	KO.SA.*KE.TI	C1	117a7	ko-sa-ma-to	+		C
24=SI	*KE.KI.RU	C1	94b2	si-ki-ro	+		C
24=SO	DI.ZA.*KE	C1	1a2	di-za-so	K	N	C
24=ZA	*KE.KI.RU	C1	94b2	za-ki-ri-jo	K	N	C
25=*22	KA.*NU.TI	C1	97a3	ka-*22-to	+		C
25=JA	I.TA.*NU	C1	28b6	i-ta-ja	K	N	C
25=KA	MI.*NU.TE	C4	86a5,95a2,95b2,	mi-ka-to	K	N	C
25=KA	MI.*NU.TE	C4	86a5,95a2,95b2,	mi-ka-ta	PK	QN	C
25=MA	KA.*NU.TI	C1	97a3	ka-ma-to	+		C
25=NI	DA.MI.*NU	C1	117a8	da-mi-ni-jo	PK	EP	C
25=NI	KA.*NU.TI	C1	97a3	ka-ni-to	K		C
25=O	*NU.DU.WA	C1	40.1	o-du-we	K		C
25=QA	TI.*NU.JA	C1	115b2	ti-qa-jo	PK	N	C
25=SA	KA.*NU.TI	C1	97a3	ka-sa-to	MPK	N	C
26=DA	*NA.DA.RE	C1	117a5	da-da-re-jo-de	K	P	C
26=KI	*NA.DA.RE	C1	117a5	ki-da-ro	K	N	C
26=KO	DA.*NA.SI	C1	126a1	da-ko-so	K	N	C
26=KU	I.*NA.WA	C1	PH6.1(IV16)	i-ku-wo-i-pi	K		C
26=MA	TI.TA.*NA	C1	HTW220(CRV5)	ti-ta-ma	K		C
26=NA	A.RA.*NA.RE	C1	1a4,47b1?	a-ra-na-ro	K	N	C
26=NA	TA.*NA.TI	C3A1	7a4,10b4,98a2,	ta-na-to	K	N	C
26=NO	*NA.DA.RE	C1	117a5	no-da-ro	K	N	C
26=O	*NA.DA.RE	C1	117a5	o-da-ra-o	K		C
26=QA	*NA.DA.RE	C1	117a5	qa-da-ro	K	N	C
26=QA	DI.*NA.RO	* C1	108.2	di-qa-ra	K	N	C
26=QI	I.*NA.JA	* C1	PKZ11(I4)	i-qi-jo	K		C
26=QI	I.*NA.JA	* C1	PKZ11(I4)	i-qi-ja	K		C
26=QO	I.*NA.JA	* C1	PKZ11(I4)	i-qo-jo	PK		C
26=QO	KA.RO.*NA	C1	11a2	ka-ro-qo	MPK	N	C
26=SA	I.*NA.WA	C1	PH6.1(IV16)	i-sa-wo	K		C
26=SI	TA.WE.*NA	C1	10b1	ta-we-si-jo	K	N	C
26=SO	DI.WE.*NA	C2	93a1,102.3	di-we-so	K	N	C
26=TA	TA.*NA.TI	C3A1	7a4,10b4,98a2,	ta-ta-ta	K	PN	C
26=TA	I.*NA.JA	* C1	PKZ11(I4)	i-ta-ja	K	N	C
26=TU	*NA.DA.RE	C1	117a5	tu-da-ra	K	N	C
28=DA	A.RA.*WI	= C1	87.5	a-ra-da-jo	K	N	C
28=KO	A.RA.*WI	= C1	87.5	a-ra-ko	K	N	C
28=PO	DU.RU.*WI	C1	25a4	du-ru-po	K	N	C
28=RU	A.RA.*WI	= C1	87.5	a-ra-ru-ja	K		C

Appendix C

Hypoth.	Linear A	Code	Reference	Linear B	Code		
28=SI	A.RA.*WI	=C1	87.5	a-ra-si-jo	K	N	C
29=*49	*KA.SA.RU	C1	10b3	*49-sa-ro	+		C
29=A	*KA.SA.RU	C1	10b3	a-sa-ro	K	N	C
29=A	*KA.NU.TI	C1	97a3	a-nu-to-jo	K	N	C
29=A	*KA.NU.TI	C1	97a3	a-nu-to	TK	N	C
29=DE	A.*KA.RU	C2	2.1,86a1,86b1?	a-de-ra$_2$	+		C
29=DI	A.*KA.RU	C2	2.1,86a1,86b1?	a-di-ri-jo	K	N	C
29=DU	*KA.SA.RU	C1	10b3	du-sa-ro	K	N	C
29=E	*KA.SA.RU	C1	10b3	e-sa-re-we	K	Q	C
29=JA	*KA.SA.RU	C1	10b3	ja-sa-ro	K	N	C
29=KA	*KA.SA.RU	C1	10b3	ka-sa-ro	K		C
29=KA	A.*KA.RU	C2	2.1,86a1,86b1?	a-ka-re-u	PK	N	C
29=KE	A.*KA.RU	C2	2.1,86a1,86b1?	a-ke-ra-wo	PK	N	C
29=KI	A.*KA.RU	C2	2.1,86a1,86b1?	a-ki-re-u	K	N	C
29=KI	A.*KA.RU	C2	2.1,86a1,86b1?	a-ki-ri-ja	+		C
29=KO	A.*KA.RU	C2	2.1,86a1,86b1?	a-ko-ro	PK		C
29=KO	A.*KA.RU	C2	2.1,86a1,86b1?	a-ko-ra-jo	K	N	C
29=KU	A.*KA.RU	C2	2.1,86a1,86b1?	a-ku-ri-jo	K	N	C
29=MA	*KA.RO.NA	C1	11a2	ma-ro-ne	K	N	C
29=MI	*KA.SA.RU	C1	10b3	mi-sa-ra-jo	K	N	C
29=NA	A.*KA.RU	C2	2.1,86a1,86b1?	a-na-re-u	+		C
29=NO	*KA.SA.RU	C1	10b3	no-sa-ro	K	N	C
29=PA	A.*KA.RU	C2	2.1,86a1,86b1?	a-pa-re-u	K	N	CX
29=PE	A.*KA.RU	C2	2.1,86a1,86b1?	a-pe-re	K		C
29=PI	A.*KA.RU	C2	2.1,86a1,86b1?	a-pi-re-jo	K	N	C
29=PI	A.*KA.RU	C2	2.1,86a1,86b1?	a-pi-ra-wo	K	N	C
29=QA	*KA.SA.RU	C1	10b3	qa-sa-ro-we	K	P	C
29=QI	A.*KA.RU	C2	2.1,86a1,86b1?	a-qi-ru	K	N	C
29=QI	A.*KA.RU	C2	2.1,86a1,86b1?	a-qi-ro	K	N	C
29=RA	A.*KA.RU	C2	2.1,86a1,86b1?	a-ra-ru-wo-a	K		C
29=RA	A.*KA.RU	C2	2.1,86a1,86b1?	a-ra-ru-ja	K		C
29=SA	A.*KA.RU	C2	2.1,86a1,86b1?	a-sa-ro	K	N	C
29=TI	A.*KA.RU	C2	2.1,86a1,86b1?	a-ti-ro	K	N	C
29=TO	A.*KA.RU	C2	2.1,86a1,86b1?	a-to-re-u	K	N	C
29=WO	A.*KA.RU	C2	2.1,86a1,86b1?	a-wo-ro	K	N	C
30=A	*DA.KU.NA	C1	103.4	a-ku-na-i	+		C
30=A$_3$	*DA.TA.RA	C1	6a1	a$_3$-ta-ro-we	PK	N	C
30=A$_3$	*DA.TA.RE	C2	88.5,62.2*	a$_3$-ta-ro-we	PK	N	C
30=DA	*DA.MI.NU	C1	117a8	da-mi-ni-jo	PK	EP	C
30=DA	KI.*DA.RO	C1	117a9,27a4?	ki-da-ro	K	N	C
30=DO	KI.*DA.RO	C1	117a9,27a4?	ki-do-ro	K		C
30=E	NA.*DA.RE	C1	117a5	na-e-ra-ja	K	N	C
30=JA	PA.*DA.RE	*C1	10a3	pa-ja-ro	K	N	C

Hypoth.	Linear A	Code	Reference	Linear B	Code		
30=KA	*DA.TA.RE	C2	88.5,62.2*	ka-ta-ra-i	K	P	C
30=KA	*DA.TA.RA	C1	6a1	ka-ta-ra	+		C
30=KA	*DA.TA.RA	C1	6a1	ka-ta-ro	MK		C
30=KA	*DA.TA.RA	C1	6a1	ka-ta-ra-i	K	P	C
30=KA	*DA.TA.RE	C2	88.5,62.2*	ka-ta-ra	+		C
30=KA	*DA.TA.RE	C2	88.5,62.2*	ka-ta-ro	MK		C
30=KE	KI.*DA.RO	C1	117a9,27a4?	ki-ke-ro	K	N	C
30=KI	SI.*DA.RE	C2	17.3,122a5,49a4?	si-ki-ro	+		C
30=MA	KI.*DA.TA	C1	40.2	ki-ma-ta	K	N	C
30=MI	TI.*DA.TA *	C1	123b2	ti-mi-to	K		C
30=NA	PA.*DA.RE *	C1	10a3	pa-na-re-jo	PK	N	C
30=O	*DA.TA.RE	C2	88.5,62.2*	o-ta-re-wo	K	N	C
30=O	*DA.TA.RA	C1	6a1	o-ta-re-wo	K	N	C
30=O	*DA.NA.SI	C1	126a1	o-na-se-u	PK	N	C
30=O	*DA.KU.NA	C1	103.4	o-ku-no	K	N	C
30=PA	*DA.NA.SI	C1	126a1	pa-na-so	K	PN	C
30=PA	PA.*DA.RE *	C1	10a3	pa-pa-ro	PK	N	C
30=PO	*DA.MI.NU	C1	117a8	po-mi-ni-jo	K	N	C
30=PU	*DA.NA.SI	C1	126a1	pu-na-so	K	P	C
30=PU	*DA.TA.RA	C1	6a1	pu-ta-ri-ja	K		C
30=PU	*DA.TA.RE	C2	88.5,62.2*	pu-ta-ri-ja	K		C
30=QI	*DA.TA.RE	C2	88.5,62.2*	qi-ta-ro	K	N	C
30=QI	*DA.TA.RA	C1	6a1	qi-ta-ro	K	N	C
30=QI	*DA.QE.RA	C2B1	6a6,120.1,57a1	qi-qe-ro	K	N	C
30=RA	SI.*DA.RE	C2	17.3,122a5,49a4?	si-ra-ro	K	P	C
30=RI	TI.*DA.TA *	C1	123b2	ti-ri-ti-jo	K	E	C
30=RI	MA.*DA.TI *	C1	PK1.7(IV5)	ma-ri-ti-wi-jo	MPK	N	C
30=RI	TI.*DA.TA *	C1	123b2	ti-ri-to	K	P	C
30=RI	TI.*DA.TA *	C1	123b2	ti-ri-ti-ja	K	EP	C
30=RI	KI.*DA.TA	C1	40.2	ki-ri-ta	K		C
30=RU	*DA.NA.SI	C1	126a1	ru-na-so	K	N	C
30=SI	*DA.TA.RA	C1	6a1	si-ta-ro	K	N	C
30=SI	*DA.TA.RE	C2	88.5,62.2*	si-ta-ro	K	N	C
30=TA	*DA.TA.RE	C2	88.5,62.2*	ta-ta-ro	+		C
30=TA	*DA.TA.RA	C1	6a1	ta-ta-ro	+		C
30=TA	SI.*DA.RE	C2	17.3,122a5,49a4?	si-ta-ro	K	N	C
30=TO	PA.*DA.RE *	C1	10a3	pa-to-ro	K	N	C
30=U	KI.*DA.RO	C1	117a9,27a4?	ki-u-ro	K	N	C
30=WA	TI.*DA.TA *	C1	123b2	ti-wa-ti-ja	K	EN	C
30=WI	NA.*DA.RE	C1	117a5	na-wi-ro	K	N	C
30=WO	*DA.NA.SI	C1	126a1	wo-na-si	K		C
31=A	*SA.JA.MA	C1	31.3	a-ja-me	K		C
31=A	*SA.RA.RA	C1	30.3	a-ra-ru-wo-a	K		C

Appendix C

Hypoth.	Linear A		Code	Reference	Linear B	Code		
31=A	*SA.RA.RA		C1	30.3	a-ra-ru-ja	K		C
31=DE	A.*SA.RA$_2$	*	C1	89.1	a-de-ra$_2$	+		C
31=DI	A.*SA.RA$_2$	*	C1	89.1	a-di-ri-jo	K	N	C
31=JA	A.*SA.ME.NE	*	C1	ZAZ3.1	a-ja-me-no	PK		C
31=JA	*SA.MA.RO		C1A1	88.4,39.3*	ja-ma-ra	K	N	C
31=JE	I.*SA.RI		C1	PH6.4(IV16)	i-je-re-ja	PK	Q	C
31=JE	I.*SA.RI		C1	PH6.4(IV16)	i-je-re-wi-jo	K	N	C
31=KA	A.*SA.RA$_2$	*	C1	89.1	a-ka-re-u	PK	N	C
31=KA	KA.*SA.RU		C1	10b3	ka-ka-re-a$_2$	K		C
31=KA	*SA.RA.RA		C1	30.3	ka-ra-re-we	PK		C
31=KE	A.*SA.RA$_2$	*	C1	89.1	a-ke-ra-wo	PK	N	C
31=KI	A.*SA.RA$_2$	*	C1	89.1	a-ki-re-u	K	N	C
31=KI	A.*SA.RA$_2$	*	C1	89.1	a-ki-ri-ja	+		C
31=KO	A.*SA.RA$_2$	*	C1	89.1	a-ko-ro	PK		C
31=KO	A.*SA.RA$_2$	*	C1	89.1	a-ko-ra-jo	K	N	C
31=KO	A.*SA.ME.NE	*	C1	ZAZ3.1	a-ko-mo-ni-jo	K	N	C
31=KU	A.*SA.RA$_2$	*	C1	89.1	a-ku-ri-jo	K	N	C
31=MI	I.*SA.RI		C1	PH6.4(IV16)	i-mi-ri-jo	K	N	C
31=NA	A.*SA.RA$_2$	*	C1	89.1	a-na-re-u	+		C
31=PA	A.*SA.RA$_2$	*	C1	89.1	a-pa-re-u	K	N	CX
31=PA	KA.*SA.RU		C1	10b3	ka-pa-ri-jo	K	N	C
31=PE	A.*SA.RA$_2$	*	C1	89.1	a-pe-re	K		C
31=PI	A.*SA.RA$_2$	*	C1	89.1	a-pi-re-jo	K	N	C
31=PI	A.*SA.RA$_2$	*	C1	89.1	a-pi-ra-wo	K	N	C
31=QA	I.*SA.RI		C1	PH6.4(IV16)	i-qa-ro	+		C
31=QI	A.*SA.RA$_2$	*	C1	89.1	a-qi-ro	K	N	C
31=QI	A.*SA.RA$_2$	*	C1	89.1	a-qi-ru	K	N	C
31=RA	A.*SA.RA$_2$	*	C1	89.1	a-ra-ru-ja	K		C
31=RA	PA.*SA.WE.JA		C1	24a4	pa-ra-wa-jo	PK		C
31=RA	KA.*SA.RU		C1	10b3	ka-ra-re-we	PK		C
31=SA	A.*SA.RA$_2$	*	C1	89.1	a-sa-ro	K	N	C
31=SA	KA.*SA.RU		C1	10b3	ka-sa-ro	K		C
31=SA	*SA.MA.RO		C1A1	88.4,39.3*	sa-ma-ri-jo	K	N	C
31=SI	*SA.JA.MA		C1	31.3	si-ja-ma	K	N	C
31=SI	*SA.RA.RA		C1	30.3	si-ra-ro	K	P	C
31=TA	KA.*SA.RU		C1	10b3	ka-ta-ra-i	K	P	C
31=TA$_2$	KA.*SA.RU		C1	10b3	ka-ta$_2$-ro	+		C
31=TI	A.*SA.RA$_2$	*	C1	89.1	a-ti-ro	K	N	C
31=TO	A.*SA.ME.NE	*	C1	ZAZ3.1	a-to-mo-na	K	N	C
31=TO	A.*SA.RA$_2$	*	C1	89.1	a-to-re-u	K	N	C
31=TO	KA.*SA.RU		C1	10b3	ka-to-ro	K	N	C
31=WA	KA.*SA.RU		C1	10b3	ka-wa-ro	K	N	C
31=WE	I.*SA.RI		C1	PH6.4(IV16)	i-we-ro	K	N	C

Hypoth.	Linear A	Code	Reference	Linear B	Code		
31=WO	A.*SA.RA₂	* C1	89.1	*a-wo-ro*	K	N	C
31=ZA	I.*SA.RI	C1	PH6.4(IV16)	*i-za-re*	K	N	C
32=JA	PA.*JA.RE	C2B2	8b4,88.4,29.2,	*pa-ja-ro*	K	N	C
32=JA	TE.*JA.RE	* C1	117a5	*te-ja-ro*	K	N	CX
32=KE	I.*JA.TE	C1	PHZ4(II12)	*i-ke-ta*	K	N	C
32=MI	TE.*JA.RE	* C1	117a5	*te-mi-ro*	K	N	C
32=NA	PA.*JA.RE	C2B2	8b4,88.4,29.2,	*pa-na-re-jo*	PK	N	C
32=NU	KU.PA.*JA	C1	116a1	*ku-pa-nu-we-to*	K	N	C
32=PA	TE.*JA.RE	* C1	117a5	*te-pa-ra*	K	P	C
32=PA	PA.*JA.RE	C2B2	8b4,88.4,29.2,	*pa-pa-ro*	PK	N	C
32=PE	I.*JA.TE	C1	PHZ4(II12)	*i-pe-ta*	+		C
32=PO	*JA.KU.TI	C1	KN1b1(IV1)	*po-ku-ta*	PK	Q	C
32=QE	*JA.RE.MI	C1	87.3	*qe-re-ma-o*	PK	N	C
32=RA	I.*JA.TE	C1	PHZ4(II12)	*i-ra-ta*	PK	N	C
32=RO	I.*JA.TE	C1	PHZ4(II12)	*i-ro-to*	K	N	C
32=RO	TE.*JA.RE	* C1	117a5	*te-ro-ri-jo*	K	N	C
32=RO	KU.PA.*JA	C1	116a1	*ku-pa-ro*	K		C
32=SA	KU.PA.*JA	C1	116a1	*ku-pa-sa*	K	P	C
32=TO	PA.*JA.RE	C2B2	8b4,88.4,29.2,	*pa-to-ro*	K	N	C
33=PA₃	DA.RU.*33	C1	7b2	*da-ru-pa₃*	K	N	C
34=*65	A.*PU₂.NA	C1	14.3	*a-*65-na*	K	N	C
34=KU	A.*PU₂.NA	C1	14.3	*a-ku-na-i*	+		C
34=MA	A.*PU₂.NA	C1	14.3	*a-ma-no*	K	N	C
34=PA₃	A.*PU₂.NA	C1	14.3	*a-pa₃-no*	K	N	C
34=TA	A.*PU₂.NA	C1	14.3	*a-ta-no*	K	N	C
39=TO	PA.I.*TO	C2	97a3,120.6,	*pa-i-to*	K	P	C
43=PA	RA.*43.TI	C2	17.1,19.1	*ra-pa-to*	K		C
43=SA	RA.*43.TI	C2	17.1,19.1	*ra-sa-to*	K	QP	C
43=SU	RA.*43.TI	C2	17.1,19.1	*ra-su-ti-jo*	K	E	C
43=WO	RA.*43.TI	C2	17.1,19.1	*ra-wo-ti-jo*	K	N	C
51=A	*DI.DE.RU	C3	86a3,95a4,95b4	*a-de-ra₂*	+		C
51=A	*DI.NA.RO	* C1	108.2	*a-na-re-u*	+		C
51=A₃	*DI.KI.SE	C2	87.3,117b2	*a₃-ki-si-jo*	K	N	C
51=DE	*DI.KI.SE	C2	87.3,117b2	*de-ki-si-wo*	PK	N	C
51=DU	WA.*DI.NI	C2	HTW208a(CRIV1),	*wa-du-na*	K	N	C
51=E	*DI.KI.SE	C2	87.3,117b2	*e-ki-si-jo*	K	E	C
51=E	DO.*DI.RA	C2	HTW212a(CRIV11),	*do-e-ra*	PK	Q	C
51=E	DO.*DI.RA	C2	HTW212a(CRIV11),	*do-e-ro*	PK	Q	C
51=PA	*DI.NA.RO	* C1	108.2	*pa-na-re-jo*	PK	N	C
51=PI	WI.*DI.NA	C1	28a5	*wi-pi-no-o*	K	N	C
51=QA	U.*DI.MI	C1	117a4	*u-qa-mo*	K	PN	C
51=RA	WI.*DI.NA	C1	28a5	*wi-ra-ne*	+		C
51=RI	WI.*DI.NA	C1	28a5	*wi-ri-ne-we*	K	QN	C

Appendix C

Hypoth.	Linear A	Code	Reference	Linear B	Code		
51=RI	WI.*DI.NA	C1	28a5	wi-ri-ni-jo	K		C
51=SO	DU.TA.*DI	* C1	19.3	du-ta-so	K	N	C
51=TA	KI.*DI.NI	* C1	93a2	ki-ta-no	K		C
51=TO	KI.*DI.NI	* C1	93a2	ki-to-ne	K		C
51=TO	KI.*DI.NI	* C1	93a2	ki-to-na	K		C
52=*49	*A.SA.RA₂	* C1	89.1	*49-sa-ro	+		C
52=A	*A.SA.RA₂	* C1	89.1	a-sa-ro	K	N	C
52=A	*A.RA.NA.RE	C1	1a4,47b1?	a-ra-na-ro	K	N	C
52=A	*A.KA.RU	C2	2.1,86a1,86b1?	a-ka-re-u	PK	N	C
52=A₃	*A.KA.RU	C2	2.1,86a1,86b1?	a₃-ka-ra	K	N	C
52=DI	*A.WE.SU	C1	118.3	di-we-so	K	N	C
52=DU	*A.SA.RA₂	* C1	89.1	du-sa-ro	K	N	C
52=E	*A.SA.RA₂	* C1	89.1	e-sa-re-we	K	Q	C
52=E	*A.RA.WI	= C1	87.5	e-ra-wo	PK		C
52=E	*A.KA.RU	C2	2.1,86a1,86b1?	e-ka-ra-e-we	K	Q	C
52=E	*A.PU₂.NA	C1	14.3	e-pu₂-no	K		C
52=I	I.DA.*A	+ C1	KOZ1b	i-da-i-jo	PK	N	C
52=JA	*A.SA.RA₂	* C1	89.1	ja-sa-ro	K	N	C
52=KA	*A.SA.RA₂	* C1	89.1	ka-sa-ro	K		C
52=KA	*A.KA.RU	C2	2.1,86a1,86b1?	ka-ka-re-a₂	K		C
52=KI	*A.RI.NI.TA	C1	25a3	ki-ri-ne-to	K	N	C
52=KU	*A.TA.I	* C1	PRZ1b(I17)	ku-ta-i-jo	K	N	C
52=KU	*A.KA.RU	C2	2.1,86a1,86b1?	ku-ka-ro	K	N	C
52=MA	*A.RA.PI	# C1	87.5	ma-ra-pi-jo	K	N	C
52=MI	*A.SA.RA₂	* C1	89.1	mi-sa-ra-jo	K	N	C
52=MU	*A.KA.RU	C2	2.1,86a1,86b1?	mu-ka-ra	K	N	C
52=NO	*A.SA.RA₂	* C1	89.1	no-sa-ro	K	N	C
52=PA	*A.RA.WI	= C1	87.5	pa-ra-wa-jo	PK		C
52=PO	*A.KU.TU	C1	TY3b7(IV9)	po-ku-ta	PK	Q	C
52=PU₂	*A.RU.DA.RA	C1	28b5,62.1?	pu₂-ru-da-ro	K	N	C
52=QA	*A.SA.RA₂	* C1	89.1	qa-sa-ro-we	K	P	C
52=SA	*A.KA.RU	C2	2.1,86a1,86b1?	sa-ka-ri-jo	K	N	C
52=SE	*A.RI.NI.TA	C1	25a3	se-ri-na-ta	K	N	C
52=TA	*A.WE.SU	C1	118.3	ta-we-si-jo	K	N	C
52=TE	PA.SI.*A	* C1	45b3	pa-si-te-o-i	K	G	C
52=WE	*A.WE.SU	C1	118.3	we-we-si-jo	PK	N	C
52=WO	*A.KA.RU	C2	2.1,86a1,86b1?	wo-ka-re	K		C
53=JA	PA.*RA.NE	C2	115a4,115b1,	pa-ja-ni-jo	K		C
53=JA	PA.*RA.NE	C2	115a4,115b1,	pa-ja-ni	+		C
53=KA	PA.*RA.NE	C2	115a4,115b1,	pa-ka-na	K		C
53=KA	A.*RA.WI	= C1	87.5	a-ka-wo	PK	N	C
53=KA	A.*RA.WI	= C1	87.5	a-ka-wi-ja-de	K	PN	C
53=KE	A.*RA.WI	= C1	87.5	a-ke-wo	K	N	C

Hypoth.	Linear A	Code	Reference	Linear B	Code		
53=KU	A.*RA.WI	= C1	87.5	a-ku-wo	K		C
53=RA	A.*RA.NA.RE	C1	1a4,47b1?	a-ra-na-ro	K	N	C
53=RO	A.*RA.WI	= C1	87.5	a-ro-we	K		C
53=RO	SI.KI.*RA	C1	8a4	si-ki-ro	+		C
53=SI	A.*RA.WI	= C1	87.5	a-si-wi-jo	MPK	N	C
53=TA	A.*RA.WI	= C1	87.5	a-ta-wo	PK	N	C
53=TA	KU.*RA.I	* C1	117a2	ku-ta-i-jo	K	N	C
53=TO	SI.KI.*RA	C1	8A4	si-ki-to	K	N	C
53=WE	*RA.RE.*RA	C1	HTW206B(CRIV8)	we-re-we	K	Q	C
53=WI	PA.*RA.NE	C2	115a4,115b1,	pa-wi-no	K	N	C
54=*83	QA.*RE.TO	C1	132.1,111a1?	qa-*83-to	K	N	C
54=JO	SI.DA.*RE	C2	17.3,122a5,49a4?	si-da-jo	K		C
54=KA	KA.*RE.RO	C1	HTW203(CRIV18)	ka-ka-re-a_2	K		C
54=KA	A.*RE.SA.NA + C1		TEZ2	a-ka-sa-no	K	N	C
54=KU	A.*RE.DA.I	* C1	29.5	a-ku-do-i	K	P	CX
54=MA	KI.*RE.TA_2	C2	129.1,85b1	ki-ma-to	K	N	C
54=MA	KI.*RE.TA_2	C2	129.1,85b1	ki-ma-ta	K	N	C
54=NE	TE.JA.*RE	* C1	117a5	te-ja-ne	+		C
54=NI	PA.JA.*RE	C2B2	8b4,88.4,29.2,	pa-ja-ni	+		C
54=NI	PA.JA.*RE	C2B2	8b4,88.4,29.2,	pa-ja-ni-jo	K		C
54=PA	KA.*RE.RO	C1	HTW203(CRIV18)	ka-pa-ri-jo	K	N	C
54=PO	U.*RE.WI	C1	25a2	u-po-we	K		C
54=PTE	RA.*RE.RA	C1	HTW206b(CRIV8)	ra-pte-re	PK	Q	C
54=RA	KA.*RE.RO	C1	HTW203(CRIV18)	ka-ra-re-we	PK		C
54=RA_2	QA.*RE.TO	C1	132.1,111a1?	qa-ra_2-ti-jo	K	N	C
54=RI	KI.*RE.TA_2	C2	129.1,85b1	ki-ri-ta	K		C
54=RI	KI.*RE.TA_2	C2	129.1,85b1	ki-ri-te-wi-ja	PK	Q	C
54=RO	TE.JA.*RE	* C1	117a5	te-ja-ro	K	N	CX
54=RO	PA.JA.*RE	C2B2	8b4,88.4,29.2,	pa-ja-ro	K	N	C
54=SA	KA.*RE.RO	C1	HTW203(CRIV18)	ka-sa-ro	K		C
54=SO	PA.JA.*RE	C2B2	8b4,88.4,29.2,	pa-ja-so	K	N	C
54=TA	KA.*RE.RO	C1	HTW203(CRIV18)	ka-ta-ra-i	K	P	C
54=TA	KA.*RE.RO	C1	HTW203(CRIV18)	ka-ta-ra	+		C
54=TA	KA.*RE.RO	C1	HTW203(CRIV18)	ka-ta-ro	MK		C
54=TA_2	KA.*RE.RO	C1	HTW203(CRIV18)	ka-ta_2-ro	+		C
54=TO	KA.*RE.RO	C1	HTW203(CRIV18)	ka-to-ro	K	N	C
54=WA	KA.*RE.RO	C1	HTW203(CRIV18)	ka-wa-ro	K	N	C
55=DE	A.KA.*RU	C2	2.1,86a1,86b1?	a-ka-de	K	N	C
55=I	A.KA.*RU	C2	2.1,86a1,86b1?	a-ka-i-jo	K	N	C
55=KA	*RU.MA.TA	C1B1	99b2,29.1	ka-ma-to	+		C
55=KE	*RU.MA.TA	C1B1	99b2,29.1	ke-ma-ta	K		C
55=KI	*RU.MA.TA	C1B1	99b2,29.1	ki-ma-to	K	N	C
55=KI	*RU.MA.TA	C1B1	99b2,29.1	ki-ma-ta	K	N	C

Appendix C

Hypoth.	Linear A		Code	Reference	Linear B	Code		
55=KU	A.*RU.DA.RA		C1	28b5,62.1?	a-ku-di-ri-jo	K	N	C
55=NO	KA.SA.*RU		C1	10b3	ka-sa-no	K	N	C
55=PA₃	A.*RU.DA.RA		C1	28b5,62.1?	a-pa₃-da-ro	K	N	CX
55=RE	A.KA.*RU		C2	2.1,86a1,86b1?	a-ka-re-u	PK	N	C
55=RO	A.*RU.DA.RA		C1	28b5,62.1?	a-ro-do-ro-o	K	GPN	C
55=RO	QA.QA.*RU		C3A1	93a4,118.2,122b3,	qa-qa-ro	K	N	C
55=RO	KA.SA.*RU		C1	10b3	ka-sa-ro	K		C
55=RU	KU.*RU.KU		C1	87.4	ku-ru-ka	K	N	C
55=SA	*RU.MA.TA		C1B1	99b2,29.1	sa-ma-ti-ja	K	N	C
55=TA	A.KA.*RU		C2	2.1,86a1,86b1?	a-ka-ta-jo	PK	N	C
55=TO	A.KA.*RU		C2	2.1,86a1,86b1?	a-ka-to	K	N	C
55=TO	A.KA.*RU		C2	2.1,86a1,86b1?	a-ka-to-wa	K	N	C
55=TO	KA.SA.*RU		C1	10b3	ka-sa-to	MPK	N	C
55=TU	DU.*RU.WI		C1	25a4	du-tu-wa	+		C
55=WI	A.KA.*RU		C2	2.1,86a1,86b1?	a-ka-wi-ja-de	K	PN	C
55=WO	A.KA.*RU		C2	2.1,86a1,86b1?	a-ka-wo	PK	N	C
56=A₃	*PI.TE.RI	*	C1	PKZ11b(I4)	a₃-te-re	K		C
56=A₃	*PI.TA.JA		C1	6a2	a₃-ta-jo	K	N	C
56=A₃	*PI.TA.RA	*	C1	96a4	a₃-ta-ro-we	PK	N	C
56=DA	A.RA.*PI	#	C1	87.5	a-ra-da-jo	K	N	C
56=DI	*PI.TA.KA.SE		C1	21.1	di-ta-ka-so	K	N	C
56=DI	*PI.TA.KE.SI		C1	87.2	di-ta-ka-so	K	N	C
56=I	*PI.TA.JA		C1	6a2	i-ta-ja	K	N	C
56=KA	*PI.TA.RA	*	C1	96a4	ka-ta-ra	+		C
56=KA	A.RA.*PI	#	C1	87.5	a-ra-ka-jo	K	N	C
56=KA	*PI.TA.RA	*	C1	96a4	ka-ta-ra-i	K	P	C
56=KA	*PI.TA.RA	*	C1	96a4	ka-ta-ro	MK		C
56=KO	A.RA.*PI	#	C1	87.5	a-ra-ko	K	N	C
56=KU	*PI.TE.RI	*	C1	PKZ11b(I4)	ku-te-ro	K	N	C
56=O	*PI.TA.RA	*	C1	96a4	o-ta-re-wo	K	N	C
56=PA	*PI.TA.JA		C1	6a2	pa-ta-ja	K		C
56=PE	*PI.TE.RI	*	C1	PKZ11b(I4)	pe-te-re-wa	K		C
56=PU	*PI.TA.RA	*	C1	96a4	pu-ta-ri-ja	K		C
56=PU	*PI.TE.RI	*	C1	PKZ11b(I4)	pu-te-ri-ja	K		C
56=PU₂	*PI.TE.RI	*	C1	PKZ11b(I4)	pu₂-te-re	PK	Q	C
56=QI	*PI.TA.RA	*	C1	96a4	qi-ta-ro	K	N	C
56=QO	*PI.TE.RI	*	C1	PKZ11b(I4)	qo-te-ro	PK	N	C
56=RU	A.RA.*PI	#	C1	87.5	a-ra-ru-ja	K		C
56=RU	A.RA.*PI	#	C1	87.5	a-ra-ru-wo-a	K		C
56=SI	A.RA.*PI	#	C1	87.5	a-ra-si-jo	K	N	C
56=SI	*PI.TA.RA	*	C1	96a4	si-ta-ro	K	N	C
56=TA	*PI.TA.RA	*	C1	96a4	ta-ta-ro	+		C
56=U	*PI.TA.JA		C1	6a2	u-ta-jo-jo	K	N	C

Hypoth.	Linear A	Code	Reference	Linear B	Code		
56=U	*PI.TA.JA	C1	6a2	u-ta-jo	K		C
57=A	*SI.KI.RA	C1	8a4	a-ki-re-u	K	N	C
57=A	*SI.KI.RA	C1	8a4	a-ki-ri-ja	+		C
57=A$_3$	*SI.KI.NE	* C1	116a5	a$_3$-ki-no-o	K		C
57=DA	*SI.DA.RE	C2	17.3,122a5,49a4?	da-da-re-jo-de	K	P	C
57=DI	*SI.KI.NE	* C1	116a5	di-ki-nu-wo	K	N	C
57=E	*SI.KI.NE	* C1	116a5	e-ki-no	K	N	C
57=E	*SI.MI.TA	C1	96a2	e-mi-to	+		C
57=JO	DA.NA.*SI	C1	126a1	da-na-jo	K	N	C
57=KI	*SI.DA.RE	C2	17.3,122a5,49a4?	ki-da-ro	K	N	C
57=MO	DA.NA.*SI	C1	126a1	da-na-mo	K		C
57=NO	*SI.DA.RE	C2	17.3,122a5,49a4?	no-da-ro	K	N	C
57=O	*SI.DA.RE	C2	17.3,122a5,49a4?	o-da-ra-o	K		C
57=PI	*SI.KI.NE	* C1	116a5	pi-ki-nu-wo	K	N	C
57=QA	*SI.DA.RE	C2	17.3,122a5,49a4?	qa-da-ro	K	N	C
57=SA	MA.*SI.DU	C1	43.1	ma-sa-de	K	P	C
57=SI	MA.*SI.DU	C1	43.1	ma-si-dwo	K		C
57=SI	*SI.KI.RA	C1	8a4	si-ki-ro	+		C
57=SI	*SI.MI.TA	C1	96a2	si-mi-te-u	+		C
57=TI	*SI.MI.TA	C1	96a2	ti-mi-to	K		C
57=TO	*SI.TU.NE	* C1	HTW221a(CRV4)	to-tu-no	K	N	C
57=TU	*SI.DA.RE	C2	17.3,122a5,49a4?	tu-da-ra	K	N	C
57=WE	PA.*SI.A	* C1	45b3	pa-we-a	K		C
57=ZA	*SI.KI.RA	C1	8a4	za-ki-ri-jo	K	N	C
58=RA$_2$	QA.*RA$_2$.WA	C1	86a3	qa-ra$_2$-wo	K	N	C
58=RO	A.SA.*RA$_2$	* C1	89.1	a-sa-ro	K	N	C
58=WA	U.*RA$_2$.TI	* C1	108.3	u-wa-ta	PK	N	C
59=*64	A.*SU.JA	C1	11a3	a-*64-jo	PK	N	C
59=DI	A.*SU.JA	C1	11a3	a-di-je-wo	K	N	C
59=MO	*SU.NI.KA	C2	HTW204a(CRIV2),	mo-ni-ko	K	N	C
59=NI	A.*SU.JA	C1	11a3	a-ni-ja	PK		C
59=PO	*SU.NI.KA	C2	HTW204a(CRIV2),	po-ni-ki-ja	K		C
59=PO	*SU.NI.KA	C2	HTW204a(CRIV2),	po-ni-ke-a	K		C
59=QA	*SU.NI.KA	C2	HTW204a(CRIV2),	qa-ni-ko	K	N	C
59=RE	A.*SU.JA	C1	11a3	a-re-jo	K	N	C
59=RI	A.*SU.JA	C1	11a3	a-ri-ja-wo	K	N	C
59=RO$_2$	A.*SU.JA	C1	11a3	a-ro$_2$-jo	K		C
59=SA	DU.*SU.NI	C1	108.2	du-sa-ni	K	N	C
59=TA	KU.NI.*SU	C4	10a1,86a1,95a3,	ku-ni-ta	K	Q	C
59=TE	A.*SU.JA	C1	11a3	a-te-jo	K	QN	C
59=TI	A.*SU.JA	C1	11a3	a-ti-jo	K	N	C
60=KA	KU.*NI.SU	C4	10a1,86a1,95a3,	ku-ka-so	K	N	C
60=KE	KU.*NI.SU	C4	10a1,86a1,95a3,	ku-ke-so	K	N	C

Appendix C

Hypoth.	Linear A	Code	Reference	Linear B	Code		
60=MI	TI.*NI.TA	C1	27a1	*ti-mi-to*	K		C
60=MI	KU.*NI.SU	C4	10a1,86a1,95a3,	*ku-mi-so*	K	N	C
60=NI	KU.DO.*NI	C2	13.4,85a4	*ku-do-ni-ja*	K	P	C
60=PA	KU.*NI.SU	C4	10a1,86a1,95a3,	*ku-pa-sa*	K	P	C
60=RI	TI.*NI.TA	C1	27a1	*ti-ri-ti-jo*	K	E	C
60=RI	TI.*NI.TA	C1	27a1	*ti-ri-to*	K	P	C
60=RU	KU.*NI.SU	C4	10a1,86a1,95a3,	*ku-ru-so*	PK		C
60=TA	KU.*NI.SU	C4	10a1,86a1,95a3,	*ku-ta-si-jo*	K	N	C
60=WA	TI.*NI.TA	C1	27a1	*ti-wa-ti-ja*	K	EN	C
61=DA	*NE.MI.NA	C1A1	115a3,135a1	*da-mi-ni-jo*	PK	EP	C
61=JA	PA.RA.*NE	C2	115a4,115b1,	*pa-ra-ja*	PK		C
61=JA	PA.TA.*NE	C2	94b1,122a6	*pa-ta-ja*	K		C
61=KU	PA.RA.*NE	C2	115a4,115b1,	*pa-ra-ku-ja*	K		C
61=PO	*NE.MI.NA	C1A1	115a3,135a1	*po-mi-ni-jo*	K	N	C
61=RO	SI.KI.*NE	* C1	116a5	*si-ki-ro*	+		C
61=TI	PA.TA.*NE	C2	94b1,122a6	*pa-ta-ti-jo*	K		C
61=TI	PA.RA.*NE	C2	115a4,115b1,	*pa-ra-ti-jo*	K	N	C
61=TO	SI.KI.*NE	* C1	116a5	*si-ki-to*	K	N	C
61=TO	PA.RA.*NE	C2	115a4,115b1,	*pa-ra-to*	K	N	C
61=U	PA.RA.*NE	C2	115a4,115b1,	*pa-ra-u-jo*	K	N	C
61=WA	PA.RA.*NE	C2	115a4,115b1,	*pa-ra-wa-jo*	PK		C
62=A	*QA.NU.MA	* C1	116a6	*a-nu-mo*	K	N	C
62=A	*QA.KU.RE	* C1	HTW217a1(CRIV4)	*a-ku-ri-jo*	K	N	C
62=A	*QA.RE.TO	C1	132.1,111a1?	*a-re-ta$_2$*	K		C
62=A	*QA.RE.TO	C1	132.1,111a1?	*a-re-ta-wo*	K	N	C
62−DA	*QA.*QA.RU	C3A1	93A4,118.2,122B3	*da-da-re-jo-de*	K	P	C
62=DI	*QA.*QA.RU	C3A1	93a4,118.2,122b3,	*di-qa-ra*	K	N	C
62=E	*QA.RE.TO	C1	132.1,111A1?	*e-re-ta*	PK	Q	C
62=KA	*QA.*QA.RU	C3A1	93A4,118.2,122B3	*ka-ka-re-a$_2$*	K		C
62=KO	*QA.KU.RE	* C1	HTW217a1(CRIV4)	*ko-ku-ro*	K	N	C
62=KO	*QA.RE.TO	C1	132.1,111a1?	*ko-re-te*	PK	Q	C
62=O	*QA.RE.TO	C1	132.1,111a1?	*o-re-te-wo*	K	QN	C
62=PA	*QA.*QA.RU	C3A1	93A4,118.2,122B3	*pa-pa-ro*	PK	N	C
62=QA	*QA.RA$_2$.WA	C1	86a3	*qa-ra$_2$-wo*	K	N	C
62=QA	*QA.*QA.RU	C3A1	93a4,118.2,122b3,	*qa-qa-ro*	K	N	C
62=TE	*QA.RE.TO	C1	132.1,111a1?	*te-re-ta*	PK	Q	C
62=WE	*QA.*QA.RU	C3A1	93A4,118.2,122B3	*we-we-ro*	K	N	C
63=DA	KI.*63.RE	C1	37.4	*ki-da-ro*	K	N	C
63=DO	KI.*63.RE	C1	37.4	*ki-do-ro*	K		C
63=KE	KI.*63.RE	C1	37.4	*ki-ke-ro*	K	N	C
63=U	KI.*63.RE	C1	37.4	*ki-u-ro*	K	N	C
65=KA	A.*65.TE	C1	96a2	*a-ka-to*	K	N	C
65=KA	A.*65.TE	C1	96a2	*a-ka-ta-jo*	PK	N	C

Hypoth.	Linear A	Code	Reference	Linear B	Code		
65=KE	A.*65.TE	C1	96a2	a-ke-ta	PK	N	C
65=KO	A.*65.TE	C1	96a2	a-ko-to	K	N	C
65=MO	A.*65.TE	C1	96a2	a-mo-te	K		C
65=MO	A.*65.TE	C1	96a2	a-mo-ta	PK		C
65=NA	A.*65.TE	C1	96a2	a-na-ta	K		C
65=NA	A.*65.TE	C1	96a2	a-na-to	K		C
65=NE	A.*65.TE	C1	96a2	a-ne-te-wa	K	N	C
65=NU	A.*65.TE	C1	96a2	a-nu-to-jo	K	N	C
65=NU	A.*65.TE	C1	96a2	a-nu-to	TK	N	C
65=PA	A.*65.TE	C1	96a2	a-pa-ta-wa	K	P	C
65=PO	A.*65.TE	C1	96a2	a-po-te	K		C
65=QA	A.*65.TE	C1	96a2	a-qa-to	K	N	C
65=QO	A.*65.TE	C1	96a2	a-qo-ta	K		C
65=RE	A.*65.TE	C1	96a2	a-re-ta$_2$	K		C
65=RE	A.*65.TE	C1	96a2	a-re-ta-wo	K	N	C
65=WO	A.*65.TE	C1	96a2	a-wo-ti-jo	K	N	C
65=ZE	A.*65.TE	C1	96a2	a-ze-ta	K	N	C
65=ZE	A.*65.TE	C1	96a2	a-ze-to	K		C
68=*22	DA.*68.TE	C1	34.1	da-*22-to	EK	P	C
68=*22	DA.*68.TE	C1	34.1	da-*22-ti-jo	K	E	C
68=*49	TU.*68.MA	* C1	117a3	tu-*49-mi	K	N	C
68=DA	A.RA.*68	C1	122b3,87.5?,	a-ra-da-jo	K	N	C
68=KA	A.RA.*68	C1	122b3,87.5?,	a-ra-ka-jo	K	N	C
68=KO	A.RA.*68	C1	122b3,87.5?,	a-ra-ko	K	N	C
68=O	DA.*68.TE	C1	34.1	da-o-ta	K	N	C
68=RU	A.RA.*68	C1	122b3,87.5?,	a-ra-ru-ja	K		C
68=RU	A.RA.*68	C1	122b3,87.5?,	a-ra-ru-wo-a	K		C
68=SI	A.RA.*68	C1	122b3,87.5?,	a-ra-si-jo	K	N	C
69=RI	PI.*69.TE	C1	116a4	pi-ri-to-jo	+		C
69=RI	PI.*69.TE	C1	116a4	pi-ri-te	+		C
69=RI	PI.*69.TE	C1	116a4	pi-ri-to-wo	K	N	C
69=WA	U.*69.SI	C2	15.1,140.1	u-wa-si-jo	K	N	C
72=A	*RI.MI.SI	C1	119.2	a-mi-si-ja	K		C
72=A	*RI.TE.I.JA	* C1	HTZ158b(II7)	a-te-i-ja-ta	K	N	C
72=DI	A.*RI.NI.TA	C1	25a3	a-di-nwa-ta	K	N	C
72=KA	*RI.TA.MA	C1	115a1	ka-ta-mi-jo	K	E	CX
72=KU	*RI.MI.SI	C1	119.2	ku-mi-so	K	N	C
72=MA	KI.*RI.TA$_2$	C2	114a1,121.1	ki-ma-ta	K	N	C
72=MA	KI.*RI.TA$_2$	C2	114a1,121.1	ki-ma-to	K	N	C
72=QA	*RI.MI.SI	C1	119.2	qa-mi-si-jo	K	N	C
72=RI	KI.*RI.TA$_2$	C2	114a1,121.1	ki-ri-te-wi-ja-i	K	Q	C
72=RI	KI.*RI.TA$_2$	C2	114a1,121.1	ki-ri-te-wi-ja	PK	Q	C
72=RI	KI.*RI.TA$_2$	C2	114a1,121.1	ki-ri-ta-i	K		C

Appendix C

Hypoth.	Linear A	Code	Reference	Linear B	Code		
72=RI	KI.*RI.TA$_2$	C2	114a1,121.1	ki-ri-ta	K		C
72=TI	*RI.TA.MA	C1	115a1	ti-ta-ma	K		C
72=WO	I.SA.*RI	C1	PH6.4(IV16)	i-sa-wo	K	N	C
74=A	*TA.NA.TI	C3A1	7a4,10b4,98a2,	a-na-ta	K		C
74=A	*TA.NA.TI	C3A1	7a4,10b4,98a2,	a-na-to	K		C
74=DA	DA.*TA.RE	C2	88.5,62.2*	da-da-re-jo-de	K	P	C
74=DA	DA.*TA.RA	C1	6a1	da-da-re-jo-de	K	P	C
74=DI	PI.*TA.JA	C1	6a2	pi-di-jo	K	Q	C
74=DO	U.*TA.RO *	C1	116a1	u-do-ro	PK		C
74=DO	SI.MI.*TA	C1	96a2	si-mi-do	+		C
74=DU	U.*TA.RO *	C1	116a1	u-du-ru-wo	K	P	C
74=I	DA.*TA.RA	C1	6a1	da-i-ra	K		C
74=I	DA.*TA.RE	C2	88.5,62.2*	da-i-ra	K		C
74=JA	DA.*TA.RE	C2	88.5,62.2*	da-ja-ro	K		C
74=JA	PA.*TA.NE	C2	94b1,122a6	pa-ja-ni-jo	K		C
74=JA	DA.*TA.RA	C1	6a1	da-ja-ro	K		C
74=JA	PA.*TA.NE	C2	94b1,122a6	pa-ja-ni	+		C
74=KA	PA.*TA.NE	C2	94b1,122a6	pa-ka-na	K		C
74=KA	A.*TA.I *	C1	PRZ1b(I17)	a-ka-i-jo	K	N	C
74=MU	TI.*TA.NA	C1	HTW220(CRV5)	ti-mu-nu-we	K	N	C
74=NO	RU.MA.*TA	C1B1	99b2,29.1	ru-ma-no	K	N	C
74=PA	U.*TA.RO *	C1	116a1	u-pa-ra	K	N	C
74=PA	KI.DA.*TA	C1	40.2	ki-da-pa	K	P	C
74=PI	U.*TA.RO *	C1	116a1	u-pi-ri-jo	K		CX
74=PO	I.*TA.NU	C1	28b6	i-po-no	K		C
74=PU	*TA.NA.TI	C3A1	7a4,10b4,98a2,	pu-na-to	K	N	C
74=PU$_2$	DA.*TA.RE	C2	88.5,62.2*	da-pu$_2$-ra	K	N	CX
74=PU$_2$	DA.*TA.RA	C1	6a1	da-pu$_2$-ra	K	N	CX
74=RA$_2$	KI.*TA.I	C1	123a1	ki-ra$_2$-i-jo	K	N	C
74=RE	A.*TA.I *	C1	PRZ1b(I17)	a-re-i-jo	PK	QN	C
74=RI	PI.*TA.JA	C1	6a2	pi-ri-je	K		C
74=RO	KI.DA.*TA	C1	40.2	ki-da-ro	K	N	C
74=TA	*TA.NA.TI	C3A1	7a4,10b4,98a2,	ta-na-to	K	N	C
74=TE	SI.MI.*TA	C1	96a2	si-mi-te-u	+		C
74=TE	A.*TA.I *	C1	PRZ1b(I17)	a-te-i-ja-ta	K	N	C
74=TO	*TA.NA.TI	C3A1	7a4,10b4,98a2,	to-na-ta	K	N	C
74=TO	DA.*TA.RA	C1	6a1	da-to-ro	K	N	C
74=TO	DA.*TA.RE	C2	88.5,62.2*	da-to-ro	K	N	C
74=WA	*TA.NA.TI	C3A1	7a4,10b4,98a2,	wa-na-ta-jo	PK	N	C
74=WE	DA.*TA.RE	C2	88.5,62.2*	da-we-ro	K	QN	C
74=WE	DA.*TA.RA	C1	6a1	da-we-ro	K	QN	C
74=WI	PA.*TA.NE	C2	94b1,122a6	pa-wi-no	K	N	C
74=WI	*TA.NA.TI	C3A1	7a4,10b4,98a2,	wi-na-to	K	PN	C

Minoan Linear A

Hypoth.	Linear A		Code	Reference	Linear B	Code		
74=WO	I.KU.*TA	*	C1	35.1	i-ku-wo-i-pi	K		C
74=ZA	PI.*TA.RA	*	C1	96a4	pi-za-ra	K		C
75=RO	QA.RA$_2$.*WA		C1	86a3	qa-ra$_2$-ro	K	N	C
75=TI	QA.RA$_2$.*WA		C1	86a3	qa-ra$_2$-ti-jo	K	N	C
75=WO	QA.RA$_2$.*WA		C1	86a3	qa-ra$_2$-wo	K	N	C
76=A	*MI.NU.TE		C4	86a5,95a2,95b2,	a-nu-to-jo	K	N	C
76=A	*MI.NU.TE		C4	86a5,95a2,95b2,	a-nu-to	TK	N	C
76=KA	*MI.DA.NI	*	C1	41.4	ka-da-no	K	N	C
76=KI	SI.*MI.TA		C1	96a2	si-ki-to	K	N	C
76=MI	SI.*MI.TA		C1	96a2	si-mi-te-u	+		C
76=MI	DA.*MI.NU		C1	117a8	da-mi-ni-jo	PK	EP	C
76=NI	SI.*MI.TA		C1	96a2	si-ni-to	K	N	C
76=TE	DA.*MI.NU		C1	117a8	da-te-ne-ja	K	N	C
76=U	DA.*MI.NU		C1	117a8	da-u-no	K	N	CX
76=WA	DA.*MI.NU		C1	117a8	da-wa-no	K	N	C
76=WI	RI.*MI.SI		C1	119.2	ri-wi-so	K	N	C
77=*64	A.*SE.JA		C1	115a4	a-*64-jo	PK	N	C
77=DI	A.*SE.JA		C1	115a4	a-di-je-wo	K	N	C
77=DI	PA.*SE.JA		C3	93a8,	pa-di-jo	K	N	C
77=JO	RA.TI.*SE		C1	6b2	ra-ti-jo	K	E	C
77=NI	A.*SE.JA		C1	115a4	a-ni-ja	PK		C
77=NU	DI.KI.*SE		C2	87.3,117b2	di-ki-nu-wo	K	N	C
77=PO	*SE.KU.TU		C1	115a3	po-ku-ta	PK	Q	C
77=RA	PA.*SE.JA		C3	93a8,	pa-ra-ja	PK		C
77=RE	A.*SE.JA		C1	115a4	a-re-jo	K	N	C
77=RI	A.*SE.JA		C1	115a4	a-ri-ja-wo	K	N	C
77=RO$_2$	A.*SE.JA		C1	115a4	a-ro$_2$-jo	K		C
77=SA	PA.*SE.JA		C3	93a8,	pa-sa-ja	K		C
77=TA	PA.*SE.JA		C3	93a8,	pa-ta-ja	K		C
77=TE	A.*SE.JA		C1	115a4	a-te-jo	K	QN	C
77=TI	A.*SE.JA		C1	115a4	a-ti-jo	K	N	C
78=A	*TI.TA.NA		C1	HTW220(CRV5)	a-ta-no	K	N	C
78=AU	*TI.TA.NA		C1	HTW220(CRV5)	au-ta-na	+		C
78=DE	*TI.*TI.KU		C2	35a1,ZAZ3.2#	de-de-ko-wo	K		CX
78=KA	*TI.NI.TA		C1	27a1	ka-ni-to	K		C
78=KA	*TI.TA.NA		C1	HTW220(CRV5)	ka-ta-no	PK	N	C
78=KA	*TI.TA.NA		C1	HTW220(CRV5)	ka-ta-ni-ja	K		CX
78=KI	*TI.TA.NA		C1	HTW220(CRV5)	ki-ta-no	K		C
78=KU	*TI.NI.TA		C1	27a1	ku-ni-ta	K	Q	C
78=NA	A.*TI.KI.TA.A		C1	TYZ4	a-na-ki-ti	K	N	C
78=O	*TI.DA.TA	*	C1	123b2	o-da-tu-we-ta	K		C
78=RA	A.*TI.KI.TA.A		C1	TYZ4	a-ra-ka-te-ja	K	Q	C
78=RU	*TI.DA.TA	*	C1	123b2	ru-da-to	+		C

Appendix C

Hypoth.	Linear A	Code	Reference	Linear B	Code		
78=SA	*TI.MA.RU.WI.TE	C1	PU1.1	sa-ma-ri-wa-ta	K	N	C
78=SE	KA.NU.*TI	C1	97a3	ka-nu-se-u	K	N	C
78=SI	*TI.NI.TA	C1	27a1	si-ni-to	K	N	C
78=TO	TA.NA.*TI	C3A1	7a4,10b4,98a2,	ta-na-to	K	N	C
78=U	*TI.TA.NA	C1	HTW220(CRV5)	u-ta-no	K	P	C
78=U	*TI.TA.NA	C1	HTW220(CRV5)	u-ta-ni-jo	K	E	C
78=U	*TI.TA.NA	C1	HTW220(CRV5)	u-ta-no	K	N	C
78=WA	*TI.DU.NI	C1	49a4	wa-du-na	K	N	C
78=WA	*TI.*TI.KU	C2	35A1,ZAZ3.2#	wa-wa-ka	K	Q	C
79=TO	*79.TU.NE	C3	7b1,87.1,117b1	to-tu-no	K	N	C
80=A	*80.TE.JA *	C1	PK1.4(IV5)	a-te-jo	K	QN	C
80=E	*80.TE.JA *	C1	PK1.4(IV5)	e-te-jo	+		C
80=PO	*80.TI.NI *	C1	93a6	po-ti-ni-ja	MPK	G	C
80=TO	*80.TE.JA *	C1	PK1.4(IV5)	to-te-ja	K	Q	C
85=RO	I.QA.*85	C2	44b1,131.2	i-qa-ro	+		C
86=TA	KI.RI.*TA₂	C2	114a1,121.1	ki-ri-ta	K		C
86=TE	KI.RI.*TA₂	C2	114a1,121.1	ki-ri-te-wi-ja	PK	Q	C
91=A	*QE.KU.RE	C1	20.2	a-ku-ri-jo	K	N	C
91=DA	DA.*QE.RA	C2B1	6a6,120.1,57a1	da-da-re-jo-de	K	P	C
91=DE	*QE.DE.MI.NU	C2	MA1a(IV10),	de-de-me-na	K		C
91=I	DA.*QE.RA	C2B1	6a6,120.1,57a1	da-i-ra	K		C
91=JA	PA.TA.*QE	C1	31.6	pa-ta-ja	K		C
91=JA	DA.*QE.RA	C2B1	6a6,120.1,57a1	da-ja-ro	K		C
91=KA	TU.*QE.NU	C1	25a3	tu-ka-na	K	N	C
91=KO	*QE.KU.RE	C1	20.2	ko-ku-ro	K	N	C
91=KU	*QE.SU.PU	C1	87.4	ku-su-pa	K		C
91=NA	TU.*QE.NU	C1	25a3	tu-na-no	K		C
91=PU₂	DA.*QE.RA	C2B1	6a6,120.1,57a1	da-pu₂-ra	K	N	CX
91=RI	KA.PA.*QE	C1	6a4	ka-pa-ri-jo	K	N	C
91=SO	KA.PA.*QE	C1	6a4	ka-pa-so	+		C
91=TI	PA.TA.*QE	C1	31.6	pa-ta-ti-jo	K		C
91=TO	DA.*QE.RA	C2B1	6a6,120.1,57a1	da-to-ro	K	N	C
91=TO	*QE.TU.NE	C1	12.3	to-tu-no	K	N	C
91=WE	DA.*QE.RA	C2B1	6a6,120.1,57a1	da-we-ro	K	QN	C
91=WI	TU.*QE.NU	C1	25a3	tu-wi-no	K		C
92=*22	*TE.JA.RE *	C1	117a5	*22-ja-ro	K		CX
92=DA	*TE.JA.RE *	C1	117a5	da-ja-ro	K		C
92=DI	I.JA.*TE	C1	PHZ4(II12)	i-ja-di	K		CX
92=KU	*TE.JA.RE *	C1	117a5	ku-ja-ro	K	N	C
92=MI	*TE.JA.RE *	C1	117a5	mi-ja-ro	K	N	C
92=PA	*TE.JA.RE *	C1	117a5	pa-ja-ro	K	N	C
92=QO	*TE.JA.RE *	C1	117a5	qo-ja-ro	K		CX
92=TE	*TE.JA.RE *	C1	117a5	te-ja-ro	K	N	CX

Hypoth.	Linear A	Code	Reference	Linear B	Code		
92=ZA	PI.*TE.RI	* C1	PKZ11b(I4)	*pi-za-ra*	K		C
93=A	*DU.PA₃.NA	C1	115b2	*a-pa₃-no*	K	N	C
93=DWO	MA.SI.*DU	C1	43.1	*ma-si-dwo*	K		C
93=KA	*DU.PA₃.NA	C1	115b2	*ka-pa₃-no*	K	N	C
93=KE	I.*DU.TI	* C1	104.2	*i-ke-ta*	K	N	C
93=KO	*DU.RU.WI	C1	25a4	*ko-ru-we-ja*	K		C
93=KU	I.*DU.WI	* C1	MA1a(IV10)	*i-ku-wo-i-pi*	K		C
93=MU	TI.*DU.NI	C1	49a4	*ti-mu-nu-we*	K	N	C
93=NO	A.*DU.ZA	* C1	PK1.2(IV5)	*a-no-zo-jo*	K	N	C
93=PE	I.*DU.TI	* C1	104.2	*i-pe-ta*	+		C
93=RA	I.*DU.TI	* C1	104.2	*i-ra-ta*	PK	N	C
93=RO	I.*DU.TI	* C1	104.2	*i-ro-to*	K	N	C
93=RO	A.*DU.ZA	* C1	PK1.2(IV5)	*a-ro-za*	+		C
93=RO	A.*DU.ZA	* C1	PK1.2(IV5)	*a-ro-zo*	K		C
93=SA	I.*DU.WI	* C1	MA1a(IV10)	*i-sa-wo*	K	N	C
93=TA	A.*DU.ZA	* C1	PK1.2(IV5)	*a-ta-ze-u*	K	N	C
94=JA	TA.*WE.NA	C1	10b1	*ta-ja-no*	+		C
94=KI	DI.*WE.NA	C2	93a1,102.3	*di-ki-nu-wo*	K	N	C
94=MI	A.*WE.SU	C1	118.3	*a-mi-si-ja*	K		C
94=PA	TA.*WE.NA	C1	10b1	*ta-pa-no*	K		C
94=RA	TA.*WE.NA	C1	10b1	*ta-ra-nu*	PK		C
94=RA	A.*WE.SU	C1	118.3	*a-ra-si-jo*	K	N	C
94=WA	A.*WE.SU	C1	118.3	*a-wa-so*	K	N	C
95=DA	RU.*MA.TA	C1B1	99b2,29.1	*ru-da-to*	+		C
95=KA	KU.RU.*MA	* C1	115b3	*ku-ru-ka*	K	N	C
95=KA	SA.*MA.RO	C1A1	88.4,39.3*	*sa-ka-ri-jo*	K	N	C
95=KI	RU.*MA.TA	C1B1	99b2,29.1	*ru-ki-to*	K	P	C
95=KI	RU.*MA.TA	C1B1	99b2,29.1	*ru-ki-ti-ja*	K	EN	C
95=MA	SA.*MA.RO	C1A1	88.4,39.3*	*sa-ma-ri-jo*	K	N	C
95=MA	*MA.SI.DU	C1	43.1	*ma-si-dwo*	K		C
95=NO	KU.RU.*MA	* C1	115b3	*ku-ru-no*	+		C
95=O	*MA.DA.TI	* C1	PK1.7(IV5)	*o-da-tu-we-ta*	K		C
95=QA	SA.*MA.RO	C1A1	88.4,39.3*	*sa-qa-re-jo*	K	QN	C
95=RA	I.DA.*MA.TE	C2	ARZ1(V17III),	*i-da-ra-ta*	K		C
95=RU	*MA.DA.TI	* C1	PK1.7(IV5)	*ru-da-to*	+		C
95=SO	KU.RU.*MA	* C1	115b3	*ku-ru-so*	PK		C
95=U	SA.*MA.RO	C1A1	88.4,39.3*	*sa-u-ri-jo*	K	N	C
95=ZA	SA.*MA.RO	C1A1	88.4,39.3*	*sa-za-ro*	+		C
95=ZE	SA.*MA.RO	C1A1	88.4,39.3*	*sa-ze-ro*	K	N	C
96=A₃	*96.KI.TA	C1	29.4	*a₃-ki-ta*	K	N	C
96=DA	A.RA.*96	* C1	109.4	*a-ra-da-jo*	K	N	C
96=DE	DE.*96.KU	C1	93a6	*de-de-ko-wo*	K		CX
96=KA	A.RA.*96	* C1	109.4	*a-ra-ka-jo*	K	N	C

Appendix C

Hypoth.	Linear A		Code	Reference	Linear B	Code		
96=KO	A.RA.*96	*	C1	109.4	a-ra-ko	K	N	C
96=ME	*96.KI.TA		C1	29.4	me-ki-ti	+		C
96=PO	*96.KI.TA		C1	29.4	po-ki-te	K	N	C
96=RU	A.RA.*96	*	C1	109.4	a-ra-ru-ja	K		C
96=RU	*96.KI.TA		C1	29.4	ru-ki-ti-ja	K	EN	C
96=RU	*96.KI.TA		C1	29.4	ru-ki-to	K	P	C
96=RU	A.RA.*96	*	C1	109.4	a-ra-ru-wo-ja	PK		C
96=SI	*96.KI.TA		C1	29.4	si-ki-to	K	N	C
96=SI	A.RA.*96	*	C1	109.4	a-ra-si-jo	K	N	C
96=U	DE.*96.KU		C1	93a6	de-u-ki-jo-jo	K		C
96=WE	KU.RE.*96		C1A1	117b1,39.2	ku-re-we	PK	QE	C
97=A	*U.MI.NA.SI		C2	28a1,117a1	a-mi-ni-so	PK	P	C
97=A	*U.MI.NA.SI		C2	28a1,117a1	a-mi-ni-si-ja	K	E	C
97=A₃	*U.TA.RO	*	C1	116a1	a₃-ta-ro-we	PK	N	C
97=DO	*U.RE.WI		C1	25a2	do-re-we	K	N	C
97=KA	*U.TA.RO	*	C1	116a1	ka-ta-ro	MK		C
97=KA	*U.TA.RO	*	C1	116a1	ka-ta-ra-i	K	P	C
97=KA	*U.TA.RO	*	C1	116a1	ka-ta-ra	+		C
97=KE	*U.RE.WI		C1	25a2	ke-re-wa	K		C
97=KO	*U.RE.WI		C1	25a2	ko-re-wo	K	N	C
97=KO	KA.*U.DE.TA		C1	13.1	ka-ko-de-ta	K		C
97=KU	*U.RE.WI		C1	25a2	ku-re-we	PK	QE	C
97=O	*U.TA.RO	*	C1	116a1	o-ta-re-wo	K	N	C
97=PTE	*U.RE.WI		C1	25a2	pte-re-wa	K		C
97=PU	*U.RE.WI		C1	25a2	pu-re-wa	K	N	C
97=PU	*U.TA.RO	*	C1	116a1	pu-ta-ri-ja	K		C
97=QA	*U.RA₂.TI	*	C1	108.3	qa-ra₂-ti-jo	K	N	C
97=QE	*U.RE.WI		C1	25a2	qe-re-wa	K	N	C
97=QI	*U.TA.RO	*	C1	116a1	qi-ta-ro	K	N	C
97=SI	*U.TA.RO	*	C1	116a1	si-ta-ro	K	N	C
97=TA	*U.TA.RO	*	C1	116a1	ta-ta-ro	+		C
97=WE	*U.RE.WI		C1	25a2	we-re-we	K	Q	C
98=A	*KU.PA₃.NU		C9	1a3,3.6,88.3,88.4,	a-pa₃-no	K	N	C
98=DA	QA.*KU.RE	*	C1	HTW217a1(CRIV4)	qa-da-ro	K	N	C
98=KA	A.*KU.TU		C1	TY3b7(IV9)	a-ka-ta-jo	PK	N	C
98=KA	A.*KU.TU		C1	TY3b7(IV9)	a-ka-to	K		C
98=KA	*KU.PA₃.NA.TU		C2	47a1,119.3	ka-pa₃-na-to	K	N	C
98=KA	*KU.PA₃.NU		C9	1a3,3.6,88.3,	ka-pa₃-no	K	N	C
98=KA	*KU.RU.*KU		C1	87.4	ku-ru-ka	K	N	C
98=KE	I.*KU.TA	*	C1	35.1	i-ke-ta	K	N	C
98=KE	*KU.RA.I	*	C1	117a2	ke-ra-i-ja-pi	K		C
98=KE	A.*KU.TU		C1	TY3b7(IV9)	a-ke-ta	PK	N	C
98=KO	A.*KU.TU		C1	TY3b7(IV9)	a-ko-to	K	N	C

Minoan Linear A

Hypoth.	Linear A	Code	Reference	Linear B	Code		
98=KU	*KU.DO.NI	C2	13.4,85a4	ku-do-ni-ja	K	P	C
98=KU	*KU.RU.*KU	C1	87.4	ku-ru-ka	K	N	C
98=MI	DA.*KU.NA	C1	103.4	da-mi-ni-jo	PK	EP	C
98=MI	*KU.NI.SU	C4	10a1,86a1,95a3,	mi-ni-so	K	N	C
98=MO	I.*KU.RI.NA	C1	90.1	i-mo-ro-ne-u	K	N	C
98=MO	A.*KU.TU	C1	TY3b7(IV9)	a-mo-te	K		C
98=MO	A.*KU.TU	C1	TY3b7(IV9)	a-mo-ta	PK		C
98=NA	A.*KU.TU	C1	TY3b7(IV9)	a-na-ta	K		C
98=NA	A.*KU.TU	C1	TY3b7(IV9)	a-na-to	K		C
98=NA	KA.*KU.PA	C3	16.1,	ka-na-po	K	N	C
98=NE	A.*KU.TU	C1	TY3b7(IV9)	a-ne-te-wa	K	N	C
98=NU	A.*KU.TU	C1	TY3b7(IV9)	a-nu-to	TK	N	C
98=NU	A.*KU.TU	C1	TY3b7(IV9)	a-nu-to-jo	K	N	C
98=PA	A.*KU.TU	C1	TY3b7(IV9)	a-pa-ta-wa	K	P	C
98=PE	I.*KU.TA *	C1	35.1	i-pe-ta	+		C
98=PO	A.*KU.TU	C1	TY3b7(IV9)	a-po-te	K		C
98=QA	A.*KU.TU	C1	TY3b7(IV9)	a-qa-to	K	N	C
98=QA	QA.*KU.RE *	C1	HTW217a1(CRIV4)	qa-qa-ro	K	N	C
98=QO	A.*KU.TU	C1	TY3b7(IV9)	a-qo-ta	K		C
98=RA	I.*KU.TA *	C1	35.1	i-ra-ta	PK	N	C
98=RA	JA.*KU.TI	C1	KN1b1(IV1)	ja-ra-to	K	N	CX
98=RA$_2$	QA.*KU.RE *	C1	HTW217a1(CRIV4)	qa-ra$_2$-ro	K	N	C
98=RE	A.*KU.TU	C1	TY3b7(IV9)	a-re-ta$_2$	K		C
98=RE	A.*KU.TU	C1	TY3b7(IV9)	a-re-ta-wo	K	N	C
98=RI	KA.*KU.PA	C3	16.1,	ka-ri-pi-jo	+		C
98=RO	I.*KU.TA *	C1	35.1	i-ro-to	K	N	C
98=SA	QA.*KU.RE *	C1	HTW217a1(CRIV4)	qa-sa-ro-we	K	P	C
98=SI	QA.*KU.RE *	C1	HTW217a1(CRIV4)	qa-si-re-wi-ja	PK		C
98=TA	*KU.PA.JA	C1	116a1	ta-pa-jo	K		CX
98=TE	DA.*KU.NA	C1	103.4	da-te-ne-ja	K	N	C
98=U	DA.*KU.NA	C1	103.4	da-u-no	K	N	CX
98=WA	DA.*KU.NA	C1	103.4	da-wa-no	K	N	C
98=WA	QE.*KU.RE	C1	20.2	qe-wa-ra	K		CX
98=WO	A.*KU.TU	C1	TY3b7(IV9)	a-wo-ti-jo	K	N	C
98=WO	SE.*KU.TU	C1	115a3	se-wo-to	K		C
98=ZE	A.*KU.TU	C1	TY3b7(IV9)	a-ze-ta	K	N	C
98=ZE	A.*KU.TU	C1	TY3b7(IV9)	a-ze-to	K		C
100=*49	*I.SA.RI	C1	PH6.4(IV16)	*49-sa-ro	+		C
100=A	*I.SA.RI	C1	PH6.4(IV16)	a-sa-ro	K	N	C
100=A	*I.TA.NU	C1	28b6	a-ta-no	K	N	C
100=A	*I.KI.RA	C1	25a5	a-ki-re-u	K	N	C
100=A	*I.KI.RA	C1	25a5	a-ki-ri-ja	+		C
100=AU	*I.TA.NU	C1	28b6	au-ta-na	+		C

Appendix C

Hypoth.	Linear A	Code		Reference	Linear B	Code		
100=DA	*I.NA.JA	*	C1	PKZ11(I4)	da-na-jo	K	N	C
100=DU	*I.SA.RI		C1	PH6.4(IV16)	du-sa-ro	K	N	C
100=E	*I.SA.RI		C1	PH6.4(IV16)	e-sa-re-we	K	Q	C
100=I	PA.*I.TO		C2	97a3,120.6,	pa-i-to	K	P	C
100=I	PA.*I.TO		C2	97a3,120.6,	pa-i-ti-jo	K	E	C
100=JA	*I.SA.RI		C1	PH6.4(IV16)	ja-sa-ro	K	N	C
100=KA	*I.SA.RI		C1	PH6.4(IV16)	ka-sa-ro	K		C
100=KA	*I.TA.NU		C1	28b6	ka-ta-ni-ja	K		CX
100=KA	*I.TA.NU		C1	28b6	ka-ta-no	PK	N	C
100=KE	PA.*I.TO		C2	97a3,120.6,	pa-ke-ta	K	N	C
100=KI	*I.DA.PA₃		C1	PH6.4(IV16)	ki-da-pa	K	P	C
100=KI	*I.TA.NU		C1	28b6	ki-ta-no	K		C
100=MA	*I.NA.JA	*	C1	PKZ11(I4)	ma-na-je-u	K	QN	C
100=MI	*I.SA.RI		C1	PH6.4(IV16)	mi-sa-ra-jo	K	N	C
100=NO	*I.SA.RI		C1	PH6.4(IV16)	no-sa-ro	K	N	C
100=NO	KU.RA.*I	*	C1	117a2	ku-ra-no	K	N	C
100=NO	KI.TA.*I		C1	123a1	ki-ta-no	K		C
100=NO	A.TA.*I	*	C1	PRZ1b(I17)	a-ta-no	K	N	C
100=O	*I.DU.WI	*	C1	MA1a(IV10)	o-du-we	K		C
100=O	A.TA.*I	*	C1	PRZ1b(I17)	a-ta-o	PK	N	C
100=O	*I.NA.JA	*	C1	PKZ11(I4)	o-na-jo	PK	N	C
100=PO	*I.KU.TA	*	C1	35.1	po-ku-ta	PK	Q	C
100=QA	*I.SA.RI		C1	PH6.4(IV16)	qa-sa-ro-we	K	P	C
100=QI	*I.JA.TE		C1	PHZ4(II12)	qi-ja-to	K	N	C
100=QO	*I.JA.TE		C1	PHZ4(II12)	qo-ja-te	K		C
100=RA	PA.*I.TO		C2	97a3,120.6,	pa-ra-to	K	N	C
100=RA	PA.*I.TO		C2	97a3,120.6,	pa-ra-ti-jo	K	N	C
100=RE	*I.NA.JA	*	C1	PKZ11(I4)	re-na-jo	K	EPN	CX
100=SI	PA.*I.TO		C2	97a3,120.6,	pa-si-te-o-i	K	G	C
100=SI	*I.KI.RA		C1	25a5	si-ki-ro	+		C
100=SO	MA.*I.MI		C1	89.2	ma-so-mo	K	P	C
100=SU	*I.JA.TE		C1	PHZ4(II12)	su-ja-to	K		C
100=TA	PA.*I.TO		C2	97a3,120.6,	pa-ta-ti-jo	K		C
100=U	*I.TA.NU		C1	28b6	u-ta-no	K	N	C
100=U	*I.TA.NU		C1	28b6	u-ta-no	K	P	C
100=U	*I.TA.NU		C1	28b6	u-ta-ni-jo	K	E	C
100=WI	*I.DA.MA.TE		C2	ARZ1(V17III),	wi-da-ma-ta₂	K	N	C
100=WI	*I.NA.JA	*	C1	PKZ11(I4)	wi-na-jo	K	N	C
100=WO	A.TA.*I	*	C1	PRZ1b(I17)	a-ta-wo	PK	N	C
100=ZA	PA.*I.TO		C2	97a3,120.6,	pa-za-ti	K	N	C
100=ZA	*I.KI.RA		C1	25a5	za-ki-ri-jo	K	N	C
100=ZE	A.TA.*I	*	C1	PRZ1b(I17)	a-ta-ze-u	K	N	C
101=A	*DO.DI.RA		C2	HTW212a(CRIV11),	a-di-ri-jo	K	N	C

176   Minoan Linear A

Hypoth.	Linear A	Code	Reference	Linear B	Code		
101=DO	KU.*DO.NI	C2	13.4,85a4	ku-do-ni-ja	K	P	C
101=KA	KU.*DO.NI	C2	13.4,85a4	ku-ka-no	K	N	C
101=PA	KU.*DO.NI	C2	13.4,85a4	ku-pa-nu-we-to	K	N	C
101=RA	KU.*DO.NI	C2	13.4,85a4	ku-ra-no	K	N	C
101=RU	KU.*DO.NI	C2	13.4,85a4	ku-ru-no	+		C
101=TU	DU.*DO.WA	C1	36.2	du-tu-wa	+		C
102=QA	DI.*DE.RU	C3	86a3,95a4,95b4	di-qa-ra	K	N	C
103=A	*KI.RE.TA$_2$	C2	129.1,85b1	a-re-ta$_2$	K		C
103=A	*KI.RE.TA$_2$	C2	129.1,85b1	a-re-ta-wo	K	N	C
103=DA	*KI.DA.RO	C1	117a9,27a4?	da-da-re-jo-de	K	P	C
103=DA	*KI.*KI.RA.JA	C1	85b1	da-da-re-jo-de	K	P	C
103=DI	*KI.WE.SI	C1	TY3a1(IV9)	di-we-so	K	N	C
103=DO	DI.*KI.SE	C2	87.3,117b2	di-do-si	PK		C
103=E	*KI.RE.TA$_2$	C2	129.1,85b1	e-re-ta	PK	Q	C
103=JE	I.*KI.RA	C1	25a5	i-je-re-ja	PK	Q	C
103=KA	*KI.*KI.RA.JA	C1	85B1	ka-ka-re-a$_2$	K		C
103=KI	SI.*KI.RA	C1	8a4	si-ki-ro	+		C
103=KI	*KI.DA.RO	C1	117a9,27a4?	ki-da-ro	K	N	C
103=KI	*KI.RI.TA$_2$	C2	114a1,121.1	ki-ri-te-wi-ja	PK	Q	C
103=KI	*KI.RI.TA$_2$	C2	114a1,121.1	ki-ri-ta	K		C
103=KO	*KI.RE.TA$_2$	C2	129.1,85b1	ko-re-te	PK	Q	C
103=KU	*KI.TA.I	C1	123a1	ku-ta-i-jo	K	N	C
103=MA	*KI.RI.TA$_2$	C2	114a1,121.1	ma-ri-ti-wi-jo	MPK	N	C
103=MI	I.*KI.RA	C1	25a5	i-mi-ri-jo	K	N	C
103=MI	A.TI.*KI.TA.A	C1	TYZ4	a-ti-mi-te	PK	G	C
103=NO	*KI.DA.RO	C1	117a9,27a4?	no-da-ro	K	N	C
103=O	*KI.RE.TA$_2$	C2	129.1,85b1	o-re-te-wo	K	QN	C
103=O	*KI.DA.RO	C1	117a9,27a4?	o-da-ra-o	K		C
103=O	*KI.DA.TA	C1	40.2	o-da-tu-we-ta	K		C
103=PA$_3$	*KI.RI.TA$_2$	C2	114a1,121.1	pa$_3$-ri-to	K	N	C
103=PE	*KI.RI.TA$_2$	C2	114a1,121.1	pe-ri-ta	K	N	C
103=PE	*KI.RI.TA$_2$	C2	114a1,121.1	pe-ri-to	K	N	C
103=PI	*KI.RI.TA$_2$	C2	114a1,121.1	pi-ri-to-wo	K	N	C
103=PI	*KI.RI.TA$_2$	C2	114a1,121.1	pi-ri-to-jo	+		C
103=PI	*KI.RI.TA$_2$	C2	114a1,121.1	pi-ri-te	+		C
103=QA	*KI.DA.RO	C1	117a9,27a4?	qa-da-ro	K	N	C
103=QA	I.*KI.RA	C1	25a5	i-qa-ro	+		C
103=RA	SI.*KI.RA	C1	8a4	si-ra-ro	K	P	C
103=RA	SI.*KI.NE	*C1	116a5	si-ra-no	K	N	C
103=RU	*KI.DA.TA	C1	40.2	ru-da-to	+		C
103=TA	SI.*KI.RA	C1	8a4	si-ta-ro	K	N	C
103=TA	*KI.WE.SI	C1	TY3a1(IV9)	ta-we-si-jo	K	N	C
103=TE	*KI.RE.TA$_2$	C2	129.1,85b1	te-re-ta	PK	Q	C

Appendix C

Hypoth.	Linear A	Code		Reference	Linear B	Code		
103=TI	KE.*KI.RU	C1		94b2	*ke-ti-ro*	PK	N	C
103=TI	*KI.RI.TA$_2$	C2		114a1,121.1	*ti-ri-to*	K	P	C
103=TI	*KI.RI.TA$_2$	C2		114a1,121.1	*ti-ri-ti-jo*	K	E	C
103=TO	KE.*KI.RU	C1		94b2	*ke-to-ro*	K	N	C
103=TU	*KI.DA.RO	C1		117a9,27a4?	*tu-da-ra*	K	N	C
103=WE	DI.*KI.SE	C2		87.3,117b2	*di-we-so*	K	N	C
103=WE	*KI.WE.SI	C1		TY3a1(IV9)	*we-we-si-jo*	PK	N	C
103=WE	I.*KI.RA	C1		25a5	*i-we-ro*	K	N	C
103=ZA	DI.*KI.SE	C2		87.3,117b2	*di-za-so*	K	N	C
103=ZA	I.*KI.RA	C1		25a5	*i-za-re*	K	N	C
114=DE	PA.*114.I	*	C1	43.1	*pa-de-i*	K	GN	C
150=QA	U.*150.MA	*	C1	PHW17a(III16)	*u-qa-mo*	K	PN	C
153=MA	RU.*153.NA	*	C1	11b3	*ru-ma-no*	K	N	C
153=TA$_2$	RU.*153.NA	*	C1	11b3	*ru-ta$_2$-no*	K	N	C

APPENDIX D

This appendix presents the "evidence" supporting the phonetic values of each of the "random" decipherments. The first decipherment is based on the values brought over from Linear B. The remaining nine are deliberately erroneous and serve as a control sample to help determine whether the "evidence" supporting the use of the Linear B values in Linear A has any statistical significance. For a full explanation see Chapter Three.

Two types of evidence are presented for each decipherment. The first class of evidence is "orthographic" or "inflectional" alternations within Linear A: final alternations such as DA.TA.RA / DA.TA.RE, initial alternation such as KU.DO.NI / KA.U.DO.NI, and medial alternations such as DI.RA.DI.NA / DI.RE.DI.NA. I have cited alternations in the random decipherments which resemble the alternations cited as confirmation for the values taken from Linear B. Most involve a pair of signs which have the same consonant but a different vowel. The format for printing the Linear A words is the same as in Appendix A.

The second kind of "evidence" is parallels with Linear B. The presentation of these parallels follows the format of Appendix B. Only complete sign-groups have been cited. For the Linear A sign-groups, the L numbers are listed in square brackets.

The phonetic values used for each decipherment are listed in the following table. The method of constructing these "random" phonetic values is explained on page 74.

The Ten Decipherments

Sign	1	2	3	4	5	6	7	8	9	10
1	PA_3	RA_2	ME	DE	DO	WA	QA	SE	PI	RO
2	PA	SA	RU	DI	MA	KA	TU	DU	KI	SI
6	TU	DU	KI	SI	PA	SA	RU	DI	MA	KA
7	SO	7	7	7	7	7	7	7	7	7
8	8	SO	8	8	8	8	8	8	8	8
20	20	20	20	20	PU_2	KE	JE	20	20	TO
21	21	21	SO	21	21	21	21	21	21	21
22	RO	PA_3	RA_2	ME	DE	DO	WA	QA	SE	PI
23	ZA	23	23	WI	23	23	23	TA_2	KO	PU
24	KE	JE	24	24	TO	24	24	24	24	PU_2
25	NU	NE	U	NI	SU	TE	MI	QE	WE	RI
26	NA	KU	RE	DA	TI	JA	RA	TA	I	A
28	WI	28	28	28	TA_2	KO	PU	ZA	28	28
29	KA	TU	DU	KI	SI	PA	SA	RU	DI	MA
30	DA	TI	JA	RA	TA	I	A	NA	KU	RE
31	SA	RU	DI	MA	KA	TU	DU	KI	SI	PA
32	JA	RA	TA	I	A	NA	KU	RE	DA	TI
33	33	33	33	SO	33	33	33	33	33	33
34	PU_2	KE	JE	34	34	TO	34	34	34	34
37	37	37	37	37	SO	37	37	37	37	37
39	TO	39	39	39	39	PU_2	KE	JE	39	39
41	41	WI	41	41	41	TA_2	KO	PU	ZA	41
43	43	43	43	43	43	SO	43	43	43	43
45	KO	PU	ZA	45	45	WI	45	45	45	TA_2
51	DI	MA	KA	TU	DU	KI	SI	PA	SA	RU
52	A	NA	KU	RE	DA	TI	JA	RA	TA	I
53	RA	TA	I	A	NA	KU	RE	DA	TI	JA
54	RE	DA	TI	JA	RA	TA	I	A	NA	KU
55	RU	DI	MA	KA	TU	DU	KI	SI	PA	SA
56	PI	RO	PA_3	RA_2	ME	DE	DO	WA	QA	SE
57	SI	PA	SA	RU	DI	MA	KA	TU	DU	KI
58	RA_2	ME	DE	DO	WA	QA	SE	PI	RO	PA_3
59	SU	TE	MI	QE	WE	RI	NU	NE	U	NI
60	NI	SU	TE	MI	QE	WE	RI	NU	NE	U
61	NE	U	NI	SU	TE	MI	QE	WE	RI	NU
62	QA	SE	PI	RO	PA_3	RA_2	ME	DE	DO	WA

The Ten Decipherments (cont.)

Sign	1	2	3	4	5	6	7	8	9	10
64	PU	ZA	64	64	WI	64	64	64	TA$_2$	KO
67	67	67	67	67	67	67	SO	67	67	67
68	68	TA$_2$	KO	PU	ZA	68	68	WI	68	68
69	69	TO	69	69	69	69	PU$_2$	KE	JE	69
72	RI	NU	NE	U	NI	SU	TE	MI	QE	WE
74	TA	I	A	NA	KU	RE	DA	TI	JA	RA
75	WA	QA	SE	PI	RO	PA$_3$	RA$_2$	ME	DE	DO
76	MI	QE	WE	RI	NU	NE	U	NI	SU	TE
77	SE	PI	RO	PA$_3$	RA$_2$	ME	DE	DO	WA	QA
78	TI	JA	RA	TA	I	A	NA	KU	RE	DA
79	79	79	TO	79	79	79	79	PU$_2$	KE	JE
80	80	PU$_2$	KE	JE	80	80	TO	80	80	80
81	JE	81	81	TO	81	81	81	81	PU$_2$	KE
83	83	83	PU$_2$	KE	JE	83	83	TO	83	83
84	ME	DE	DO	WA	QA	SE	PI	RO	PA$_3$	RA$_2$
85	85	85	TA$_2$	KO	PU	ZA	85	85	WI	85
86	TA$_2$	KO	PU	ZA	86	86	WI	86	86	86
87	87	87	87	PU$_2$	KE	JE	87	87	TO	87
88	88	88	WI	88	88	88	TA$_2$	KO	PU	ZA
90	90	90	90	90	90	90	90	SO	90	90
91	QE	WE	RI	NU	NE	U	NI	SU	TE	MI
92	TE	MI	QE	WE	RI	NU	NE	U	NI	SU
93	DU	KI	SI	PA	SA	RU	DI	MA	KA	TU
94	WE	RI	NU	NE	U	NI	SU	TE	MI	QE
95	MA	KA	TU	DU	KI	SI	PA	SA	RU	DI
96	96	96	96	TA$_2$	KO	PU	ZA	96	96	WI
97	U	NI	SU	TE	MI	QE	WE	RI	NU	NE
98	KU	RE	DA	TI	JA	RA	TA	I	A	NA
100	I	A	NA	KU	RE	DA	TI	JA	RA	TA
101	DO	WA	QA	SE	PI	RO	PA$_3$	RA$_2$	ME	DE
102	DE	DO	WA	QA	SE	PI	RO	PA$_1$	RA$_2$	ME
103	KI	SI	PA	SA	RU	DI	MA	KA	TU	DU
114	114	114	114	114	114	114	114	114	SO	114
120	120	120	120	120	120	120	120	120	120	SO

Appendix D

DECIPHERMENT 1 (Linear B Values)

Alternations within Linear A

A.TI.KA.A.MI.KO	#	C1	ZAW2.1(III8)	[52.78.29.52.76.45]
A.TI.KI.TA.A		C1	TYZ4(II18)	[52.78.103.74.52]
DA.TA.RA		C1	6A1	[30.74.53]
DA.TA.RE		C2	88.5,62.2*	[30.74.54]
I.41.NA.MA	*	B1	APZ2a1(I13)	[100.41.26.95]
I.41.NA.MI.NA	#	C1	PKZ10(I6)	[100.41.26.76.26]
JA.SA.SA.RA.MA.NA	*	C1	KNZ10a(I8)	[32.31.31.53.95.26]
JA.SA.SA.RA.ME	*	C2	PSZ2c(I1),TLZ1(I16)	[32.31.31.53.84]
KA.U.DE.TA		C1	13.1	[29.97.102.74]
KA.U.DO.NI		C1	26b2	[29.97.101.60]
KI.RE.TA.NA		C3A1	8a5,108.1,120.4,2.3	[103.54.74.26]
KI.RE.TA$_2$		C2	129.1,85b1	[103.54.86]
KU.PA$_3$.NA.TU		C2	47a1,119.3	[98.1.26.6]
KU.PA$_3$.NU		C9	1a3,3.6,88.3,88.4,117a3,	[98.1.25]
PI.TA.KA.SE		C1	21.1	[56.74.29.77]
PI.TA.KE.SI		C1	87.2	[56.74.24.57]
SU.KI.RI.TA	#	A1	PHW18	[59.103.72.74]
SU.KI.RI.TE.I.JA	#	C1	HTZ158B(I17)	[59.103.72.92.100.32]
WA.TU.MA.RE	*	C1	128a2	[75.6.95.54]
WA.TU.MI	*	C1	HTW206a(CRIV8)	[75.6.76]
JA.DI.KI.TE.TE.PI	*	C1	PKZ8a(I3)	[32.51.103.92.92.56]
A.DI.KI.TE.TE.PI	*	C1	PKZ11A(I4)	[52.51.103.92.92.56]
JA.TA.I.88.U.JA		C1	APZ1(I14)	[32.74.100.88.97.32]
A.TA.I.88.WA.JA		C3	KOZ1A,PKZ12A(I5),	[52.74.100.88.75.32]
KU.DO.NI		C2	13.4,85A4	[98.101.60]
KA.U.DO.NI		C1	26b2	[29.97.101.60]
QA.KU.RE	*	C1	HTW217a1(CRIV4)	[62.98.54]
QE.KU.RE		C1	20.2	[91.98.54]
A.SA.SA.RA.ME	*	C2	PKZ11b(I4),PRZ1c(I17)	[52.31.31.53.84]
JA.SA.SA.RA.ME	*	C2	PSZ2c(I1),TLZ1(I16)	[32.31.31.53.84]
DI.RA.DI.NA		A1	PH1a1(IV13)	[51.53.51.26]
DI.RE.DI.NA		C1	98a2	[51.54.51.26]

DECIPHERMENT 1 (cont.)

Alternations within Linear A

A.SU.JA	C1	11a3	[52.59.32]
A.SE.JA	C1	115a4	[52.77.32]
KI.RE.TA2	C2	129.1,85b1	[103.54.86]
KI.RI.TA2	C2	114a1,121.1	[103.72.86]

Parallels with Linear B

A.KA.RU [52.29.55]	C2	2.1,86a1,86b1?	*a-ka-re-u*	PK	N	C
A.RA.NA.RE [52.53.26.54]	C1	1a4,47b1?	*a-ra-na-ro*	K	N	C
A.RE.SA.NA [52.54.31.26]	+C1	TEZ2	*a-re-sa-ni-e*	P		C
A.SA.RA2 [52.31.58]	*C1	89.1	*a-sa-ro*	K	N	C
DA.MI.NU [30.76.25]	C1	117A8	*da-mi-ni-jo*	PK	EP	C
DI.DE.RU [51.102.55]	C3	86a3,95a4,95b4	*di-de-ro*	K+	N	C
I.JA.TE [100.32.92]	C1	PHZ4(II12)	*i-ja-te*	P	Q	C
I.KU.TA [100.98.74]	*C1	35.1	*i-ku-to*	M	N	C
KA.NU.TI [29.25.78]	C1	97a3	*ka-nu-ta-jo*	P	N	C
KA.SA.RU [29.31.55]	C1	10b3	*ka-sa-ro*	K		C
KI.DA.RO [103.30.22]	C1	117a9,27a4?	*ki-da-ro*	K	N	C
KI.RI.TA$_2$ [103.72.86]	C2	114a1.121.1	*ki-ri-ta*	K		C
KU.DO.NI [98.101.60]	C2	13.4,85a4	*ku-do-ni-ja*	K	P	C
KU.RU.KU [98.55.98]	C1	87.4	*ku-ru-ka*	K	N	C
MA.SI.DU [95.57.93]	C1	43.1	*ma-si-dwo*	K		C
PA.I.TO [2.100.39]	C2	97a3,120.6	*pa-i-to*	K	P	C
PA.JA.RE [2.32.54]	C2B2	8b4,88.4,29.2,	*pa-ja-ro*	K	N	C

DECIPHERMENT 1 (cont.)

Parallels with Linear B

QA.QA.RU [62.62.55]		C3A1	93a4,118.2,122b3,	*qa-qa-ro*	K	N C
QA.RA$_2$.WA [62.58.75]		C1	86a3	*qa-ra$_2$-wo*	K	N C
SA.MA.RO [31.95.22]		C1A1	88.4,39.3*	*sa-ma-ri-jo*	K	N C
SI.KI.RA [57.103.53]		C1	8a4	*si-ki-ro*	+	C
SI.MI.TA [57.76.74]		C1	96a2	*si-mi-te-u*	+	C
SU.KI.RI.TA [59.103.72.74]	#	C1	PHW18	*su-ki-ri-ta*	K	P C
TA.NA.TI [74.26.78]		C3A1	7A4,10B4,98A2,	*ta-na-to*	K	N C
TE.JA.RE [92.32.54]	*	C1	117a5	*te-ja-ro*	K	N CX

DECIPHERMENT 2 (Random)

Alternations within Linear A

NA.DI.TI.TA		C1	28b5,62.1?	[52.55.30.53]
NA.DI.TA	*	B1	11a1	[52.55.53]
SA.I.U		C2	94b1,122a6	[2.74.61]
SA.I.WE		C1	31.6	[2.74.91]
RO.I.TU.PI		C1	21.1	[56.74.29.77]
RO.I.TA	*	C1	96a4	[56.74.53]
TA.KU.DU.TE.KE.QE	*	B1	PK1(IV5)	[53.26.6.59.34.76]
TA.KU.DA	*	D1	47b1	[53.26.54]
RE.DA.96		C1A1	117b1,39.2	[98.54.96]
RU.DA.96		C1	20.4	[31.54.96]
RE.DI.KA	*	C1	115b3	[98.55.95]
RI.DI.KA		C1	118.4	[94.55.95]
A.SA.85	*	C1	PA1(IV7)	[100.2.85]
A.SE.85		C2	44b1,131.2	[100.62.85]

Parallels with Linear B

A.KU.RA [100.26.32]	*	C1	PKZ11(I4)	*a-ku-ri-jo*	K	N	C
A.RE.I [100.98.74]	*	C1	35.1	*a-re-i-jo*	PK	QN	C
A.TI.RA2 [100.30.1]		C1	PH6.4(IV16)	*a-ti-ro*	K	N	C
SI.KI.RE [103.93.98]	*	D1	27a4	*si-ki-ro*	+		C
SI.NU.KO [103.72.86]		C2	114a1,121.1	*si-nu-ke*	K	N	C
TI.RI.TI [30.94.30]		C4	10a5,85a2,93a7,	*ti-ri-ti-ja*	K	EP	C
TI.TA2.MI [30.68.92]		C1	34.1	*ti-ta-ma*	K		C

DECIPHERMENT 3 (Random)

Alternations within Linear A

KU.MA.JA.I		C1	28b5,62.1?	[52.55.30.53]	
KU.MA.I	*	B1	11a1	[52.55.53]	
KU.DI.DO.NI	*	C1	ZAZ3.1	[52.31.84.61]	
KU.DI.DE	*	C1	89.1	[52.31.58]	
KU.DI.DI.I.DO	*	C2	PKZ11b(I4),PRZ1c(I17)	[52.31.31.53.84]	
JA.DA.RE		C1	103.4	[30.98.26]	
JA.DA.RO.NI		C1B1	103.4,103.2	[30.98.77.61]	
TU.DU.NA.MI	*	C1	PK1.7(IV5)	[95.29.100.59]	
TU.DU.NE.QE		C1	87.1,117a1	[95.29.72.92]	
RE.JA.TI		C1	117a5	[26.30.54]	
RU.JA.TI	*	C1B1	10a3	[2.30.54]	
DA.TI.96		C1A1	117b1,39.2	[98.54.96]	
DI.TI.96		C1	20.4	[31.54.96]	
DA.TI.96		C1A1	117b1,39.2	[98.54.96]	
DA.TU.96		C1	20.1	[98.95.96]	

Parallels with Linear B

DA.MA.TU [98.55.95]	*	C1	115b3	*da-ma-te*	P	Q	C	
KA.PA.RO [51.103.77]		C2	87.3,117b2	*ka-pa-ri-jo*	K	N	C	
KE.RA.TE [80.78.60]	*	C1	93a6	*ke-ra-ti-jo-jo*	P		C	
PA.JA.RA$_2$ [103.30.22]		C1	117a9,27a4?	*pa-ja-ro*	K	N	C	
PA.PA.RE [103.103.26]		C1	88.2	*pa-pa-ro*	PK	N	C	
RA.U.TA [78.25.32]		C1	115b2	*ra-u-ta*	P	N	C	
SI.MI.TE [93.59.60]		C1	108.2	*si-mi-te-u*	+		C	

DECIPHERMENT 4 (Random)

Alternations within Linear A

RA.NA.A	C1	6a1 [30.74.53]	
RA.NA.JA	C2	88.5,62.2* [30.74.54]	
KU.RA.DU.WE	C2	ARZ1(V17III),ARZ2(V17iv)	[100.30.95.92]
KU.RA.DE	C1	PH6.4(IV16) [100.30.1]	
KI.ME.DA	C1	11a2 [29.22.26]	
KI.ME.DE	C1	31.3 [29.22.1]	
TI.DE.NI	C9	1a3,3.6,88.3,88.4,117a3, [98.1.25]	
TI.DE.NE.I	C1	24a1 [98.1.94.32]	
DA.RA.JA	C1	117a5 [26.30.54]	
DI.RA.JA *	C1	10a3 [2.30.54]	
RA.NA.A	C1	6a1 [30.74.53]	
RA$_2$.NA.A *	C1	96a4 [56.74.53]	
RA.NA.A	C1	6a1 [30.74.53]	
RA.NU.A	C2B1	6a6,120.1,57a1 [30.91.53]	
TU.A.TU.DA	A1	PH1a1(IV13) [51.53.51.26]	
TU.JA.TU.DA	C1	98a2 [51.54.51.26]	
RE.DI.A.SU	C2	96a1,96b1 [52.2.53.61]	
RE.DU.A.SI *	B1	SKZ1(II25) [52.95.53.6]	
RU.SI.SU *	C1	HTW221a(CRV4) [57.6.61]	
RU.SA.SU *	C1	116a5 [57.103.61]	

Parallels with Linear B

DU.RU.PA [95.57.93]	C1	43.1	*du-ru-po*	K	N	C
TA.RA.NA [78.30.74]	* C1	123b2	*ta-ra-nu*	PK		C
TA.TA.TI [78.78.98]	C2	35a1,ZAZ3.2#+	*ta-ta-ta*	K	PN	C

Appendix D

DECIPHERMENT 5 (Random)

Alternations within Linear A

DA.RA.TA.RE	*	C1	29.5	[52.54.30.100]
DA.RA.TE.DI.DU.88	*	B1	KNZ13(V14)	[52.54.61.57.51.88]
RE.TA.DA	+	C1	KOZ1b	[100.30.52]
RE.TA.DO		C1	PH6.4(IV16)	[100.30.1]
RE.SA.TE.DI		C1	13.5	[100.93.61.57]
RE.SA.TA2	*	C1	MA1a(IV10)	[100.93.28]
RU.DU.QE	*	C1	93a2	[103.51.60]
RO.DU.QE		C2	HTW208a(CRIV1),	[75.51.60]
MI.SO.23		C3	10a2,10a4,85a3	[97.37.23]
MI.SE.23		C2	122a1,122b3	[97.102.23]

Parallels with Linear B

DA.NA.KO [52.53.96]	*	C1	109.4	da-na-ko	P	N	C
DA.NA.ME [52.53.56]	#	C1	87.5	da-na-mo	K		C
I.KU.TI [78.74.26]		C1	HTW220(CRV5)	i-ku-to	M	N	C
KA.RA.KO [31.54.96]		C1	20.4	ka-ra-ko	M		CX
MI.RA.TA2 [97.54.28]		C1	25a2	mi-ra-ti-ja	P	QE	C
NE.WE.WI [91.59.64]		C1	87.4	ne-we-wi-ja	P	QE	C
PA3.JA.RA [62.98.54]	*	C1	HTW217a1(CRIV4)	pa-ja-ro	K	N	C
SI.JA.MA [29.98.2]		C3	16.1,HTW215a,	si-ja-ma	K	N	C
TA.ZA.RI [30.68.92]		C1	34.1	ta-za-ro	K	N	C
TI.TA.RA [26.30.54]		C1	117a5	ti-ta-ra	P	N	C

DECIPHERMENT 6 (Random)

Alternations within Linear A

TI.RE.DA.88.PA₃.NA	*	C3	PKZ12a(I5),TLZ1(I16),	[52.74.100.88.75.32]
TI.RE.DA.88.PI.PA	+	C1	ZAZ3.2	[52.74.100.88.102.29]
NA.TU.TU.KU.SI.JA	*	C1	KNZ10a(I8)	[32.31.31.53.95.26]
NA.TU.TU.KU.SE	*	C2	PSZ2c(I1),TLZ1(I16)	[32.31.31.53.84]
U.SA.MI		C1	12.3	[91.6.61]
U.SA.MA	*	C1	PHW14a(III13)	[91.6.57]
SA.DU.TE.ME.SE	*	C1	128a1	[6.55.25.77.84]
SA.DU.TU.QA.-.TA	*	C1	KOZ1b	[6.55.31.58.160.54]

Parallels with Linear B

A.RE.JA [78.74.26]		C1	HTW220(CRV5)	*a-re-jo*	K	N	C
I.JA.MA [30.26.57]		C1	126a1	*i-ja-me-i*	P	N	C
I.MI.RA.A [30.61.98.78]		C1	117a8	*i-mi-ri-jo*	K	N	C
KA.MA.TI [2.57.52]	*	C1	45b3	*ka-ma-ti-jo-jo*	T	N	C
KA.NA.TA [2.32.54]		C2B2	8b4,88.4,29.2,	*ka-na-to*	M		C
KO.KI.JA [28.51.26]		C1	28a5	*ko-ki-jo*	P	N	C
PA.RA.KA [29.98.2]		C3	16.1,HTW215a,	*pa-ra-ko*	P	N	C
QE.TA.KO [97.54.28]		C1	25a2	*qe-ta-ko*	P	N	C

DECIPHERMENT 7 (Random)

Alternations within Linear A

JA.DA.TI.TA₂.RA₂.KU	*	C3	PKZ12a(I5),TLZ1(I16),	[52.74.100.88.75.32]
JA.DA.TI.TA₂.RO.SA	+	C1	ZAZ3.2	[52.74.100.88.102.29]
SI.RA.WA	*	C1	108.2	[51.26.22]
SI.RA.WE		C6	9a3,9b5,16.1,25a1,	[51.26.97]
PA₃.SI.RA	*	C1	HTW210a(CRIV13)	[101.51.26]
PA₃.SI.RE		C2	HTW212a(CRIV11),	[101.51.53]
KU.DU.DU.RE.PA.RA	*	C1	KNZ10a(I8)	[32.31.31.53.95.26]
KU.DU.DU.RE.PI	*	C2	PSZ2c(I1),TLZ1(I16)	[32.31.31.53.84]
MA.MA.RA		C1	88.2	[103.103.26]
MA.MA.RE.KU		C1	85b1	[103.103.53.32]
PA.SA.TI.NU	*	C1	PK1.7(IV5)	[95.29.100.59]
PA.SA.TE.NE		C2	87.1,117a1	[95.29.72.92]
PA₃.SI.RA	*	C1	HTW210a(CRIV13)	[101.51.26]
PU.SI.RA		C1	28a5	[28.51.26]

Parallels with Linear B

A.RA.KA [30.26.57]	C1	126a1	*a-ra-ko*	K	N	C
A.TA.RA [30.98.26]	C1	103.4	*a-ta-ra*	M		C
DI.PI.SI [93.84.51]	C1	19.3	*di-pi-si-jo*	P	GQ	C
DI.QA.RA [93.1.26]	C1	115b2	*di-qa-ra*	K	N	C
KA.U.DA [57.76.74]	C1	96a2	*ka-u-da*	K	PN	C
MA.MA.RA [103.103.26]	C1	88.2	*ma-ma-ro*	P	N	C

DECIPHERMENT 8 (Random)

Alternations within Linear A

RA.DA.WA	#	C1	87.5	[52.53.56]
RA.DA.WI		C1	122b3,87.5?,109.4?	[52.53.68]
RA.KI.KI.DA.RO	*	C2	PKZ11b(I4),PRZ1c(I17)	[52.31.31.53.84]
RA.KI.KO.SA.JA	*	C1	GOW1a1(III10)	[52.31.88.95.100]
JA.NA.SA.U		C2	ARZ1(V17III),ARZ2(V17iv)	[100.30.95.92]
JA.NA.SE		C1	PH6.4(IV16)	[100.30.1]
I.SE.TA.DI		C2	47a1,119.3	[98.1.26.6]
I.SE.TE.RE		C1	24a1	[98.1.94.32]
WA.TI.RE		C1	6a2	[56.74.32]
WA.TI.RU.DO		C1	21.1	[56.74.29.77]
TA.NA.A		C1	117a5	[26.30.54]
TU.NA.A		C2	17.3,122a5,49a4?	[57.30.54]
KA.NA.TI		C1	40.2	[103.30.74]
KU.NA.TI	*	C1	123b2	[78.30.74]
RE.PA.KA.U.U.WA	*	C1	PKZ8a(I3)	[32.51.103.92.92.56]
RA.PA.KA.U.U.WA	*	C1	PKZ11a(I4)	[52.51.103.92.92.56]
RA.KI.KI.DA.RO	*	C2	PKZ11b(I4),PRZ1c(I17)	[52.31.31.53.84]
RE.KI.KI.DA.RO	*	C2	PSZ2c(I1),TLZ1(I16)	[32.31.31.53.84]
KA.A.TI.TA		C3A1	8a5,108.1,120.4,2.3	[103.54.74.26]
KU.TI.TA		C1	HTW220(CRV5)	[78.74.26]
KU.NA.TI	*	C1	123b2	[78.30.74]
KU.NU.TI		C1	27a1	[78.60.74]
JA.DU.85	*	C1	PA1(IV7)	[100.2.85]
JA.DE.85		C2	44b1,131.2	[100.62.85]

Parallels with Linear B

KA.NA.TI [103.30.74]		C1	40.2	*ka-na-to*	M		C
KA.PA.NU [103.51.60]	*	C1	93a2	*ka-pa₃-no*	K	N	C
MA.NA.SA [93.30.95]	*	C1	6A4	*ma-na-sa*	P	G	CX
MA.RO.PA [93.84.51]		C1	19.3	*ma-ro-pi*	P	P	C
RA₂.PA.DA [101.51.53]		C2	HTW212a(CRIV11),	*ra-pa-do*	P	N	C
RA₂.PA.TA [101.51.26]	*	C1	HTW210a(CRIV13)	*ra-pa-to*	K		C
RA.TI.JA [52.74.100]	*	C1	PRZ1b(I17)	*ra-ti-jo*	K	E	C

DECIPHERMENT 9 (Random)

Alternations within Linear A

TA.SI.PA₃.RI	*	C1	ZAZ3.1	[52.31.84.61]
TA.SI.PU.RU.RA	*	C1	GOW1a1(III10)	[52.31.88.95.100]
RA.KA.RI.DU		C1	13.5	[100.93.61.57]
RA.KA.RE	*	C1	104.2	[100.93.78]
RA.I.DA	*	C1	PKZ11(I4)	[100.26.32]
RA.I.DE		C1	PH6.1(IV16)	[100.26.75]
QA.JA.DA		C1	6a2	[56.74.32]
QA.JA.DI.WA		C1	21.1	[56.74.29.77]
TA.JA.RA	*	C1	PRZ1b(I17)	[52.74.100]
TU.JA.RA		C1	123a1	[103.74.100]
TA.U.DA		C1	11a3	[52.59.32]
TA.WA.DA		C1	115a4	[52.77.32]

Parallels with Linear B

A.ME.NE [98.101.60]		C2	13.4,85a4	*a-me-no*	P	N	C
A.PA.RU [98.55.95]	*	C1	115b3	*a-pa-re-u*	K	N	CX
A.PI.MI.DA [98.1.94.32]		C1	24a1	*a-pi-me-de*	PK	N	C
A.TI.RA [98.53.100]	*	C1	117a2	*a-ti-ro*	K	N	C
DE.MA.SU [75.6.76]	*	C1	HTW206a(CRIV8)	*de-ma-si*	K	Q	C
KA.PA₃.SA [93.84.51]		C1	19.3	*ka-pa-so*	+		C
KA.U.NE [93.59.60]		C1	108.2	*ka-u-no*	T	N	C
KU.TE.TI [30.91.53]		C2B1	6a6,120.1,57a1	*ku-te-ta-jo*	P		C
ME.SA.TI [101.51.53]		C2	HTW212a(CRIV11),	*me-sa-ta*	K		C
TE.QA.JA [91.56.74]		C1	6a6	*te-qa-ja*	PK	N	C
TE.U.TA2 [91.59.64]		C1	87.4	*te-u-to*	PK	N	C
WE.KA.DE [25.93.75]		C1	40.1	*we-ka-di-jo*	K	N	C

DECIPHERMENT 10 (Random)

Alternations within Linear A

I.PA.RE.MA		C1	MAW5a1(III12)	[52.31.30.29]
I.PA.RA₂.NU	*	C1	ZAZ3.1	[52.31.84.61]
I.PA.PA₃	*	C1	89.1	[52.31.58]
I.PA.PA.JA.RA₂	*	C2	PKZ11b(I4),PRZ1c(I17)	[52.31.31.53.84]
DE.RU.A	*	C1	HTW210a(CRIV13)	[101.51.26]
DE.RU.JA		C2	HTW212a(CRIV11),	[101.51.53]
DU.DU.A		C1	88.2	[103.103.26]
DU.DU.JA.TI		C1	85b1	[103.103.53.32]
DU.RE.RA		C1	40.2	[103.30.74]
DA.RE.RA	*	C1	123b2	[78.30.74]
DU.RU.U	*	C1	93a2	[103.51.60]
DO.RU.U		C2	HTW208a(CRIV1),	[75.51.60]
SI.TI.KU		C2B2	8b4,88.4,29.2,TY3a4(IV9)	[2.32.54]
SU.TI.KU	*	C1	117a5	[92.32.54]
RU.QE.A		C2	93a1,102.3	[51.94.26]
RA.QE.A		C1	10b1	[74.94.26]
TU.RA.RU	*	C1	19.3	[93.74.51]
TU.RA2.RU		C1	19.3	[93.84.51]

Parallels with Linear B

I.RA.TA [52.74.100]	*	C1	PRZ1b(I17)	i-ra-ta	PK	N	C
MA.NA.SI [29.98.2]		C3	16.1,HTW215a,	ma-na-sa	P	G	CX
SI.RA.NU [2.74.61]		C2	94b1,122a6	si-ra-no	K	N	C
TA.NA.WE.A [101.96.34]		C1	90.1	ta-na-wa	P		C
WA.NA.KU [62.98.54]	*	C1	HTW217a1(CRIV4)	wa-na-ka	PK	QN	C
WI.DU.RA [96.103.74]		C1	29.4	wi-du-ro	K	N	C

APPENDIX E

Linear A Sign Frequency

This appendix presents statistics on the frequency of the individual Linear A signs. The first and second tables are based on the entire Linear A corpus, the first organized by L number, the second by total frequency. The third table includes only the Hagia Triada tablets (HT 1-154), the fourth everything else. These last two tables are printed on facing pages to facilitate comparison of the behavior of signs at Hagia Triada and elsewhere.

The first column gives the L number of the Linear A sign accompanied in parenthesis by the corresponding Linear B phonetic value. Columns two through seven contain the total frequency, the initial frequency, the frequency as initial in words perhaps incomplete at the beginning, the medial frequency, the frequency as final in words perhaps incomplete at the end, and the final frequency. Column eight states as a percentage the frequency of this sign relative to all signs in the current table. The sum of all figures in the column is 100.0%. The last three columns contain the percentage of the occurrences of this sign which are securely initial, medial and final. These figures are computed from columns three, five and seven only. Their sum for each sign is 100.0%.

These figures are based on the Raison-Pope *Index du linéaire A* but can not be reproduced simply by counting the signs in the center column of that index since each sign-group has been counted only once regardless of how often it occurs. The common "totaling word" 98-22 contributes only one to the counts for L22 and L98. Statistics compiled on different principles may differ significantly from these.[1]

---

[1] If a sequence of signs occurs intact and also with a bracket at either end the incomplete group is assumed identical to the complete. Thus 97-57 and]97-57[are counted as one. Where Raison-Pope give variant readings (separated by a slash) I have counted the more likely. I have not segregated dotted signs and queried signs. In most cases I have treated (,) as a word-divider and have supplied tentative division within very long strings of signs, but in no case have I treated such cases as securely initial or final. Occasionally the Raison-Pope index fails to list a sign-group under each of its signs (2-32-54[missing under 54, 93-84-51 missing under 93, etc.), and six sign-groups, though cited, are not incorporated in the index (TEZ2, TLZ1, TYZ4, PHW20, PU1.1, PHW18).

All Linear A

Sign	Tot.	Init.	]—	Med.	—[	Fin.	Tot.	Init.	Med.	Fin.
1(PA₃)	21	4	1	7	2	7	1.20%	22.2%	38.9%	38.9%
2(PA)	46	20	2	15	1	8	2.63%	46.5%	34.9%	18.6%
3	2	0	0	0	0	2	0.11%	0.0%	0.0%	100.0%
4	1	1	0	0	0	0	0.06%	100.0%	0.0%	0.0%
6(TU)	40	10	3	14	3	10	2.29%	29.4%	41.2%	29.4%
7(SO)	1	1	0	0	0	0	0.06%	100.0%	0.0%	0.0%
8	1	1	0	0	0	0	0.06%	100.0%	0.0%	0.0%
9	2	0	0	2	0	0	0.11%	0.0%	100.0%	0.0%
10	3	1	1	1	0	0	0.17%	50.0%	50.0%	0.0%
14	2	0	0	0	0	2	0.11%	0.0%	0.0%	100.0%
20	4	1	0	1	0	2	0.23%	25.0%	25.0%	50.0%
21	1	1	0	0	0	0	0.06%	100.0%	0.0%	0.0%
22(RO)	21	3	0	7	0	11	1.20%	14.3%	33.3%	52.4%
23(ZA)	10	0	1	4	0	5	0.57%	0.0%	44.4%	55.6%
24(KE)	6	1	0	2	0	3	0.34%	16.7%	33.3%	50.0%
25(NU)	23	2	1	12	2	6	1.32%	10.0%	60.0%	30.0%
26(NA)	73	6	3	33	3	28	4.18%	9.0%	49.3%	41.8%
27	2	1	1	0	0	0	0.11%	100.0%	0.0%	0.0%
28(WI)	12	2	2	2	2	4	0.69%	25.0%	25.0%	50.0%
29(KA)	52	20	2	14	3	13	2.98%	42.6%	29.8%	27.7%
30(DA)	57	24	2	23	2	6	3.26%	45.3%	43.4%	11.3%
31(SA)	47	15	3	21	3	5	2.69%	36.6%	51.2%	12.2%
32(JA)	60	15	5	14	3	23	3.44%	28.8%	26.9%	44.2%
33	1	0	0	0	0	1	0.06%	0.0%	0.0%	100.0%
34(PU₂)	6	0	0	4	0	2	0.34%	0.0%	66.7%	33.3%
35	2	1	0	0	0	1	0.11%	50.0%	0.0%	50.0%
36	2	2	0	0	0	0	0.11%	100.0%	0.0%	0.0%
37	1	0	0	1	0	0	0.06%	0.0%	100.0%	0.0%
39(TO)	4	0	0	1	1	2	0.23%	0.0%	33.3%	66.7%
41	11	1	2	5	2	1	0.63%	14.3%	71.4%	14.3%
42	2	1	0	0	1	0	0.11%	100.0%	0.0%	0.0%
43	1	0	0	1	0	0	0.06%	0.0%	100.0%	0.0%
44	2	1	0	0	0	1	0.11%	50.0%	0.0%	50.0%
45(KO)	8	5	0	1	0	2	0.46%	62.5%	12.5%	25.0%
51(DI)	51	10	3	22	2	14	2.92%	21.7%	47.8%	30.4%
52(A)	72	53	7	7	0	5	4.12%	81.5%	10.8%	7.7%
53(RA)	62	7	4	22	7	22	3.55%	13.7%	43.1%	43.1%
54(RE)	55	3	4	19	6	23	3.15%	6.7%	42.2%	51.1%
55(RU)	51	7	7	20	3	14	2.92%	17.1%	48.8%	34.1%
56(PI)	21	8	3	4	2	4	1.20%	50.0%	25.0%	25.0%

All Linear A (cont.)

Sign	Tot.	Init.	]—	Med.	—[	Fin.	Tot.	Init.	Med.	Fin.
57(SI)	46	13	8	10	3	12	2.63%	37.1%	28.6%	34.3%
58(RA₂)	13	0	0	5	3	5	0.74%	0.0%	50.0%	50.0%
59(SU)	31	10	4	7	3	7	1.78%	41.7%	29.2%	29.2%
60(NI)	28	3	1	7	3	14	1.60%	12.5%	29.2%	58.3%
61(NE)	24	2	0	7	2	13	1.37%	9.1%	31.8%	59.1%
62(QA)	17	10	2	3	0	2	0.97%	66.7%	20.0%	13.3%
63	3	0	0	3	0	0	0.17%	0.0%	100.0%	0.0%
64(PU)	9	4	1	0	1	3	0.52%	57.1%	0.0%	42.9%
65	3	0	0	2	0	1	0.17%	0.0%	66.7%	33.3%
66	3	2	0	0	0	1	0.17%	66.7%	0.0%	33.3%
67	1	0	0	1	0	0	0.06%	0.0%	100.0%	0.0%
68	7	0	1	3	1	2	0.40%	0.0%	60.0%	40.0%
69	4	1	0	3	0	0	0.23%	25.0%	75.0%	0.0%
72(RI)	23	3	0	13	2	5	1.32%	14.3%	61.9%	23.8%
74(TA)	64	7	8	29	2	18	3.67%	13.0%	53.7%	33.3%
75(WA)	17	7	1	3	1	5	0.97%	46.7%	20.0%	33.3%
76(MI)	36	7	3	16	1	9	2.06%	21.9%	50.0%	28.1%
77(SE)	18	1	0	7	2	8	1.03%	6.3%	43.8%	50.0%
78(TI)	59	10	2	21	1	25	3.38%	17.9%	37.5%	44.6%
79	4	3	0	1	0	0	0.23%	75.0%	25.0%	0.0%
80	6	5	0	1	0	0	0.34%	83.3%	16.7%	0.0%
81(JE)	4	2	0	0	2	0	0.23%	100.0%	0.0%	0.0%
82	2	0	0	0	0	2	0.11%	0.0%	0.0%	100.0%
83	6	2	2	0	0	2	0.34%	50.0%	0.0%	50.0%
84(ME)	14	1	1	5	1	6	0.80%	8.3%	41.7%	50.0%
85	7	0	1	1	1	4	0.40%	0.0%	20.0%	80.0%
86(TA₂)	8	2	0	0	0	6	0.46%	25.0%	0.0%	75.0%
87	6	3	0	1	0	2	0.34%	50.0%	16.7%	33.3%
88	11	0	1	6	2	2	0.63%	0.0%	75.0%	25.0%
90	1	0	0	0	0	1	0.06%	0.0%	0.0%	100.0%
91(QE)	22	12	1	3	1	5	1.26%	60.0%	15.0%	25.0%
92(TE)	35	5	1	9	2	18	2.00%	15.6%	28.1%	56.3%
93(DU)	41	9	3	17	2	10	2.35%	25.0%	47.2%	27.8%
94(WE)	23	4	2	13	2	2	1.32%	21.1%	68.4%	10.5%
95(MA)	52	11	2	23	2	14	2.98%	22.9%	47.9%	29.2%
96	13	1	1	5	0	6	0.74%	8.3%	41.7%	50.0%
97(U)	26	17	3	3	1	2	1.49%	77.3%	13.6%	9.1%
98(KU)	54	19	4	19	3	9	3.09%	40.4%	40.4%	19.1%
99	3	3	0	0	0	0	0.17%	100.0%	0.0%	0.0%
100(I)	65	28	1	18	1	17	3.72%	44.4%	28.6%	27.0%

All Linear A (cont.)

Sign	Tot.	Init.	]—	Med.	—[	Fin.	Tot.	Init.	Med.	Fin.
101(DO)	15	8	0	6	0	1	0.86%	53.3%	40.0%	6.7%
102(DE)	15	3	1	8	2	1	0.86%	25.0%	66.7%	8.3%
103(KI)	45	16	3	18	2	6	2.58%	40.0%	45.0%	15.0%
111	3	0	0	0	0	3	0.17%	0.0%	0.0%	100.0%
114	1	0	0	1	0	0	0.06%	0.0%	100.0%	0.0%
120	1	0	0	1	0	0	0.06%	0.0%	100.0%	0.0%
126	1	0	0	0	0	1	0.06%	0.0%	0.0%	100.0%
134	1	0	0	1	0	0	0.06%	0.0%	100.0%	0.0%
135	4	0	0	2	1	1	0.23%	0.0%	66.7%	33.3%
138	1	0	0	0	0	1	0.06%	0.0%	0.0%	100.0%
143	2	0	1	1	0	0	0.11%	0.0%	100.0%	0.0%
144	2	0	0	2	0	0	0.11%	0.0%	100.0%	0.0%
145	1	0	0	0	0	1	0.06%	0.0%	0.0%	100.0%
147	1	0	0	0	1	0	0.06%	0.0%	0.0%	0.0%
150	1	0	0	1	0	0	0.06%	0.0%	100.0%	0.0%
151	2	1	0	1	0	0	0.11%	50.0%	50.0%	0.0%
152	1	0	0	1	0	0	0.06%	0.0%	100.0%	0.0%
153	1	0	0	1	0	0	0.06%	0.0%	100.0%	0.0%

All Linear A Sorted by Frequency

Sign	Tot.	Init.	]—	Med.	—[	Fin.	Tot.	Init.	Med.	Fin.
26(NA)	73	6	3	33	3	28	4.18%	9.0%	49.3%	41.8%
52(A)	72	53	7	7	0	5	4.12%	81.5%	10.8%	7.7%
100(I)	65	28	1	18	1	17	3.72%	44.4%	28.6%	27.0%
74(TA)	64	7	8	29	2	18	3.67%	13.0%	53.7%	33.3%
53(RA)	62	7	4	22	7	22	3.55%	13.7%	43.1%	43.1%
32(JA)	60	15	5	14	3	23	3.44%	28.8%	26.9%	44.2%
78(TI)	59	10	2	21	1	25	3.38%	17.9%	37.5%	44.6%
30(DA)	57	24	2	23	2	6	3.26%	45.3%	43.4%	11.3%
54(RE)	55	3	4	19	6	23	3.15%	6.7%	42.2%	51.1%
98(KU)	54	19	4	19	3	9	3.09%	40.4%	40.4%	19.1%
29(KA)	52	20	2	14	3	13	2.98%	42.6%	29.8%	27.7%
95(MA)	52	11	2	23	2	14	2.98%	22.9%	47.9%	29.2%
51(DI)	51	10	3	22	2	14	2.92%	21.7%	47.8%	30.4%
55(RU)	51	7	7	20	3	14	2.92%	17.1%	48.8%	34.1%
31(SA)	47	15	3	21	3	5	2.69%	36.6%	51.2%	12.2%
2(PA)	46	20	2	15	1	8	2.63%	46.5%	34.9%	18.6%
57(SI)	46	13	8	10	3	12	2.63%	37.1%	28.6%	34.3%
103(KI)	45	16	3	18	2	6	2.58%	40.0%	45.0%	15.0%
93(DU)	41	9	3	17	2	10	2.35%	25.0%	47.2%	27.8%
6(TU)	40	10	3	14	3	10	2.29%	29.4%	41.2%	29.4%
76(MI)	36	7	3	16	1	9	2.06%	21.9%	50.0%	28.1%
92(TE)	35	5	1	9	2	18	2.00%	15.6%	28.1%	56.3%
59(SU)	31	10	4	7	3	7	1.78%	41.7%	29.2%	29.2%
60(NI)	28	3	1	7	3	14	1.60%	12.5%	29.2%	58.3%
97(U)	26	17	3	3	1	2	1.49%	77.3%	13.6%	9.1%
61(NE)	24	2	0	7	2	13	1.37%	9.1%	31.8%	59.1%
25(NU)	23	2	1	12	2	6	1.32%	10.0%	60.0%	30.0%
72(RI)	23	3	0	13	2	5	1.32%	14.3%	61.9%	23.8%
94(WE)	23	4	2	13	2	2	1.32%	21.1%	68.4%	10.5%
91(QE)	22	12	1	3	1	5	1.26%	60.0%	15.0%	25.0%
1(PA_3)	21	4	1	7	2	7	1.20%	22.2%	38.9%	38.9%
22(RO)	21	3	0	7	0	11	1.20%	14.3%	33.3%	52.4%
56(PI)	21	8	3	4	2	4	1.20%	50.0%	25.0%	25.0%
77(SE)	18	1	0	7	2	8	1.03%	6.3%	43.8%	50.0%
62(QA)	17	10	2	3	0	2	0.97%	66.7%	20.0%	13.3%
75(WA)	17	7	1	3	1	5	0.97%	46.7%	20.0%	33.3%
101(DO)	15	8	0	6	0	1	0.86%	53.3%	40.0%	6.7%
102(DE)	15	3	1	8	2	1	0.86%	25.0%	66.7%	8.3%
84(ME)	14	1	1	5	1	6	0.80%	8.3%	41.7%	50.0%
58(RA_2)	13	0	0	5	3	5	0.74%	0.0%	50.0%	50.0%

All Linear A Sorted by Frequency (cont.)

Sign	Tot.	Init.	]—	Med.	—[	Fin.	Tot.	Init.	Med.	Fin.
96	13	1	1	5	0	6	0.74%	8.3%	41.7%	50.0%
28(WI)	12	2	2	2	2	4	0.69%	25.0%	25.0%	50.0%
41	11	1	2	5	2	1	0.63%	14.3%	71.4%	14.3%
88	11	0	1	6	2	2	0.63%	0.0%	75.0%	25.0%
23(ZA)	10	0	1	4	0	5	0.57%	0.0%	44.4%	55.6%
64(PU)	9	4	1	0	1	3	0.52%	57.1%	0.0%	42.9%
45(KO)	8	5	0	1	0	2	0.46%	62.5%	12.5%	25.0%
86(TA$_2$)	8	2	0	0	0	6	0.46%	25.0%	0.0%	75.0%
68	7	0	1	3	1	2	0.40%	0.0%	60.0%	40.0%
85	7	0	1	1	1	4	0.40%	0.0%	20.0%	80.0%
24(KE)	6	1	0	2	0	3	0.34%	16.7%	33.3%	50.0%
34(PU$_2$)	6	0	0	4	0	2	0.34%	0.0%	66.7%	33.3%
80	6	5	0	1	0	0	0.34%	83.3%	16.7%	0.0%
83	6	2	2	0	0	2	0.34%	50.0%	0.0%	50.0%
87	6	3	0	1	0	2	0.34%	50.0%	16.7%	33.3%
20	4	1	0	1	0	2	0.23%	25.0%	25.0%	50.0%
39(TO)	4	0	0	1	1	2	0.23%	0.0%	33.3%	66.7%
69	4	1	0	3	0	0	0.23%	25.0%	75.0%	0.0%
79	4	3	0	1	0	0	0.23%	75.0%	25.0%	0.0%
81(JE)	4	2	0	0	2	0	0.23%	100.0%	0.0%	0.0%
135	4	0	0	2	1	1	0.23%	0.0%	66.7%	33.3%
10	3	1	1	1	0	0	0.17%	50.0%	50.0%	0.0%
63	3	0	0	3	0	0	0.17%	0.0%	100.0%	0.0%
65	3	0	0	2	0	1	0.17%	0.0%	66.7%	33.3%
66	3	2	0	0	0	1	0.17%	66.7%	0.0%	33.3%
99	3	3	0	0	0	0	0.17%	100.0%	0.0%	0.0%
111	3	0	0	0	0	3	0.17%	0.0%	0.0%	100.0%
3	2	0	0	0	0	2	0.11%	0.0%	0.0%	100.0%
9	2	0	0	2	0	0	0.11%	0.0%	100.0%	0.0%
14	2	0	0	0	0	2	0.11%	0.0%	0.0%	100.0%
27	2	1	1	0	0	0	0.11%	100.0%	0.0%	0.0%
35	2	1	0	0	0	1	0.11%	50.0%	0.0%	50.0%
36	2	2	0	0	0	0	0.11%	100.0%	0.0%	0.0%
42	2	1	0	0	1	0	0.11%	100.0%	0.0%	0.0%
44	2	1	0	0	0	1	0.11%	50.0%	0.0%	50.0%
82	2	0	0	0	0	2	0.11%	0.0%	0.0%	100.0%
143	2	0	1	1	0	0	0.11%	0.0%	100.0%	0.0%
144	2	0	0	2	0	0	0.11%	0.0%	100.0%	0.0%
151	2	1	0	1	0	0	0.11%	50.0%	50.0%	0.0%
4	1	1	0	0	0	0	0.06%	100.0%	0.0%	0.0%

All Linear A Sorted by Frequency (cont.)

Sign	Tot.	Init.	]—	Med.	—[	Fin.	Tot.	Init.	Med.	Fin.
7(SO)	1	1	0	0	0	0	0.06%	100.0%	0.0%	0.0%
8	1	1	0	0	0	0	0.06%	100.0%	0.0%	0.0%
21	1	1	0	0	0	0	0.06%	100.0%	0.0%	0.0%
33	1	0	0	0	0	1	0.06%	0.0%	0.0%	100.0%
37	1	0	0	1	0	0	0.06%	0.0%	100.0%	0.0%
43	1	0	0	1	0	0	0.06%	0.0%	100.0%	0.0%
67	1	0	0	1	0	0	0.06%	0.0%	100.0%	0.0%
90	1	0	0	0	0	1	0.06%	0.0%	0.0%	100.0%
114	1	0	0	1	0	0	0.06%	0.0%	100.0%	0.0%
120	1	0	0	1	0	0	0.06%	0.0%	100.0%	0.0%
126	1	0	0	0	0	1	0.06%	0.0%	0.0%	100.0%
134	1	0	0	1	0	0	0.06%	0.0%	100.0%	0.0%
138	1	0	0	0	0	1	0.06%	0.0%	0.0%	100.0%
145	1	0	0	0	0	1	0.06%	0.0%	0.0%	100.0%
147	1	0	0	0	1	0	0.06%	0.0%	0.0%	0.0%
150	1	0	0	1	0	0	0.06%	0.0%	100.0%	0.0%
152	1	0	0	1	0	0	0.06%	0.0%	100.0%	0.0%
153	1	0	0	1	0	0	0.06%	0.0%	100.0%	0.0%

Minoan Linear A

Hagia Triada Tablets Only

Sign	Tot.	Init.	]—	Med.	—[	Fin.	Tot.	Init.	Med.	Fin.
1(PA₃)	14	4	0	5	1	4	1.29%	30.8%	38.5%	30.8%
2(PA)	29	17	1	6	0	5	2.68%	60.7%	21.4%	17.9%
3	1	0	0	0	0	1	0.09%	0.0%	0.0%	100.0%
4	1	1	0	0	0	0	0.09%	100.0%	0.0%	0.0%
6(TU)	27	8	3	5	2	9	2.50%	36.4%	22.7%	40.9%
7(SO)	1	1	0	0	0	0	0.09%	100.0%	0.0%	0.0%
8	1	1	0	0	0	0	0.09%	100.0%	0.0%	0.0%
9	2	0	0	2	0	0	0.18%	0.0%	100.0%	0.0%
10	1	0	1	0	0	0	0.09%	0.0%	0.0%	0.0%
14	0	0	0	0	0	0	0.00%	0.0%	0.0%	0.0%
20	0	0	0	0	0	0	0.00%	0.0%	0.0%	0.0%
21	1	1	0	0	0	0	0.09%	100.0%	0.0%	0.0%
22(RO)	17	1	0	7	0	9	1.57%	5.9%	41.2%	52.9%
23(ZA)	6	0	0	2	0	4	0.55%	0.0%	33.3%	66.7%
24(KE)	6	1	0	2	0	3	0.55%	16.7%	33.3%	50.0%
25(NU)	15	2	1	8	0	4	1.39%	14.3%	57.1%	28.6%
26(NA)	36	5	1	10	1	19	3.33%	14.7%	29.4%	55.9%
27	2	1	1	0	0	0	0.18%	100.0%	0.0%	0.0%
28(WI)	8	2	1	0	2	3	0.74%	40.0%	0.0%	60.0%
29(KA)	33	18	1	6	1	7	3.05%	58.1%	19.4%	22.6%
30(DA)	42	22	1	14	1	4	3.88%	55.0%	35.0%	10.0%
31(SA)	27	15	2	5	1	4	2.50%	62.5%	20.8%	16.7%
32(JA)	26	4	0	5	0	17	2.40%	15.4%	19.2%	65.4%
33	1	0	0	0	0	1	0.09%	0.0%	0.0%	100.0%
34(PU₂)	4	0	0	2	0	2	0.37%	0.0%	50.0%	50.0%
35	2	1	0	0	0	1	0.18%	50.0%	0.0%	50.0%
36	2	2	0	0	0	0	0.18%	100.0%	0.0%	0.0%
37	1	0	0	1	0	0	0.09%	0.0%	100.0%	0.0%
39(TO)	3	0	0	1	0	2	0.28%	0.0%	33.3%	66.7%
41	0	0	0	0	0	0	0.00%	0.0%	0.0%	0.0%
42	2	1	0	0	1	0	0.18%	100.0%	0.0%	0.0%
43	1	0	0	1	0	0	0.09%	0.0%	100.0%	0.0%
44	1	1	0	0	0	0	0.09%	100.0%	0.0%	0.0%
45(KO)	5	4	0	0	0	1	0.46%	80.0%	0.0%	20.0%
51(DI)	28	8	1	9	1	9	2.59%	30.8%	34.6%	34.6%
52(A)	26	22	1	1	0	2	2.40%	88.0%	4.0%	8.0%
53(RA)	42	5	2	15	3	17	3.88%	13.5%	40.5%	45.9%
54(RE)	37	2	3	10	4	18	3.42%	6.7%	33.3%	60.0%
55(RU)	36	5	3	13	2	13	3.33%	16.1%	41.9%	41.9%
56(PI)	10	6	0	3	0	1	0.92%	60.0%	30.0%	10.0%

All but Hagia Triada Tablets

Sign	Tot.	Init.	]—	Med.	—[	Fin.	Tot.	Init.	Med.	Fin.
1(PA₃)	7	0	1	2	1	3	1.00%	0.0%	40.0%	60.0%
2(PA)	22	7	1	9	1	4	3.13%	35.0%	45.0%	20.0%
3	1	0	0	0	0	1	0.14%	0.0%	0.0%	100.0%
4	0	0	0	0	0	0	0.00%	0.0%	0.0%	0.0%
6(TU)	13	2	0	9	1	1	1.85%	16.7%	75.0%	8.3%
7(SO)	0	0	0	0	0	0	0.00%	0.0%	0.0%	0.0%
8	0	0	0	0	0	0	0.00%	0.0%	0.0%	0.0%
9	0	0	0	0	0	0	0.00%	0.0%	0.0%	0.0%
10	2	1	0	1	0	0	0.28%	50.0%	50.0%	0.0%
14	2	0	0	0	0	2	0.28%	0.0%	0.0%	100.0%
20	4	1	0	1	0	2	0.57%	25.0%	25.0%	50.0%
21	0	0	0	0	0	0	0.00%	0.0%	0.0%	0.0%
22(RO)	4	2	0	0	0	2	0.57%	50.0%	0.0%	50.0%
23(ZA)	4	0	1	2	0	1	0.57%	0.0%	66.7%	33.3%
24(KE)	0	0	0	0	0	0	0.00%	0.0%	0.0%	0.0%
25(NU)	8	0	0	4	2	2	1.14%	0.0%	66.7%	33.3%
26(NA)	39	1	2	25	2	9	5.55%	2.9%	71.4%	25.7%
27	0	0	0	0	0	0	0.00%	0.0%	0.0%	0.0%
28(WI)	4	0	1	2	0	1	0.57%	0.0%	66.7%	33.3%
29(KA)	20	3	1	8	2	6	2.84%	17.6%	47.1%	35.3%
30(DA)	16	3	1	9	1	2	2.28%	21.4%	64.3%	14.3%
31(SA)	20	0	1	16	2	1	2.84%	0.0%	94.1%	5.9%
32(JA)	37	11	5	10	3	8	5.26%	37.9%	34.5%	27.6%
33	0	0	0	0	0	0	0.00%	0.0%	0.0%	0.0%
34(PU₂)	2	0	0	2	0	0	0.28%	0.0%	100.0%	0.0%
35	0	0	0	0	0	0	0.00%	0.0%	0.0%	0.0%
36	0	0	0	0	0	0	0.00%	0.0%	0.0%	0.0%
37	0	0	0	0	0	0	0.00%	0.0%	0.0%	0.0%
39(TO)	1	0	0	0	1	0	0.14%	0.0%	0.0%	0.0%
41	11	1	2	5	2	1	1.56%	14.3%	71.4%	14.3%
42	0	0	0	0	0	0	0.00%	0.0%	0.0%	0.0%
43	0	0	0	0	0	0	0.00%	0.0%	0.0%	0.0%
44	1	0	0	0	0	1	0.14%	0.0%	0.0%	100.0%
45(KO)	3	1	0	1	0	1	0.43%	33.3%	33.3%	33.3%
51(DI)	24	3	2	13	1	5	3.41%	14.3%	61.9%	23.8%
52(A)	47	32	6	6	0	3	6.69%	78.0%	14.6%	7.3%
53(RA)	21	2	2	7	4	6	2.99%	13.3%	46.7%	40.0%
54(RE)	22	1	1	9	3	8	3.13%	5.6%	50.0%	44.4%
55(RU)	15	2	4	7	1	1	2.13%	20.0%	70.0%	10.0%
56(PI)	11	2	3	1	2	3	1.56%	33.3%	16.7%	50.0%

Hagia Triada Tablets Only (cont.)

Sign	Tot.	Init.	]—	Med.	—[	Fin.	Tot.	Init.	Med.	Fin.
57(SI)	29	9	4	6	3	7	2.68%	40.9%	27.3%	31.8%
58(RA$_2$)	10	0	0	4	3	3	0.92%	0.0%	57.1%	42.9%
59(SU)	20	8	1	4	2	5	1.85%	47.1%	23.5%	29.4%
60(NI)	22	1	0	5	3	13	2.03%	5.3%	26.3%	68.4%
61(NE)	19	2	0	5	2	10	1.76%	11.8%	29.4%	58.8%
62(QA)	15	9	2	2	0	2	1.39%	69.2%	15.4%	15.4%
63	3	0	0	3	0	0	0.28%	0.0%	100.0%	0.0%
64(PU)	7	3	1	0	0	3	0.65%	50.0%	0.0%	50.0%
65	3	0	0	2	0	1	0.28%	0.0%	66.7%	33.3%
66	3	2	0	0	0	1	0.28%	66.7%	0.0%	33.3%
67	0	0	0	0	0	0	0.00%	0.0%	0.0%	0.0%
68	3	0	0	2	0	1	0.28%	0.0%	66.7%	33.3%
69	2	0	0	2	0	0	0.18%	0.0%	100.0%	0.0%
72(RI)	12	2	0	8	1	1	1.11%	18.2%	72.7%	9.1%
74(TA)	42	6	4	16	1	15	3.88%	16.2%	43.2%	40.5%
75(WA)	5	2	0	0	0	3	0.46%	40.0%	0.0%	60.0%
76(MI)	25	6	3	9	0	7	2.31%	27.3%	40.9%	31.8%
77(SE)	13	1	0	6	0	6	1.20%	7.7%	46.2%	46.2%
78(TI)	33	6	1	8	0	18	3.05%	18.8%	25.0%	56.3%
79	4	3	0	1	0	0	0.37%	75.0%	25.0%	0.0%
80	1	1	0	0	0	0	0.09%	100.0%	0.0%	0.0%
81(JE)	2	2	0	0	0	0	0.18%	100.0%	0.0%	0.0%
82	2	0	0	0	0	2	0.18%	0.0%	0.0%	100.0%
83	5	2	2	0	0	1	0.46%	66.7%	0.0%	33.3%
84(ME)	9	1	1	4	0	3	0.83%	12.5%	50.0%	37.5%
85	4	0	1	1	0	2	0.37%	0.0%	33.3%	66.7%
86(TA$_2$)	6	0	0	0	0	6	0.55%	0.0%	0.0%	100.0%
87	5	3	0	0	0	2	0.46%	60.0%	0.0%	40.0%
88	1	0	0	0	0	1	0.09%	0.0%	0.0%	100.0%
90	1	0	0	0	0	1	0.09%	0.0%	0.0%	100.0%
91(QE)	19	10	1	3	1	4	1.76%	58.8%	17.6%	23.5%
92(TE)	17	5	1	1	0	10	1.57%	31.3%	6.3%	62.5%
93(DU)	31	9	1	11	2	8	2.87%	32.1%	39.3%	28.6%
94(WE)	15	2	2	9	0	2	1.39%	15.4%	69.2%	15.4%
95(MA)	32	9	1	11	1	10	2.96%	30.0%	36.7%	33.3%
96	11	1	1	3	0	6	1.02%	10.0%	30.0%	60.0%
97(U)	18	12	1	3	0	2	1.66%	70.6%	17.6%	11.8%
98(KU)	41	18	4	12	2	5	3.79%	51.4%	34.3%	14.3%
99	2	2	0	0	0	0	0.18%	100.0%	0.0%	0.0%
100(I)	32	11	1	6	0	14	2.96%	35.5%	19.4%	45.2%

All but Hagia Triada Tablets (cont.)

Sign	Tot.	Init.	]—	Med.	—[	Fin.	Tot.	Init.	Med.	Fin.
57(SI)	19	5	5	4	0	5	2.70%	35.7%	28.6%	35.7%
58(RA$_2$)	3	0	0	1	0	2	0.43%	0.0%	33.3%	66.7%
59(SU)	12	3	3	3	1	2	1.71%	37.5%	37.5%	25.0%
60(NI)	7	2	1	2	0	2	1.00%	33.3%	33.3%	33.3%
61(NE)	5	0	0	2	0	3	0.71%	0.0%	40.0%	60.0%
62(QA)	2	1	0	1	0	0	0.28%	50.0%	50.0%	0.0%
63	0	0	0	0	0	0	0.00%	0.0%	0.0%	0.0%
64(PU)	2	1	0	0	1	0	0.28%	100.0%	0.0%	0.0%
65	0	0	0	0	0	0	0.00%	0.0%	0.0%	0.0%
66	0	0	0	0	0	0	0.00%	0.0%	0.0%	0.0%
67	1	0	0	1	0	0	0.14%	0.0%	100.0%	0.0%
68	4	0	1	1	1	1	0.57%	0.0%	50.0%	50.0%
69	2	1	0	1	0	0	0.28%	50.0%	50.0%	0.0%
72(RI)	11	1	0	5	1	4	1.56%	10.0%	50.0%	40.0%
74(TA)	22	1	4	13	1	3	3.13%	5.9%	76.5%	17.6%
75(WA)	12	5	1	3	1	2	1.71%	50.0%	30.0%	20.0%
76(MI)	12	1	0	8	1	2	1.71%	9.1%	72.7%	18.2%
77(SE)	7	0	0	2	2	3	1.00%	0.0%	40.0%	60.0%
78(TI)	29	5	1	14	1	8	4.13%	18.5%	51.9%	29.6%
79	0	0	0	0	0	0	0.00%	0.0%	0.0%	0.0%
80	5	4	0	1	0	0	0.71%	80.0%	20.0%	0.0%
81(JE)	2	0	0	0	2	0	0.28%	0.0%	0.0%	0.0%
82	0	0	0	0	0	0	0.00%	0.0%	0.0%	0.0%
83	1	0	0	0	0	1	0.14%	0.0%	0.0%	100.0%
84(ME)	5	0	0	1	1	3	0.71%	0.0%	25.0%	75.0%
85	3	0	0	0	1	2	0.43%	0.0%	0.0%	100.0%
86(TA$_2$)	2	2	0	0	0	0	0.28%	100.0%	0.0%	0.0%
87	2	1	0	1	0	0	0.28%	50.0%	50.0%	0.0%
88	10	0	1	6	2	1	1.42%	0.0%	85.7%	14.3%
90	0	0	0	0	0	0	0.00%	0.0%	0.0%	0.0%
91(QE)	4	2	0	0	0	2	0.57%	50.0%	0.0%	50.0%
92(TE)	18	0	0	8	2	8	2.56%	0.0%	50.0%	50.0%
93(DU)	11	0	2	6	0	3	1.56%	0.0%	66.7%	33.3%
94(WE)	8	2	0	4	2	0	1.14%	33.3%	66.7%	0.0%
95(MA)	21	3	1	12	1	4	2.99%	15.8%	63.2%	21.1%
96	2	0	0	2	0	0	0.28%	0.0%	100.0%	0.0%
97(U)	10	6	2	0	1	1	1.42%	85.7%	0.0%	14.3%
98(KU)	16	2	0	8	1	5	2.28%	13.3%	53.3%	33.3%
99	1	1	0	0	0	0	0.14%	100.0%	0.0%	0.0%
100(I)	33	17	0	12	1	3	4.69%	53.1%	37.5%	9.4%

Hagia Triada Tablets Only (cont.)

Sign	Tot.	Init.	]—	Med.	—[	Fin.	Tot.	Init.	Med.	Fin.
101(DO)	8	4	0	4	0	0	0.74%	50.0%	50.0%	0.0%
102(DE)	12	3	1	6	1	1	1.11%	30.0%	60.0%	10.0%
103(KI)	32	14	2	10	2	4	2.96%	50.0%	35.7%	14.3%
111	3	0	0	0	0	3	0.28%	0.0%	0.0%	100.0%
114	1	0	0	1	0	0	0.09%	0.0%	100.0%	0.0%
120	1	0	0	1	0	0	0.09%	0.0%	100.0%	0.0%
126	1	0	0	0	0	1	0.09%	0.0%	0.0%	100.0%
134	0	0	0	0	0	0	0.00%	0.0%	0.0%	0.0%
135	0	0	0	0	0	0	0.00%	0.0%	0.0%	0.0%
138	1	0	0	0	0	1	0.09%	0.0%	0.0%	100.0%
143	0	0	0	0	0	0	0.00%	0.0%	0.0%	0.0%
144	0	0	0	0	0	0	0.00%	0.0%	0.0%	0.0%
145	0	0	0	0	0	0	0.00%	0.0%	0.0%	0.0%
147	0	0	0	0	0	0	0.00%	0.0%	0.0%	0.0%
150	0	0	0	0	0	0	0.00%	0.0%	0.0%	0.0%
151	0	0	0	0	0	0	0.00%	0.0%	0.0%	0.0%
152	1	0	0	1	0	0	0.09%	0.0%	100.0%	0.0%
153	1	0	0	1	0	0	0.09%	0.0%	100.0%	0.0%

All but Hagia Triada Tablets (cont.)

Sign	Tot.	Init.	]—	Med.	—[	Fin.	Tot.	Init.	Med.	Fin.
101(DO)	7	4	0	2	0	1	1.00%	57.1%	28.6%	14.3%
102(DE)	3	0	0	2	1	0	0.43%	0.0%	100.0%	0.0%
103(KI)	14	2	1	8	0	3	1.99%	15.4%	61.5%	23.1%
111	0	0	0	0	0	0	0.00%	0.0%	0.0%	0.0%
114	0	0	0	0	0	0	0.00%	0.0%	0.0%	0.0%
120	0	0	0	0	0	0	0.00%	0.0%	0.0%	0.0%
126	0	0	0	0	0	0	0.00%	0.0%	0.0%	0.0%
134	1	0	0	1	0	0	0.14%	0.0%	100.0%	0.0%
135	4	0	0	2	1	1	0.57%	0.0%	66.7%	33.3%
138	0	0	0	0	0	0	0.00%	0.0%	0.0%	0.0%
143	2	0	1	1	0	0	0.28%	0.0%	100.0%	0.0%
144	2	0	0	2	0	0	0.28%	0.0%	100.0%	0.0%
145	1	0	0	0	0	1	0.14%	0.0%	0.0%	100.0%
147	1	0	0	0	1	0	0.14%	0.0%	0.0%	0.0%
150	1	0	0	1	0	0	0.14%	0.0%	100.0%	0.0%
151	2	1	0	1	0	0	0.28%	50.0%	50.0%	0.0%
152	0	0	0	0	0	0	0.00%	0.0%	0.0%	0.0%
153	0	0	0	0	0	0	0.00%	0.0%	0.0%	0.0%

APPENDIX F

Linear B Sign Frequency

This appendix consists of tabulations of the frequency of Linear B signs in words of various classes. The statistics reflect only the sign-groups listed in Morpurgo (1961).[1] Each distinct sign-group is counted once, no matter how many times it is repeated within Linear B. These statistics, therefore, differ from those compiled on different principles. For the subdivisions into personal names and place names a possible identification has been counted equally with a more secure one. A sign-group therefore may occasionally be counted both as a name and a place, but the same sign-group is never counted more than once in a single table.

These statistics can make no claim to finality. Recent joins and improved readings, especially at Knossos, will modify the figures. Moreover, the difficulty of deciding whether a Linear B sign-group is a name, a place, or something else should not be underestimated. At least for the common signs, however, these figures are unlikely to be altered significantly.

---

[1] Words missing in Morpurgo but found in the latest edition of *The Knossos Tablets* are included in **Appendices B, C, and D**, but not in the frequency counts in Appendices F and G.

All Sign-Groups (16834 Signs)

Sign	Total	Initial	Medial	Final	Total	Initial	Medial	Final
a	627	568	27	32	3.72%	90.59%	4.31%	5.10%
e	543	397	87	59	3.23%	73.11%	16.02%	10.87%
i	324	113	119	92	1.92%	34.88%	36.73%	28.40%
o	418	219	50	149	2.48%	52.39%	11.96%	35.65%
u	428	61	194	173	2.54%	14.25%	45.33%	40.42%
a_2	67	28	19	20	0.40%	41.79%	28.36%	29.85%
a_3	51	48	3	0	0.30%	94.12%	5.88%	0.00%
da	244	96	120	28	1.45%	39.34%	49.18%	11.48%
de	191	48	56	87	1.13%	25.13%	29.32%	45.55%
di	125	76	41	8	0.74%	60.80%	32.80%	6.40%
do	147	45	72	30	0.87%	30.61%	48.98%	20.41%
du	73	29	36	8	0.43%	39.73%	49.32%	10.96%
dwe	4	0	2	2	0.02%	0.00%	50.00%	50.00%
dwo	7	3	1	3	0.04%	42.86%	14.29%	42.86%
ja	559	32	194	333	3.32%	5.72%	34.70%	59.57%
je	76	7	56	13	0.45%	9.21%	73.68%	17.11%
jo	724	16	104	604	4.30%	2.21%	14.36%	83.43%
ka	435	200	167	68	2.58%	45.98%	38.39%	15.63%
ke	422	126	237	59	2.51%	29.86%	56.16%	13.98%
ki	241	86	130	25	1.43%	35.68%	53.94%	10.37%
ko	449	154	161	134	2.67%	34.30%	35.86%	29.84%
ku	181	118	50	13	1.08%	65.19%	27.62%	7.18%
ma	249	103	112	34	1.48%	41.37%	44.98%	13.65%
me	274	111	135	28	1.63%	40.51%	49.27%	10.22%
mi	140	37	85	18	0.83%	26.43%	60.71%	12.86%
mo	145	17	51	77	0.86%	11.72%	35.17%	53.10%
mu	30	16	14	0	0.18%	53.33%	46.67%	0.00%
na	258	33	145	80	1.53%	12.79%	56.20%	31.01%
ne	237	46	106	85	1.41%	19.41%	44.73%	35.86%
ni	193	21	149	23	1.15%	10.88%	77.20%	11.92%
no	355	32	92	231	2.11%	9.01%	25.92%	65.07%
nu	90	9	62	19	0.53%	10.00%	68.89%	21.11%
nwa	14	1	10	3	0.08%	7.14%	71.43%	21.43%
pa	276	140	112	24	1.64%	50.72%	40.58%	8.70%
pa_3	35	17	13	5	0.21%	48.57%	37.14%	14.29%
pe	208	108	86	14	1.24%	51.92%	41.35%	6.73%
pi	296	85	132	79	1.76%	28.72%	44.59%	26.69%
po	254	156	70	28	1.51%	61.42%	27.56%	11.02%
pte	13	5	6	2	0.08%	38.46%	46.15%	15.38%
pu	94	57	28	9	0.56%	60.64%	29.79%	9.57%
pu_2	42	14	24	4	0.25%	33.33%	57.14%	9.52%
qa	116	59	34	23	0.69%	50.86%	29.31%	19.83%
qe	135	57	43	35	0.80%	42.22%	31.85%	25.93%
qi	54	20	29	5	0.32%	37.04%	53.70%	9.26%
qo	147	32	75	40	0.87%	21.77%	51.02%	27.21%

All Sign-Groups (cont.)

Sign	Total	Initial	Medial	Final	Total	Initial	Medial	Final
ra	582	113	346	123	3.46%	19.42%	59.45%	21.13%
ra₂	40	0	22	18	0.24%	0.00%	55.00%	45.00%
ra₃	9	0	4	5	0.05%	0.00%	44.44%	55.56%
re	459	73	296	90	2.73%	15.90%	64.49%	19.61%
ri	426	53	322	51	2.53%	12.44%	75.59%	11.97%
ro	590	33	227	330	3.50%	5.59%	38.47%	55.93%
ro₂	20	0	9	11	0.12%	0.00%	45.00%	55.00%
ru	168	48	105	15	1.00%	28.57%	62.50%	8.93%
sa	191	60	89	42	1.13%	31.41%	46.60%	21.99%
se	116	22	74	20	0.69%	18.97%	63.79%	17.24%
si	298	58	166	74	1.77%	19.46%	55.70%	24.83%
so	201	10	69	122	1.19%	4.98%	34.33%	60.70%
su	60	32	25	3	0.36%	53.33%	41.67%	5.00%
ta	608	102	219	287	3.61%	16.78%	36.02%	47.20%
ta₂	12	0	2	10	0.07%	0.00%	16.67%	83.33%
te	501	121	250	130	2.98%	24.15%	49.90%	25.95%
ti	304	62	198	44	1.81%	20.39%	65.13%	14.47%
to	510	98	145	267	3.03%	19.22%	28.43%	52.35%
tu	119	57	50	12	0.71%	47.90%	42.02%	10.08%
two	1	0	1	0	0.01%	0.00%	100.00%	0.00%
wa	310	85	136	89	1.84%	27.42%	43.87%	28.71%
we	393	71	151	171	2.33%	18.07%	38.42%	43.51%
wi	221	63	141	17	1.31%	28.51%	63.80%	7.69%
wo	436	84	152	200	2.59%	19.27%	34.86%	45.87%
za	47	15	16	16	0.28%	31.91%	34.04%	34.04%
ze	36	14	16	6	0.21%	38.89%	44.44%	16.67%
zo	62	8	19	35	0.37%	12.90%	30.65%	56.45%
*18	4	1	1	2	0.02%	25.00%	25.00%	50.00%
*19	1	0	0	1	0.01%	0.00%	0.00%	100.00%
*22	11	3	7	1	0.07%	27.27%	63.64%	9.09%
*34	12	7	4	1	0.07%	58.33%	33.33%	8.33%
*35	8	5	2	1	0.05%	62.50%	25.00%	12.50%
*47	8	7	1	0	0.05%	87.50%	12.50%	0.00%
*49	3	1	2	0	0.02%	33.33%	66.67%	0.00%
*63	1	0	1	0	0.01%	0.00%	100.00%	0.00%
*64	4	0	4	0	0.02%	0.00%	100.00%	0.00%
*65	16	0	11	5	0.10%	0.00%	68.75%	31.25%
*79	5	0	3	2	0.03%	0.00%	60.00%	40.00%
*82	11	3	5	3	0.07%	27.3%	45.5%	27.3%
*83	12	3	8	1	0.07%	25.00%	66.67%	8.33%
*85	21	20	1	0	0.12%	95.24%	4.76%	0.00%
*86	4	0	3	1	0.02%	0.00%	75.00%	25.00%
*88	1	0	0	1	0.01%	0.00%	0.00%	100.00%

All Complete Sign-Groups (11726 Signs)

Sign	Total	Initial	Medial	Final	Total	Initial	Medial	Final
a	450	416	16	18	3.84%	92.44%	3.56%	4.00%
e	393	277	72	44	3.35%	70.48%	18.32%	11.20%
i	206	75	83	48	1.76%	36.41%	40.29%	23.30%
o	306	155	36	115	2.61%	50.65%	11.76%	37.58%
u	315	35	150	130	2.69%	11.11%	47.62%	41.27%
a_2	58	21	18	19	0.49%	36.21%	31.03%	32.76%
a_3	44	43	1	0	0.38%	97.73%	2.27%	0.00%
da	167	56	94	17	1.42%	33.53%	56.29%	10.18%
de	133	29	42	62	1.13%	21.80%	31.58%	46.62%
di	90	51	35	4	0.77%	56.67%	38.89%	4.44%
do	92	29	54	9	0.78%	31.52%	58.70%	9.78%
du	48	20	26	2	0.41%	41.67%	54.17%	4.17%
dwe	3	0	2	1	0.03%	0.00%	66.67%	33.33%
dwo	3	1	0	2	0.03%	33.33%	0.00%	66.67%
ja	395	11	151	233	3.37%	2.78%	38.23%	58.99%
je	53	0	50	3	0.45%	0.00%	94.34%	5.66%
jo	507	3	78	426	4.32%	0.59%	15.38%	84.02%
ka	282	119	126	37	2.40%	42.20%	44.68%	13.12%
ke	303	82	189	32	2.58%	27.06%	62.38%	10.56%
ki	161	53	101	7	1.37%	32.92%	62.73%	4.35%
ko	328	110	129	89	2.80%	33.54%	39.33%	27.13%
ku	121	80	36	5	1.03%	66.12%	29.75%	4.13%
ma	164	58	90	16	1.40%	35.37%	54.88%	9.76%
me	177	64	103	10	1.51%	36.16%	58.19%	5.65%
mi	92	22	63	7	0.78%	23.91%	68.48%	7.61%
mo	92	13	36	43	0.78%	14.13%	39.13%	46.74%
mu	22	12	10	0	0.19%	54.55%	45.45%	0.00%
na	174	15	102	57	1.48%	8.62%	58.62%	32.76%
ne	160	28	86	46	1.36%	17.50%	53.75%	28.75%
ni	122	0	116	6	1.04%	0.00%	95.08%	4.92%
no	247	11	76	160	2.11%	4.45%	30.77%	64.78%
nu	59	3	52	4	0.50%	5.08%	88.14%	6.78%
nwa	8	0	6	2	0.07%	0.00%	75.00%	25.00%
pa	191	97	81	13	1.63%	50.79%	42.41%	6.81%
pa_3	24	13	9	2	0.20%	54.17%	37.50%	8.33%
pe	166	84	75	7	1.42%	50.60%	45.18%	4.22%
pi	223	62	104	57	1.90%	27.80%	46.64%	25.56%
po	193	117	59	17	1.65%	60.62%	30.57%	8.81%
pte	9	2	6	1	0.08%	22.22%	66.67%	11.11%
pu	63	42	19	2	0.54%	66.67%	30.16%	3.17%
pu_2	29	10	18	1	0.25%	34.48%	62.07%	3.45%
qa	73	38	23	12	0.62%	52.05%	31.51%	16.44%
qe	90	39	36	15	0.77%	43.33%	40.00%	16.67%
qi	41	15	26	0	0.35%	36.59%	63.41%	0.00%
qo	106	19	62	25	0.90%	17.92%	58.49%	23.58%

All Complete Sign-Groups (cont.)

Sign	Total	Initial	Medial	Final	Total	Initial	Medial	Final
ra	398	63	262	73	3.39%	15.83%	65.83%	18.34%
ra_2	32	0	19	13	0.27%	0.00%	59.38%	40.63%
ra_3	9	0	4	5	0.08%	0.00%	44.44%	55.56%
re	316	38	232	46	2.69%	12.03%	73.42%	14.56%
ri	288	25	253	10	2.46%	8.68%	87.85%	3.47%
ro	411	11	186	214	3.51%	2.68%	45.26%	52.07%
ro_2	16	0	7	9	0.14%	0.00%	43.75%	56.25%
ru	118	26	85	7	1.01%	22.03%	72.03%	5.93%
sa	130	39	71	20	1.11%	30.00%	54.62%	15.38%
se	76	8	58	10	0.65%	10.53%	76.32%	13.16%
si	194	34	120	40	1.65%	17.53%	61.86%	20.62%
so	134	4	50	80	1.14%	2.99%	37.31%	59.70%
su	43	22	19	2	0.37%	51.16%	44.19%	4.65%
ta	428	53	172	203	3.65%	12.38%	40.19%	47.43%
ta_2	9	0	2	7	0.08%	0.00%	22.22%	77.78%
te	352	66	206	80	3.00%	18.75%	58.52%	22.73%
ti	203	35	150	18	1.73%	17.24%	73.89%	8.87%
to	366	67	113	186	3.12%	18.31%	30.87%	50.82%
tu	85	42	41	2	0.72%	49.41%	48.24%	2.35%
two	1	0	1	0	0.01%	0.00%	100.00%	0.00%
wa	217	55	111	51	1.85%	25.35%	51.15%	23.50%
we	272	37	110	125	2.32%	13.60%	40.44%	45.96%
wi	159	44	110	5	1.36%	27.67%	69.18%	3.14%
wo	300	47	113	140	2.56%	15.67%	37.67%	46.67%
za	29	7	11	11	0.25%	24.14%	37.93%	37.93%
ze	24	9	11	4	0.20%	37.50%	45.83%	16.67%
zo	48	6	18	24	0.41%	12.50%	37.50%	50.00%
*18	2	1	0	1	0.02%	50.00%	0.00%	50.00%
*19	1	0	0	1	0.01%	0.00%	0.00%	100.00%
*22	5	0	5	0	0.04%	0.00%	100.00%	0.00%
*34	9	6	3	0	0.08%	66.67%	33.33%	0.00%
*35	6	4	2	0	0.05%	66.67%	33.33%	0.00%
*47	5	4	1	0	0.04%	80.00%	20.00%	0.00%
*49	3	1	2	0	0.03%	33.33%	66.67%	0.00%
*63	1	0	1	0	0.01%	0.00%	100.00%	0.00%
*64	3	0	3	0	0.03%	0.00%	100.00%	0.00%
*65	12	0	10	2	0.10%	0.00%	83.33%	16.67%
*79	4	0	2	2	0.03%	0.00%	50.00%	50.00%
*82	7	1	4	2	0.06%	14.3%	57.1%	28.6%
*83	6	0	6	0	0.05%	0.00%	100.00%	0.00%
*85	16	16	0	0	0.14%	100.00%	0.00%	0.00%
*86	3	0	3	0	0.03%	0.00%	100.00%	0.00%
*88	1	0	0	1	0.01%	0.00%	0.00%	100.00%

All Knossos Sign-Groups (8579 Signs)

Sign	Total	Initial	Medial	Final	Total	Initial	Medial	Final
a	341	307	7	27	3.97%	90.03%	2.05%	7.92%
e	224	183	21	20	2.61%	81.70%	9.38%	8.93%
i	166	61	66	39	1.93%	36.75%	39.76%	23.49%
o	171	97	21	53	1.99%	56.73%	12.28%	30.99%
u	186	40	77	69	2.17%	21.51%	41.40%	37.10%
a₂	4	2	0	2	0.05%	50.00%	0.00%	50.00%
a₃	26	24	2	0	0.30%	92.31%	7.69%	0.00%
da	160	73	68	19	1.87%	45.63%	42.50%	11.88%
de	86	26	20	40	1.00%	30.23%	23.26%	46.51%
di	75	47	22	6	0.87%	62.67%	29.33%	8.00%
do	81	25	33	23	0.94%	30.86%	40.74%	28.40%
du	53	21	24	8	0.62%	39.62%	45.28%	15.09%
dwe	4	0	2	2	0.05%	0.00%	50.00%	50.00%
dwo	4	2	0	2	0.05%	50.00%	0.00%	50.00%
ja	287	27	86	174	3.35%	9.41%	29.97%	60.63%
je	35	7	18	10	0.41%	20.00%	51.43%	28.57%
jo	375	10	41	324	4.37%	2.67%	10.93%	86.40%
ka	227	105	78	44	2.65%	46.26%	34.36%	19.38%
ke	173	64	78	31	2.02%	36.99%	45.09%	17.92%
ki	132	54	61	17	1.54%	40.91%	46.21%	12.88%
ko	217	78	77	62	2.53%	35.94%	35.48%	28.57%
ku	115	79	24	12	1.34%	68.70%	20.87%	10.43%
ma	126	55	46	25	1.47%	43.65%	36.51%	19.84%
me	135	60	53	22	1.57%	44.44%	39.26%	16.30%
mi	88	26	49	13	1.03%	29.55%	55.68%	14.77%
mo	98	9	30	59	1.14%	9.18%	30.61%	60.20%
mu	16	6	10	0	0.19%	37.50%	62.50%	0.00%
na	146	24	81	41	1.70%	16.44%	55.48%	28.08%
ne	112	26	46	40	1.31%	23.21%	41.07%	35.71%
ni	115	16	81	18	1.34%	13.91%	70.43%	15.65%
no	179	20	30	129	2.09%	11.17%	16.76%	72.07%
nu	64	8	40	16	0.75%	12.50%	62.50%	25.00%
nwa	8	1	4	3	0.09%	12.50%	50.00%	37.50%
pa	155	77	59	19	1.81%	49.68%	38.06%	12.26%
pa₃	33	17	11	5	0.38%	51.52%	33.33%	15.15%
pe	84	48	30	6	0.98%	57.14%	35.71%	7.14%
pi	125	38	53	34	1.46%	30.40%	42.40%	27.20%
po	122	79	26	17	1.42%	64.75%	21.31%	13.93%
pte	6	4	1	1	0.07%	66.67%	16.67%	16.67%
pu	60	36	15	9	0.70%	60.00%	25.00%	15.00%
pu₂	21	6	11	4	0.24%	28.57%	52.38%	19.05%
qa	81	47	21	13	0.94%	58.02%	25.93%	16.05%
qe	66	30	16	20	0.77%	45.45%	24.24%	30.30%
qi	29	16	9	4	0.34%	55.17%	31.03%	13.79%
qo	71	16	34	21	0.83%	22.54%	47.89%	29.58%

All Knossos Sign-Groups (cont.)

Sign	Total	Initial	Medial	Final	Total	Initial	Medial	Final
ra	289	66	156	67	3.37%	22.84%	53.98%	23.18%
ra$_2$	13	0	6	7	0.15%	0.00%	46.15%	53.85%
ra$_3$	0	0	0	0	0.00%	0.00%	0.00%	0.00%
re	199	37	112	50	2.32%	18.59%	56.28%	25.13%
ri	219	38	148	33	2.55%	17.35%	67.58%	15.07%
ro	305	19	80	206	3.56%	6.23%	26.23%	67.54%
ro$_2$	13	0	5	8	0.15%	0.00%	38.46%	61.54%
ru	94	33	49	12	1.10%	35.11%	52.13%	12.77%
sa	110	38	46	26	1.28%	34.55%	41.82%	23.64%
se	53	13	27	13	0.62%	24.53%	50.94%	24.53%
si	172	43	90	39	2.00%	25.00%	52.33%	22.67%
so	120	5	23	92	1.40%	4.17%	19.17%	76.67%
su	46	27	16	3	0.54%	58.70%	34.78%	6.52%
ta	347	71	105	171	4.04%	20.46%	30.26%	49.28%
ta$_2$	10	0	2	8	0.12%	0.00%	20.00%	80.00%
te	219	68	87	64	2.55%	31.05%	39.73%	29.22%
ti	150	30	87	33	1.75%	20.00%	58.00%	22.00%
to	285	47	60	178	3.32%	16.49%	21.05%	62.46%
tu	60	34	17	9	0.70%	56.67%	28.33%	15.00%
two	0	0	0	0	0.00%	0.00%	0.00%	0.00%
wa	153	41	63	49	1.78%	26.80%	41.18%	32.03%
we	190	43	73	74	2.21%	22.63%	38.42%	38.95%
wi	103	40	54	9	1.20%	38.83%	52.43%	8.74%
wo	188	42	49	97	2.19%	22.34%	26.06%	51.60%
za	29	10	8	11	0.34%	34.48%	27.59%	37.93%
ze	19	5	11	3	0.22%	26.32%	57.89%	15.79%
zo	41	7	10	24	0.48%	17.07%	24.39%	58.54%
*18	4	1	1	2	0.05%	25.00%	25.00%	50.00%
*19	1	0	0	1	0.01%	0.00%	0.00%	100.00%
*22	10	3	6	1	0.12%	30.00%	60.00%	10.00%
*34	5	2	2	1	0.06%	40.00%	40.00%	20.00%
*35	2	1	1	0	0.02%	50.00%	50.00%	0.00%
*47	7	7	0	0	0.08%	100.00%	0.00%	0.00%
*49	3	1	2	0	0.03%	33.33%	66.67%	0.00%
*63	0	0	0	0	0.00%	0.00%	0.00%	0.00%
*64	2	0	2	0	0.02%	0.00%	100.00%	0.00%
*65	11	0	8	3	0.13%	0.00%	72.73%	27.27%
*79	3	0	2	1	0.03%	0.00%	66.67%	33.33%
*82	2	1	1	0	0.02%	50.0%	50.0%	0.0%
*83	10	3	6	1	0.12%	30.00%	60.00%	10.00%
*85	7	6	1	0	0.08%	85.71%	14.29%	0.00%
*86	2	0	2	0	0.02%	0.00%	100.00%	0.00%
*88	0	0	0	0	0.00%	0.00%	0.00%	0.00%

Knossos Names (3334 Signs)

Sign	Total	Initial	Medial	Final	Total	Initial	Medial	Final
a	150	145	2	3	4.50%	96.67%	1.33%	2.00%
e	51	44	6	1	1.53%	86.27%	11.76%	1.96%
i	49	25	23	1	1.47%	51.02%	46.94%	2.04%
o	44	23	5	16	1.32%	52.27%	11.36%	36.36%
u	98	15	32	51	2.94%	15.31%	32.65%	52.04%
a_2	0	0	0	0	0.00%	0.00%	0.00%	0.00%
a_3	14	14	0	0	0.42%	100.00%	0.00%	0.00%
da	72	29	35	8	2.16%	40.28%	48.61%	11.11%
de	23	7	8	8	0.69%	30.43%	34.78%	34.78%
di	38	21	15	2	1.14%	55.26%	39.47%	5.26%
do	25	7	11	7	0.75%	28.00%	44.00%	28.00%
du	29	13	12	4	0.87%	44.83%	41.38%	13.79%
dwe	0	0	0	0	0.00%	0.00%	0.00%	0.00%
dwo	1	1	0	0	0.03%	100.00%	0.00%	0.00%
ja	73	11	39	23	2.19%	15.07%	53.42%	31.51%
je	12	2	9	1	0.36%	16.67%	75.00%	8.33%
jo	163	1	13	149	4.89%	0.61%	7.98%	91.41%
ka	91	38	44	9	2.73%	41.76%	48.35%	9.89%
ke	60	18	35	7	1.80%	30.00%	58.33%	11.67%
ki	48	18	26	4	1.44%	37.50%	54.17%	8.33%
ko	78	28	23	27	2.34%	35.90%	29.49%	34.62%
ku	43	30	9	4	1.29%	69.77%	20.93%	9.30%
ma	55	22	28	5	1.65%	40.00%	50.91%	9.09%
me	42	15	21	6	1.26%	35.71%	50.00%	14.29%
mi	31	12	16	3	0.93%	38.71%	51.61%	9.68%
mo	34	4	10	20	1.02%	11.76%	29.41%	58.82%
mu	10	3	7	0	0.30%	30.00%	70.00%	0.00%
na	68	10	48	10	2.04%	14.71%	70.59%	14.71%
ne	36	7	23	6	1.08%	19.44%	63.89%	16.67%
ni	32	3	25	4	0.96%	9.38%	78.13%	12.50%
no	84	8	11	65	2.52%	9.52%	13.10%	77.38%
nu	30	3	26	1	0.90%	10.00%	86.67%	3.33%
nwa	6	0	4	2	0.18%	0.00%	66.67%	33.33%
pa	48	27	20	1	1.44%	56.25%	41.67%	2.08%
pa_3	16	6	8	2	0.48%	37.50%	50.00%	12.50%
pe	35	24	11	0	1.05%	68.57%	31.43%	0.00%
pi	38	19	18	1	1.14%	50.00%	47.37%	2.63%
po	38	22	9	7	1.14%	57.89%	23.68%	18.42%
pte	1	1	0	0	0.03%	100.00%	0.00%	0.00%
pu	20	14	4	2	0.60%	70.00%	20.00%	10.00%
pu_2	8	3	4	1	0.24%	37.50%	50.00%	12.50%
qa	38	23	12	3	1.14%	60.53%	31.58%	7.89%
qe	18	12	6	0	0.54%	66.67%	33.33%	0.00%
qi	15	9	6	0	0.45%	60.00%	40.00%	0.00%
qo	42	8	24	10	1.26%	19.05%	57.14%	23.81%

Knossos Names (cont.)

Sign	Total	Initial	Medial	Final	Total	Initial	Medial	Final
ra	107	19	69	19	3.21%	17.76%	64.49%	17.76%
ra₂	5	0	4	1	0.15%	0.00%	80.00%	20.00%
ra₃	0	0	0	0	0.00%	0.00%	0.00%	0.00%
re	64	12	42	10	1.92%	18.75%	65.63%	15.63%
ri	82	11	66	5	2.46%	13.41%	80.49%	6.10%
ro	165	1	33	131	4.95%	0.61%	20.00%	79.39%
ro₂	4	0	1	3	0.12%	0.00%	25.00%	75.00%
ru	37	13	18	6	1.11%	35.14%	48.65%	16.22%
sa	50	20	27	3	1.50%	40.00%	54.00%	6.00%
se	23	3	17	3	0.69%	13.04%	73.91%	13.04%
si	57	19	33	5	1.71%	33.33%	57.89%	8.77%
so	63	0	6	57	1.89%	0.00%	9.52%	90.48%
su	17	12	4	1	0.51%	70.59%	23.53%	5.88%
ta	162	26	49	87	4.86%	16.05%	30.25%	53.70%
ta₂	5	0	1	4	0.15%	0.00%	20.00%	80.00%
te	63	20	34	9	1.89%	31.75%	53.97%	14.29%
ti	52	11	33	8	1.56%	21.15%	63.46%	15.38%
to	134	12	32	90	4.02%	8.96%	23.88%	67.16%
tu	25	12	12	1	0.75%	48.00%	48.00%	4.00%
two	0	0	0	0	0.00%	0.00%	0.00%	0.00%
wa	73	18	41	14	2.19%	24.66%	56.16%	19.18%
we	42	9	17	16	1.26%	21.43%	40.48%	38.10%
wi	49	25	21	3	1.47%	51.02%	42.86%	6.12%
wo	83	13	16	54	2.49%	15.66%	19.28%	65.06%
za	13	3	6	4	0.39%	23.08%	46.15%	30.77%
ze	6	1	5	0	0.18%	16.67%	83.33%	0.00%
zo	16	2	2	12	0.48%	12.50%	12.50%	75.00%
*18	3	1	0	2	0.09%	33.33%	0.00%	66.67%
*19	1	0	0	1	0.03%	0.00%	0.00%	100.00%
*22	1	0	1	0	0.03%	0.00%	100.00%	0.00%
*34	3	2	1	0	0.09%	66.67%	33.33%	0.00%
*35	0	0	0	0	0.00%	0.00%	0.00%	0.00%
*47	1	1	0	0	0.03%	100.00%	0.00%	0.00%
*49	3	1	2	0	0.09%	33.33%	66.67%	0.00%
*63	0	0	0	0	0.00%	0.00%	0.00%	0.00%
*64	1	0	1	0	0.03%	0.00%	100.00%	0.00%
*65	7	0	6	1	0.21%	0.00%	85.71%	14.29%
*79	1	0	0	1	0.03%	0.00%	0.00%	100.00%
*82	2	1	1	0	0.06%	50.0%	50.0%	0.0%
*83	3	0	3	0	0.09%	0.00%	100.00%	0.00%
*85	2	2	0	0	0.06%	100.00%	0.00%	0.00%
*86	2	0	2	0	0.06%	0.00%	100.00%	0.00%
*88	0	0	0	0	0.00%	0.00%	0.00%	0.00%

Knossos Place-Names (368 Signs)

Sign	Total	Initial	Medial	Final	Total	Initial	Medial	Final
a	10	10	0	0	2.72%	100.00%	0.00%	0.00%
e	6	4	0	2	1.63%	66.67%	0.00%	33.33%
i	10	0	4	6	2.72%	0.00%	40.00%	60.00%
o	5	3	0	2	1.36%	60.00%	0.00%	40.00%
u	7	3	4	0	1.90%	42.86%	57.14%	0.00%
a₂	0	0	0	0	0.00%	0.00%	0.00%	0.00%
a₃	0	0	0	0	0.00%	0.00%	0.00%	0.00%
da	16	11	3	2	4.35%	68.75%	18.75%	12.50%
de	20	1	0	19	5.43%	5.00%	0.00%	95.00%
di	2	2	0	0	0.54%	100.00%	0.00%	0.00%
do	5	1	4	0	1.36%	20.00%	80.00%	0.00%
du	5	1	4	0	1.36%	20.00%	80.00%	0.00%
dwe	0	0	0	0	0.00%	0.00%	0.00%	0.00%
dwo	0	0	0	0	0.00%	0.00%	0.00%	0.00%
ja	13	0	5	8	3.53%	0.00%	38.46%	61.54%
je	0	0	0	0	0.00%	0.00%	0.00%	0.00%
jo	13	1	5	7	3.53%	7.69%	38.46%	53.85%
ka	10	5	4	1	2.72%	50.00%	40.00%	10.00%
ke	2	0	0	2	0.54%	0.00%	0.00%	100.00%
ki	3	1	2	0	0.82%	33.33%	66.67%	0.00%
ko	8	1	5	2	2.17%	12.50%	62.50%	25.00%
ku	7	5	2	0	1.90%	71.43%	28.57%	0.00%
ma	7	4	3	0	1.90%	57.14%	42.86%	0.00%
me	0	0	0	0	0.00%	0.00%	0.00%	0.00%
mi	3	0	3	0	0.82%	0.00%	100.00%	0.00%
mo	7	0	1	6	1.90%	0.00%	14.29%	85.71%
mu	1	0	1	0	0.27%	0.00%	100.00%	0.00%
na	8	0	8	0	2.17%	0.00%	100.00%	0.00%
ne	2	1	1	0	0.54%	50.00%	50.00%	0.00%
ni	7	0	7	0	1.90%	0.00%	100.00%	0.00%
no	4	0	1	3	1.09%	0.00%	25.00%	75.00%
nu	0	0	0	0	0.00%	0.00%	0.00%	0.00%
nwa	1	0	1	0	0.27%	0.00%	100.00%	0.00%
pa	9	3	5	1	2.45%	33.33%	55.56%	11.11%
pa₃	3	3	0	0	0.82%	100.00%	0.00%	0.00%
pe	1	0	1	0	0.27%	0.00%	100.00%	0.00%
pi	1	0	0	1	0.27%	0.00%	0.00%	100.00%
po	0	0	0	0	0.00%	0.00%	0.00%	0.00%
pte	0	0	0	0	0.00%	0.00%	0.00%	0.00%
pu	2	2	0	0	0.54%	100.00%	0.00%	0.00%
pu₂	1	0	1	0	0.27%	0.00%	100.00%	0.00%
qa	5	4	1	0	1.36%	80.00%	20.00%	0.00%
qe	0	0	0	0	0.00%	0.00%	0.00%	0.00%
qi	1	1	0	0	0.27%	100.00%	0.00%	0.00%
qo	0	0	0	0	0.00%	0.00%	0.00%	0.00%

Knossos Place-Names (cont.)

Sign	Total	Initial	Medial	Final	Total	Initial	Medial	Final
ra	17	6	7	4	4.62%	35.29%	41.18%	23.53%
ra₂	0	0	0	0	0.00%	0.00%	0.00%	0.00%
ra₃	0	0	0	0	0.00%	0.00%	0.00%	0.00%
re	4	1	2	1	1.09%	25.00%	50.00%	25.00%
ri	14	5	8	1	3.80%	35.71%	57.14%	7.14%
ro	6	0	3	3	1.63%	0.00%	50.00%	50.00%
ro₂	0	0	0	0	0.00%	0.00%	0.00%	0.00%
ru	5	1	4	0	1.36%	20.00%	80.00%	0.00%
sa	9	4	3	2	2.45%	44.44%	33.33%	22.22%
se	1	1	0	0	0.27%	100.00%	0.00%	0.00%
si	5	4	1	0	1.36%	80.00%	20.00%	0.00%
so	17	1	6	10	4.62%	5.88%	35.29%	58.82%
su	4	2	1	1	1.09%	50.00%	25.00%	25.00%
ta	15	2	10	3	4.08%	13.33%	66.67%	20.00%
ta₂	0	0	0	0	0.00%	0.00%	0.00%	0.00%
te	2	1	1	0	0.54%	50.00%	50.00%	0.00%
ti	6	2	4	0	1.63%	33.33%	66.67%	0.00%
to	19	2	4	13	5.16%	10.53%	21.05%	68.42%
tu	3	3	0	0	0.82%	100.00%	0.00%	0.00%
two	0	0	0	0	0.00%	0.00%	0.00%	0.00%
wa	8	3	2	3	2.17%	37.50%	25.00%	37.50%
we	9	0	3	6	2.45%	0.00%	33.33%	66.67%
wi	3	1	2	0	0.82%	33.33%	66.67%	0.00%
wo	5	0	0	5	1.36%	0.00%	0.00%	100.00%
za	0	0	0	0	0.00%	0.00%	0.00%	0.00%
ze	0	0	0	0	0.00%	0.00%	0.00%	0.00%
zo	0	0	0	0	0.00%	0.00%	0.00%	0.00%
*18	0	0	0	0	0.00%	0.00%	0.00%	0.00%
*19	0	0	0	0	0.00%	0.00%	0.00%	0.00%
*22	1	0	1	0	0.27%	0.00%	100.00%	0.00%
*34	0	0	0	0	0.00%	0.00%	0.00%	0.00%
*35	0	0	0	0	0.00%	0.00%	0.00%	0.00%
*47	4	4	0	0	1.09%	100.00%	0.00%	0.00%
*49	0	0	0	0	0.00%	0.00%	0.00%	0.00%
*63	0	0	0	0	0.00%	0.00%	0.00%	0.00%
*64	0	0	0	0	0.00%	0.00%	0.00%	0.00%
*65	1	0	1	0	0.27%	0.00%	100.00%	0.00%
*79	0	0	0	0	0.00%	0.00%	0.00%	0.00%
*82	0	0	0	0	0.00%	0.00%	0.00%	0.00%
*83	4	1	3	0	1.09%	25.00%	75.00%	0.00%
*85	1	1	0	0	0.27%	100.00%	0.00%	0.00%
*86	0	0	0	0	0.00%	0.00%	0.00%	0.00%
*88	0	0	0	0	0.00%	0.00%	0.00%	0.00%

All Pylos Sign-Groups (8467 Signs)

Sign	Total	Initial	Medial	Final	Total	Initial	Medial	Final
a	313	288	20	5	3.70%	92.01%	6.39%	1.60%
e	332	228	67	37	3.92%	68.67%	20.18%	11.14%
i	156	57	50	49	1.84%	36.54%	32.05%	31.41%
o	253	123	29	101	2.99%	48.62%	11.46%	39.92%
u	257	23	117	117	3.04%	8.95%	45.53%	45.53%
a_2	61	26	18	17	0.72%	42.62%	29.51%	27.87%
a_3	28	27	1	0	0.33%	96.43%	3.57%	0.00%
da	83	26	48	9	0.98%	31.33%	57.83%	10.84%
de	104	21	36	47	1.23%	20.19%	34.62%	45.19%
di	49	30	19	0	0.58%	61.22%	38.78%	0.00%
do	74	25	42	7	0.87%	33.78%	56.76%	9.46%
du	20	10	10	0	0.24%	50.00%	50.00%	0.00%
dwe	1	0	1	0	0.01%	0.00%	100.00%	0.00%
dwo	3	1	1	1	0.04%	33.33%	33.33%	33.33%
ja	278	5	109	164	3.28%	1.80%	39.21%	58.99%
je	44	0	42	2	0.52%	0.00%	95.45%	4.55%
jo	375	6	62	307	4.43%	1.60%	16.53%	81.87%
ka	210	92	92	26	2.48%	43.81%	43.81%	12.38%
ke	255	67	155	33	3.01%	26.27%	60.78%	12.94%
ki	108	31	71	6	1.28%	28.70%	65.74%	5.56%
ko	238	78	90	70	2.81%	32.77%	37.82%	29.41%
ku	67	42	24	1	0.79%	62.69%	35.82%	1.49%
ma	123	46	66	11	1.45%	37.40%	53.66%	8.94%
me	149	58	83	8	1.76%	38.93%	55.70%	5.37%
mi	55	11	39	5	0.65%	20.00%	70.91%	9.09%
mo	54	8	22	24	0.64%	14.81%	40.74%	44.44%
mu	15	10	5	0	0.18%	66.67%	33.33%	0.00%
na	113	11	67	35	1.33%	9.73%	59.29%	30.97%
ne	121	24	56	41	1.43%	19.83%	46.28%	33.88%
ni	81	3	73	5	0.96%	3.70%	90.12%	6.17%
no	170	10	58	102	2.01%	5.88%	34.12%	60.00%
nu	28	2	23	3	0.33%	7.14%	82.14%	10.71%
nwa	6	0	6	0	0.07%	0.00%	100.00%	0.00%
pa	128	65	55	8	1.51%	50.78%	42.97%	6.25%
pa_3	2	0	2	0	0.02%	0.00%	100.00%	0.00%
pe	126	62	56	8	1.49%	49.21%	44.44%	6.35%
pi	176	43	82	51	2.08%	24.43%	46.59%	28.98%
po	137	86	39	12	1.62%	62.77%	28.47%	8.76%
pte	8	1	6	1	0.09%	12.50%	75.00%	12.50%
pu	36	19	15	2	0.43%	52.78%	41.67%	5.56%
pu_2	17	8	9	0	0.20%	47.06%	52.94%	0.00%
qa	34	9	14	11	0.40%	26.47%	41.18%	32.35%
qe	69	27	28	14	0.81%	39.13%	40.58%	20.29%
qi	23	3	19	1	0.27%	13.04%	82.61%	4.35%
qo	82	17	44	21	0.97%	20.73%	53.66%	25.61%

All Pylos Sign-Groups (cont.)

Sign	Total	Initial	Medial	Final	Total	Initial	Medial	Final
ra	278	49	181	48	3.28%	17.63%	65.11%	17.27%
ra$_2$	27	0	16	11	0.32%	0.00%	59.26%	40.74%
ra$_3$	9	0	4	5	0.11%	0.00%	44.44%	55.56%
re	281	39	199	43	3.32%	13.88%	70.82%	15.30%
ri	203	14	169	20	2.40%	6.90%	83.25%	9.85%
ro	294	13	146	135	3.47%	4.42%	49.66%	45.92%
ro$_2$	9	0	4	5	0.11%	0.00%	44.44%	55.56%
ru	75	16	57	2	0.89%	21.33%	76.00%	2.67%
sa	79	21	43	15	0.93%	26.58%	54.43%	18.99%
se	58	8	43	7	0.69%	13.79%	74.14%	12.07%
si	136	15	85	36	1.61%	11.03%	62.50%	26.47%
so	81	6	45	30	0.96%	7.41%	55.56%	37.04%
su	13	7	6	0	0.15%	53.85%	46.15%	0.00%
ta	272	33	111	128	3.21%	12.13%	40.81%	47.06%
ta$_2$	3	0	1	2	0.04%	0.00%	33.33%	66.67%
te	295	61	159	75	3.48%	20.68%	53.90%	25.42%
ti	153	32	110	11	1.81%	20.92%	71.90%	7.19%
to	230	52	88	90	2.72%	22.61%	38.26%	39.13%
tu	55	20	31	4	0.65%	36.36%	56.36%	7.27%
two	1	0	1	0	0.01%	0.00%	100.00%	0.00%
wa	168	49	76	43	1.98%	29.17%	45.24%	25.60%
we	205	31	76	98	2.42%	15.12%	37.07%	47.80%
wi	119	24	90	5	1.41%	20.17%	75.63%	4.20%
wo	256	43	103	110	3.02%	16.80%	40.23%	42.97%
za	22	6	8	8	0.26%	27.27%	36.36%	36.36%
ze	16	8	5	3	0.19%	50.00%	31.25%	18.75%
zo	21	2	12	7	0.25%	9.52%	57.14%	33.33%
*18	0	0	0	0	0.00%	0.00%	0.00%	0.00%
*19	0	0	0	0	0.00%	0.00%	0.00%	0.00%
*22	0	0	0	0	0.00%	0.00%	0.00%	0.00%
*34	7	5	2	0	0.08%	71.43%	28.57%	0.00%
*35	6	4	1	1	0.07%	66.67%	16.67%	16.67%
*47	0	0	0	0	0.00%	0.00%	0.00%	0.00%
*49	0	0	0	0	0.00%	0.00%	0.00%	0.00%
*63	1	0	1	0	0.01%	0.00%	100.00%	0.00%
*64	3	0	3	0	0.04%	0.00%	100.00%	0.00%
*65	4	0	3	1	0.05%	0.00%	75.00%	25.00%
*79	2	0	1	1	0.02%	0.00%	50.00%	50.00%
*82	8	2	3	3	0.09%	25.0%	37.5%	37.5%
*83	2	0	2	0	0.02%	0.00%	100.00%	0.00%
*85	11	11	0	0	0.13%	100.00%	0.00%	0.00%
*86	2	0	1	1	0.02%	0.00%	50.00%	50.00%
*88	0	0	0	0	0.00%	0.00%	0.00%	0.00%

Pylos Names (3515 Signs)

Sign	Total	Initial	Medial	Final	Total	Initial	Medial	Final
a	129	128	1	0	3.67%	99.22%	0.78%	0.00%
e	109	88	19	2	3.10%	80.73%	17.43%	1.83%
i	52	23	19	10	1.48%	44.23%	36.54%	19.23%
o	100	46	11	43	2.84%	46.00%	11.00%	43.00%
u	152	6	56	90	4.32%	3.95%	36.84%	59.21%
a_2	17	9	6	2	0.48%	52.94%	35.29%	11.76%
a_3	17	17	0	0	0.48%	100.00%	0.00%	0.00%
da	38	11	23	4	1.08%	28.95%	60.53%	10.53%
de	30	10	11	9	0.85%	33.33%	36.67%	30.00%
di	12	5	7	0	0.34%	41.67%	58.33%	0.00%
do	35	8	23	4	1.00%	22.86%	65.71%	11.43%
du	13	6	7	0	0.37%	46.15%	53.85%	0.00%
dwe	0	0	0	0	0.00%	0.00%	0.00%	0.00%
dwo	1	0	1	0	0.03%	0.00%	100.00%	0.00%
ja	69	1	33	35	1.96%	1.45%	47.83%	50.72%
je	16	0	16	0	0.46%	0.00%	100.00%	0.00%
jo	189	0	25	164	5.38%	0.00%	13.23%	86.77%
ka	97	43	41	13	2.76%	44.33%	42.27%	13.40%
ke	97	34	61	2	2.76%	35.05%	62.89%	2.06%
ki	37	6	29	2	1.05%	16.22%	78.38%	5.41%
ko	121	34	42	45	3.44%	28.10%	34.71%	37.19%
ku	30	15	14	1	0.85%	50.00%	46.67%	3.33%
ma	64	27	36	1	1.82%	42.19%	56.25%	1.56%
me	57	17	40	0	1.62%	29.82%	70.18%	0.00%
mi	17	6	11	0	0.48%	35.29%	64.71%	0.00%
mo	24	6	11	7	0.68%	25.00%	45.83%	29.17%
mu	10	6	4	0	0.28%	60.00%	40.00%	0.00%
na	40	4	26	10	1.14%	10.00%	65.00%	25.00%
ne	50	11	22	17	1.42%	22.00%	44.00%	34.00%
ni	26	0	23	3	0.74%	0.00%	88.46%	11.54%
no	76	1	22	53	2.16%	1.32%	28.95%	69.74%
nu	10	0	9	1	0.28%	0.00%	90.00%	10.00%
nwa	1	0	1	0	0.03%	0.00%	100.00%	0.00%
pa	41	17	24	0	1.17%	41.46%	58.54%	0.00%
pa_3	2	0	2	0	0.06%	0.00%	100.00%	0.00%
pe	41	25	15	1	1.17%	60.98%	36.59%	2.44%
pi	46	24	21	1	1.31%	52.17%	45.65%	2.17%
po	45	29	12	4	1.28%	64.44%	26.67%	8.89%
pte	1	1	0	0	0.03%	100.00%	0.00%	0.00%
pu	15	13	2	0	0.43%	86.67%	13.33%	0.00%
pu_2	5	3	2	0	0.14%	60.00%	40.00%	0.00%
qa	19	4	8	7	0.54%	21.05%	42.11%	36.84%
qe	30	12	13	5	0.85%	40.00%	43.33%	16.67%
qi	10	2	8	0	0.28%	20.00%	80.00%	0.00%
qo	46	6	32	8	1.31%	13.04%	69.57%	17.39%

Pylos Names (cont.)

Sign	Total	Initial	Medial	Final	Total	Initial	Medial	Final
ra	104	20	70	14	2.96%	19.23%	67.31%	13.46%
ra₂	5	0	3	2	0.14%	0.00%	60.00%	40.00%
ra₃	1	0	1	0	0.03%	0.00%	100.00%	0.00%
re	108	19	79	10	3.07%	17.59%	73.15%	9.26%
ri	92	3	83	6	2.62%	3.26%	90.22%	6.52%
ro	156	6	67	83	4.44%	3.85%	42.95%	53.21%
ro₂	5	0	2	3	0.14%	0.00%	40.00%	60.00%
ru	38	11	26	1	1.08%	28.95%	68.42%	2.63%
sa	36	10	24	2	1.02%	27.78%	66.67%	5.56%
se	19	3	15	1	0.54%	15.79%	78.95%	5.26%
si	44	8	33	3	1.25%	18.18%	75.00%	6.82%
so	39	1	22	16	1.11%	2.56%	56.41%	41.03%
su	5	3	2	0	0.14%	60.00%	40.00%	0.00%
ta	189	20	79	90	5.38%	10.58%	41.80%	47.62%
ta₂	0	0	0	0	0.00%	0.00%	0.00%	0.00%
te	78	19	51	8	2.22%	24.36%	65.38%	10.26%
ti	60	14	39	7	1.71%	23.33%	65.00%	11.67%
to	80	17	24	39	2.28%	21.25%	30.00%	48.75%
tu	32	13	17	2	0.91%	40.63%	53.13%	6.25%
two	1	0	1	0	0.03%	0.00%	100.00%	0.00%
wa	99	32	48	19	2.82%	32.32%	48.48%	19.19%
we	86	9	33	44	2.45%	10.47%	38.37%	51.16%
wi	38	17	19	2	1.08%	44.74%	50.00%	5.26%
wo	124	18	39	67	3.53%	14.52%	31.45%	54.03%
za	6	1	5	0	0.17%	16.67%	83.33%	0.00%
ze	5	1	4	0	0.14%	20.00%	80.00%	0.00%
zo	9	2	4	3	0.26%	22.22%	44.44%	33.33%
*18	0	0	0	0	0.00%	0.00%	0.00%	0.00%
*19	0	0	0	0	0.00%	0.00%	0.00%	0.00%
*22	0	0	0	0	0.00%	0.00%	0.00%	0.00%
*34	2	1	1	0	0.06%	50.00%	50.00%	0.00%
*35	1	1	0	0	0.03%	100.00%	0.00%	0.00%
*47	0	0	0	0	0.00%	0.00%	0.00%	0.00%
*49	0	0	0	0	0.00%	0.00%	0.00%	0.00%
*63	1	0	1	0	0.03%	0.00%	100.00%	0.00%
*64	3	0	3	0	0.09%	0.00%	100.00%	0.00%
*65	1	0	1	0	0.03%	0.00%	100.00%	0.00%
*79	1	0	0	1	0.03%	0.00%	0.00%	100.00%
*82	4	2	1	1	0.11%	50.0%	25.0%	25.0%
*83	2	0	2	0	0.06%	0.00%	100.00%	0.00%
*85	4	4	0	0	0.11%	100.00%	0.00%	0.00%
*86	0	0	0	0	0.00%	0.00%	0.00%	0.00%
*88	0	0	0	0	0.00%	0.00%	0.00%	0.00%

Pylos Place-Names (1061 Signs)

Sign	Total	Initial	Medial	Final	Total	Initial	Medial	Final
a	47	37	9	1	4.43%	78.72%	19.15%	2.13%
e	48	30	6	12	4.52%	62.50%	12.50%	25.00%
i	20	3	12	5	1.89%	15.00%	60.00%	25.00%
o	17	10	3	4	1.60%	58.82%	17.65%	23.53%
u	29	7	18	4	2.73%	24.14%	62.07%	13.79%
a_2	13	10	3	0	1.23%	76.92%	23.08%	0.00%
a_3	5	4	1	0	0.47%	80.00%	20.00%	0.00%
da	10	5	3	2	0.94%	50.00%	30.00%	20.00%
de	29	1	3	25	2.73%	3.45%	10.34%	86.21%
di	1	1	0	0	0.09%	100.00%	0.00%	0.00%
do	6	0	6	0	0.57%	0.00%	100.00%	0.00%
du	0	0	0	0	0.00%	0.00%	0.00%	0.00%
dwe	0	0	0	0	0.00%	0.00%	0.00%	0.00%
dwo	0	0	0	0	0.00%	0.00%	0.00%	0.00%
ja	54	0	17	37	5.09%	0.00%	31.48%	68.52%
je	0	0	0	0	0.00%	0.00%	0.00%	0.00%
jo	28	0	11	17	2.64%	0.00%	39.29%	60.71%
ka	26	7	19	0	2.45%	26.92%	73.08%	0.00%
ke	28	6	21	1	2.64%	21.43%	75.00%	3.57%
ki	17	2	15	0	1.60%	11.76%	88.24%	0.00%
ko	19	6	12	1	1.79%	31.58%	63.16%	5.26%
ku	3	2	1	0	0.28%	66.67%	33.33%	0.00%
ma	13	6	7	0	1.23%	46.15%	53.85%	0.00%
me	10	6	4	0	0.94%	60.00%	40.00%	0.00%
mi	9	1	8	0	0.85%	11.11%	88.89%	0.00%
mo	2	1	1	0	0.19%	50.00%	50.00%	0.00%
mu	2	1	1	0	0.19%	50.00%	50.00%	0.00%
na	15	2	8	5	1.41%	13.33%	53.33%	33.33%
ne	23	7	8	8	2.17%	30.43%	34.78%	34.78%
ni	12	1	11	0	1.13%	8.33%	91.67%	0.00%
no	20	1	12	7	1.89%	5.00%	60.00%	35.00%
nu	3	0	3	0	0.28%	0.00%	100.00%	0.00%
nwa	0	0	0	0	0.00%	0.00%	0.00%	0.00%
pa	19	10	8	1	1.79%	52.63%	42.11%	5.26%
pa_3	0	0	0	0	0.00%	0.00%	0.00%	0.00%
pe	14	6	6	2	1.32%	42.86%	42.86%	14.29%
pi	41	7	15	19	3.86%	17.07%	36.59%	46.34%
po	15	7	6	2	1.41%	46.67%	40.00%	13.33%
pte	0	0	0	0	0.00%	0.00%	0.00%	0.00%
pu	5	2	3	0	0.47%	40.00%	60.00%	0.00%
pu_2	5	2	3	0	0.47%	40.00%	60.00%	0.00%
qa	1	0	0	1	0.09%	0.00%	0.00%	100.00%
qe	7	3	2	2	0.66%	42.86%	28.57%	28.57%
qi	1	0	1	0	0.09%	0.00%	100.00%	0.00%
qo	6	4	1	1	0.57%	66.67%	16.67%	16.67%

Pylos Place-Names (cont.)

Sign	Total	Initial	Medial	Final	Total	Initial	Medial	Final
ra	48	6	35	7	4.52%	12.50%	72.92%	14.58%
ra₂	4	0	2	2	0.38%	0.00%	50.00%	50.00%
ra₃	2	0	1	1	0.19%	0.00%	50.00%	50.00%
re	44	5	35	4	4.15%	11.36%	79.55%	9.09%
ri	28	5	22	1	2.64%	17.86%	78.57%	3.57%
ro	27	1	15	11	2.54%	3.70%	55.56%	40.74%
ro₂	0	0	0	0	0.00%	0.00%	0.00%	0.00%
ru	6	2	4	0	0.57%	33.33%	66.67%	0.00%
sa	13	6	6	1	1.23%	46.15%	46.15%	7.69%
se	8	2	6	0	0.75%	25.00%	75.00%	0.00%
si	11	2	6	3	1.04%	18.18%	54.55%	27.27%
so	11	2	5	4	1.04%	18.18%	45.45%	36.36%
su	1	1	0	0	0.09%	100.00%	0.00%	0.00%
ta	19	2	13	4	1.79%	10.53%	68.42%	21.05%
ta₂	2	0	0	2	0.19%	0.00%	0.00%	100.00%
te	47	10	18	19	4.43%	21.28%	38.30%	40.43%
ti	17	4	13	0	1.60%	23.53%	76.47%	0.00%
to	26	2	15	9	2.45%	7.69%	57.69%	34.62%
tu	7	0	7	0	0.66%	0.00%	100.00%	0.00%
two	0	0	0	0	0.00%	0.00%	0.00%	0.00%
wa	31	5	11	15	2.92%	16.13%	35.48%	48.39%
we	24	0	11	13	2.26%	0.00%	45.83%	54.17%
wi	25	3	22	0	2.36%	12.00%	88.00%	0.00%
wo	31	3	22	6	2.92%	9.68%	70.97%	19.35%
za	3	2	0	1	0.28%	66.67%	0.00%	33.33%
ze	0	0	0	0	0.00%	0.00%	0.00%	0.00%
zo	0	0	0	0	0.00%	0.00%	0.00%	0.00%
*18	0	0	0	0	0.00%	0.00%	0.00%	0.00%
*19	0	0	0	0	0.00%	0.00%	0.00%	0.00%
*22	0	0	0	0	0.00%	0.00%	0.00%	0.00%
*34	0	0	0	0	0.00%	0.00%	0.00%	0.00%
*35	0	0	0	0	0.00%	0.00%	0.00%	0.00%
*47	0	0	0	0	0.00%	0.00%	0.00%	0.00%
*49	0	0	0	0	0.00%	0.00%	0.00%	0.00%
*63	0	0	0	0	0.00%	0.00%	0.00%	0.00%
*64	0	0	0	0	0.00%	0.00%	0.00%	0.00%
*65	0	0	0	0	0.00%	0.00%	0.00%	0.00%
*79	0	0	0	0	0.00%	0.00%	0.00%	0.00%
*82	2	0	1	1	0.19%	0.0%	50.0%	50.0%
*83	0	0	0	0	0.00%	0.00%	0.00%	0.00%
*85	0	0	0	0	0.00%	0.00%	0.00%	0.00%
*86	1	0	0	1	0.09%	0.00%	0.00%	100.00%
*88	0	0	0	0	0.00%	0.00%	0.00%	0.00%

APPENDIX G

Sign Frequency by Word Class

In this appendix the information tabulated in Appendix F is organized in such a way as to bring out significant variation between various subclasses of the Linear B vocabulary. For each Linear B sign, the frequencies are broken down into seven classes:
 a) Place names at Pylos.
 b) Personal names at Pylos.
 c) Everything at Pylos.
 d) Everything in Linear B.
 e) Everything at Knossos.
 f) Personal names at Knossos.
 g) Place names at Knossos.

In addition to the absolute counts (as initial, medial, final, and total), the relative frequency of the sign *within each class* is calculated. The sign *i*, for example, occurs 20 times in Pylos toponyms which accounts for 1.89% of the signs in such words. This same sign occurs 10 times in Knossos toponyms, but this amounts to 2.72% of the signs in that class of words.

The bar graphs printed at the right, facing each table, allow one to grasp at a glance the relative frequency of a sign in each of the seven classes. The graphs read from left to right in the order described above. Pylos place names are at the left, Knossos place names at the right. The left side may reflect a mainland substratum, the right a Cretan substratum.

Sign Frequency by Word Class

		PY Topon.	PY Anthr.	PY All	All SG's	KN All	KN Anthr.	KN Topon.
a	Percent	4.43%	3.67%	3.70%	3.72%	3.97%	4.50%	2.72%
	Total	47	129	313	627	341	150	10
	Initial	37	128	288	568	307	145	10
	Medial	9	1	20	27	7	2	0
	Final	1	0	5	32	27	3	0
e	Percent	4.52%	3.10%	3.92%	3.23%	2.61%	1.53%	1.63%
	Total	48	109	332	543	224	51	6
	Initial	30	88	228	397	183	44	4
	Medial	6	19	67	87	21	6	0
	Final	12	2	37	59	20	1	2
i	Percent	1.89%	1.48%	1.84%	1.92%	1.93%	1.47%	2.72%
	Total	20	52	156	324	166	49	10
	Initial	3	23	57	113	61	25	0
	Medial	12	19	50	119	66	23	4
	Final	5	10	49	92	39	1	6
o	Percent	1.60%	2.84%	2.99%	2.48%	1.99%	1.32%	1.36%
	Total	17	100	253	418	171	44	5
	Initial	10	46	123	219	97	23	3
	Medial	3	11	29	50	21	5	0
	Final	4	43	101	149	53	16	2
u	Percent	2.73%	4.32%	3.04%	2.54%	2.17%	2.94%	1.90%
	Total	29	152	257	428	186	98	7
	Initial	7	6	23	61	40	15	3
	Medial	18	56	117	194	77	32	4
	Final	4	90	117	173	69	51	0
V	Percent	15.17%	15.42%	15.48%	13.90%	12.68%	11.76%	10.33%
	Total	161	542	1311	2340	1088	392	38
	Initial	87	291	719	1358	688	252	20
	Medial	48	106	283	477	192	68	8
	Final	26	145	309	505	208	72	10

Appendix G

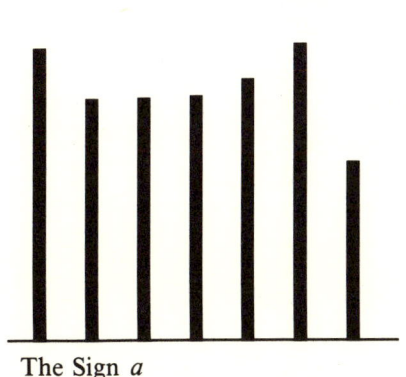
The Sign *a*

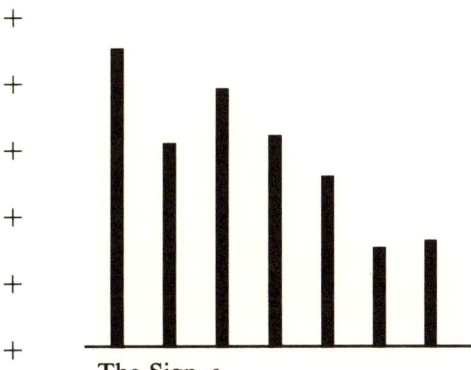
The Sign *e*

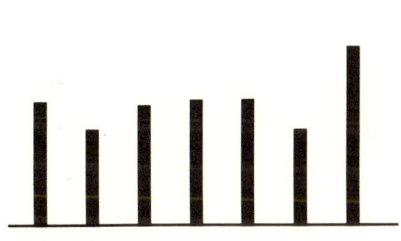
The Sign *i*

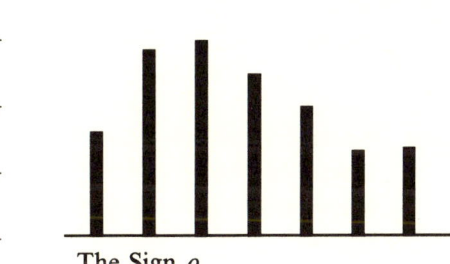
The Sign *o*

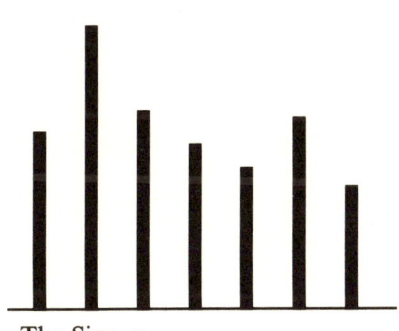
The Sign *u*

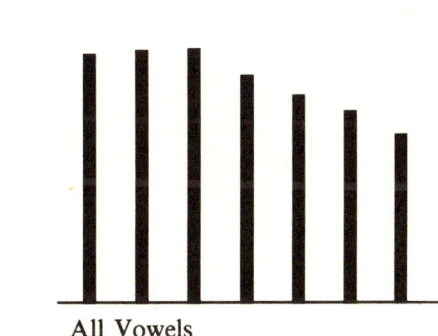
All Vowels

Sign Frequency by Word Class

		PY Topon.	PY Anthr.	PY All	All SG's	KN All	KN Anthr.	KN Topon.
da	Percent	0.94%	1.08%	0.98%	1.45%	1.87%	2.16%	4.35%
	Total	10	38	83	244	160	72	16
	Initial	5	11	26	96	73	29	11
	Medial	3	23	48	120	68	35	3
	Final	2	4	9	28	19	8	2
de	Percent	2.73%	0.85%	1.23%	1.13%	1.00%	0.69%	5.43%
	Total	29	30	104	191	86	23	20
	Initial	1	10	21	48	26	7	1
	Medial	3	11	36	56	20	8	0
	Final	25	9	47	87	40	8	19
di	Percent	0.09%	0.34%	0.58%	0.74%	0.87%	1.14%	0.54%
	Total	1	12	49	125	75	38	2
	Initial	1	5	30	76	47	21	2
	Medial	0	7	19	41	22	15	0
	Final	0	0	0	8	6	2	0
do	Percent	0.57%	1.00%	0.87%	0.87%	0.94%	0.75%	1.36%
	Total	6	35	74	147	81	25	5
	Initial	0	8	25	45	25	7	1
	Medial	6	23	42	72	33	11	4
	Final	0	4	7	30	23	7	0
du	Percent	0.00%	0.37%	0.24%	0.43%	0.62%	0.87%	1.36%
	Total	0	13	20	73	53	29	5
	Initial	0	6	10	29	21	13	1
	Medial	0	7	10	36	24	12	4
	Final	0	0	0	8	8	4	0
d-	Percent	4.34%	3.64%	3.90%	4.63%	5.30%	5.61%	13.04%
	Total	46	128	330	780	455	187	48
	Initial	7	40	112	294	192	77	16
	Medial	12	71	155	325	167	81	11
	Final	27	17	63	161	96	29	21

Appendix G

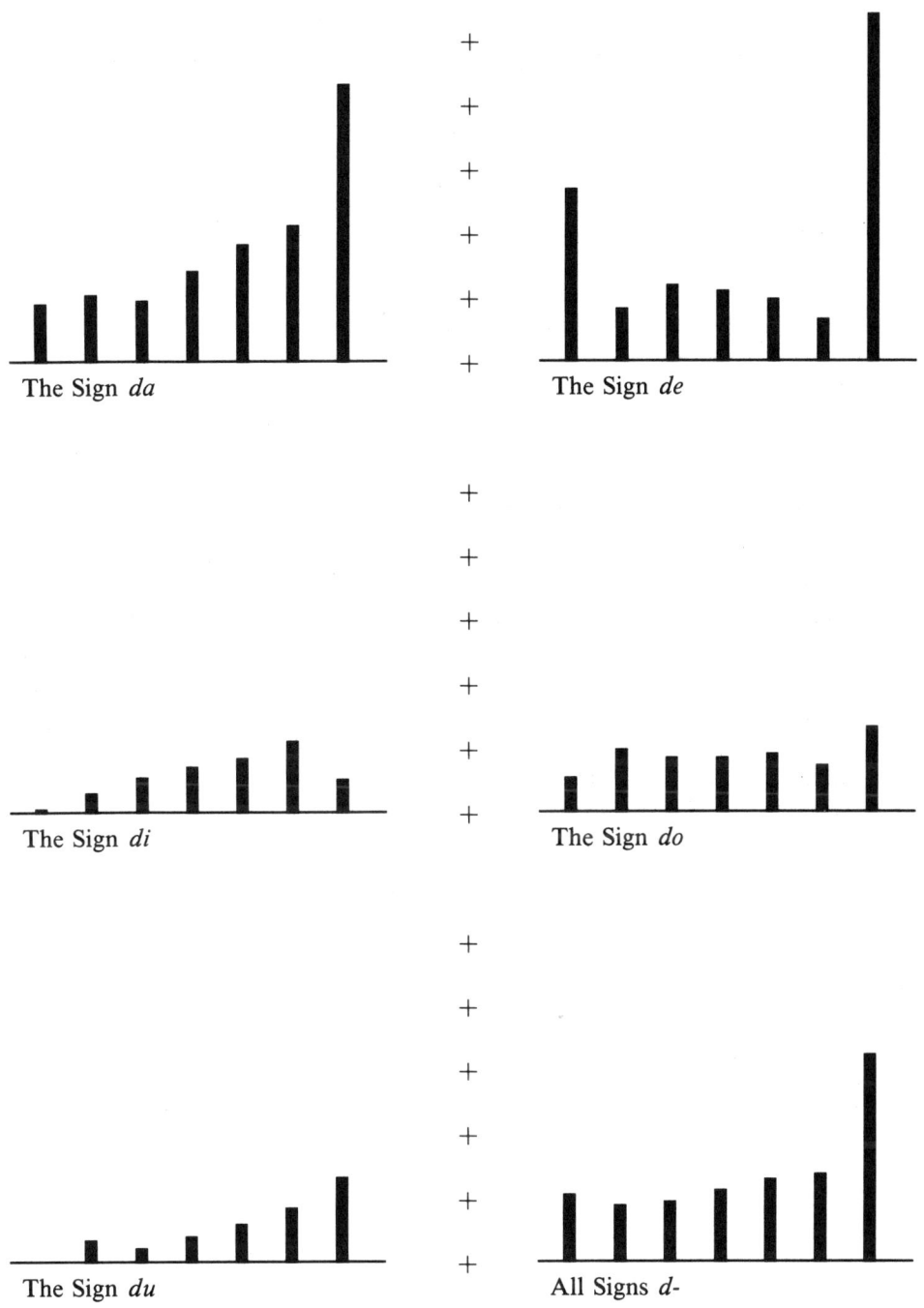

Sign Frequency by Word Class

		PY Topon.	PY Anthr.	PY All	All SG's	KN All	KN Anthr.	KN Topon.
ja	Percent	5.09%	1.96%	3.28%	3.32%	3.35%	2.19%	3.53%
	Total	54	69	278	559	287	73	13
	Initial	0	1	5	32	27	11	0
	Medial	17	33	109	194	86	39	5
	Final	37	35	164	333	174	23	8
je	Percent	0.00%	0.46%	0.52%	0.45%	0.41%	0.36%	0.00%
	Total	0	16	44	76	35	12	0
	Initial	0	0	0	7	7	2	0
	Medial	0	16	42	56	18	9	0
	Final	0	0	2	13	10	1	0
jo	Percent	2.64%	5.38%	4.43%	4.30%	4.37%	4.89%	3.53%
	Total	28	189	375	724	375	163	13
	Initial	0	0	6	16	10	1	1
	Medial	11	25	62	104	41	13	5
	Final	17	164	307	604	324	149	7
j-	Percent	7.73%	7.80%	8.23%	8.07%	8.12%	7.44%	7.07%
	Total	82	274	697	1359	697	248	26
	Initial	0	1	11	55	44	14	1
	Medial	28	74	213	354	145	61	10
	Final	54	199	473	950	508	173	15

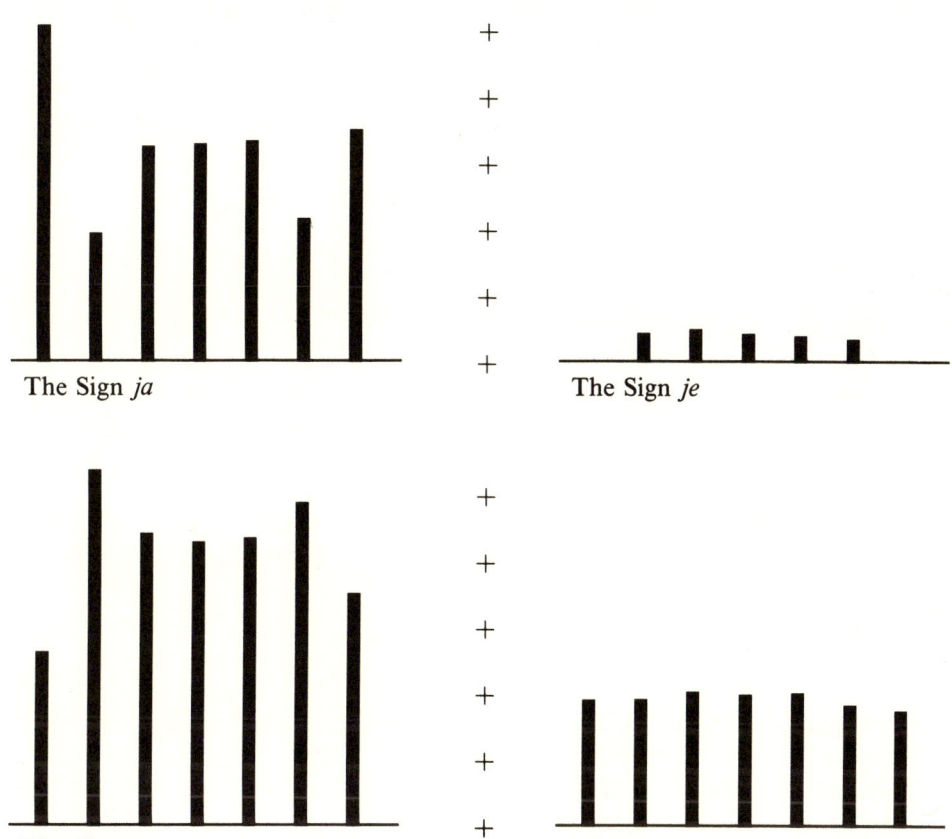

Sign Frequency by Word Class

		PY Topon.	PY Anthr.	PY All	All SG's	KN All	KN Anthr.	KN Topon.
ka	Percent	2.45%	2.76%	2.48%	2.58%	2.65%	2.73%	2.72%
	Total	26	97	210	435	227	91	10
	Initial	7	43	92	200	105	38	5
	Medial	19	41	92	167	78	44	4
	Final	0	13	26	68	44	9	1
ke	Percent	2.64%	2.76%	3.01%	2.51%	2.02%	1.80%	0.54%
	Total	28	97	255	422	173	60	2
	Initial	6	34	67	126	64	18	0
	Medial	21	61	155	237	78	35	0
	Final	1	2	33	59	31	7	2
ki	Percent	1.60%	1.05%	1.28%	1.43%	1.54%	1.44%	0.82%
	Total	17	37	108	241	132	48	3
	Initial	2	6	31	86	54	18	1
	Medial	15	29	71	130	61	26	2
	Final	0	2	6	25	17	4	0
ko	Percent	1.79%	3.44%	2.81%	2.67%	2.53%	2.34%	2.17%
	Total	19	121	238	449	217	78	8
	Initial	6	34	78	154	78	28	1
	Medial	12	42	90	161	77	23	5
	Final	1	45	70	134	62	27	2
ku	Percent	0.28%	0.85%	0.79%	1.08%	1.34%	1.29%	1.90%
	Total	3	30	67	181	115	43	7
	Initial	2	15	42	118	79	30	5
	Medial	1	14	24	50	24	9	2
	Final	0	1	1	13	12	4	0
k-	Percent	8.77%	10.87%	10.37%	10.26%	10.07%	9.60%	8.15%
	Total	93	382	878	1728	864	320	30
	Initial	23	132	310	684	380	132	12
	Medial	68	187	432	745	318	137	13
	Final	2	63	136	299	166	51	5

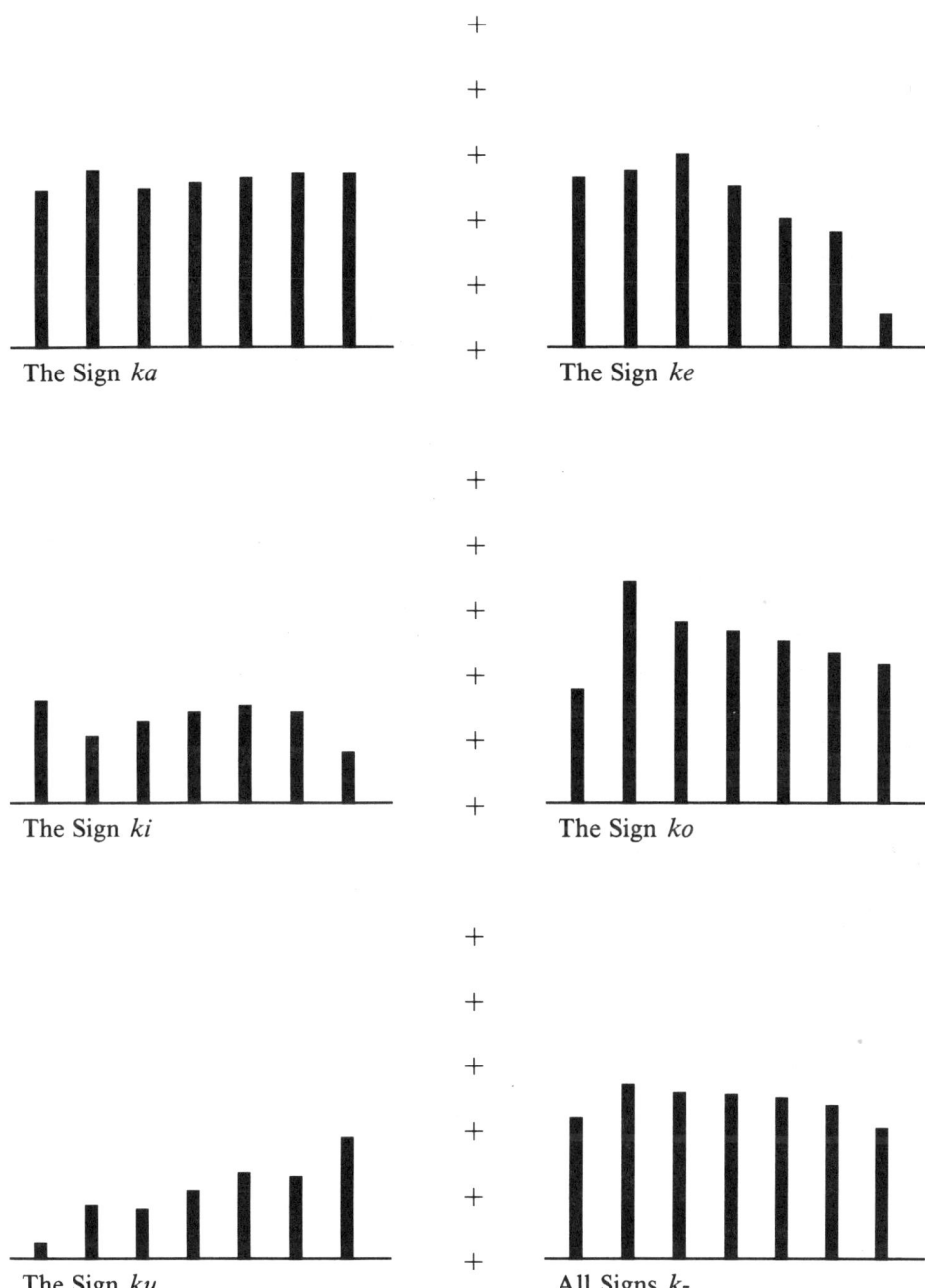

Sign Frequency by Word Class

		PY Topon.	PY Anthr.	PY All	All SG's	KN All	KN Anthr.	KN Topon.
ma	Percent	1.23%	1.82%	1.45%	1.48%	1.47%	1.65%	1.90%
	Total	13	64	123	249	126	55	7
	Initial	6	27	46	103	55	22	4
	Medial	7	36	66	112	46	28	3
	Final	0	1	11	34	25	5	0
me	Percent	0.94%	1.62%	1.76%	1.63%	1.57%	1.26%	0.00%
	Total	10	57	149	274	135	42	0
	Initial	6	17	58	111	60	15	0
	Medial	4	40	83	135	53	21	0
	Final	0	0	8	28	22	6	0
mi	Percent	0.85%	0.48%	0.65%	0.83%	1.03%	0.93%	0.82%
	Total	9	17	55	140	88	31	3
	Initial	1	6	11	37	26	12	0
	Medial	8	11	39	85	49	16	3
	Final	0	0	5	18	13	3	0
mo	Percent	0.19%	0.68%	0.64%	0.86%	1.14%	1.02%	1.90%
	Total	2	24	54	145	98	34	7
	Initial	1	6	8	17	9	4	0
	Medial	1	11	22	51	30	10	1
	Final	0	7	24	77	59	20	6
mu	Percent	0.19%	0.28%	0.18%	0.18%	0.19%	0.30%	0.27%
	Total	2	10	15	30	16	10	1
	Initial	1	6	10	16	6	3	0
	Medial	1	4	5	14	10	7	1
	Final	0	0	0	0	0	0	0
m-	Percent	3.39%	4.89%	4.68%	4.98%	5.40%	5.16%	4.89%
	Total	36	172	396	838	463	172	18
	Initial	15	62	133	284	156	56	4
	Medial	21	102	215	397	188	82	8
	Final	0	8	48	157	119	34	6

Appendix G

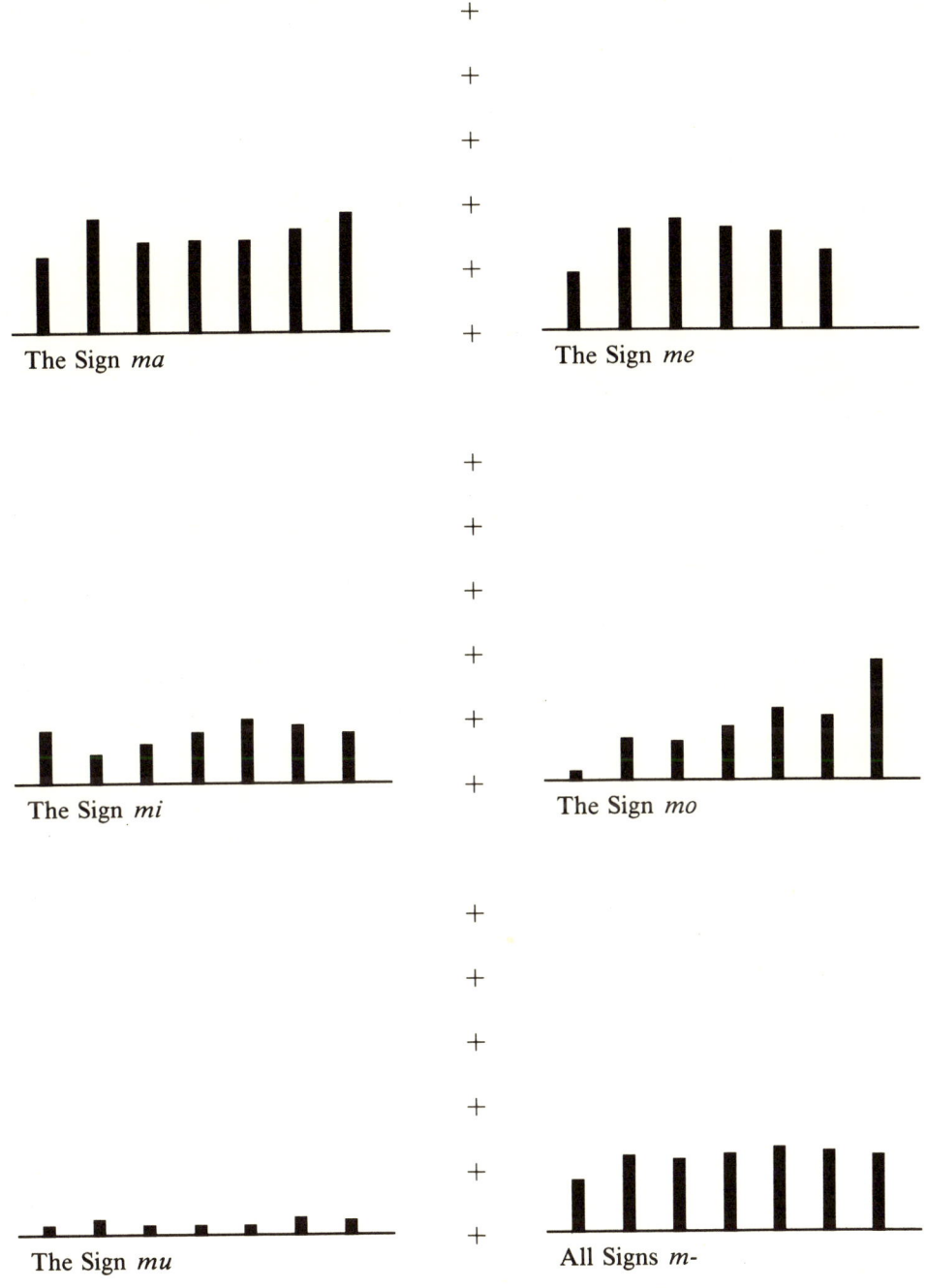

Sign Frequency by Word Class

		PY Topon.	PY Anthr.	PY All	All SG's	KN All	KN Anthr.	KN Topon.
na	Percent	1.41%	1.14%	1.33%	1.53%	1.70%	2.04%	2.17%
	Total	15	40	113	258	146	68	8
	Initial	2	4	11	33	24	10	0
	Medial	8	26	67	145	81	48	8
	Final	5	10	35	80	41	10	0
ne	Percent	2.17%	1.42%	1.43%	1.41%	1.31%	1.08%	0.54%
	Total	23	50	121	237	112	36	2
	Initial	7	11	24	46	26	7	1
	Medial	8	22	56	106	46	23	1
	Final	8	17	41	85	40	6	0
ni	Percent	1.13%	0.74%	0.96%	1.15%	1.34%	0.96%	1.90%
	Total	12	26	81	193	115	32	7
	Initial	1	0	3	21	16	3	0
	Medial	11	23	73	149	81	25	7
	Final	0	3	5	23	18	4	0
no	Percent	1.89%	2.16%	2.01%	2.11%	2.09%	2.52%	1.09%
	Total	20	76	170	355	179	84	4
	Initial	1	1	10	32	20	8	0
	Medial	12	22	58	92	30	11	1
	Final	7	53	102	231	129	65	3
nu	Percent	0.28%	0.28%	0.33%	0.53%	0.75%	0.90%	0.00%
	Total	3	10	28	90	64	30	0
	Initial	0	0	2	9	8	3	0
	Medial	3	9	23	62	40	26	0
	Final	0	1	3	19	16	1	0
n-	Percent	6.88%	5.75%	6.06%	6.73%	7.18%	7.50%	5.71%
	Total	73	202	513	1133	616	250	21
	Initial	11	16	50	141	94	31	1
	Medial	42	102	277	554	278	133	17
	Final	20	84	186	438	244	86	3

Appendix G

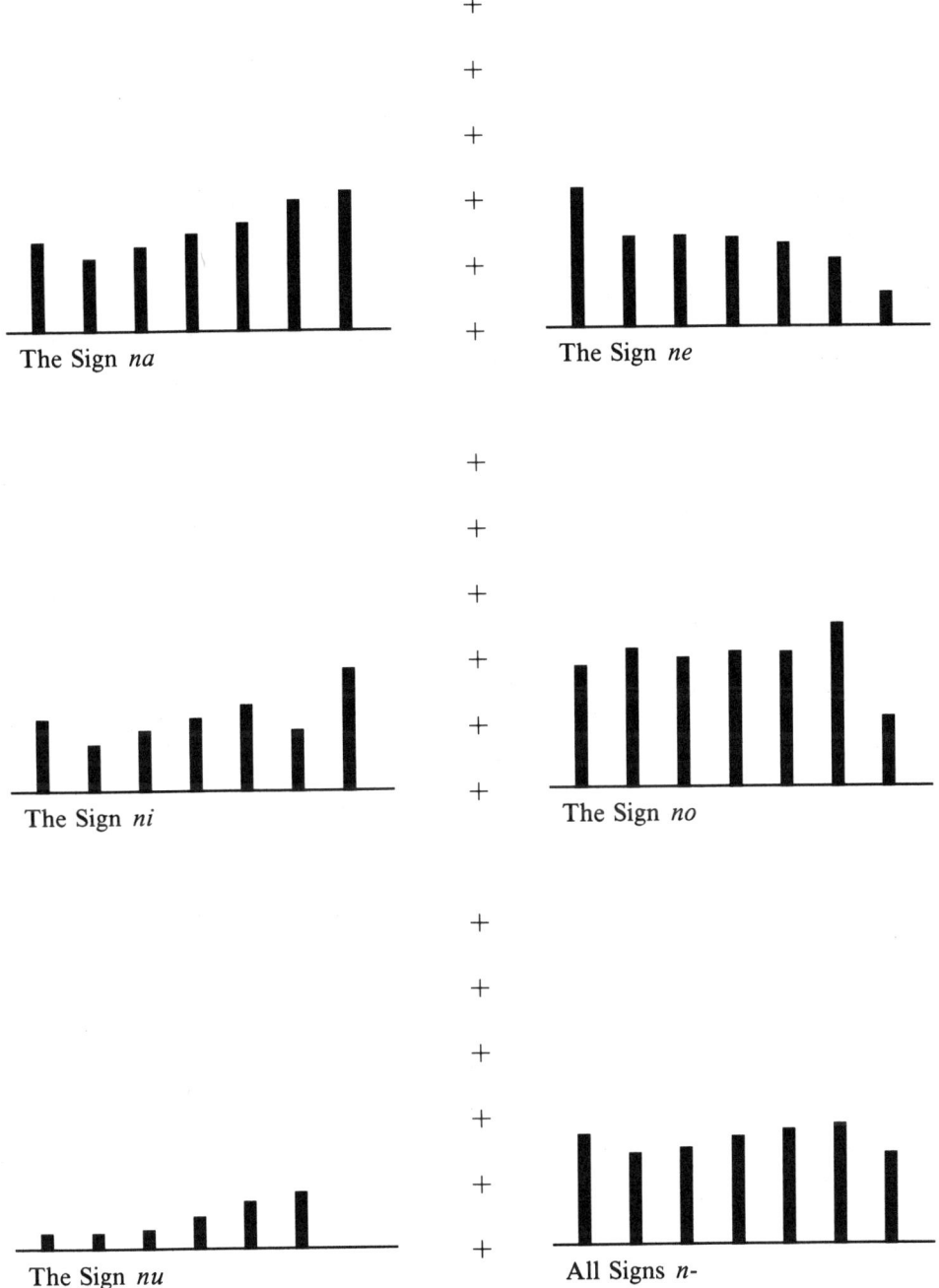

Sign Frequency by Word Class

		PY Topon.	PY Anthr.	PY All	All SG's	KN All	KN Anthr.	KN Topon.
pa	Percent	1.79%	1.17%	1.51%	1.64%	1.81%	1.44%	2.45%
	Total	19	41	128	276	155	48	9
	Initial	10	17	65	140	77	27	3
	Medial	8	24	55	112	59	20	5
	Final	1	0	8	24	19	1	1
pe	Percent	1.32%	1.17%	1.49%	1.24%	0.98%	1.05%	0.27%
	Total	14	41	126	208	84	35	1
	Initial	6	25	62	108	48	24	0
	Medial	6	15	56	86	30	11	1
	Final	2	1	8	14	6	0	0
pi	Percent	3.86%	1.31%	2.08%	1.76%	1.46%	1.14%	0.27%
	Total	41	46	176	296	125	38	1
	Initial	7	24	43	85	38	19	0
	Medial	15	21	82	132	53	18	0
	Final	19	1	51	79	34	1	1
po	Percent	1.41%	1.28%	1.62%	1.51%	1.42%	1.14%	0.00%
	Total	15	45	137	254	122	38	0
	Initial	7	29	86	156	79	22	0
	Medial	6	12	39	70	26	9	0
	Final	2	4	12	28	17	7	0
pu	Percent	0.47%	0.43%	0.43%	0.56%	0.70%	0.60%	0.54%
	Total	5	15	36	94	60	20	2
	Initial	2	13	19	57	36	14	2
	Medial	3	2	15	28	15	4	0
	Final	0	0	2	9	9	2	0
p-	Percent	8.86%	5.35%	7.12%	6.70%	6.36%	5.37%	3.53%
	Total	94	188	603	1128	546	179	13
	Initial	32	108	275	546	278	106	5
	Medial	38	74	247	428	183	62	6
	Final	24	6	81	154	85	11	2

Appendix G

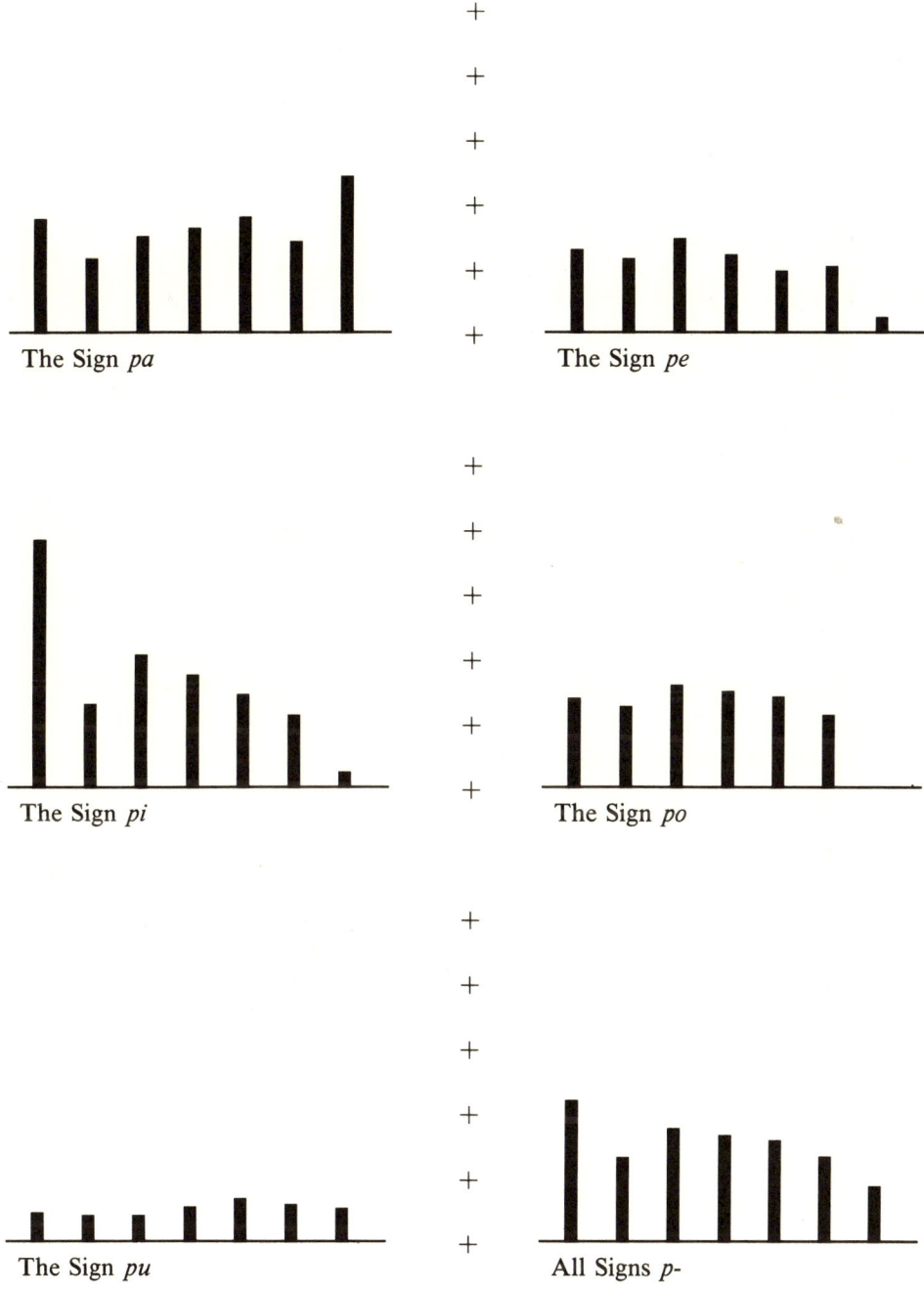

Sign Frequency by Word Class

		PY Topon.	PY Anthr.	PY All	All SG's	KN All	KN Anthr.	KN Topon.
qa	Percent	0.09%	0.54%	0.40%	0.69%	0.94%	1.14%	1.36%
	Total	1	19	34	116	81	38	5
	Initial	0	4	9	59	47	23	4
	Medial	0	8	14	34	21	12	1
	Final	1	7	11	23	13	3	0
qe	Percent	0.66%	0.85%	0.81%	0.80%	0.77%	0.54%	0.00%
	Total	7	30	69	135	66	18	0
	Initial	3	12	27	57	30	12	0
	Medial	2	13	28	43	16	6	0
	Final	2	5	14	35	20	0	0
qi	Percent	0.09%	0.28%	0.27%	0.32%	0.34%	0.45%	0.27%
	Total	1	10	23	54	29	15	1
	Initial	0	2	3	20	16	9	1
	Medial	1	8	19	29	9	6	0
	Final	0	0	1	5	4	0	0
qo	Percent	0.57%	1.31%	0.97%	0.87%	0.83%	1.26%	0.00%
	Total	6	46	82	147	71	42	0
	Initial	4	6	17	32	16	8	0
	Medial	1	32	44	75	34	24	0
	Final	1	8	21	40	21	10	0
q-	Percent	1.41%	2.99%	2.46%	2.69%	2.88%	3.39%	1.63%
	Total	15	105	208	452	247	113	6
	Initial	7	24	56	168	109	52	5
	Medial	4	61	105	181	80	48	1
	Final	4	20	47	103	58	13	0

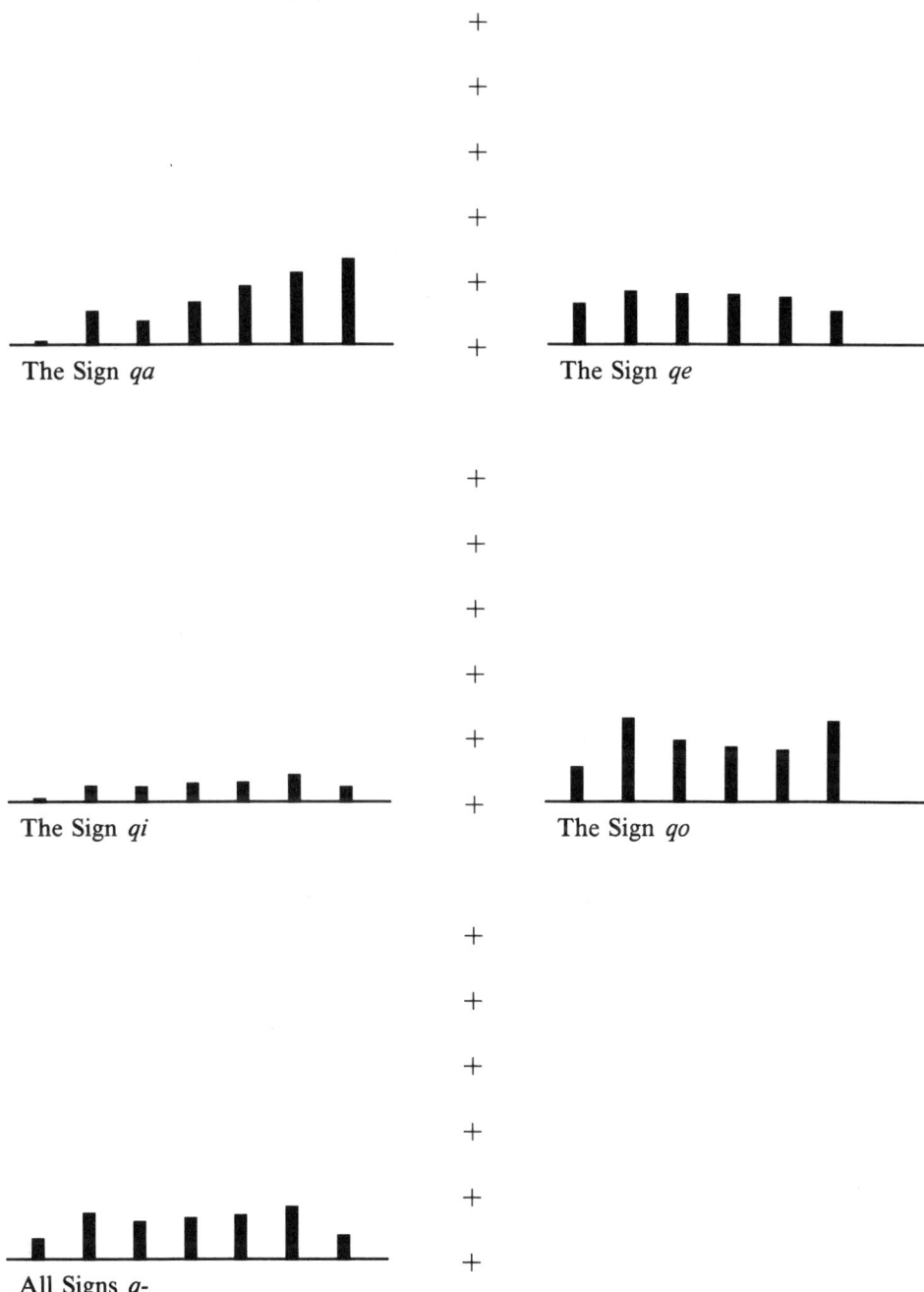

Sign Frequency by Word Class

		PY Topon.	PY Anthr.	PY All	All SG's	KN All	KN Anthr.	KN Topon.
ra	Percent	4.52%	2.96%	3.28%	3.46%	3.37%	3.21%	4.62%
	Total	48	104	278	582	289	107	17
	Initial	6	20	49	113	66	19	6
	Medial	35	70	181	346	156	69	7
	Final	7	14	48	123	67	19	4
re	Percent	4.15%	3.07%	3.32%	2.73%	2.32%	1.92%	1.09%
	Total	44	108	281	459	199	64	4
	Initial	5	19	39	73	37	12	1
	Medial	35	79	199	296	112	42	2
	Final	4	10	43	90	50	10	1
ri	Percent	2.64%	2.62%	2.40%	2.53%	2.55%	2.46%	3.80%
	Total	28	92	203	426	219	82	14
	Initial	5	3	14	53	38	11	5
	Medial	22	83	169	322	148	66	8
	Final	1	6	20	51	33	5	1
ro	Percent	2.54%	4.44%	3.47%	3.50%	3.56%	4.95%	1.63%
	Total	27	156	294	590	305	165	6
	Initial	1	6	13	33	19	1	0
	Medial	15	67	146	227	80	33	3
	Final	11	83	135	330	206	131	3
ru	Percent	0.57%	1.08%	0.89%	1.00%	1.10%	1.11%	1.36%
	Total	6	38	75	168	94	37	5
	Initial	2	11	16	48	33	13	1
	Medial	4	26	57	105	49	18	4
	Final	0	1	2	15	12	6	0
r-	Percent	14.42%	14.17%	13.36%	13.22%	12.89%	13.65%	12.50%
	Total	153	498	1131	2225	1106	455	46
	Initial	19	59	131	320	193	56	13
	Medial	111	325	752	1296	545	228	24
	Final	23	114	248	609	368	171	9

Appendix G

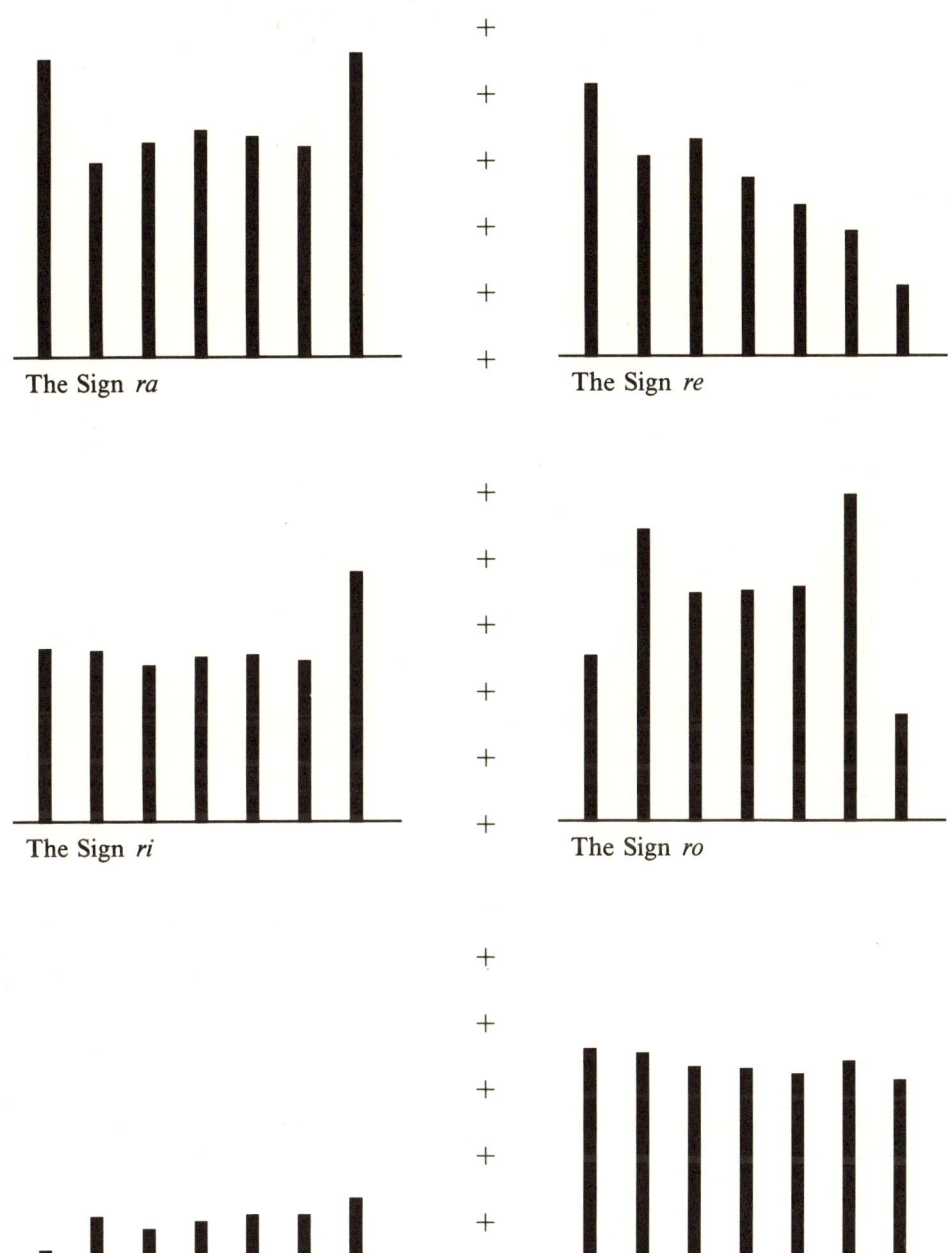

The Sign *ra*

The Sign *re*

The Sign *ri*

The Sign *ro*

The Sign *ru*

All Signs *r-*

Sign Frequency by Word Class

		PY Topon.	PY Anthr.	PY All	All SG's	KN All	KN Anthr.	KN Topon.
sa	Percent	1.23%	1.02%	0.93%	1.13%	1.28%	1.50%	2.45%
	Total	13	36	79	191	110	50	9
	Initial	6	10	21	60	38	20	4
	Medial	6	24	43	89	46	27	3
	Final	1	2	15	42	26	3	2
se	Percent	0.75%	0.54%	0.69%	0.69%	0.62%	0.69%	0.27%
	Total	8	19	58	116	53	23	1
	Initial	2	3	8	22	13	3	1
	Medial	6	15	43	74	27	17	0
	Final	0	1	7	20	13	3	0
si	Percent	1.04%	1.25%	1.61%	1.77%	2.00%	1.71%	1.36%
	Total	11	44	136	298	172	57	5
	Initial	2	8	15	58	43	19	4
	Medial	6	33	85	166	90	33	1
	Final	3	3	36	74	39	5	0
so	Percent	1.04%	1.11%	0.96%	1.19%	1.40%	1.89%	4.62%
	Total	11	39	81	201	120	63	17
	Initial	2	1	6	10	5	0	1
	Medial	5	22	45	69	23	6	6
	Final	4	16	30	122	92	57	10
su	Percent	0.09%	0.14%	0.15%	0.36%	0.54%	0.51%	1.09%
	Total	1	5	13	60	46	17	4
	Initial	1	3	7	32	27	12	2
	Medial	0	2	6	25	16	4	1
	Final	0	0	0	3	3	1	1
s-	Percent	4.15%	4.07%	4.33%	5.14%	5.84%	6.30%	9.78%
	Total	44	143	367	866	501	210	36
	Initial	13	25	57	182	126	54	12
	Medial	23	96	222	423	202	87	11
	Final	8	22	88	261	173	69	13

Appendix G

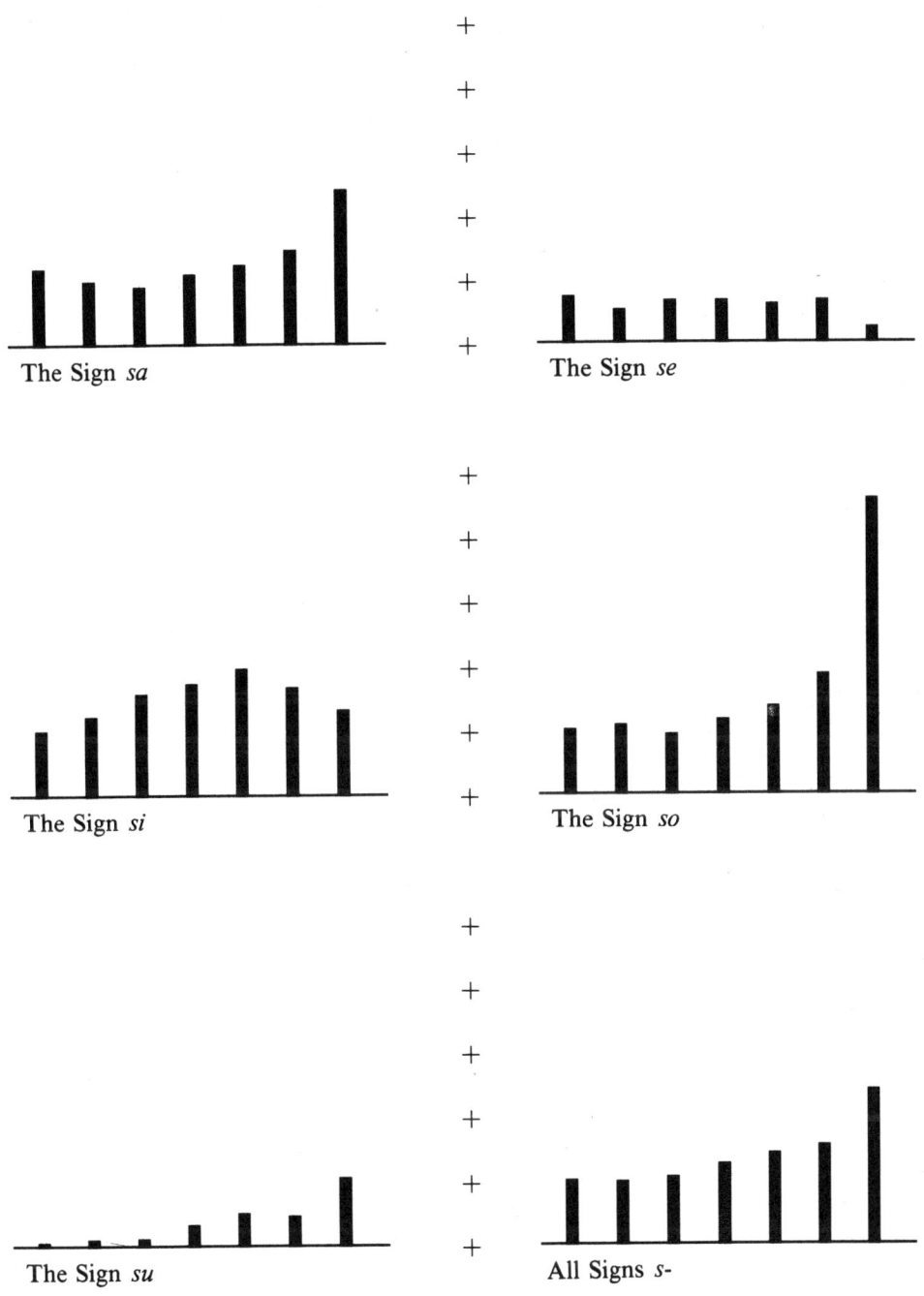

Sign Frequency by Word Class

		PY Topon.	PY Anthr.	PY All	All SG's	KN All	KN Anthr.	KN Topon.
ta	Percent	1.79%	5.38%	3.21%	3.61%	4.04%	4.86%	4.08%
	Total	19	189	272	608	347	162	15
	Initial	2	20	33	102	71	26	2
	Medial	13	79	111	219	105	49	10
	Final	4	90	128	287	171	87	3
te	Percent	4.43%	2.22%	3.48%	2.98%	2.55%	1.89%	0.54%
	Total	47	78	295	501	219	63	2
	Initial	10	19	61	121	68	20	1
	Medial	18	51	159	250	87	34	1
	Final	19	8	75	130	64	9	0
ti	Percent	1.60%	1.71%	1.81%	1.81%	1.75%	1.56%	1.63%
	Total	17	60	153	304	150	52	6
	Initial	4	14	32	62	30	11	2
	Medial	13	39	110	198	87	33	4
	Final	0	7	11	44	33	8	0
to	Percent	2.45%	2.28%	2.72%	3.03%	3.32%	4.02%	5.16%
	Total	26	80	230	510	285	134	19
	Initial	2	17	52	98	47	12	2
	Medial	15	24	88	145	60	32	4
	Final	9	39	90	267	178	90	13
tu	Percent	0.66%	0.91%	0.65%	0.71%	0.70%	0.75%	0.82%
	Total	7	32	55	119	60	25	3
	Initial	0	13	20	57	34	12	3
	Medial	7	17	31	50	17	12	0
	Final	0	2	4	12	9	1	0
t-	Percent	10.93%	12.49%	11.87%	12.13%	12.37%	13.08%	12.23%
	Total	116	439	1005	2042	1061	436	45
	Initial	18	83	198	440	250	81	10
	Medial	66	210	499	862	356	160	19
	Final	32	146	308	740	455	195	16

Appendix G

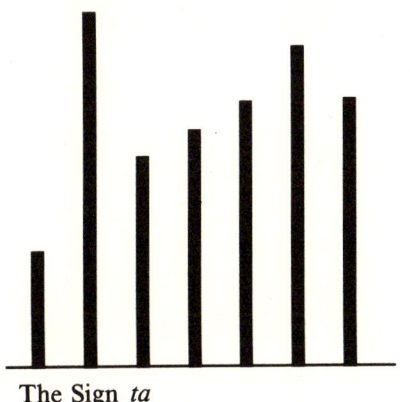

The Sign *ta*

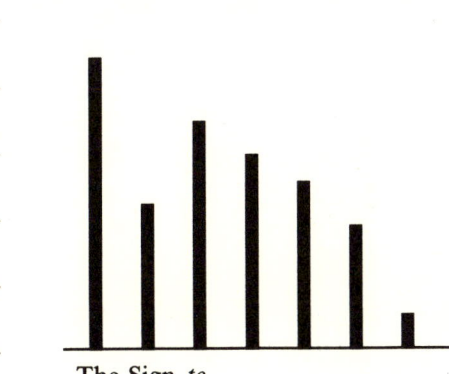

The Sign *te*

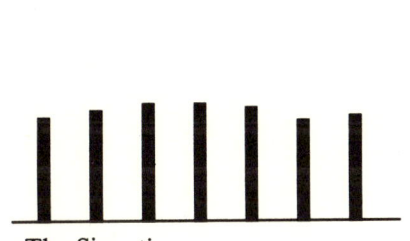

The Sign *ti*

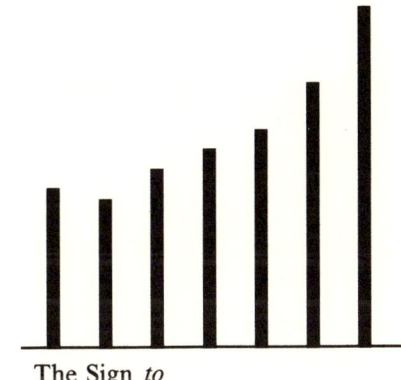

The Sign *to*

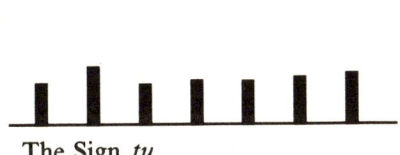

The Sign *tu*

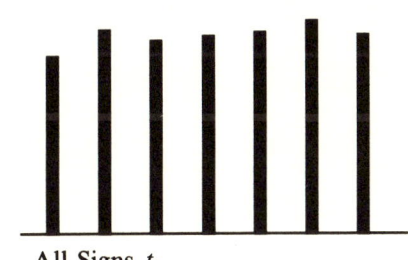

All Signs *t-*

Sign Frequency by Word Class

		PY Topon.	PY Anthr.	PY All	All SG's	KN All	KN Anthr.	KN Topon.
wa	Percent	2.92%	2.82%	1.98%	1.84%	1.78%	2.19%	2.17%
	Total	31	99	168	310	153	73	8
	Initial	5	32	49	85	41	18	3
	Medial	11	48	76	136	63	41	2
	Final	15	19	43	89	49	14	3
we	Percent	2.26%	2.45%	2.42%	2.33%	2.21%	1.26%	2.45%
	Total	24	86	205	393	190	42	9
	Initial	0	9	31	71	43	9	0
	Medial	11	33	76	151	73	17	3
	Final	13	44	98	171	74	16	6
wi	Percent	2.36%	1.08%	1.41%	1.31%	1.20%	1.47%	0.82%
	Total	25	38	119	221	103	49	3
	Initial	3	17	24	63	40	25	1
	Medial	22	19	90	141	54	21	2
	Final	0	2	5	17	9	3	0
wo	Percent	2.92%	3.53%	3.02%	2.59%	2.19%	2.49%	1.36%
	Total	31	124	256	436	188	83	5
	Initial	3	18	43	84	42	13	0
	Medial	22	39	103	152	49	16	0
	Final	6	67	110	200	97	54	5
w-	Percent	10.46%	9.87%	8.83%	8.08%	7.39%	7.41%	6.79%
	Total	111	347	748	1360	634	247	25
	Initial	11	76	147	303	166	65	4
	Medial	66	139	345	580	239	95	7
	Final	34	132	256	477	229	87	14

Appendix G

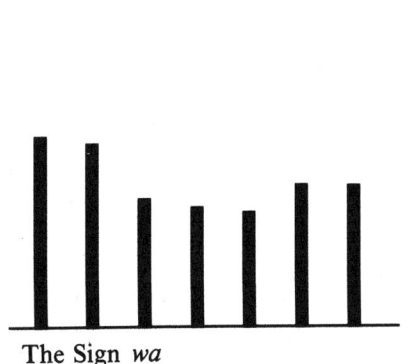

The Sign *wa*

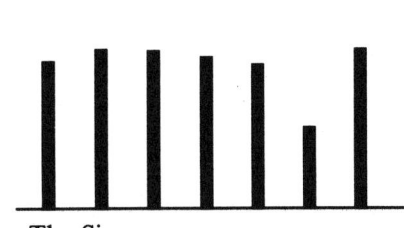

The Sign *we*

The Sign *wi*

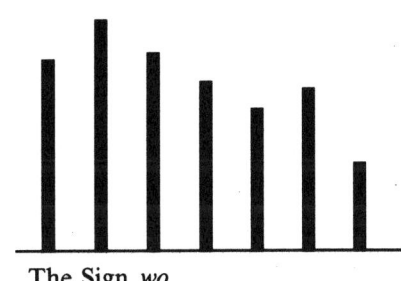

The Sign *wo*

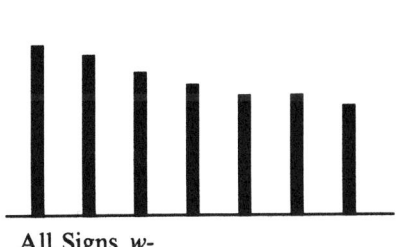

All Signs *w-*

Sign Frequency by Word Class

		PY Topon.	PY Anthr.	PY All	All SG's	KN All	KN Anthr.	KN Topon.
za	Percent	0.28%	0.17%	0.26%	0.28%	0.34%	0.39%	0.00%
	Total	3	6	22	47	29	13	0
	Initial	2	1	6	15	10	3	0
	Medial	0	5	8	16	8	6	0
	Final	1	0	8	16	11	4	0
ze	Percent	0.00%	0.14%	0.19%	0.21%	0.22%	0.18%	0.00%
	Total	0	5	16	36	19	6	0
	Initial	0	1	8	14	5	1	0
	Medial	0	4	5	16	11	5	0
	Final	0	0	3	6	3	0	0
zo	Percent	0.00%	0.26%	0.25%	0.37%	0.48%	0.48%	0.00%
	Total	0	9	21	62	41	16	0
	Initial	0	2	2	8	7	2	0
	Medial	0	4	12	19	10	2	0
	Final	0	3	7	35	24	12	0
z-	Percent	0.28%	0.57%	0.70%	0.86%	1.04%	1.05%	0.00%
	Total	3	20	59	145	89	35	0
	Initial	2	4	16	37	22	6	0
	Medial	0	13	25	51	29	13	0
	Final	1	3	18	57	38	16	0

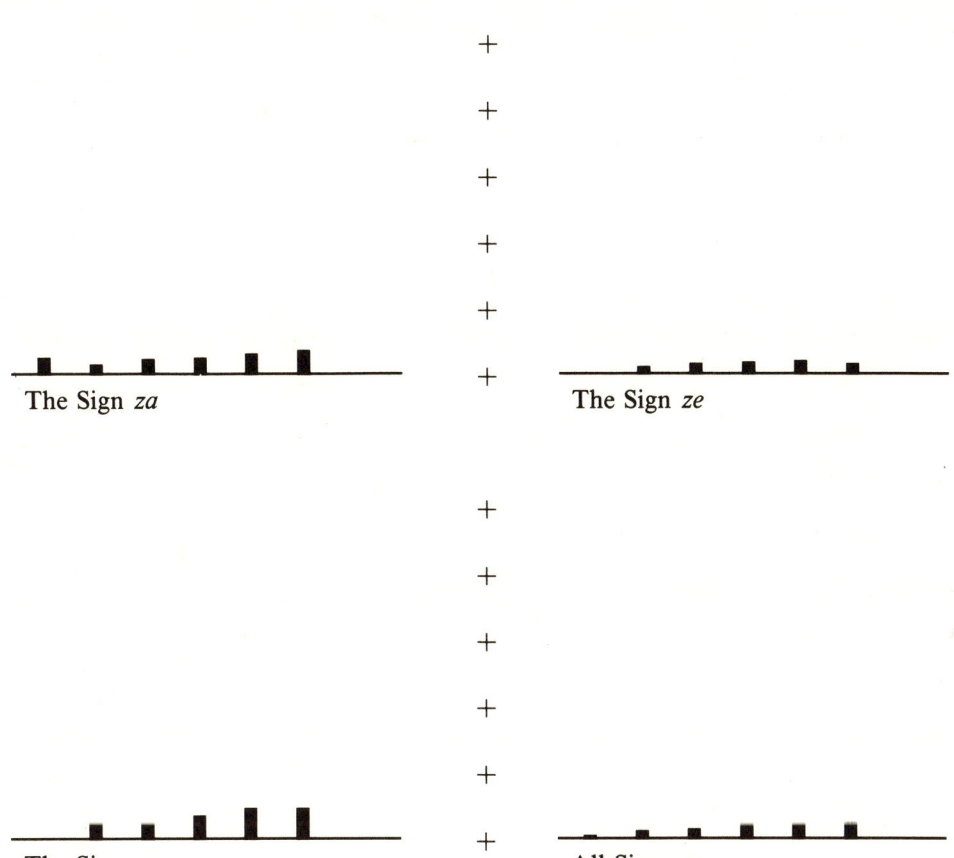

Sign Frequency by Word Class

		PY Topon.	PY Anthr.	PY All	All SG's	KN All	KN Anthr.	KN Topon.
*18	Percent	0.00%	0.00%	0.00%	0.02%	0.05%	0.09%	0.00%
	Total	0	0	0	4	4	3	0
	Initial	0	0	0	1	1	1	0
	Medial	0	0	0	1	1	0	0
	Final	0	0	0	2	2	2	0
*19	Percent	0.00%	0.00%	0.00%	0.01%	0.01%	0.03%	0.00%
	Total	0	0	0	1	1	1	0
	Initial	0	0	0	0	0	0	0
	Medial	0	0	0	0	0	0	0
	Final	0	0	0	1	1	1	0
*22	Percent	0.00%	0.00%	0.00%	0.07%	0.12%	0.03%	0.27%
	Total	0	0	0	11	10	1	1
	Initial	0	0	0	3	3	0	0
	Medial	0	0	0	7	6	1	1
	Final	0	0	0	1	1	0	0
*34	Percent	0.00%	0.06%	0.08%	0.07%	0.06%	0.09%	0.00%
	Total	0	2	7	12	5	3	0
	Initial	0	1	5	7	2	2	0
	Medial	0	1	2	4	2	1	0
	Final	0	0	0	1	1	0	0
*35	Percent	0.00%	0.03%	0.07%	0.05%	0.02%	0.00%	0.00%
	Total	0	1	6	8	2	0	0
	Initial	0	1	4	5	1	0	0
	Medial	0	0	1	2	1	0	0
	Final	0	0	1	1	0	0	0
*47	Percent	0.00%	0.00%	0.00%	0.05%	0.08%	0.03%	1.09%
	Total	0	0	0	8	7	1	4
	Initial	0	0	0	7	7	1	4
	Medial	0	0	0	1	0	0	0
	Final	0	0	0	0	0	0	0

Sign Frequency by Word Class

		PY Topon.	PY Anthr.	PY All	All SG's	KN All	KN Anthr.	KN Topon.
*49	Percent	0.00%	0.00%	0.00%	0.02%	0.03%	0.09%	0.00%
	Total	0	0	0	3	3	3	0
	Initial	0	0	0	1	1	1	0
	Medial	0	0	0	2	2	2	0
	Final	0	0	0	0	0	0	0
*63	Percent	0.00%	0.03%	0.01%	0.01%	0.00%	0.00%	0.00%
	Total	0	1	1	1	0	0	0
	Initial	0	0	0	0	0	0	0
	Medial	0	1	1	1	0	0	0
	Final	0	0	0	0	0	0	0
*64	Percent	0.00%	0.09%	0.04%	0.02%	0.02%	0.03%	0.00%
	Total	0	3	3	4	2	1	0
	Initial	0	0	0	0	0	0	0
	Medial	0	3	3	4	2	1	0
	Final	0	0	0	0	0	0	0
*65	Percent	0.00%	0.03%	0.05%	0.10%	0.13%	0.21%	0.27%
	Total	0	1	4	16	11	7	1
	Initial	0	0	0	0	0	0	0
	Medial	0	1	3	11	8	6	1
	Final	0	0	1	5	3	1	0
*79	Percent	0.00%	0.03%	0.02%	0.03%	0.03%	0.03%	0.00%
	Total	0	1	2	5	3	1	0
	Initial	0	0	0	0	0	0	0
	Medial	0	0	1	3	2	0	0
	Final	0	1	1	2	1	1	0
*82	Percent	0.19%	0.11%	0.09%	0.07%	0.02%	0.06%	0.00%
	Total	2	4	8	11	2	2	0
	Initial	0	2	2	3	1	1	0
	Medial	1	1	3	5	1	1	0
	Final	1	1	3	3	0	0	0

Sign Frequency by Word Class

		PY Topon.	PY Anthr.	PY All	All SG's	KN All	KN Anthr.	KN Topon.
*83	Percent	0.00%	0.06%	0.02%	0.07%	0.12%	0.09%	1.09%
	Total	0	2	2	12	10	3	4
	Initial	0	0	0	3	3	0	1
	Medial	0	2	2	8	6	3	3
	Final	0	0	0	1	1	0	0
*85	Percent	0.00%	0.11%	0.13%	0.12%	0.08%	0.06%	0.27%
	Total	0	4	11	21	7	2	1
	Initial	0	4	11	20	6	2	1
	Medial	0	0	0	1	1	0	0
	Final	0	0	0	0	0	0	0
*86	Percent	0.09%	0.00%	0.02%	0.02%	0.02%	0.06%	0.00%
	Total	1	0	2	4	2	2	0
	Initial	0	0	0	0	0	0	0
	Medial	0	0	1	3	2	2	0
	Final	1	0	1	1	0	0	0
*87	Percent	0.00%	0.00%	0.00%	0.01%	0.01%	0.00%	0.00%
	Total	0	0	0	1	1	0	0
	Initial	0	0	0	0	0	0	0
	Medial	0	0	0	1	1	0	0
	Final	0	0	0	0	0	0	0
*88	Percent	0.00%	0.00%	0.00%	0.01%	0.00%	0.00%	0.00%
	Total	0	0	0	1	0	0	0
	Initial	0	0	0	0	0	0	0
	Medial	0	0	0	0	0	0	0
	Final	0	0	0	1	0	0	0
a_2	Percent	1.23%	0.48%	0.72%	0.40%	0.05%	0.00%	0.00%
	Total	13	17	61	67	4	0	0
	Initial	10	9	26	28	2	0	0
	Medial	3	6	18	19	0	0	0
	Final	0	2	17	20	2	0	0

Sign Frequency by Word Class

		PY Topon.	PY Anthr.	PY All	All SG's	KN All	KN Anthr.	KN Topon.
a_3	Percent	0.47%	0.48%	0.33%	0.30%	0.30%	0.42%	0.00%
	Total	5	17	28	51	26	14	0
	Initial	4	17	27	48	24	14	0
	Medial	1	0	1	3	2	0	0
	Final	0	0	0	0	0	0	0
dwe	Percent	0.00%	0.00%	0.01%	0.02%	0.05%	0.00%	0.00%
	Total	0	0	1	4	4	0	0
	Initial	0	0	0	0	0	0	0
	Medial	0	0	1	2	2	0	0
	Final	0	0	0	2	2	0	0
dwo	Percent	0.00%	0.03%	0.04%	0.04%	0.05%	0.03%	0.00%
	Total	0	1	3	7	4	1	0
	Initial	0	0	1	3	2	1	0
	Medial	0	1	1	1	0	0	0
	Final	0	0	1	3	2	0	0
nwa	Percent	0.00%	0.03%	0.07%	0.08%	0.09%	0.18%	0.27%
	Total	0	1	6	14	8	6	1
	Initial	0	0	0	1	1	0	0
	Medial	0	1	6	10	4	4	1
	Final	0	0	0	3	3	2	0
pa_3	Percent	0.00%	0.06%	0.02%	0.21%	0.38%	0.48%	0.82%
	Total	0	2	2	35	33	16	3
	Initial	0	0	0	17	17	6	3
	Medial	0	2	2	13	11	8	0
	Final	0	0	0	5	5	2	0
pte	Percent	0.00%	0.03%	0.09%	0.08%	0.07%	0.03%	0.00%
	Total	0	1	8	13	6	1	0
	Initial	0	1	1	5	4	1	0
	Medial	0	0	6	6	1	0	0
	Final	0	0	1	2	1	0	0

Sign Frequency by Word Class

		PY Topon.	PY Anthr.	PY All	All SG's	KN All	KN Anthr.	KN Topon.
pu_2	Percent	0.47%	0.14%	0.20%	0.25%	0.24%	0.24%	0.27%
	Total	5	5	17	42	21	8	1
	Initial	2	3	8	14	6	3	0
	Medial	3	2	9	24	11	4	1
	Final	0	0	0	4	4	1	0
ra_2	Percent	0.38%	0.14%	0.32%	0.24%	0.15%	0.15%	0.00%
	Total	4	5	27	40	13	5	0
	Initial	0	0	0	0	0	0	0
	Medial	2	3	16	22	6	4	0
	Final	2	2	11	18	7	1	0
ra_3	Percent	0.19%	0.03%	0.11%	0.05%	0.00%	0.00%	0.00%
	Total	2	1	9	9	0	0	0
	Initial	0	0	0	0	0	0	0
	Medial	1	1	4	4	0	0	0
	Final	1	0	5	5	0	0	0
ro_2	Percent	0.00%	0.14%	0.11%	0.12%	0.15%	0.12%	0.00%
	Total	0	5	9	20	13	4	0
	Initial	0	0	0	0	0	0	0
	Medial	0	2	4	9	5	1	0
	Final	0	3	5	11	8	3	0
ta_2	Percent	0.19%	0.00%	0.04%	0.07%	0.12%	0.15%	0.00%
	Total	2	0	3	12	10	5	0
	Initial	0	0	0	0	0	0	0
	Medial	0	0	1	2	2	1	0
	Final	2	0	2	10	8	4	0
two	Percent	0.00%	0.03%	0.01%	0.01%	0.00%	0.00%	0.00%
	Total	0	1	1	1	0	0	0
	Initial	0	0	0	0	0	0	0
	Medial	0	1	1	1	0	0	0
	Final	0	0	0	0	0	0	0

APPENDIX H

This appendix presents the Linear A sign-groups transliterated according to the values listed on page 67 and Figures 5 and 6. Since I have printed L numbers for each sign-group, I have not hesitated to introduce some "speculative" phonetic values in this appendix. Most controversial are: L57 as SI, L83 as AI, and L79 as QI. For these values see Chapter Four.

The explanation of the code in the second column is as follows.

*	Reading of Raison-Pope but not Brice.
?	Reading of Brice only.
+	Inscription not in Brice.
#	More likely variant reading
=	Less likely variant reading.
A	Sign-group incomplete at beginning
B	Sign-group incomplete at end.
C	Complete sign-group.
D	Sign-group incomplete both at beginning and end.

The number following the letter indicates how many times the sign-group occurs in the corresponding state of preservation. The code C2A1 means "twice complete and once incomplete at the beginning."

References follow the system of Raison-Pope (1971) with the addition of Brice's (1961) reference in parenthesis. A comma terminates an incomplete list of references.

Minoan Linear A

Transliteration	L Numbers	Code	Reference
A.DA	52.30	C1	TY3b5(IV9)
A.DA.SI.QE	52.30.57.91	? C1	IV9a3
A.DE	52.102	? C1	IV10b
A.DI	52.51	? C3	I4a,I5a,II1
A.DI.DA.KI.TI.PA.KU	52.51.30.103.78.2.98	* D1	KNZ6(II1)
A.DI.KI.TE	52.51.103.92	* B1	PKZ12a(I5)
A.DI.KI.TE.TE.PI	52.51.103.92.92.56	* C1	PKZ11a(I4)
A.DO.RA	52.101.53	D1	KNZ7(II2)
A.DU	52.93	C7	85a1,86a4,88.1,92.1,95b1,
A.DU.ZA	52.93.23	* C1	PK1.2(IV5)
A.I	52.100	C1	115b4
A.JA.KU	52.32.98	A1	KNZ13(V14)
A.JA.NU.MA.JA.WA	52.32.25.95.32.75	? C1	II8
A.JE	52.81	* D1	IOZ1(I15)
A.JE.12	52.81.12	? C1	I15
A.KA.NU.WE.20.DU.RA.RE	52.29.25.94.20.93.53.54	* B1	KNZ7(II2)
A.KA.RU	52.29.55	C2	2.1,86a1,86b1?
A.KO.A	52.45.52	? B1	I4b
A.KO.A.NA	52.45.52.26	* C1	PKZ11b(I4)
A.KU	52.98	C1	PA1.1(IV7)
A.KU.TU	52.98.6	C1	TY3b7(IV9)
A.MA	52.95	* C1	MA1b(IV10)
A.MA.RA.TU	52.95.53.6	* B1	SKZ1(II25)
A.NA.QA	52.26.62	A1	126a2
A.NU	52.25	* D1	PH13a1(IV17viii)
A.PA.DU.PA	52.2.93.2	= D1	PKZ12d(I5)
A.PA.RA.NE	52.2.53.61	C2	96a1,96b1
A.PA.SE.PA	52.2.77.2	# D1	PKZ12d(I5)
A.PI	52.56	C1	KNZ16(V15)
A.PU2.NA	52.34.26	C1	14.3
A.RA	52.53	? A1	IV11a
A.RA.NA.RE	52.53.26.54	C1	1a4,47b1?
A.RA.PI	52.53.56	# C1	87.5
A.RA.WI	52.53.28	= C1	87.5
A.RA.68	52.53.68	C1	122b3,87.5?,109.4?
A.RA.96	52.53.96	* C1	109.4
A.RE	52.54	? C1	29.5
A.RE.DA.I	52.54.30.100	* C1	29.5
A.RE.NE.SI.DI.88.41	52.54.61.57.51.88.41	* B1	KNZ13(V14)
A.RE.SA.NA	52.54.31.26	+ C1	TEZ2
A.RE.41.RE.NA	52.54.41.54.26	+ C1	ZAZ3.2
A.RI	52.72	C2B1	PH6.1(IV16),PH6.3(IV16),
A.RI.NI.TA	52.72.60.74	C1	25a3
A.RI.SU	52.72.59	* B1	PH13(IV17vii)
A.RU	52.55	C3	9a5,9b2,49a6,11a1?
A.RU.DA.RA	52.55.30.53	C1	28b5,62.1?
A.RU.RA	52.55.53	* B1	11a1
A.SA.DA.KA	52.31.30.29	C1	MAW5a1(III12)

Appendix H

Transliteration	L Numbers	Code	Reference
A.SA.ME.NE	52.31.84.61	* C1	ZAZ3.1
A.SA.RA2	52.31.58	* C1	89.1
A.SA.SA.RA	52.31.31.53	B1	PKZ4(I12)
A.SA.SA.RA.ME	52.31.31.53.84	* C2	PKZ11b(I4),PRZ1c(I17)
A.SA.88.MA.I	52.31.88.95.100	* C1	GOW1a1(III10)
A.SA.88.MA.I.27	52.31.88.95.100.27	? C1	III10a
A.SE	52.77	C3	93a3,132.1,ZAZ3.1+
A.SE.JA	52.77.32	C1	115a4
A.SE.KO	52.77.45	? A1	24a4
A.SI	52.57	? D1	51a3
A.SI.JA.KA	52.57.32.29	C2	28a1,28b1
A.SU.JA	52.59.32	C1	11a3
A.TA.I	52.74.100	* C1	PRZ1b(I17)
A.TA.I.88	52.74.100.88	? C1	I16
A.TA.I.88.DE.KA	52.74.100.88.102.29	+ C1	ZAZ3.2
A.TA.I.88.WA.JA	52.74.100.88.75.32	* C3	PKZ12a(I5),TLZ1(I16),
A.TA.NU.WI.JA.WA	52.74.25.28.32.75	* B1	HTZ159(II8)
A.TI.KA.A	52.78.29.52	? C1	III8.1
A.TI.KA.A.MI.KO	52.78.29.52.76.45	# C1	ZAW2.1(III8)
A.TI.KI.TA.A	52.78.103.74.52	C1	TYZ4(II18)
A.TU	52.6	C1	87.5
A.TU.RI.SI.20	52.6.72.57.20	? C1	II4
A.TU.WE.SI.TI	52.6.94.57.78	* C1	KNZ5(II4)
A.U	52.97	? A1	46b2
A.WA.TI.NA.RA2	52.75.78.26.58	? C1	II13
A.WE.SU	52.94.59	C1	118.3
A.20.DA.85	52.20.30.85	= C1	SIZ1
A.20.KA.A.MI.KO	52.20.29.52.76.45	= C1	ZAW2.1(III8)
A.41.DA.85	52.41.30.85	# C1	SIZ1
A.65.TE	52.65.92	C1	96a2
A.68.—.NA.MA.MA.TI.TI	52.68.160.26.95.95.78.78	* C1	HTZ155(V7)
A.89.TU	52.89.6	? C1	IV14.1
A.120.ZA	52.120.23	? C1	IV5.2
A.151.TU.134.RA	52.151.6.134.53	* C1	PH2.1(IV14)
AI.KI.TA2	83.103.86	A1	122b2
AI.TI.KA.A	83.78.29.52	? A1	4.1
AI.TI.KA.A.RE	83.78.29.52.54	* D1	4.1
AI.TU	83.6	C4	9a2,9b3,119.4,122a6
AI.TU.JA	83.6.32	C1	115b3
DA.—.KU	30.160.98	? B1	IV6C
DA.DE.KU	30.102.98	? C1	127a2
DA.DU.MA.TA	30.93.95.74	C1	95a1
DA.I	30.100	C1	12.6,29.5?
DA.KA	30.29	C6	HTW226(CRIII3),
DA.KI.TI.NE.KU	30.103.78.61.98	? C1	II1
DA.KU.NA	30.98.26	C1	103.4
DA.KU.SE.NE	30.98.77.61	C1B1	103.4,103.2
DA.KU.SE.NE.TI	30.98.77.61.78	C1	104.1
DA.ME	30.84	C5	86a4,95a2,95b2,106.3,

Transliteration	L Numbers	Code	Reference
DA.MI.NU	30.76.25	C1	117a8
DA.NA.SI	30.26.57	C1	126a1
DA.NE.KU.TI	30.61.98.78	C1	117a8
DA.PA3	30.1	B1	79.1,6b5?
DA.QE.RA	30.91.53	C2B1	6a6,120.1,57a1
DA.RA	30.53	* D1	PH7b3(IV17iii)
DA.RE	30.54	C5	7a4,10b1,85a5,122b4,
DA.RU.NE.PA	30.55.61.2	* C1	98b2
DA.RU.NE.TE	30.55.61.92	? C1	98b2
DA.RU.33	30.55.33	C1	7b2
DA.SA	30.31	? C1	V17ii
DA.SI.DI.JA	30.57.51.32	A1	126a3
DA.SI.85	30.57.85	C4	13.5,85a3,99b1,122a2
DA.SU	30.59	* B1	9b1
DA.SU.RA	30.59.53	? C1	9b1
DA.TA.RA	30.74.53	C1	6a1
DA.TA.RE	30.74.54	C2	88.5,62.2*
DA.TA.RO	30.74.22	? C1	116a1
DA.TI	30.78	? A1	IV11b1
DA.TU	30.6	C1	123a6
DA.U.120.I	30.97.120.100	C1	120.3
DA.WA.—.DU.WA.NA	30.75.160.93.75.26	? C1	I8b
DA.WA.—.DU.WA.145	30.75.160.93.75.145	* C1	KNZ10b(I8)
DA.WE.DA	30.94.30	C4	10a5,85a2,93a7,122a7
DA.68.TE	30.68.92	C1	34.1
DE.DI	102.51	C1	94b2
DE.NU.RA.JA	102.25.53.32	C1	115a1
DE.PA3	102.1	? A1	11b1
DE.SI	102.57	* D1	51a3
DE.96.KU	102.96.98	C1	93a6
DI.AI	51.83	* C1	HTW217a1(CRIV4)
DI.DE	51.102	? C1	86b3
DI.DE.RU	51.102.55	C3	86a3,95a4,95b4
DI.DI.KA.SE	51.51.29.77	+ C1	ZAZ3.1
DI.JA.I	51.32.100	A1	29.3
DI.KA.TU	51.29.6	B1	52a2
DI.KI.SE	51.103.77	C2	87.3,117b2
DI.NA.RO	51.26.22	* C1	108.2
DI.NA.U	51.26.97	C6	9a3,9b5,16.1,25a1,
DI.PA.JA	51.2.32	* A1	PH7a1(IV17iii)
DI.PA.PU	51.2.64	? D1	IV17iii1
DI.RA.DI.NA	51.53.51.26	A1	PH1a1(IV13)
DI.RE.DI.NA	51.54.51.26	C1	98a2
DI.WE.NA	51.94.26	C2	93a1,102.3
DI.ZA.DO.82	51.23.101.82	? C1	II5
DI.ZA.KE	51.23.24	C1	1a2
DO.DI	101.51	* C1	HTW209a(CRIV10)
DO.DI.NA	101.51.26	* C1	HTW210a(CRIV13)
DO.DI.NA.SU.KA	101.51.26.59.29	? C1	CRIV13a
DO.DI.RA	101.51.53	C2	HTW212a(CRIV11),

Transliteration	L Numbers	Code	Reference
DO.DI.SU.KA	101.51.59.29	? C1	CRIV10a
DO.DU	101.93	C1	99b2
DO.RA	101.53	C1	PHW20
DO.SU	101.59	C1	1a2
DO.96.DI	101.96.51	C1	101.1
DO.96.PU2	101.96.34	C1	25a4
DU.—.JA	93.160.32	? C1	IV13a1
DU.DA.MA	93.30.95	C1	6b4
DU.DO.WA	93.101.75	C1	36.2
DU.JA	93.32	C1	7a3
DU.KU.PA3.NA.TU.NA.TE	93.98.1.26.6.26.92	#D1	APZ2b1(I13)
DU.ME.DI	93.84.51	C1	19.3
DU.NE.MI	93.61.76	A1	127a1
DU.PA3.NA	93.1.26	C1	115b2
DU.PI.I.NA	93.56.100.26	? C1	123b5
DU.RA	93.53	* A1	MA2a(IV11)
DU.RU.WI	93.55.28	C1	25a4
DU.SU	93.59	? D1	62.3
DU.SU.NI	93.59.60	C1	108.2
DU.TA.DI	93.74.51	* C1	19.3
DU.TA2.NI	93.86.60	? C1	103.1
DU.65.A	93.65.52	C1	15.1
I.A.SI	100.52.57	? B1	I7
I.DA.A	100.30.52	+ C1	KOZ1b
I.DA.MA.TE	100.30.95.92	C2	ARZ1(V17III),ARZ2(V17iv)
I.DA.PA3	100.30.1	C1	PH6.4(IV16)
I.DO.RI.NI.TA	100.101.72.60.74	C1	PH6.2(IV16)
I.DU.NE.SI	100.93.61.57	C1	13.5
I.DU.TI	100.93.78	* C1	104.2
I.DU.TI.TI	100.93.78.78	? C1	104.2
I.DU.WI	100.93.28	* C1	MA1a(IV10)
I.JA	100.32	B1	KNZ10b(I8)
I.JA.TE	100.32.92	C1	PHZ4(II12)
I.KA	100.29	C3A1	26b4,91.1,102.4,93a9
I.KI.RA	100.103.53	C1	25a5
I.KU.PA3.NA.TU.NA.TE	100.98.1.26.6.26.92	= D1	APZ2b(I13)
I.KU.RI.NA	100.98.72.26	C1	90.1
I.KU.SU	100.98.59	? C1	35.1
I.KU.TA	100.98.74	* C1	35.1
I.MI.SA.RA	100.76.31.53	A1	27a3
I.NA.JA	100.26.32	* C1	PKZ11(I4)
I.NA.JA.PA.SI	100.26.32.2.57	? A1	I4d
I.NA.JA.RE.NU	100.26.32.54.25	? B1	I13a2
I.NA.JA.RE.68	100.26.32.54.68	* B1	APZ2a2(I13)
I.NA.WA	100.26.75	C1	PH6.1(IV16)
I.PA.85	100.2.85	* C1	PA1(IV7)
I.PI.NA.MA	100.56.26.95	? B1	I13a1
I.PI.NA.MI.NA	100.56.26.76.26	= C1	PKZ10(I6)

Minoan Linear A

Transliteration	L Numbers	Code	Reference
I.QA.85	100.62.85	C2	44b1,131.2
I.RA2	100.58	C6	HTW225(CRIII1),
I.RU.JA	100.55.32	? C1	7a2
I.SA.RI	100.31.72	C1	PH6.4(IV16)
I.SI	100.57	? C1	IV13c
I.SU.KI	100.59.103	? C1	II7a
I.TA	100.74	? C1	25b1
I.TA.NU	100.74.25	C1	28b6
I.TI	100.78	* C1	62.3
I.TI.KU.DU	100.78.98.93	? C1	62.3
I.TI.TI.KU.NI	100.78.78.98.60	C1	96a1
I.WI	100.28	= D1	78
I.41.NA.MA	100.41.26.95	* B1	APZ2a1(I13)
I.41.NA.MA.SI.RU.TE	100.41.26.95.57.55.92	+ C1	KOZ1c
I.41.NA.MI.NA	100.41.26.76.26	# C1	PKZ10(I6)
I.88	100.88	C1	HTW228(CRIII4)
I.122	100.122	? C1	102.2
I.126	100.126	* C1	102.2,25b2#
JA.—.WI.DA.RA	32.160.28.30.53	? C1	I10
JA.DI	32.51	C1	PHW16a(III15)
JA.DI.KI.TE.TE.PI	32.51.103.92.92.56	* C1	PKZ8a(I3)
JA.DI.RA.TI	32.51.53.78	* C1	KN1a1(IV1)
JA.DU	32.93	? C1	122a7
JA.DU.RI.NA.TI	32.93.72.26.78	? C1	IV1b1
JA.KI.JA	32.103.32	? D1	IV17vii1
JA.KI.PA3	32.103.1	* B1	PH13.2(IV17)
JA.KU	32.98	C1	MA2b2(IV11)
JA.KU.TI	32.98.78	C1	KN1b1(IV1)
JA.MA	32.95	* A1	MA2c2(IV11)
JA.MA.U.PI	32.95.97.56	? A1	IV11c2
JA.ME	32.84	* C2	28a4,28b1
JA.MI.DA.RE	32.76.30.54	C1	122a4
JA.NU	32.25	* D1	KNZ6
JA.PA	32.2	? A1	I7
JA.PA.TA.I.DA.88.DI	32.2.74.100.30.88.51	* D1	PKZ9(I7)
JA.QE	32.91	A1	KNZ17(I9)
JA.RA	32.53	? C1	III3
JA.RE.MI	32.54.76	C1	87.3
JA.SA.SA.RA	32.31.31.53	? C2B1	I1.2,I16,I8a
JA.SA.SA.RA.MA.NA	32.31.31.53.95.26	* C1	KNZ10a(I8)
JA.SA.SA.RA.ME	32.31.31.53.84	* C2	PSZ2c(I1),TLZ1(I16)
JA.SI	32.57	C1	KNZ4(II3)
JA.TA.I.88	32.74.100.88	B1	APZ1(I14)
JA.13.RI	32.13.72	? C1	V12.1
JA.48	32.48	? C2	28a4,28b1
JA.135.TU.KU	32.135.6.98	+ C2	LAZ1,LAZ1
JA.138	32.138	C1	119.4
JA.143.TA.A.NA.NE	32.143.74.52.26.61	* A1	KNZ7(II2)
JE.AI	81.83	C1	94a4
JE.DE.MA	81.102.95	? C1	III16a

Transliteration	L Numbers	Code	Reference
JE.DI	81.51	C4	8a1,36.1,122b1,140.1
KA.—.QE	29.160.91	? C1	140.3
KA.—.TU	29.160.6	? C1	47a1
KA.DU.MA.NE	29.93.95.61	C1	29.6
KA.JE	29.81	D1	KN?22a2(IV12)
KA.KU	29.98	C1	62.2
KA.KU.PA	29.98.2	C3	16.1,HTW215a(CRIV6),
KA.ME	29.84	? C1	140.3
KA.NA	29.26	C1B1	23a1,123b4
KA.NU.TI	29.25.78	C1	97a3
KA.PA	29.2	C4B2	6a1,8b3,94a1,102.1,105.1,
KA.PA.QE	29.2.91	C1	6a4
KA.QE	29.91	* C1	140.3
KA.RA	29.53	# C1	9b2
KA.RA2	29.58	D1	139.3
KA.RE.RO	29.54.22	C1	HTW203(CRIV18)
KA.RI.QE	29.72.91	? C1	IV5.1
KA.RI.63.I	29.72.63.100	C1	98a4
KA.RO	29.22	? D1	45a1
KA.RO.NA	29.22.26	C1	11a2
KA.RO.PA3	29.22.1	C1	31.3
KA.RU	29.55	C1B1	97a1,75.1,84.1?
KA.SA.RU	29.31.55	C1	10b3
KA.SU	29.59	* C1	PK1.1(IV5)
KA.TI	29.78	C1A1	63.1,126b3*
KA.U.DE.TA	29.97.102.74	C1	13.1
KA.U.DO.NI	29.97.101.60	C1	26b2
KA.WA	29.75	? C1	V16
KA.21.RU	29.21.55	? C1	115a5
KA.66	29.66	= C1	9b2,V4?
KA.96	29.96	C1	88.3
KE.KI.RU	24.103.55	C1	94b2
KE.96.RI	24.96.72	= D1	KNZ19.1(I11)
KE.96.96	24.96.96	? D1	I11.1
KI.DA	103.30	* B2	27a4,47a4
KI.DA.RO	103.30.22	C1	117a9,27a4?
KI.DA.SU	103.30.59	? B1	47a4
KI.DA.TA	103.30.74	C1	40.2
KI.DE.MA.PI.NA	103.102.95.56.26	? C1	31.4
KI.DE.MA.9.NA	103.102.95.9.26	* C1	31.4
KI.DI	103.51	? C1	93a2
KI.DI.NI	103.51.60	* C1	93a2
KI.DU.KU	103.93.98	* D1	27a4
KI.KI.NA	103.103.26	C1	88.2
KI.KI.RA.JA	103.103.53.32	C1	85b1
KI.MI	103.76	? D1	54a2
KI.MI.RA2	103.76.58	* D1	54a3
KI.RA	103.53	C1	103.5
KI.RE	103.54	A1	ZA1a1(IV4),120.4?
KI.RE.JA.TU	103.54.32.6	? C1	I3.2

Transliteration	L Numbers		Code	Reference
KI.RE.TA.NA	103.54.74.26		C3A1	8a5,108.1,120.4,2.3
KI.RE.TA2	103.54.86		C2	129.1,85b1
KI.RI.TA2	103.72.86		C2	114a1,121.1
KI.RO	103.22		C13B1	1a1,15.4,30.4,34.6,88.3,
KI.RU	103.55		C1	MIZ1(II22iv)
KI.TA.I	103.74.100		C1	123a1
KI.TE.TE	103.92.92	?	B1	I4a
KI.TE.TE.PI	103.92.92.56	?	C1	I3.2
KI.WE.SI	103.94.57		C1	TY3a1(IV9)
KI.63.RE	103.63.54		C1	37.4
KI.111.KU	103.111.98	?	D1	27a4
KO.A.DU.WA	45.52.93.75		C1	TY3b6(IV9)
KO.JA	45.32		C1	119.2
KO.RU	45.55		C1	23a5
KO.SA.KE.TI	45.31.24.78		C1	117a7
KO.WE	45.94		C1	11a3,62.5?
KU.DA	98.30		C1	122a8
KU.DO	98.101	?	A1	64.1
KU.DO.NA	98.101.26	*	D1	64.1
KU.DO.NI	98.101.60		C2	13.4,85a4
KU.DU	98.93	?	A1	51b1
KU.KA	98.29	?	C1	110a1
KU.KU.DA.RA	98.98.30.53		C1	117a7
KU.MA.RO	98.95.22		A1	96a5
KU.MA.96	98.95.96		C1	20.1
KU.ME.TA	98.84.74		A1	51b1
KU.MI	98.76	*	C1	110a1
KU.MI.NA.QE	98.76.26.91		C1D1	HTW214a(CRIV5),54a2
KU.NI	98.60		D1	83.3
KU.NI.SU	98.60.59		C4	10a1,86a1,95a3,95b3,86b1?
KU.PA	98.2		C1	HTW220a(CRV5),110a2?
KU.PA.JA	98.2.32		C1	116a1
KU.PA3.NA.TU	98.1.26.6		C2	47a1,119.3
KU.PA3.NA.TU.NA	98.1.26.6.26	?	D1	I13b1
KU.PA3.NU	98.1.25		C9	1a3,3.6,88.3,88.4,117a3,
KU.PA3.WE.JA	98.1.94.32		C1	24a1
KU.RA.I	98.53.100	*	C1	117a2
KU.RA.27	98.53.27	?	C1	117a2
KU.RE	98.54	*	B1	39.3
KU.RE.96	98.54.96		C1A1	117b1,39.2
KU.RO	98.22		C30A5	9a6,9b6,11a3,11b5,13.7,
KU.RU.KU	98.55.98		C1	87.4
KU.RU.MA	98.55.95	*	C1	115b3
KU.RU.MA.I	98.55.95.100	?	C1	115b3
KU.TA	98.74		B1	115b4
MA.DA.TI	95.30.78	*	C1	PK1.7(IV5)
MA.DI	95.51		C4A2	85b5,97a4,118.1,
MA.I.MI	95.100.76		C1	89.2
MA.KA.I.SU	95.29.100.59	*	C1	PK1.7(IV5)
MA.KA.RI.TE	95.29.72.92		C2	87.1,117a1

Appendix H 263

Transliteration	L Numbers	Code	Reference
MA.KA.SI.SU	95.29.57.59	? C1	IV5.7
MA.RE	95.54	* C2	55a1,PH19.2+
MA.RI	95.72	B1	128a4
MA.RI.TA2	95.72.86	? C1	90.3
MA.RU	95.55	C1	117a3
MA.SI	95.57	A1	5.2
MA.SI.DU	95.57.93	C1	43.1
MA.TE.TI	95.92.78	? C1	IV5.7
MA.WE.RE.I	95.94.54.100	* C1	6b2
MA.3	95.3	C2	6a3,102.3,97a6?
MA.10.RE.SA	95.10.54.31	* A1	PH10a(IV17ii)
ME.RU	84.55	* D1	46a1
ME.TE	84.92	? A1	94a4
ME.ZA	84.23	C2	10a5,85b3,154bis.1?
MI.DA	76.30	A1	27b1,41.3?
MI.DA.NI	76.30.60	* C1	41.4
MI.DE	76.102	+B1	PH19.2
MI.KA	76.29	B1	135a2
MI.KI.SE.NA	76.103.77.26	C1	26a2
MI.NU.MI	76.25.76	A1	47a6
MI.NU.TE	76.25.92	C4	86a5,95a2,95b2,106.1
MI.RU.SU.RA.RE	76.55.59.53.54	? C1	117a4
MI.RU.TA.RA.RE	76.55.74.53.54	* C1	117a4
MI.TA	76.74	A1	128a3
MI.TI	76.78	? A1	61.1
MI.TI.SA	76.78.31	? C1	31.1
MI.TI.TI.NE	76.78.78.61	? C2	V9,V7
MI.TU	76.6	C2	117a2,135a2
MI.68.TA	76.68.74	? B1	IV12a1
NA.A.PA3	26.52.1	+A1	KNZ20
NA.DA.RE	26.30.54	C1	117a5
NA.NE.MI	26.61.76	? D1	V1
NA.MI.85	26.76.85	B1	KNZ19.2(I11)
NA.QA.SI	26.62.57	? D1	I16
NA.SI	26.57	A1	APZ2a1(I13)
NA.TI	26.78	C1	97a4,111b3?
NA.WI	26.28	* B1	111b3
NA.68.NE	26.68.61	? B1	135a3
NA.111	26.111	C1A1	155a2,115a2*
NA.152.NE	26.152.61	* C1	135a3
NE.MI.NA	61.76.26	C1A1	115a3,135a1
NE.NI	61.60	B1	89.5
NI.RA	60.53	B1	PH11a2(IV17iv)
NI.SI	60.57	* B1	140.2
NI.TI.JA	60.78.32	=D1	PH9a+
NI.41	60.41	* C1	KNW26(III17)
NI.67.JA	60.67.32	#D1	PH9a+
NU.DU.WA	25.93.75	C1	40.1
NU.PA3	25.1	? A1	I3.2
NU.PU	25.64	? D1	IV17,VII1

Minoan Linear A

Transliteration	L Numbers	Code		Reference
NU.TI	25.78		A1	84.2
NU.WI	25.28		C2	115a2,115b2
PA.DA.RE	2.30.54	*	C1	10a3
PA.DA.SU	2.30.59	?	C1	20.1
PA.DA.SU.TI	2.30.59.78	?	C1	104.3
PA.DE	2.102		C3	9a2,9b2,122a5
PA.I	2.100	?	B1	I4d
PA.I.KI	2.100.103		D1	73.2
PA.I.TO	2.100.39		C2	97a3,120.6,122a2?
PA.JA	2.32		C2A1	41.4,PH1b1(IV13),MA4b
PA.JA.RE	2.32.54		C2B2	8b4,88.4,29.2,TY3a4(IV9)
PA.JA.SA	2.32.31		D1	PH11b1(IV17iv)
PA.KA	2.29	*	C1	85b3
PA.KE	2.24	?	C1	98a4
PA.MI	2.76	?	B1	IV9b4
PA.PA	2.2	?	C2	II19i,III10b
PA.PA3	2.1	?	C1	41.3
PA.RA	2.53		C1	128a1,PH3a3(IV15)?
PA.RA.NE	2.53.61		C2	115a4,115b1,HTW221a(CRV4)?
PA.RA.TU	2.53.6	?	C1	128a1
PA.RI	2.72	*	C2	PH3a3(IV15),PKZ11d(I4)
PA.RO.—.TI	2.22.160.78	*	C1	104.3
PA.RO.SU	2.22.59	*	C1	20.1
PA.SA.RI.JA	2.31.72.32	?	C1	24a4
PA.SA.WE.JA	2.31.94.32		C1	24a4
PA.SE	2.77		C2	18.1,27b4
PA.SE.JA	2.77.32		C3	93a8,HTW201(CRIV15)
PA.SI.A	2.57.52	*	C1	45b3
PA.TA.DA	2.74.30	*	B1	HT?170.3
PA.TA.DA.DU.PU2.RE	2.74.30.93.34.54	*	B1	HTZ160(II9)
PA.TA.NE	2.74.61		C2	94b1,122a6
PA.TA.QE	2.74.91		C1	31.6
PA.TA.SA.DU.PU2.RE	2.74.31.93.34.54	?	C1	II9
PA.114.I	2.114.100	*	C1	43.1
PA3.DA.RE	1.30.54	?	A1	IV6a2
PA3.KA.RA.TI	1.29.53.78		C1	8a1
PA3.NI	1.60		C2	85a2,102.2
PA3.NI.NA	1.60.26		C3	6b6,93a1,93a8
PA3.NU.TI.NE	1.25.78.61	?	C1	V13
PA3.87	1.87		C1	8b2
PA3.135	1.135	*	A1	PKZ8a(I3)
PI.—.DO	56.160.101	#	C1	TY3a2(IV9)
PI.DI.RI.KI	56.51.72.103	?	D1	IV17iii1
PI.JA.SU.MA.TI.TI.14	56.32.59.95.78.78.14	#	A1	HTZ157
PI.JA.TA.MA.TI.TI.14	56.32.74.95.78.78.14	=	A1	HTZ157
PI.MA.RE	56.95.54	?	A1	55a1
PI.ME.DO	56.84.101	?	C1	IV9b2
PI.MI.NA.TE	56.76.26.92	?	A1	I13a2
PI.PA.JA.TA.RI.I.TE.RI	56.2.32.74.72.100.92.72		D1	KNZ13(V14)
PI.PI	56.56	?	C2	85a1,97a1

Transliteration	L Numbers	Code	Reference
PI.SA	56.31	* C2	123b2,113.2#
PI.TA.JA	56.74.32	C1	6a2
PI.TA.KA.SE	56.74.29.77	C1	21.1
PI.TA.KE.SI	56.74.24.57	C1	87.2
PI.TA.RA	56.74.53	* C1	96a4
PI.TE.RI	56.92.72	* C1	PKZ11b(I4)
PI.TE.ZA	56.92.23	? C1	I4b
PI.69.TE	56.69.92	C1	116a4
PI.96.RI	56.96.72	# D1	KNZ19(I11)
PU.KO	64.45	C1	31.1
PU.MA.KU	64.95.98	* D1	139.1
PU.PI	64.56	# B1	TY2.1(IV8)
PU.RA2	64.58	C2A1	28a3,116a2,49a1
PU.WI	64.28	= B1	TY2.1(IV8)
PU.82	64.82	C2	14.1,123a3
QA.DU	62.93	A1	51b2,151.1?
QA.KU.RE	62.98.54	* C1	HTW217a1(CRIV4)
QA.NU.MA	62.25.95	* C1	116a6
QA.PA3	62.1	C1	31.2
QA.QA.RU	62.62.55	C3A1	93a4,118.2,122b3,111a2
QA.RA2.WA	62.58.75	C1	86a3
QA.RE.TO	62.54.39	C1	132.1,111a1?
QA.SA	62.31	* B1	111a1
QA.TI	62.78	* A1	61.1
QA.TI.DA	62.78.30	? C1	12.1
QA.TI.DA.TE	62.78.30.92	* C1	12.1
QA.63.I	62.63.100	C4	8a3,8b2,85b5,122a4
QA.85.RA.RE	62.85.53.54	C1	96b1
QE.DE.MI.NU	91.102.76.25	C2	MA1a(IV10),MA1b(IV10)
QE.KA	91.29	C1A1	85b2,111a1
QE.KU.RE	91.98.54	C1	20.2
QE.PI	91.56	? B1	73.3
QE.PI.TA	91.56.74	C1	6a6
QE.PU	91.64	C2	9a3,9b4
QE.RA2.U	91.58.97	C4	1a1,3.2,95a4,95b4
QE.SI	91.57	* B1	111b2
QE.SI.KA	91.57.29	? B1	111b2
QE.SU.PU	91.59.64	C1	87.4
QE.TI	91.78	C1	7a1
QE.TI.RA.DU	91.78.53.93	C1	58.1
QE.TU	91.6	A1	41.2
QE.TU.NE	91.6.61	C1	12.3
QE.TU.SI	91.6.57	* C1	PHW14a(III13)
QI.TA.DU	79.74.93	= B1	84.1
QI.TA.RA2	79.74.58	# B1	84.1
QI.TU	79.6	B1	94b5
QI.TU.NE	79.6.61	C3	7b1,87.1,117b1
RA.A	53.52	A1	PH9b
RA.DE.ME.TE	53.102.84.92	* C1	94b4
RA.KA.RU.A.NA.DA	53.29.55.52.26.30	? A1	II2

Transliteration	L Numbers	Code	Reference
RA.KI	53.103	* C1	6b5
RA.ME	53.84	* A1	PKZ12(I5)
RA.NA.RE	53.26.54	* D1	47b1
RA.NA.TU.SU.PU2.MI.WE			
	53.26.6.59.34.76.94	* B1	PK1(IV5)
RA.NA.TU.TA.DO.MI	53.26.6.74.101.76	? C1	IV5.5
RA.RA.27	53.53.27	? C1	I4c
RA.RE.RA	53.54.53	C1	HTW206b(CRIV8)
RA.RI	53.72	A1	122a1,11a1?
RA.RI.DE	53.72.102	B1	113.1
RA.TI.SE	53.78.77	C1	6b2
RA.43.TI	53.43.78	C2	17.1,19.1
RA.80.DI.KI	53.80.51.103	? C1	IV14.1
RA.88	53.88	? B1	IV17v
RA2.TI	58.78	? A1	108.3
RE.DI.SE	54.51.77	C1	85b4
RE.I	54.100	? C1	6b3
RE.RA2.DU	54.58.93	? D1	49a1
RE.RO	54.22	C1	HTW212b(CRIV11)
RE.SU	54.59	* D1	37.2
RE.TA2	54.86	A1	125.3
RE.TI	54.78	* A1	MA2b1(IV11)
RE.TU	54.6	A1	59.3
RE.ZA	54.23	C2	13.2,88.1*
RI.—.SU	72.160.59	? A1	60.1
RI.A	72.52	? C1	V2
RI.MI.SI	72.76.57	C1	119.2
RI.MI.SU.TU	72.76.59.6	? B1	49a2
RI.TA.MA	72.74.95	C1	115a1
RI.TE.I.JA	72.92.100.32	* C1	HTZ158b(II7)
RO.DA	22.30	? C1	V16
RO.I.DU.WI	22.100.93.28	? C1	IV10a
RO.KE	22.24	* C1	98a4
RO.KU	22.98	? D1	71.2
RO.SA.DA	22.31.30	? C1	V12.2
RO.WI.JA.SU	22.28.32.59	? C1	V9
RO.69.TI.DA	22.69.78.30	* C1	KNZ12(V12)
RO.135	22.135	+ B1	PH12
RU.—.PA3	55.160.1	* C1	128b2
RU.DI	55.51	* D1	141.2
RU.DO.NA	55.101.26	? C1	11b3
RU.I	55.100	* A1	HTZ158a(II7)
RU.I.KA	55.100.29	* D1	KNW3(III1)
RU.I.RU	55.100.55	# A1	24a5
RU.I.SI	55.100.57	= A1	24a5
RU.JA	55.32	* C1	KNW26a(III17)
RU.JA.SE.ME	55.32.77.84	? C1	128a1
RU.JA.TA.DI	55.32.74.51	C1	HTW208b(CRIV1)
RU.MA	55.95	B1	64.2
RU.MA.QA	55.95.62	? D1	IV17iii3

Transliteration	L Numbers		Code	Reference
RU.MA.TA	55.95.74		C1B1	99b2,29.1
RU.MA.147	55.95.147	*	D1	PH7a3(IV17iii)
RU.NA	55.26	*	A1	KN2(IV2)
RU.NI	55.60		A1	25a2
RU.SA	55.31		C1	96a3,128b2?
RU.153.NA	55.153.26	*	C1	11b3
SA.DI	31.51		C1	111b1,100.2?
SA.I.PI	31.100.56	=	D1	PSZ2a(I1)
SA.I.WI	31.100.28	=	D1	PSZ2a(I1)
SA.I.41	31.100.41	#	D1	PSZ2a(I1)
SA.JA.MA	31.32.95		C1	31.3
SA.KI	31.103	*	C1	115b4
SA.MA	31.95		C3	6b5,10a1,52a1,39.3?
SA.MA.RO	31.95.22		C1A1	88.4,39.3*
SA.QE.WE	31.91.94		C1	11b4
SA.RA	31.53	*	A1	62.1
SA.RA.DI	31.53.51		A1	27a5
SA.RA.RA	31.53.53		C1	30.3
SA.RA2	31.58		C2	0B118.2,28a2,28b3,30.1,32.1,
SA.RE.96	31.54.96		C1	20.4
SA.RO	31.22		C4	9a1,17.2,19.2,42.2,25b1?
SA.RO.QE	31.22.91	*	B1	73.3
SA.RO.TE	31.22.92	?	C1	38.1
SA.RU	31.55		C5	86a2,94b2,95a3,95b1,123a4
SA.TA	31.74		C1	117a7,115b4?
SA.WI.SI	31.28.57	?	C1	29.4
SA.9.RE	31.9.54	*	C1	29.4
SA.15.ZE	31.15.16	?	C1	16.4
SA.82	31.82	*	C1	114b
SE.KU.TU	77.98.6		C1	115a3
SE.RU.RU	77.55.55	=	B1	3.4
SE.SA	77.31	?	D1	49b2
SI.—.TI	57.160.78	?	A1	IV15b3
SI.DA	57.30	?	B1	4.2
SI.DA.RE	57.30.54		C2	17.3,122a5,49a4?
SI.DU	57.93	?	A1	123b4
SI.DU	57.93		B1	110a1
SI.DU.PA.DU.PI.ZA.NA	57.93.2.93.56.23.26	*	A1	123b4
SI.DU.QA	57.93.62	?	C1	110a1
SI.I	57.100		C1	34.1
SI.I.TI	57.100.78	?	D1	III1
SI.KA	57.29		C4	HTW227(CRIII2),
SI.KI.NE	57.103.61	*	C1	116a5
SI.KI.RA	57.103.53		C1	8a4
SI.KI.TE	57.103.92	?	C1	116a5
SI.MA	57.95		C1	PHZ4(II12)
SI.MI.TA	57.76.74		C1	96a2
SI.NI	57.60	*	A1B1	140.1,TEZ1(II24)
SI.PU	57.64		D1	HTZ161(II10)
SI.RA	57.53		A1	49.5

Minoan Linear A

Transliteration	L Numbers		Code	Reference
SI.RE	57.54	*	C1B1	HT?170.3,4.2
SI.RU	57.55		C1	55a2,90.2?,PKZ11d(I4)?
SI.RU.MA.RI.TA2	57.55.95.72.86	*	C1	90.2
SI.RU.TE	57.55.92	*	A1	PKZ11d(I4)
SI.TA	57.74	*	A1	PH3a1(IV15)
SI.TI	57.78	*	D1	PH3b2(IV15)
SI.TI.NA.KA	57.78.26.29	?	B1	I16
SI.TI.SI	57.78.57	?	B1	IV15b2
SI.TU	57.6	?	C1	CRV4b
SI.TU.NE	57.6.61	*	C1	HTW221a(CRV4)
SI.TU.NE.TI	57.6.61.78		C1	PK1.1(IV5)
SI.TU.RI.RE	57.6.72.54	*	A1	3.5
SI.TU.RI.TI	57.6.72.78	?	A1	3.4
SI.159	57.159	?	B1	II24
SO.DI.RA	7.51.53		C3	9a4,9b3,122a5
SU.DU	59.93		B1	59.2
SU.DU.RI.TE	59.93.72.92	?	A1	4.2
SU.NE	59.61		B1	63.1
SU.KA	59.29	*	C2	HTW209a(CRIV10),
SU.KI	59.103	*	C1B2	HTZ158b(II7),49a3,
SU.KI.RI.TE.SE.JA	59.103.72.92.77.32	?	C1	II7b
SU.KI.WE.TA	59.103.94.74	+	A1	PHW18
SU.MA	59.95	*	C1	115a6
SU.MA.ME	59.95.84	?	D1	81.2
SU.MA.ME.KI	59.95.84.103	*	D1	81.2
SU.MA.TI.ZA.I.TE	59.95.78.23.100.92	*	A1	PK1.6(IV5)
SU.MA.TI.ZA.SI.TE	59.95.78.23.57.92	?	C1	IV5.6
SU.NI	59.60	?	A1	51a1
SU.NI.KA	59.60.29		C2	HTW204a(CRIV2),
SU.PA3.RA	59.1.53		C1	31.5
SU.PU	59.64		C1	31.2
SU.PU2.KA	59.34.29	?	C1	8b1
SU.PU2.87	59.34.87	*	C1	8b1
SU.RE	59.54	*	C1	32.3
SU.SE	59.77	?	C1	32.3
SU.WI.RE.SU	59.28.54.59	?	C1	37.1
SU.96.TA	59.96.74	*	D1	KN?22a1(IV12)
TA.DA.NE	74.30.61	?	B1	49b4
TA.DU.WE.TE	74.93.94.92	*	A1	4.2
TA.I.65	74.100.65		C3	9a4,9b4,39.1
TA.I.88	74.100.88		D1	PKZ11a(I4)
TA.NA	74.26	?	C1	120.5
TA.NA.I.88.20	74.26.100.88.20		A1	PSZ2b(I12)
TA.NA.TI	74.26.78		C3A1	7a4,10b4,98a2,49a2
TA.NE	74.61	*	D1	135b1
TA.NI	74.60	*	A1	51a1
TA.NU.A.TI	74.25.52.78	?	C1	I8a
TA.NU.RI.JA	74.25.72.32	?	D1	II16
TA.NU.144.JA	74.25.144.32	*	D1	PKZ13(II16)
TA.NU.144.TI	74.25.144.78	*	A1	KNZ10a(I8)

Transliteration	L Numbers	Code	Reference
TA.PA	74.2	C1	104.1
TA.PA3.DU	74.1.93	* C1	PRZ1a(I17)
TA.PI.SA	74.56.31	? C1	123b2
TA.PI.SI.DI	74.56.57.51	A1	4.3
TA.RA	74.53	C1	89.3,84.1?,96a4?
TA.TI	74.78	C2	26a2,97a5
TA.WE.NA	74.94.26	C1	10b1
TA2.TI.TE	86.78.92	C1	PK1.3(IV5)
TA2.TU	86.6	? A1	154bis.2
TA2.ZA	86.23	? C1	88.1
TA2.27.RE	86.27.54	? C1	IV5.2
TA2.35	86.35	? C1	26b4
TA2.80.RE	86.80.54	* C1	PK1.2(IV5)
TE.JA.RE	92.32.54	* C1	117a5
TE.KE	92.24	C1	85a5
TE.KI	92.103	C2	13.3,122a3
TE.RE.SA	92.54.31	? D1	IV17ii
TE.RO.NI	92.22.60	A1	26b2
TE.TU	92.6	C3	7a5,13.3,85b2
TE.TU.I	92.6.100	? C1	85b2
TE.88	92.88	C2	8a3,98a3
TI.DA.TA	78.30.74	* C1	123b2
TI.DU	78.93	* C1	TYZ1(V2)
TI.DU.KI	78.93.103	? B1	IV4b1
TI.DU.NI	78.93.60	C1	49a4
TI.JA	78.32	? C1	I3.2
TI.MA.RU.WI.TE	78.95.55.28.92	C1	PU1.1
TI.NA.RE	78.26.54	? A1	62.1
TI.NI	78.60	B1	51a2
TI.NI.TA	78.60.74	C1	27a1
TI.NU.JA	78.25.32	C1	115b2
TI.PA	78.2	* C1	PKZ11b(I4)
TI.PA.I	78.2.100	= D1	PKZ11c(I4)
TI.PA.SE	78.2.77	# D1	PKZ11c(I4)
TI.RE.U	78.54.97	? C1	IV13b1
TI.SA	78.31	A1	31.1,39.5?
TI.TA.NA	78.74.26	C1	HTW220(CRV5)
TI.TI.KU	78.78.98	C2	35a1,ZAZ3.2#+
TU.KI	6.103	? A1	79.2
TU.MA	6.95	C1	94b1,110b1?
TU.NU	6.25	* C1	KAZ1(V17)
TU.NU.MA	6.25.95	? C2	116a6,117a3
TU.PA	6.2	A1	112a2
TU.PA.DI.DA	6.2.51.30	C1	123b3
TU.PA.RA	6.2.53	D1	83.2
TU.PA3.KI	6.1.103	? B1	V3a
TU.QA	6.62	C1	23a4
TU.QE.NU	6.91.25	C1	25a3
TU.QI.WE.NA	6.79.94.26	C1	129.2
TU.RU.NU.SE.ME	6.55.25.77.84	* C1	128a1

Transliteration	L Numbers	Code		Reference
TU.RU.SA.RA2.—.RE	6.55.31.58.160.54	*	C1	KOZ1b
TU.SA	6.31	*	A1	79.2
TU.SU.DO	6.59.101	?	C1	49a6
TU.SU.PU2	6.59.34	*	C1	49a7
TU.TE	6.92	?	B1	IV5.4
TU.68.MA	6.68.95	*	C1	117a3
U.DE.ZA	97.102.23		C2	122a1,122b3
U.DI.MI	97.51.76		C1	117a4
U.DI.RI.KI	97.51.72.103	*	A1	PH7a2(IV17iii)
U.DU	97.93		A1	126a4,47a2?
U.JA	97.32	?	B1	I14
U.JA.RE	97.32.54	=	B1	APZ1(I14)
U.JA.SA	97.32.31	#	D1	APZ1(I14)
U.MI.NA.SI	97.76.26.57		C2	28a1,117a1
U.NA.KA.NA	97.26.29.26	*	B1	TLZ1(I16)
U.NA.KA.NA.SI	97.26.29.26.57	+	C1	KOZ1c
U.NA.KU	97.26.98	?	B1	39.3
U.NA.RU.KA	97.26.55.29	*	B1	PKZ12(I5)
U.NA.RU.KA.NA.TI.PA.SE				
	97.26.55.29.26.78.2.77	*	B1	PKZ11(I4)
U.NU.111	97.25.111		C1	26a3
U.RA2.TI	97.58.78	*	C1	108.3
U.RE.WI	97.54.28		C1	25a2
U.SU	97.59		C1D1	117a2,58.4
U.SU.—.MI	97.59.160.76	?	B1	58.4
U.TA.RO	97.74.22	*	C1	116a1
U.TA2	97.86	*	C1	103.1
U.TI	97.78		C2	10b1,MA2c2(IV11)
U.37.ZA	97.37.23		C3	10a2,10a4,85a3
U.69.SI	97.69.57		C2	15.1,140.1
U.120	97.120	?	A1	126a3
U.150.MA	97.150.95	*	C1	PHW17a(III16)
WA.DI.NI	75.51.60		C2	HTW208a(CRIV1),
WA.DU.NI.MI	75.93.60.76		C2	6b1,85b4
WA.KA.MI.ZA.RE.NA	75.29.76.23.54.26	*	B1	PK1.3(IV5)
WA.PI	75.56	?	C3	I4a,I5a,I16
WA.PI.TI.NA.RA2	75.56.78.26.58	*	C1	PHZ5(II13)
WA.TU.MA.RE	75.6.95.54	*	C1	128a2
WA.TU.MI	75.6.76	*	C1	HTW206a(CRIV8)
WA.TU.MI.RE	75.6.76.54	?	C1	128a2
WA.U.JA	75.97.32	?	A1	V11
WA.20	75.20	*	A1	PSZ2(I1)
WA.44	75.44	*	C1	PKZ11a(I4)
WA.80.MI	75.80.76	?	C1	CRIV8a
WE.JA	94.32		A1	55b2
WE.KA	94.29		C1	146.3
WE.MI	94.76		B1	PSZ1(V6)
WE.RU.MA	94.55.95		C1	118.4
WE.SE	94.77	*	C1	TY2.5(IV8)
WE.66	94.66		A1	146.2

Appendix H

Transliteration	L Numbers	Code	Reference
WI.—.DO	28.160.101	= C1	TY3a2(IV9)
WI.DI.NA	28.51.26	C1	28a5
WI.DU	28.93	A1	5.3
WI.JA.SU.MA.TI.TI.14	28.32.59.95.78.78.14	= A1	HTZ157
WI.JA.TA.MA.TI.TI.14	28.32.74.95.78.78.14	= A1	HTZ157
WI.SA	28.31	= A1	113.1
WI.TE.RO.I	28.92.22.100	* C1	25b1
WI.87	28.87	? A1	IV12b1
WI.87.MI	28.87.76	* A1	KN?22b1(IV12)
ZA.3	23.3	A1	TY3b1(IV9)
4.RA2.DI.NE	4.58.51.61	C1	6a4
8.96	8.96	C1	119.4
10.DA.DE.KU	10.30.102.98	* A1	127a2
10.KU.PA	10.98.2	* C1	HTW220b(CRV5)
12.I.WI	12.100.28	? A1	I1.1
14.JA.NA.RU	14.32.26.55	? D1	I5c
20.SA.DI	20.31.51	* C1	PHW15(III14)
20.20.KU	20.20.98	= C1	ZAZ3.2
21.TO.KU.RO	21.39.98.22	C1	122b6
27.RU	27.55	? C1A1	3.4,46a1
27.RU.RU	27.55.55	# B1	3.4
27.SI	27.57	? B1	148.2
27.WI	27.28	# D1	78.1
35.KA	35.29	C1	11b2
35.87	35.87	? C1	8b4
36.TA	36.74	C1	10b2
36.TE	36.92	C1	26a1
41.MI.NA.TE	41.76.26.92	* A1	APZ2a2(I13)
41.NA.MA.SI.RU	41.26.95.57.55	D1	TLZ1
41.RU.135.68	41.55.135.68	C1	PH2.3(IV14)
42.PA3	42.1	* C1	93a1
44.42	44.42	* B1	34.3
66.RU	66.55	C1	10a4
66.TE	66.92	C1	63.1
68.KU.NA.PA.KU.A.U	68.98.26.2.98.52.97	* D1	KNZ6(II1)
68.WI	68.28	? D1	78.1
69.SU.NE	69.59.61	? B1	135b1
69.TI.I	69.78.100	* B1	KNZ6(II1)
69.TI.12	69.78.12	? C1	II1
80.DI.KI	80.51.103	* C1	PH2.2(IV14)
80.KA.MI.SI.SI	80.29.76.57.57	? C1	IV5.3
80.KI.WE	80.103.94	* B1	KNZ12.1(V12)
80.SU.QA.RE	80.59.62.54	C1	TLZ1(I16)
80.TE.JA	80.92.32	* C1	PK1.4(IV5)
80.TI.KE	80.78.24	? C1	93a6
80.TI.NI	80.78.60	* C1	93a6
82.WA	82.75	? C1	II6ii
85.KA	85.29	A1	140.2
87.DU	87.93	C3	123b3,HTW223a(CRV1),
87.35	87.35	* C1	26b4

Minoan Linear A

Transliteration	L Numbers	Code	Reference
87.90	87.90	C1	123b1
88.NA.DI	88.26.51	A1	MA2c1(IV11)
88.SA.DU	88.31.93	? C1	III14
88.SA.RO	88.31.22	? C1	V5
89.RU.A.A	89.55.52.52	? C1	II6i
89.SA.PA3	89.31.1	? C1	IV14.4
96.KI.TA	96.103.74	C1	29.4
96.RA	96.53	D1	80.1
99.I	99.100	C2	11a4,93a5,62.5?
99.I.RU.JA	99.100.55.32	* C1	7a2
99.PI	99.56	* B1	KNZ7(II2)
111.SA.KO	111.31.45	? D1	82.2
114.I.I	114.100.100	? C1	43.2
137.DA.TI.JE	137.30.78.81	? B1	V3b
143.TO	143.39	* D1	KNZ6(II1)
151.SA.PA3	151.31.1	* C1	PH2.4(IV14)